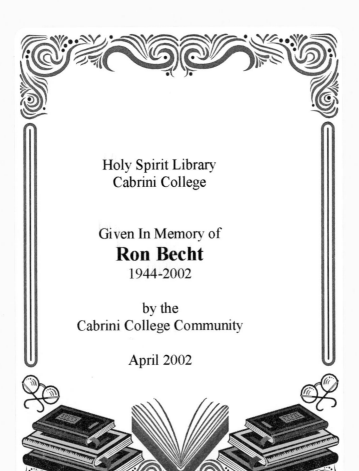

Holy Spirit Library
Cabrini College

Given In Memory of
Ron Becht
1944-2002

by the
Cabrini College Community

April 2002

Wordsworth

Frontispiece. Sir George Beaumont, *Peele Castle, c.*May 1806. The inspiration of Wordsworth's 'Elegiac Stanzas': 'I was thy Neighbour once, thou rugged Pile!'

Wordsworth

An Inner Life

Duncan Wu

BLACKWELL
Publishers

First published 2002

2 4 6 8 10 9 7 5 3 1

Blackwell Publishers Ltd
108 Cowley Road
Oxford OX4 1JF
UK

Blackwell Publishers Inc.
350 Main Street
Malden, Massachusetts 02148
USA

British Library Cataloguing in Publication Data

A CIP catalogue record for this book is available from the British Library.

Library of Congress Cataloging-in-Publication Data

Wu, Duncan
    Wordworth : an inner life / Duncan Wu.
        p.   cm.
    Includes bibliographical references and index.
    ISBN 0–631–20638–8 (alk. paper)
    1. Wordsworth, William, 1770–1850 — Criticism and interpretation.
    2. Spiritual life in literature.   3. Psychology in literature.   4. Self in
    literature.   I. Title.
    PR5888 .W8 2002
    821'.7—dc21

                                                            2001002572

Typeset in 10 on 12.5 pt Galliard by Ace Filmsetting Ltd, Frome, Somerset
Printed in Great Britain by MPG Books Ltd, Bodmin, Cornwall

This book is printed on acid-free paper.

Contents

Contents

Illustrations

Preface

This book seeks to trace the connection between Wordsworth's inner life and his poetry, as revealed in his writings from boyhood to maturity. I want to answer the question of what kind of poet Wordsworth thought himself to be at various stages in his career, how he perceived his talent, and how it was shaped and directed by external forces (most notably Coleridge). It is essentially a work of literary criticism, but because of its attention to historical and bibliographical fact I have sometimes thought of it as biography. It is not that, for my attention is on Wordsworth's *inner* life, though I have attended to the way in which his writing was shaped by the circumstances under which it was composed.

Hindsight is a distorting glass that makes the evolution of literary talent appear foreordained; the author of *Richard III*, we feel, cannot have avoided composing *Macbeth*, so obvious are connections between the two. In the unimaginable 'present' of the historical past, an artist's development is under constant threat. The enemies of promise are multifarious and ubiquitous. No one can be certain of how their talent will mature, or indeed if it can do so. The perils of drying up or failing to renew one's reserves of inspiration are ever-present. So it is that studies of Wordsworth all too frequently take it for granted that this is the poet whose great work was *The Prelude*, which was somehow destined to be written from the outset of his career. This is to disregard the history of its inception, its shifting function within Wordsworth's creative life, and its fluctuating relation to 'The Recluse'. Indeed, it is astonishing how many books concerned with Wordsworth's poetry fail to take 'The Recluse' into account, or even to mention it. So pronounced is this tendency that one almost hesitates to make it the focus of a study of Wordsworth's life and art. But we ignore it at our peril. So far as he was concerned, it was to have been the summit of his achievement. It dominated his thinking from 1798 onwards, and shaped *The Prelude* in all its forms. He knew that it would establish him as the one true philosophical poet of the age and change the world for ever, crucially altering man's relation to the world around him. Among other things, this book seeks to describe its evolution and Wordsworth's developing sense of himself as its author.

But there is another factor in all this, and that is the perspective offered by Wordsworth's juvenilia. By taking into account the poems written during his Hawkshead and Cambridge years it is possible to explain a great deal about how Wordsworth saw himself as a poet for the remainder of his career. To the best of my knowledge this is the first book-length study of the poet to take into account the comprehensive survey of the juvenile manuscripts in the relevant volume of the Cornell Wordsworth Series, published in 1997. Its appearance was one of the most important events in the literary world for some years, bringing to the canon a number of hitherto unavailable poems in a new chronological sequence. For a poet as concerned with childhood as Wordsworth it is remarkable that so little attention has been paid to his juvenilia. Indeed, the problem with many studies is the inbuilt anachronism of their reading of his childhood life through the filter of *The Prelude* – sometimes indeed *The Fourteen-Book Prelude* (1850), a much-revised view of the past it purports to describe.

Wordsworth's great autobiographical poem is a vital source for any study of his work, so integral to our understanding of him that it is probably impossible to factor it out of our thinking. The problem is that all too often our understanding of it has been untrue to its evolution and Wordsworth's reasons for writing it. This book attempts to accommodate those intentions as they existed at the time of composition. It gives considerable weight to contemporary documentary materials and manuscript drafts, many of which have been published in the Cornell Wordsworth Series. On occasion I have constructed my own transcriptions. Like other scholars I have done my fair share of speculating and conjecturing, though I believe that the evidence I have gathered to support inferences about Wordsworth's thinking sheds light on our knowledge of his life – or at least the inner life enjoyed by all artists. This book addresses Wordsworth's career up to 1813, but it cannot pretend to survey every line of every work written during that time. Acknowledging the impossibility of this, I have tried instead to give close attention to those works which may be considered representative of his thinking in the hope that in so doing I have not been guilty of distortion.

For the purposes of organizing this study I have proposed that important developments in Wordsworth's life and work may be understood through a detailed examination of three pivotal moments. The first can be dated fairly precisely to July 1787, when Wordsworth, Christopher, John and Dorothy underwent a period of delayed mourning for their parents. The death and burial of their father in 1783 had been intensely traumatic; on top of which it made the children destitute, as he left no will and no money. No doubt these factors played their part in detaining the children from confronting the emotional consequences of the events that had disrupted their lives, and the result was acute feelings of guilt, particularly in Wordsworth, that would shape his creative work from this point onwards. Indeed, the first three chapters of this book are preoccupied with guilt and betrayal as they occur in his poetry until June 1797, when a second pivotal event in his life – his momentous collaboration with Coleridge – began.

It is not possible to paint a balanced picture of Wordsworth's growth as a poet without giving Coleridge his due. The collision of temperaments and opinions during the golden year of 1797–8, which the Wordsworths spent at Alfoxden House within walking distance of Coleridge, then resident at Nether Stowey, led to a drastic and thoroughgoing reassessment, on Wordsworth's part, of his artistic aims. From being a poet of grief, he turned himself into that of 'The Recluse', a work that was to propose the redemption of humanity at large. That willed effort of self-remaking was supported by a wave of confidence provided by Coleridge. It could not last, and from July 1798 onwards Wordsworth made frequent return visits to the subjects that had earlier attracted his notice – human suffering, political injustice and emotional trauma. This retrenchment began with *The Prelude*, in which he began to question the larger project of 'The Recluse'.

The third pivotal event on which this study hinges is another death: that of John Wordsworth in February 1805. It halted composition of the thirteen-book *Prelude* and prompted Wordsworth to conduct a complete reassessment of his aims and aesthetics. The confidence that had produced the sublime transcendence of much that he had written came to seem specious in the light of that loss, and in the event he was only just able to complete *The Prelude*. He would never complete 'The Recluse'. From this point onwards his poetry was markedly different from what had preceded it. The weakening of the relationship between him and Coleridge from late 1806 onwards also contributed to this decreasing ability to write the great philosophical poem of the age. His dilemma intensified with the deaths of Catherine and Thomas Wordsworth in 1812.

I want to answer the question of what Wordsworth thought he was, how he saw himself, as far as we can judge by his writing at the time. Documentary evidence has been introduced where it is relevant, but I have always taken the view that the most important testimony is that of the poet and those closest to him, and on that account I have given priority to what can be positively determined about his thoughts and works rather than to what, so far as we know, he *didn't* think.

It has been necessary to emphasize Wordsworth's experience of grief, guilt and suffering, sometimes no doubt at the expense of other essential and important qualities such as transcendence. Wordsworth is pre-eminently the master of the immaterial, along with such poets as Vaughan and Blake. It was always an ingredient in his work, from his childhood, when he felt in danger of being engulfed by the 'abyss of idealism', to his later years. As late as 1822 he told William Ellery Channing that 'Poetry carries us up to the *infinite*, which is undefined, i e, *mystical*'.[1] Of course, this is an important ingredient of his work, but the tendency to ignore its roots in his own life experiences has led to some fundamental misunderstandings. Wordsworth's comments on visionary power need to be understood as elemental to the psychological truth of his poetry, and if at times I have appeared to underemphasize those comments it has been in an attempt to redress the balance in favour of the thesis that the primary means of understanding the nature of Wordsworthian transcendence is fully to comprehend his evolution as a writer, determined as it was in large part by the intense and enduring emotions that shaped his creative power.

---

[1]   John Beer, 'William Ellery Channing Visits the Lake Poets', *RES* 42 (1991) 211–26, p. 225.

Acknowledgements

This book could not have been undertaken without the labours of those who have revolutionized our knowledge of the poet and his works over the last three decades. In particular I pay tribute to John Finch, whose unpublished thesis has taught me a great deal about 'The Recluse' and *The Prelude* – although some of my conclusions differ from his. I am grateful also to Stephen Parrish and his co-editors on the Cornell Wordsworth Series, only now coming to its conclusion. It is an indispensable memorial to Wordsworth, and has been a constant companion. I do not take issue with its editors lightly, and have done so purely in the hope of clarifying our knowledge of his manuscripts.

I have been the grateful recipient of encouragement and help from friends and colleagues during work on this book: Paul Bauschatz, John Beer, Paul F. Betz, Ronald Britton, James A. Butler, Richard W. Clancey, Jeff Cowton, Jared Curtis, Beth Darlington, Veronica Finch, Marilyn Gaull, Stephen Gill, Sheila Gordon, Roger Green, the late George Kirby, Carol Landon, Lucy Newlyn, Constance Parrish, Catherine Payling, Mark L. Reed, Jane Renfrew, Roger Robinson, Nicholas Roe, the late Bill Ruddick, John Spedding, Jane Stabler, Gordon Thomas, Stephen Wall, the late Reginald Watters, Mary R. Wedd, the late D. G. Wilson, Sylvia Wordsworth and the late Richard Wordsworth. This book originated as a doctoral thesis supervised by the late D. F. McKenzie and Jonathan Wordsworth. I owe a debt to the Charles Lamb Society and its members for help and encouragement of various kinds. Those students I was fortunate enough to teach at the University of Glasgow, John Carroll University in Cleveland, Ohio, and the University of Oklahoma at Norman have taught me a great deal by sharing their thoughts about Wordsworth's poetry with me. This volume has provided me with a welcome opportunity of working once again with Andrew McNeillie of Blackwell Publishers in Oxford. I am grateful also to my wife Caroline, whose shrewd judgements have made this a better book than it would otherwise have been.

Parts of this book have appeared in print in different form in the following journals: the *Wordsworth Circle*, *Essays in Criticism*, the *Review of English*

Studies, Romanticism on the Net and the *Charles Lamb Bulletin*. I am grateful to their editors and publishers for permission to draw on those materials.

This volume is dedicated to three eminent British Wordsworthians, all of whom have shaped my understanding of this poetry: the late John Alban Finch, Robert S. Woof and Jonathan Wordsworth.

D. W.
Oxford,
February 2001

A Note on Texts

Throughout this volume I have quoted from standard scholarly editions. For the writings of Coleridge this means the Collected Coleridge series, and for those of Wordsworth the Cornell Wordsworth. For Coleridge's poems and plays, which at the time of writing are not yet available in J. C. C. Mays's Collected Coleridge text, I have turned to John Beer's Everyman edition, supplemented by E. H. Coleridge's Clarendon volumes for the plays. In the case of poems published by Coleridge in *Lyrical Ballads* (1798) I have quoted from the texts in the Cornell *Lyrical Ballads*. For 'The Pedlar' and its associated draft, 'Not useless do I deem', absent from the Cornell *Ruined Cottage*, I have used the texts in Jonathan Wordsworth, *The Music of Humanity* (1969). ('The Pedlar' is available in the same author's *The Borders of Vision* (1982), pp. 379–87, and *William Wordsworth: The Pedlar, Tintern Abbey, The Two-Part Prelude*, ed. Jonathan Wordsworth (Cambridge: Cambridge University Press, 1985), pp. 19–32.) When quoting from the *Five-Book Prelude* of 1804 I have had no option but to cite my own edition published in 1997; similarly, a text of the 1808 *White Doe of Rylstone* is to be found exclusively in the appendix to this volume. In the absence of the Cornell *Excursion* (forthcoming at the time of writing) I refer to the first edition of 1814; line numbers do not, therefore, correspond to those given by De Selincourt (who presents a later text).

Italics are those of the quoted text except where otherwise stated. On rare occasions I have seen fit to emend the transcriptions given by the Cornell editors, or to present my own edited texts, and I have indicated this in my notes. When doing so I have sought to present the draft as it stood on completion. To that end, deletions and overwritings are accepted and alternative readings incorporated into the text only when the original is deleted. All revisions executed at the time of the original draft are incorporated into my texts. Punctuation is authorial except where otherwise indicated.

Abbreviations

BNYPL	*Bulletin of the New York Public Library*
Bondage of Opium	Molly Lefebure, *Samuel Taylor Coleridge: A Bondage of Opium* (1974)
Borders of Vision	Jonathan Wordsworth, *William Wordsworth: The Borders of Vision* (1982)
Burton	*The Letters of Mary Wordsworth 1800–1855*, ed. Mary E. Burton (1958)
Butler *JEGP*	James A. Butler, 'Wordsworth, Cottle, and the *Lyrical Ballads*: Five Letters, 1797–1800', *JEGP* 75 (1976) 139–53
CC	*Collected Coleridge Series*, Bollingen Series 75
CC *Biographia*	*Biographia Literaria*, ed. James Engell and Walter Jackson Bate (2 vols, 1983)
CC *Friend*	*The Friend*, ed. Barbara Rooke (2 vols, 1969)
CC *Lectures 1795*	*Lectures 1795 On Politics and Religion*, ed. Lewis Patton and Peter Mann (1971)
CC *Literature*	*Lectures 1808–1819 On Literature*, ed. R. A. Foakes (2 vols, 1987)
CC *Marginalia*	*Marginalia*, ed. George Whalley and Heather Jackson (6 vols, 1980–)
CC *Table Talk*	*Table Talk*, ed. Carl Woodring (2 vols, 1990)
CC *Watchman*	*The Watchman*, ed. Lewis Patton (1970)
CLB	*Charles Lamb Bulletin*
Cornell *Benjamin*	*Benjamin the Waggoner*, ed. Paul Betz (1981)
Cornell *Borderers*	*The Borderers*, ed. Robert Osborn (1982)
Cornell *Early Poems*	*Early Poems and Fragments, 1785–1797*, ed. Carol Landon and Jared Curtis (1997)
Cornell *Evening Walk*	*An Evening Walk*, ed. James Averill (1984)
Cornell *Home at Grasmere*	*Home at Grasmere*, ed. Beth Darlington (1977)

Cornell *Lyrical Ballads*	*Lyrical Ballads and Other Poems, 1797–1800*, ed. James Butler and Karen Green (1992)
Cornell *Poems 1800–7*	*Poems, in Two Volumes, and Other Poems, 1800–1807*, ed. Jared Curtis (1985)
Cornell *Poems 1807–20*	*Shorter Poems, 1807–1820* ed. Carl H. Ketcham (1989)
Cornell *Ruined Cottage*	*The Ruined Cottage and The Pedlar*, ed. James Butler (1979)
Cornell *Salisbury Plain*	*The Salisbury Plain Poems*, ed. Stephen Gill (1975)
Cornell *Tuft*	*The Tuft of Primroses, with Other Late Poems for The Recluse*, ed. Joseph F. Kishel (1986)
Cornell *White Doe*	*The White Doe of Rylstone*, ed. Kristine Dugas (1988)
Cornell *13–Book Prelude*	*The Thirteen-Book Prelude*, ed. Mark L. Reed (2 vols., 1991)
Cornell *14–Book Prelude*	*The Fourteen-Book Prelude*, ed. W. J. B. Owen (1985)
Cornell *1799 Prelude*	*The Two-Part Prelude*, ed. Stephen Parrish (1979)
Curry	*New Letters of Robert Southey*, ed. Kenneth Curry (2 vols., 1965)
Darker Reflections	Richard Holmes, *Coleridge: Darker Reflections* (1998)
Disowned by Memory	David Bromwich, *Disowned by Memory* (1998)
Early Visions	Richard Holmes, *Coleridge: Early Visions* (1989)
EIC	*Essays in Criticism*
EY	*Letters of William and Dorothy Wordsworth: The Early Years, 1787–1805*, ed. Ernest De Selincourt, rev. Chester L. Shaver (1967)
Farington	*The Diary of Joseph Farington*, ed. Kenneth Garlick, Angus Macintyre and Kathryn Cave (16 vols, 1979–84)
Finch	John A. Finch, 'Wordsworth, Coleridge, and The Recluse, 1798–1814' (Ph.D. thesis, Cornell University,1964)
FN	*The Fenwick Notes of William Wordsworth*, ed. Jared Curtis (1993)
Gill	Stephen Gill, *William Wordsworth: A Life* (1989)
Grasmere Journals	Dorothy Wordsworth, *The Grasmere Journals*, ed. Pamela Woof (1991)

Griggs	*The Letters of Samuel Taylor Coleridge*, ed. E. L. Griggs (6 vols, 1956–71)
Howe	*The Works of William Hazlitt*, ed. P. P. Howe (21 vols, 1930–4)
Johnston	Kenneth R. Johnston, *The Hidden Wordsworth: Poet, Lover, Rebel, Spy* (1998)
Johnston, *Recluse*	Kenneth R. Johnston, *Wordsworth and The Recluse* (1984)
JEGP	*Journal of English and Germanic Philology*
Ketcham	*The Letters of John Wordsworth*, ed. Carl H. Ketcham (1969)
Little	*Barron Field's Memoirs of Wordsworth*, ed. Geoffrey Little (1975)
LY	*The Letters of William and Dorothy Wordsworth: The Later Years*, ed. Ernest De Selincourt, *i: 1821–8*, rev. Alan G. Hill (1978); *ii: 1829–34*, rev. Alan G. Hill (1982); *iii: 1835–9*, rev. Alan G. Hill (1982); *iv: 1840–53*, rev. by Alan G. Hill (1988)
Marchand	*Byron's Letters and Journals*, ed. Leslie A. Marchand (13 vols, 1973–94)
Marrs	*The Letters of Charles and Mary Anne Lamb 1796–1817*, ed. Edwin W. Marrs, Jr. (3 vols., 1975–8)
Moorman	*William Wordsworth: A Biography*, by Mary Moorman (2 vols, 1957–65)
Morley	*Henry Crabb Robinson on Books and Their Writers*, ed. Edith J. Morley (3 vols, 1938)
MY	*The Letters of William and Dorothy Wordsworth: The Middle Years*, ed. Ernest De Selincourt, *i: 1806–11*, rev. Mary Moorman (1969); *ii: 1812–20*, rev. Mary Moorman and Alan G. Hill (1970)
Norton *Prelude*	*William Wordsworth: The Prelude 1799, 1805, 1850*, ed. Jonathan Wordsworth, M. H. Abrams and Stephen Gill (1979)
Notebooks	*The Notebooks of Samuel Taylor Coleridge*, ed. Kathleen Coburn (5 vols., 1957–)
N&Q	*Notes and Queries*
OET *Prelude*	*The Prelude*, ed. Ernest de Selincourt, rev. Helen Darbishire (2nd edn, 1959)
Peacock	*The Critical Opinions of William Wordsworth*, ed. Markham L. Peacock Jr. (1950)

Prose Works	*The Prose Works of William Wordsworth*, ed. W. J. B. Owen and Jane Worthington Smyser (3 vols, 1974)
PW	*The Poetical Works of William Wordsworth*, ed. Ernest De Selincourt and Helen Darbishire (5 vols, 1940–9)
Reed i	Mark L. Reed, *Wordsworth: The Chronology of the Early Years, 1770–1799* (1967)
Reed ii	Mark L. Reed, *Wordsworth: The Chronology of the Middle Years, 1800–1815* (1975)
RES	*Review of English Studies*
Robinson Correspondence	*The Correspondence of Henry Crabb Robinson with the Wordsworth Circle (1808–1866)*, ed. Edith J. Morley (2 vols., 1927)
SIR	*Studies in Romanticism*
Supp.	*The Letters of William and Dorothy Wordsworth VIII: A Supplement of New Letters*, ed. Alan G. Hill (1993)
TLS	Times Literary Supplement
Warter	*Selections from the Letters of Robert Southey*, ed. John Wood Warter (4 vols, 1856)
WC	The Wordsworth Circle
Woof Ph.D.	Robert S. Woof, 'The Literary Relations of Wordsworth and Coleridge, 1795–1803: Five Studies' (Ph.D. thesis, University of Toronto, 1959)
WR	Duncan Wu, *Wordsworth's Reading 1770–1815* (2 vols, 1993–5)
Wu	*Selected Writings of William Hazlitt*, ed. Duncan Wu (9 vols, 1998)

1

'Perhaps my pains might be beguil'd'

Grief was the making of Wordsworth. He had lost both parents by the age of 13. His mother had died in March 1778, perhaps of pneumonia, after an illness lasting two and a half months. His father died in December 1783 after spending a night without shelter when he became lost while returning home. The loss of one's parents in early life, by whatever means, has a profoundly formative influence on the psyche of the surviving child. A year later Wordsworth started writing in response to an assignment set by his teacher, William Taylor (who would die in June 1786). His earliest surviving poem dates from 1785, and a large quantity of material survives from his time at Hawkshead and Cambridge. Given the preoccupation with childhood in his later work, the testimony of the verse written during his teenage years might be thought worth attending to, yet critics have, for the most part, been chary of it. Indeed, it is one of the ironies of literary history that the juvenile writings of this poet have been passed over in favour of his mature observations on the growth of the human mind. This is the poet who believed that 'The Child is Father of the Man', and it is partly out of deference for that view that this study argues that the key to an understanding of Wordsworth is the poetry of his boyhood.

His roots remain under-appreciated partly because he is so frequently read in the latest version of his works, which includes the juvenilia only in much revised and truncated form.[1] Arguments over the various texts of Wordsworth's

---

[1] *Wordsworth: Poetical Works*, ed. Thomas Hutchinson, revised by Ernest de Selincourt (Oxford, 1904) remains in print, and is widely used. The section entitled 'Poems written in youth' includes a drastically revised, 14-line extract from 'The Vale of Esthwaite' (text of 1815), 'Calm is all nature as a resting wheel' (text of 1807), *An Evening Walk* ('original text of 1793') and *Descriptive Sketches* (text of 1849–50), along with 'Lines written while sailing in a boat at evening' and 'Remembrance of Collins' (both texts of 1798, though deriving from a single sonnet of 1789), 'Lines left upon a seat in a Yew-Tree' (composed 1797), 'Guilt and Sorrow' (text of 1842, though deriving from a poem written in 1793)

poems have tended to centre unhelpfully on issues of literary quality.[2] It is not that this is an uninteresting subject, but that the controversy has tended to obscure something more pressing: over-reliance on the latest lifetime text of 1849–50 hinders serious appreciation of Wordsworth's literary development. At least two major critical studies published within the last decade have quoted largely, if not exclusively, from the latest texts.[3] I say this not to disparage them, but to suggest that no examination of Wordsworth's poetry can be fully sensitive to its nuances if it disregards early variants.

'The Vale of Esthwaite' was the most ambitious work of his schooldays, consisting of over 600 lines.[4] It has attracted some attention, most notably from such scholars as Geoffrey Hartman, F. W. Bateson, James Averill and Kenneth Johnston, but remains little known. This marginality doubtless owes something to the fact that it was not published until 1940 when Ernest de Selincourt published selected juvenilia in the appendix to the first volume of his *Poetical Works of Wordsworth* – a relegation that indicated de Selincourt's unease about its status. This was entirely understandable. De Selincourt's professed aim was to supply a 'sound text' of 'the six-volume edition of 1849–50',[5] which includes 'The Vale of Esthwaite' only in the form of a much revised 14–line extract. He would have admitted that by providing readers

and 'The Borderers' (text of 1842, deriving from a text of 1797–9). If there was any editorial rationale entailed in their assembly, it is not easy to work out. On the generic level, it contains works Wordsworth first composed between the ages of 17 and 29 (an unnervingly wide-ranging definition of 'youth'); on a scholarly level, it includes the earliest version of *An Evening Walk*, a poem revised right up to the final lifetime edition of 1849–50, alongside others taken directly from that final lifetime edition. There is no textual consistency to be found here.

[2] This is in no way to disparage the quality of the debate, which has been spirited and informed; see, for instance, S. M. Parrish, 'The Whig Interpretation of Literature', *TEXT* 4 (1988) 343–50 and Jack Stillinger, 'Textual Primitivism and the Editing of Wordsworth', *Studies in Romanticism* 28 (1989) 3–28. Some time before it began Stephen Gill spelt out the main issues in his 'Wordsworth's Poems: The Question of Text', *RES* 34 (1983) 172–89, and since summarized in his indispensable *Wordsworth: The Prelude* (Cambridge: Cambridge University Press, 1991), pp. 94–103.

[3] See Thomas McFarland, *William Wordsworth: Intensity and Achievement* (Oxford: Clarendon Press, 1992) and Marjean D. Purinton, *Romantic Ideology Unmasked* (Newark: University of Delaware Press, 1994). In fairness to these critics, they are clearly aware of the Cornell series, and on occasion refer to it, but for reasons of their own take de Selincourt as their primary source. In *Wordsworth's Great Period Poems* (Cambridge: Cambridge University Press, 1986) Marjorie Levinson also uses de Selincourt except for *The Prelude*, in which case she cites the Norton critical edition.

[4] The question of the poem's length is addressed in detail by Curtis and Landon, Cornell *Early Poems*, 407–13.

[5] De Selincourt's rationale is clearly explained, *PW* i p. v.

with something more substantial, he was going against the poet's own wishes. In 1997 Carol Landon and Jared Curtis published the most accurate and carefully edited text of the poem that we are ever likely to have, and it is a considerable wonder that it has, at the time of writing, received no critical attention and no review. The present study aims to demonstrate the centrality of the juvenilia to an appreciation of Wordsworth's mature work.

Curtis and Landon present a number of 'affinitive pieces' related to 'The Vale of Esthwaite', among them a description of several personified characters – Madness, Murder, Suicide, Despair and Horror. These stem from Wordsworth's enjoyment of Gothic literature, most notably Helen Maria Williams' 'Part of an Irregular Fragment, found in a dark passage of the Tower', in her *Poems* (1786).[6] As a child, it is likely that he believed in ghosts, as a number were supposed to haunt the shores of Esthwaite Water;[7] he would also have known of dilapidated Calgarth Hall on the banks of Windermere, and the two human skulls in one of its windows which, Thomas West reported in his *Guide to the Lakes* (1784), had been brought to the house by 'some ghost'.[8] Besides being the height of literary fashion, Gothicism was an integral element of folk culture in the Lakes, and it is not surprising that when he first began to write Wordsworth practised his hand at spooky episodes. But there is something else here: from the very outset of his career this poet whose realm would be that of human psychology underpinned his interest in ghosts and spectres with an accompanying fascination with extreme mental states. These early Gothic passages should not therefore be read in isolation, as they have been, but as initiating an interest in the human mind which in the fullness of time would lead to the portraits of Jenny in 'A Somersetshire Tragedy', Margaret in 'The Ruined Cottage', the Sailor in 'Adventures on Salisbury Plain', Rivers in *The Borderers*, and such characters as Harry Gill and the mad mother. In these early fragments, which derive from lines originally written in spring 1787, Madness is 'half-clad', 'Leaning from a blasted tree':

> He howled and through his shaggy hair
> His green swoln eyes did grimly glare
> Like tapers when the death bells sound
> Expiring on the grass green ground
>
>   (Madness (c) 1–4)

---

[6] See *WR* i 149.

[7] See Thompson 262.

[8] See Thomas West, *A Guide to the Lakes* (3rd edn, London, 1784), p. 64, which Wordsworth certainly knew (*WR* i 146–7). The skulls gave rise to a ballad which Wordsworth may have known; see Alexander Craig Gibson, *The Folk-Speech of Cumberland* (London, 1880), pp. 76–85.

Murder is 'Pale as the corse he slew'; Suicide 'in act to leap'; Horror's hand is 'dead-cold'.[9] Each vignette has in common a fascination with death and extremity. In the *Prelude* Wordsworth would affectionately mock this tendency in his youthful self, softening it in retrospect as he recalled that for him, 'the Yew-tree had its Ghost / That took its station there for ornament.'[10] That sepia-tinted view of his early writing fails either to provide it with a context or to make the necessary connection with the mature verse. In that sense, the critical downgrading and neglect of the juvenilia effectively began with Wordsworth himself.

Composition of 'The Vale of Esthwaite' fell into two parts. The first may be tentatively dated March–June 1787, and is characterized by a Gothic, occasionally sentimental manner modelled on such writers as Helen Maria Williams and Charlotte Smith.[11] The vignettes of Murder and Horror are typical. In the notebook in which he was working, Dove Cottage MS 3, that Gothic and sentimental style accounts for the first two-thirds of the poem, up to page 25.[12] At this point four pages are torn from the manuscript, and the poem resumes on the recto of page 30, marking its second phase, which can be dated to c.July 1787. What we find there is remarkable in the context of the later poetry: it recalls the early evening of 19 December 1783; the 13-year-old Wordsworth waits above Hawkshead on the ridge north of Borwick Lodge, a mile and a half from his school, for a horse to take him and his brothers, Richard and John, home for the holidays:

> No spot but claims the tender tear
> By joy or grief to memory dear
> One Evening when the wintry blast
> Through the sharp Hawthorn whistling pass'd
> And the poor flocks all pinch'd with cold
> Sad drooping sought the mountain fold
> Long Long upon yon steepy rock
> Alone I bore the bitter shock
> Long Long my swimming eyes did roam
> For little Horse to bear me home
> To bear me what avails my tear
> To sorrow o'er a Father's bier.
>
> ('The Vale of Esthwaite' 272–83)

[9]   Cornell *Early Poems* 534–9.
[10] *The Thirteen-Book Prelude* viii 528–9.
[11] Important influences include Smith's *Elegiac Sonnets* (first published 1784). See *WR* i 127–8, 149–50; Cornell *Early Poems* 419.
[12] I follow the pagination given by Landon and Curtis; see Cornell *Early Poems* 163.

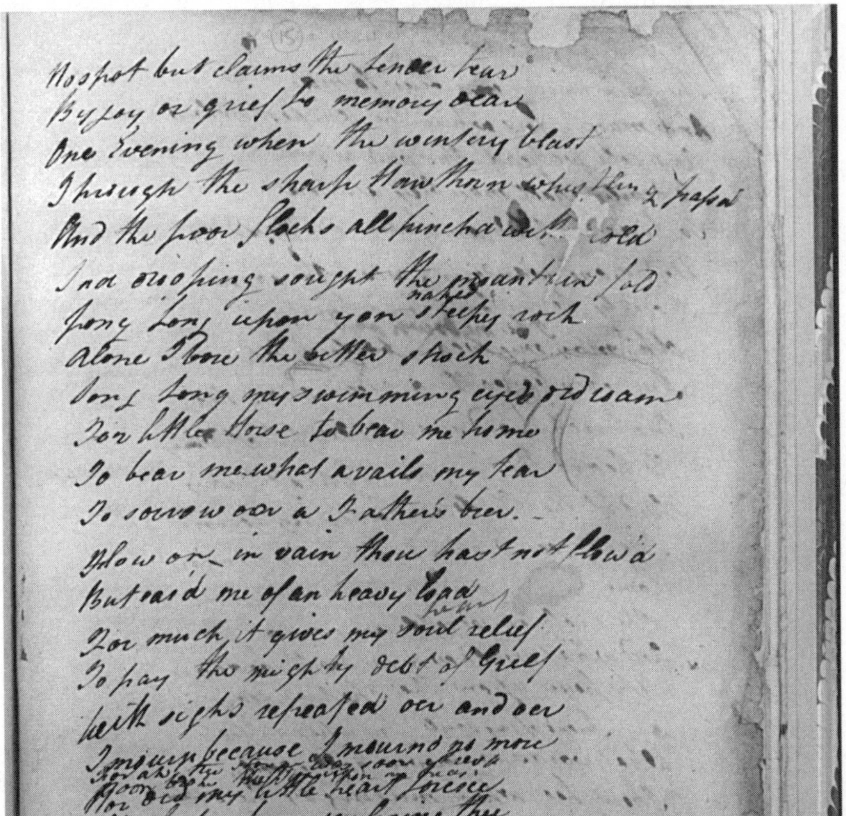

Figure 1. DC MS 3, 30r. 'The Vale of Esthwaite'; 'No spot but claims the tender tear . . .' Wordsworth's first attempt at the waiting for the horse episode, dating from *c.*July 1787.

The clunk of Wordsworth's tetrameter couplets is evidence of a self-conscious literariness underlined by their allusive manner. The 'whistling' of the wind through the hawthorn is doubly resonant, echoing both *King Lear* and James 'Ossian' Macpherson's *Temora*, where the sleeping highlanders 'thought they heard the voice of the dead. This voice of the dead, however, was perhaps no more than a shriller whistle of the winds in an old tree.'[13] The additional echo of Poor Tom's 'Through the sharp hawthorn blow the [cold] winds'[14] makes it peculiarly evocative. An acute sensitivity to nature, and its ability to accommodate our sense of the dead, is combined with the knowledge of human vulnerability before the cold, unsympathetic wind. Nature is already in this early composition a strangely divided thing, capable of both sympathy and indifference. That duality is underlined by the original reading of 'steepy rock' which in the manuscript is 'naked'.[15]

On a banal level such intimations could be explained away by the suggestion that Wordsworth was aware by the time he waited that his father was mortally ill – as indeed he probably was. But this should not obscure the important anachronism: at the time Wordsworth waited for the horses, John Wordsworth Sr was *not yet dead*. What has happened is that in retrospect the poet has anticipated his father's death, incorporating it into the 'bitter shock' of the wind and his 'swimming eyes' – as, in the present (of 1787), he feels the abandonment of an orphan. The flocks 'Sad drooping', the 'sharp Hawthorn' and the 'wintry blast' are all emotional indices of the child's state of mind in the here and now, rather than an objectively realized account of the past.

That elision of the past (1783) with the present (1787) implies some connection between the two, elucidated in the lines that follow. Without warning, Wordsworth switches from the scene above Borwick Lodge to the moment of composition, summer 1787:

> Flow on, in vain thou hast not flow'd
> But eas'd me of a heavy load
> For much it gives my soul relief
> To pay the mighty debt of Grief
> With sighs repeated o'er and o'er
> I mourn because I mourn'd no more
> For ah! the storm was soon at rest
> Soon broke the Sun upon my breast

---

[13] James Macpherson, *Temora: an ancient epic poem, with several other poems translated from the Galic language* (1763), p. 79. See WR i 92.
[14] *King Lear* III iv 46–7.
[15] See Cornell *Early Poems* 447.

Nor did my little heart foresee
– She lost a home in losing thee
Nor did it know – of thee bereft
That little more than Heav'n was left.

(ll. 284–95)

With that shift in tense, 'Flow on', the poetry turns its attention to the 'now' of 1787, three and a half years later, when Wordsworth found himself still in tears. The implied continuum between the 'bitter shock' of his father's death and what he experiences today is argued without self-indulgence: 'For much it gives my soul relief / To pay the mighty debt of Grief.' He may be recalling the stoicism of Jonson's 'On My First Son' – 'Seven years wert thou lent to me, and I thee pay, / Exacted by thy fate, on the just day' (ll. 3–4) – where the mercantile imagery suppresses an anguish that threatens constantly to erupt. But there is no sense of the repression we sense so powerfully in Jonson; instead, Wordsworth candidly assesses his response to his father's demise. He explicitly welcomes the tears he sheds now, in July 1787, as they relieve him of a 'debt of Grief' not fully rendered when he followed his father's coffin to its resting-place in Cockermouth churchyard. The 'sighs repeated o'er and o'er' appear to express feelings of culpability, even guilt, for not having adequately lamented in 1783: 'I mourn because I mourn'd no more.' That line reworks the final line of Gray's 'Sonnet on the Death of Richard West': 'And weep the more, because I weep in vain'.[16] It is a clever allusion to a work also concerned with the failure of grief adequately to express the pain of bereavement. There is guilt too in the renewed awareness that only now does Wordsworth understand the full consequences: he 'lost a home in losing thee'. This section of the 'Vale' strives to define what 'home' means, and to seek reparation for its dissolution. (In actual fact the Wordsworth children had lost their home, which had been sold with all its contents, together with John Wordsworth's land holdings, by May 1784.)

Everything here is markedly different from what precedes it – no Gothic spectres, no castles, no personified horrors. Instead of mimicking literary idioms, Wordsworth explores an inner landscape which follows the contours of his own psyche. Between the first period of composition (March–June 1787) and the second (July), some change occurred within him that turned the 'Vale' from a literary exercise into something more personal.

The explanation lies in a letter from Dorothy Wordsworth to her best friend,

---

[16] Wordsworth famously criticized the sonnet in the Preface to *Lyrical Ballads*, but it is worth bearing in mind that he exempted lines 13–14 from reproach.

Jane Pollard, dating from late July 1787.[17] This is the earliest surviving letter by either Wordsworth or his sister, but it has not always had the attention it deserves. Since their father's death Dorothy had been living with her Aunt Threlkeld in Halifax, but in May 1787 she was transplanted to her Cookson grandparents in Penrith. The Cooksons lived over their draper's shop in the market-place, and regarded the Wordsworth children as jumped-up. It gave them a self-righteous gratification to set Dorothy menial duties about the house and speak ill of her brothers. Besides anything else, they resented the money which the orphaned Wordsworths cost them. On its own this would probably have had little effect on her brother's poetry; the catalyst came at the end of the Hawkshead summer term. This would be a momentous reunion for the Wordsworth children. Dorothy had been only 6 when she had last seen her brothers and was now 14½. It would be almost like meeting for the first time. The Hawkshead term having ended on 20 June, Dorothy expected her brothers to be sent horses immediately so as to join her, but this did not happen, as she explained to Jane Pollard:

> I was for a whole week kept in expectation of my Brothers, who staid at school all that time after the vacation begun owing to the ill-nature of my Uncle who would not send horses for them because when they wrote they did not happen to mention them, and only said when they should break up which was always before sufficient. This was the beginning of my mortifications for I felt that if they had had another home to go to, they would have been behaved to in a very different manner, and received with more chearful countenances, indeed nobody but myself expressed one wish to see them, at last however they were sent for, but not till my Brother Wm had hired a horse for himself and came over because he thought some one must be ill . . . (*EY* 3–4)

The breathless, helter-skelter rhythms of Dorothy's narrative testify to the turbulent emotions underlying it. Though resident in Penrith for less than two months, she was now aware of the contempt in which she and her brothers were held by their Uncle, Christopher Crackanthorpe Cookson.[18] The delay in sending horses was its most eloquent testimony to date; what Cookson may not have realized is that it reiterated the circumstances preceding the death of John Wordsworth Sr. As in 1783, William seems to have been stranded in Hawkshead when he was desperate to leave. Such was his anxiety that he

---

[17] The connection with Dorothy's letter was first pointed out by F. W. Bateson, *Wordsworth: A Re-Interpretation* (2nd edn, London: Longman, 1956), pp. 50–3, though critics and biographers have been slow to accept it.

[18] Christopher Crackanthorpe Cookson (20 May 1745–Oct. 1799) who, on 17 July 1792, changed his surname to Crackanthorpe.

was compelled to hire a horse on his own behalf 'because he thought some one must be ill'. Dorothy is eloquent, but we may infer the elision of a good deal of mental and emotional anguish in her narrative.

It may be fair to say that the Wordsworth children had to some extent been cushioned from the full emotional impact of their orphaning in 1783. Dorothy had been looked after by kindly relatives (the family of her 'Aunt', Elizabeth Threlkeld), and her brothers had enjoyed the security provided by Ann Tyson and their school. Their ill-treatment by the unfeeling Cooksons would have provided a sudden and unwelcome reminder of their vulnerability, and re-awakened the grief that had lain dormant since their father's death:

> Many a time have Wm, J, C, and myself shed tears together, tears of the bitterest sorrow, we all of us, each day, feel more sensibly the loss we sustained when we were deprived of our parents, and each day do we receive fresh insults, you will wonder of what sort; believe me of the most mortifying kind; the insults of servants . . . (*EY* 3)

The Wordsworths, who during their parents' lives had occupied the grandest house in Cockermouth, would have felt the humiliation acutely – one un-doubtedly sanctioned, and probably encouraged, by their uncle.[19] He seems to have resented their social status, and took pleasure in rubbing their noses in the fact that they were now dependent on him. There is no escaping the fact that this letter – a brilliantly articulated account of the Wordsworth children's state at this moment – is about grief, 'tears of the bitterest sorrow', and what it means to lose a home: 'I felt that if they had had another home to go to, they would have been behaved to in a very different manner, and received with more chearful countenances.' The new and unwelcome insight of the moment was precisely that they did *not* have another home to go to. They were dependent on people who thought of them as burdensome. However devoted they had been to their parents while alive, that revelation cannot but have made them feel blameworthy for not having previously understood the consequences of their parents' deaths. The resulting guilt would have been shared, and it explains why 'Wm, J, C, and myself shed tears together.' She emphasizes that this act of expiation has taken place 'Many a time' since her brothers' arrival from Hawkshead a month or so previously (they probably joined her in late June).

---

[19] From what Dorothy says in her letter it is clear that the servants were not discouraged from insulting the Wordsworth children. Of her grandfather, Dorothy observes that he 'never speaks to us but when he scolds which is not seldom' (*EY* 4). This is a reference to William Cookson, whose bad temper may be accounted for by ill health; he died on 19 December that year at the age of 76.

As the mind created its fictions of reproach, it must have seemed to Dorothy, John, Christopher and William that the 'mighty debt' had accumulated partly through their ignorance, and that now, three and a half years later, it demanded restitution in a more complete, if delayed, act of expiation: 'I mourn because I mourn'd no more.' There is no reason to suppose that the Wordsworth children genuinely had anything to feel guilty about; their only crime was to have been innocent victims of their relatives' cruelty and vindictiveness. In her letter Dorothy repeatedly emphasizes their fresh understanding of what their parents' loss meant:

> We have been told thousands of times that we were liars but we treat such behaviour with the contempt it deserves. [We] always finish our conversations which generally take a melancholy turn, with wishing we had a father and a home. Oh! Jane, I hope it may be long ere you experience the loss of your parents, but till you feel that loss you will never know how dear to you your Sisters are . . . (*EY*5)

She observes that their hardships have brought her closer to her brothers than before – even to the point of suggesting to Jane that she will not fully appreciate her sisters until they too have been orphaned. Though new, that terrible understanding would never go away. Nearly six years later, in February 1793, Dorothy again told Jane that 'We in the same moment lost a father, a mother, a home,'[20] as if it had only just occurred. The mantra is repeated, with the same shocked numbness, almost word for word, in 'The Vale of Esthwaite': 'Nor did my little heart foresee / – She lost a home in losing thee' (ll. 292–3). The verbal echo is so close as to suggest either that Wordsworth had read Dorothy's letter or that the poem influenced her. Whichever way the influence operated, it shows how close William and Dorothy had become by July 1787.

As the correspondence with Jane Pollard suggests, Dorothy and William were traumatized by the delayed mourning of July 1787, and the circumstances that precipitated it, but it was an experience that brought dividends. For one thing, they discovered each other as if for the first time. It also sealed the bond with John and Christopher – though not with Richard, who was not party to it.[21] As Dorothy told Jane, 'I can bear the ill nature of all my relations,

---

[20]   *EY*88.

[21]   Richard had been articled to his cousin, Richard Wordsworth of Branthwaite (1752–1816), since February 1786. He remained with him until early 1789, when he moved to London, where he worked for his cousin's London attorneys, Parkin and Lambert at Gray's Inn.

for the affection of my brothers consoles me in all my Griefs.'[22] Again, it seems likely that Wordsworth read this declaration before composing the concluding lines of the 'Vale', which address Dorothy, and follow shortly after the admission that 'I must never prove / A tender parent's guardian Love' (ll. 366–7):

> Sister for whom I feel a love
> That[23] warms a Brother far above
> On you as sad she marks the scen[e]
> Why does my heart so fondly lean
> Why but because in you is giv'n
> All all my soul could wish from heav'n
> Why but because I fondly view
> All, all that heav'n has claim'd in you.
>
> ('The Vale of Esthwaite' 380–7)

Like much else in this section of the poem, these lines look forward to the later poetry, most notably the blessing of Dorothy in 'Tintern Abbey'. But where that blessing would be offered as a consolation, these early lines show Dorothy tending Wordsworth's emotional needs. Stripped of the protection of a father and a home, he finds that 'in you is giv'n / All all my soul could wish from heav'n.' Wordsworth famously puns on Dorothy's name in *The Prelude*, when he describes her as 'A gift then first bestow'd',[24] but was already at it in his schoolboy verse: as a 'gift of God', she was indeed 'from heav'n'. Again, the testimonial is witty in the Jonsonian sense,[25] in that the wordplay coyly deflects attention from the emotional subtext, while acknowledging Dorothy's indispensability.

Her presence is keenly felt as the draft moves towards its conclusion. It is full of insights doubtless drawn from conversation with her, and may have been composed in her presence. Dorothy was probably the first reader of it and was, from Wordsworth's point of view, his ideal reader. The near confla-

---

[22] *EY* 3.

[23] Landon and Curtis read 'What', which is what Wordsworth appears to have written. He would have known that it was ungrammatical, and I'm sure meant 'That', a correction I have preferred to make. See figure 2 overleaf.

[24] *The Thirteen-Book Prelude* vi 218. Perhaps recalling the *Prelude* reference, De Quincey exploited the pun in his 'Autobiographic Sketches': 'Properly, and in a spirit of prophecy, was she named *Dorothy*; in its Greek meaning, *gift of God*, well did this name prefigure the relation in which she stood to Wordsworth, the mission with which she was charged' (*Selections Grave and Gay* (14 vols, Edinburgh, 1853–60), ii 307–8).

[25] 'Farewell, thou child of my right hand', the opening phrase in Jonson's 'On My First Son', puns on the child's name, Benjamin, which in Hebrew means 'dexterous'.

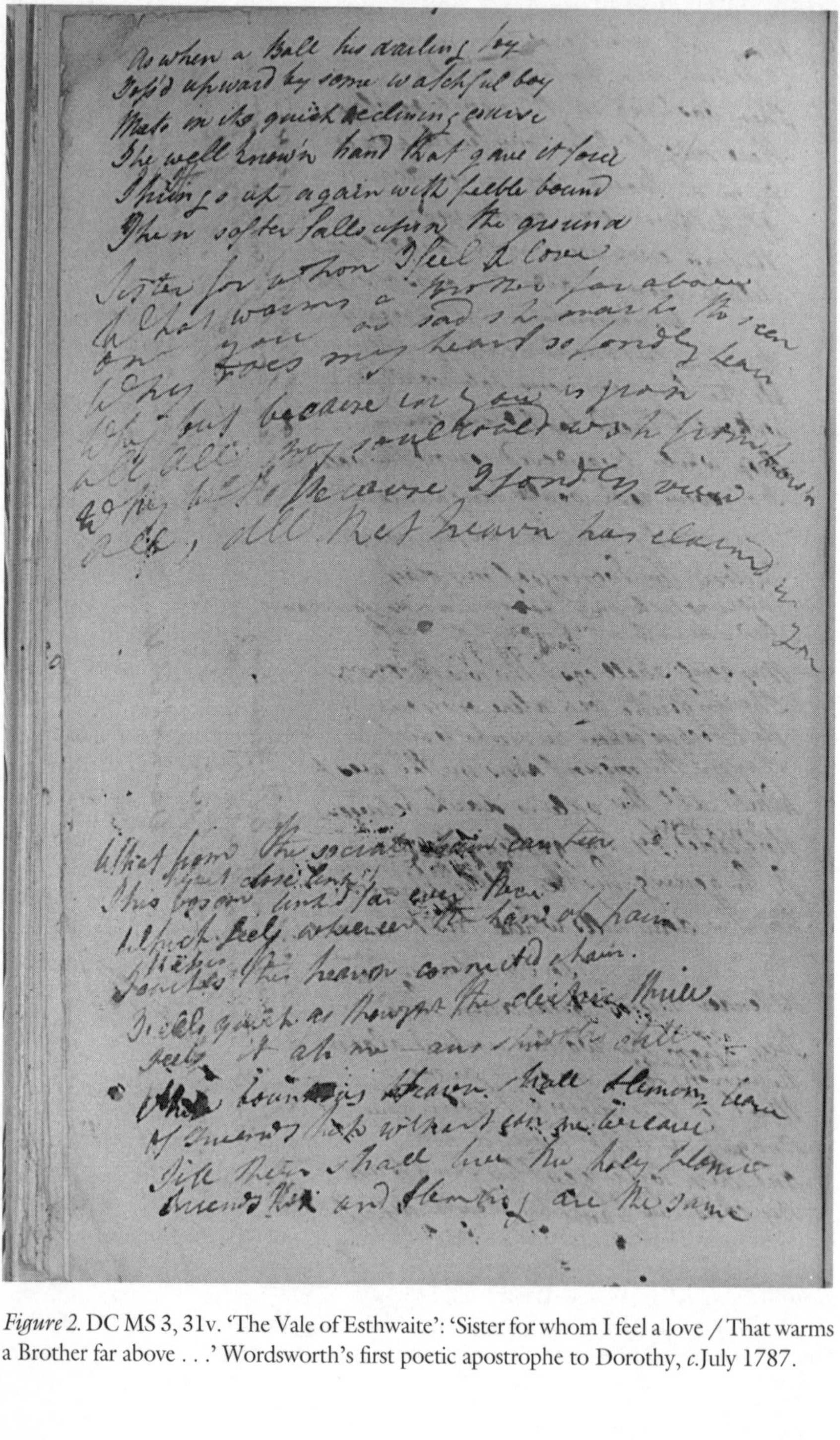

Figure 2. DC MS 3, 31v. 'The Vale of Esthwaite': 'Sister for whom I feel a love / That warms a Brother far above . . .' Wordsworth's first poetic apostrophe to Dorothy, *c.*July 1787.

tion of the waiting for the horses episode of 1783 with the grieving of summer 1787 alludes to the malignity of their Uncle Kit, and the delay in William's return that July. None of this is spelt out; indeed, the allusive manner (characteristic of the mature poet) is probably designed to prevent prying eyes from working it out. The only people who could have done so were the Wordsworth children. There was one other contemporary reader to whom Wordsworth addressed himself: John Fleming, a schoolfriend at Hawkshead, who would turn up again in *The Prelude*.[26] After declaring his love for Dorothy, Wordsworth turns to him:

> While bounteous Heav'n shall Fleming leave
> Of Friendship [?what] can me bereave
> Till then shall burn the holy flame
> Friendship and Fleming are the same.

> (ll. 394–7)

The guilt that underlies the waiting for the horses episode is mitigated in part by Fleming, whose fidelity leaves the poet 'unbereaved'. Wordsworth chooses his words with care. The movement of the verse is restorative, healing. If 'The Vale of Esthwaite' began as an attempt to out-Gothicize the Goths, the delayed mourning of July 1787 turned it into a deeply personal investigation of grief, guilt and restitution. Without being fully aware of it, Wordsworth traced an emotional course that would compel him for the rest of his poetic career.

Take, for instance, 'The Character of the Happy Warrior', where the warrior is a man

> Who, doom'd to go in company with Pain
> And Fear, and Bloodshed, miserable train!
> Turns his necessity to glorious gain;
> In face of these doth exercise a power
> Which is our human-nature's highest dower;
> Controls them and subdues, transmutes, bereaves
> Of their bad influence, and their good receives . . .

> (ll. 12–18)

Wordsworth's allusion to the recently completed *Prelude*, in which the 'mighty mind' exerts its influence on 'the outward face of things, / So molds them and endues, abstracts, combines',[27] indicates that the power attributed to the

---

[26] See *The Two-Part Prelude* ii 380–8; Fleming is discussed by Johnston, *Hidden Wordsworth* 50–1 and T. W. Thompson, *Wordsworth's Hawkshead* 117n1.
[27] *Thirteen-Book Prelude* xiii 77–9.

warrior is that of imagination. This may at first appear surprising; after twentieth-century experiences of war, no modern poet would make such claims.
But soldiering was the profession for which Wordsworth described himself as
'most inclined and . . . best qualified',[28] and consistent with this was his delight at Landor's departure in 1808 to fight alongside the Spanish army.[29]
Indeed, Wordsworth's support of the freedom fighters tells us a good deal
about his attitude towards warfare. Like Byron (oddly enough), he thought
of active service as a practical application of his political beliefs. For that reason the happy warrior is an opponent of injustice and oppression, gifted with
extraordinary ability. Not only can he transmute Pain and Fear and Blood-
shed, but in doing so he 'bereaves / Of their bad influence, and their good
receives'. That remark echoes his praise of Fleming, whose saving grace left
Wordsworth unbereaved at the end of the 'Vale'; likewise, the happy warrior
turns bereavement into a positive – even imaginative – process. It is required
because the true subject of 'The Character of the Happy Warrior' is not Nelson but John Wordsworth, whose drowning in February 1805 left William
and Dorothy grief-stricken for the first time since 1783. As William reported
to Christopher, they reacted in the same way as before: 'We have done all that
could be done to console each other by weeping together.'[30] In all likelihood,
it brought back many of the painful emotions associated with their parents'
deaths, and must have reawakened the need to expiate them. Part of that
process was the composition of poetry, and specifically 'The Recluse'; as Stephen
Gill has pointed out, John's death turned its completion into 'a trust, made
sacred by his brother's death'.[31] Like grief itself, 'The Recluse' was a duty that
demanded payment.

Wordsworth learnt other lessons through the new direction his poetry took
in July 1787. The waiting for the horses episode reveals that from an early
stage he understood the tension between memories and apparently unrelated
emotions. Such details as the whistling wind, the naked rock and solitary sheep
are ingredients in the mysterious alchemy that will resolve grief into imaginative energy. Just how precocious Wordsworth was in arguing this can be gauged
by the fact that over a century later Sigmund Freud 'discovered' the same
phenomenon, which he called a 'screen memory'. In a particularly resonant
passage in 'Screen Memories' (1899), Freud observed that 'there are some
people whose earliest recollections of childhood are concerned with everyday

---

[28] *MY* ii 2.
[29] See Peter Mann, 'Two Unpublished Letters of Robert Southey', *N&Q* NS 22 (1975)
397–9.
[30] *EY* 543.
[31] Gill 241.

and indifferent events which could not produce any emotional effect even in children, but which are recollected (*too* clearly, one is inclined to say) in every detail'. These are 'screens' for more important, associated experiences:

> What is recorded as a mnemic image is not the relevant experience itself . . . what is recorded is another psychical element closely associated with the objection- able one . . . . The result of the conflict is that, instead of the mnemic image which would have been justified by the original event, another is produced which has been to some degree associately displaced from the former one. And since the elements of the experience which aroused objection were precisely the im- portant ones, the substituted memory will necessarily lack those important ele- ments and will in consequence strike us as trivial.[32]

Memories dating from the same period as the events they screen are 'contigu- ous',[33] and as an example Freud offers that of a professor of philology 'whose earliest memories showed him a basin of ice. At the same period there oc- curred the death of his grandmother, which was a severe blow to the child. But he has no recollection of the bereavement; all that he remembers is the basin of ice.' Even at the age of 16, Wordsworth's self-analysis is sophisticated enough for us to read him in these terms. The repression of grief for his father at the time of his death in 1783 – the 'objectionable' experience, as Freud might call it – has led to 'associative displacement' in favour of the 'substi- tuted' memory of the landscape above Borwick Lodge.

I am not attempting a Freudian exposition of Wordsworth; others have done that, and with greater expertise.[34] I wish merely to suggest that the shift of gear detectable in Wordsworth's poetry from July 1787 was the result of a searching and poised act of self-examination – all the more remarkable for anticipating Freudian psychology by over a hundred years. Suppose, for a moment, that Freud had been at Wordsworth's right hand as he composed the final section of the 'Vale' in 1787, could he have elucidated the poetry in terms that would have made sense to its author? It seems unlikely. One of the hallmarks of Freud's account of screen memories is that it exploits linguistic

---

[32] *The Standard Edition of the Complete Works of Sigmund Freud* ed. James Strachey and Anna Freud (24 vols, London: Hogarth Press and the Institute of Psycho-Analysis, 1953– 74), iii 305–7.
[33] The naming of different kinds of memory according to their chronological relation to the events they screen occurs in 'Childhood and Screen Memories'; Freud, *Works* vi (1960).
[34] A number of distinguished critics, from Richard Onorato to David Ellis, have pointed out the similarity of Freud's screen memories to Wordsworth's spots of time. See also Douglas B. Wilson, *The Romantic Dream: Wordsworth and the Poetics of the Unconscious* (Lincoln: University of Nebraska Press, 1993), pp. 40–1.

counters and concepts that did not become widely understood until the twentieth century. For all the parallels in their thinking, Wordsworth and Freud (even in translation) speak different languages. Had Wordsworth in July 1787 been forced to discuss his poetry in terms that would have made sense to contemporaries, he would have spoken of 'associationism'.

The mind's tendency to associate places and emotions was widely discussed during Wordsworth's boyhood. David Hartley established an entire philosophy on the 'faculty', which was to be an important influence on Joseph Priestley and, through him, Coleridge. It is not likely that Wordsworth knew of Hartley at Hawkshead, but he had almost certainly encountered the philosophical writings of James Beattie. In his day Beattie was best known as a philosopher; he was a Professor of Moral Philosophy and Logic by the age of 25, and publication of his *Essay on Truth* in 1770 won extravagant praise (not least from Priestley) and the award of a yearly £200 pension from George III. As a schoolboy Wordsworth knew Beattie's poem *The Minstrel*, which influenced 'The Vale of Esthwaite',[35] and probably read his *Dissertations Moral and Critical* (1783), parts of which were extracted in periodicals. The *Dissertations* contains an important chapter on imagination:

> The sight of a place in which we have been happy or unhappy, renews the thoughts and the feelings that we formerly experienced there. With what rapture, after long absence, do we revisit the haunts of our childhood, and early youth! A thousand ideas, which had been for many years forgotten, now crowd upon the Imagination, and revive within us the gay passions of that romantick period. The same effect is produced, though perhaps in a fainter degree, when in a foreign land we talk of, or recollect, the place of our nativity. And from these, and other Associations of a like nature, arises in part that most important principle, the love of our country; whereof the chief objects are, our friends, and fellow-citizens . . . a fondness for the very fields and mountains, the vales, rocks, and the rivers, which formed the scenery of our first amusements and adventures.[36]

That Wordsworth waited twice for the horses, in 1783 and 1787, is elided in the poem and easily overlooked. But Beattie's comments remind us that the corresponding episode in the 'Vale' is inspired by a return visit to 'a place in which we have been happy or unhappy'. The key to screen memories lies in that distinctively Freudian concept of repression; Beattie provides an eighteenth-century substitute for this mechanism when he suggests that the return to the ridge above Borwick Lodge revived 'A thousand ideas, which had been

[35]   *WR* i 10–11.
[36]   James Beattie, *Dissertations Moral and Critical* (London, 1783), p. 87.

for many years forgotten'. Whatever else it is about, the waiting for the horses episode in the 'Vale' is concerned with feelings that its narrator had 'forgotten'. Significantly, Wordsworth had not previously written about his parents; nowhere in the considerable collection of extant verse composed between 1785 and July 1787 does he mention them. Circumstances had detained him and his siblings from a full expression of grief, and there was a price to be paid for that. The return to the ridge reiterated the events of December 1783 and brought about a confrontation with emotions suppressed since his father's death. He and his brothers remained in Hawkshead until, as Dorothy reveals, he 'hired a horse for himself and came over because he thought some one must be ill'. That reflects a genuine anxiety about her, while indicating something of his personal distress at the time.

Although Beattie declares an interest in 'happy or unhappy' experiences in the past, the main thrust of his argument concerns favourable associations that give rise to a 'love of our country'. So it is that, in lines that follow those describing the wait for the horses, Wordsworth envisages his return to the Lake District in old age and an encounter with a young boy.

> Perhaps my pains might be beguil'd
> By some fond vacant-gazing child
> He the long wondrous tale would hear
> Without a proud fastidious ear
> And while I wandered round the vale
> [From] every rock would hang a tale.
> With equal prattling half as dear
> Call tale from tale and tear from tear[37] . . .
>
> ('The Vale of Esthwaite' 348–53)

So closely does this follow Beattie that it is hard to believe that Wordsworth did not have him in mind as he wrote. Within the space of twenty lines he will go on to celebrate his affection for 'our friends, and fellow-citizens' in the form of Dorothy and Fleming, but before he does so he describes his 'fondness for the very fields and mountains, the vales, rocks, and the rivers, which formed the scenery of our first amusements and adventures'. As in Beattie, the landscape assumes importance from its associations: 'And while I wandered round the vale / [From] every rock would hang a tale.' This is decisive in resolving the poem's thematic argument, for the same mechanism that had

---

[37] The Cornell editors omit the last couplet from their reading text. My examination of the manuscript suggests that it is contemporary with the original draft, and that being undeleted it is not an alternative reading but part of the main text. I therefore include it here. Cf. Cornell *Early Poems* 450–1.

led to the reawakened grief of 1787 leads to renewed affection for the countryside. This is not, after all, a poem about the destructive effects of early trauma; on the contrary – Wordsworth envisages himself as an old man weeping with emotion as he recalls the past, a process that, as he claims, 'beguiles' his 'pain'.

Associationism is so fundamental to Coleridge's thought, and much that Wordsworth wrote after 1798, that it is sometimes implied, if not stated, that he knew nothing about it before he met Coleridge. That could not be more wrong. It is present in his thinking from at least July 1787, and would resurface frequently in the poetry of succeeding years. One of the revelations of the juvenilia, irrespective of their literary merit, is that they contain, in advanced form, many of the concepts associated with Wordsworth's post-Coleridgean work. The price of their comparatively late admission to the canon has been a widespread failure to appreciate his intellectual precocity. No doubt 'The Recluse' and *The Prelude* were uniquely the product of Coleridge's influence, but they are also the culmination of an aesthetic talent predicated by 'The Vale of Esthwaite'.

Wordsworth seems to have lost heart in the 'Vale' shortly after drafting the address to Dorothy. The manuscript has scorch marks on some leaves and burns along its edges. We can only conjecture as to why. It would have been monstrous had Uncle Kit thrown it to the flames, though it was not beyond him to have done such a thing. He probably did not wish to encourage any thought his nephew might have of writing poetry, and would hardly have been delighted by the later passages of the 'Vale'. But it is more likely that the notebook was thrown on the fire by Wordsworth himself and rescued by his sister. He had reason to feel dissatisfied, no doubt aware by the time he had finished of the clumsiness of the Gothic and sentimental passages. If so, he was overlooking the achievement of the last 120 odd lines. At any rate, whatever disappointment he may have felt with the poem would have been temporary.

Until publication of the Cornell edition in 1997, it was known only to a handful of scholars that when copying extracts from the 'Vale' at Cambridge in 1788, Wordsworth titled one of them 'Vale longum vale'.[38] The Latin pun reminds us that the poem announces Wordsworth's temporary farewell to the Lake District. (It was concluded during his last vacation before leaving for Cambridge.) The title of the extract, exclusive to that fair copy, indicates that from the vantage-point of 1788 he understood the poem to have concluded an important episode in his creative and emotional development. He now understood how to write directly about important events in his personal life;

---

[38] Cornell *Early Poems* 492.

and on an emotional level, he had begun to resolve the grief arising from his parents' deaths. The fair copy extracts he made from the scorched manuscript in 1788 fill about a quarter of his substantial Cambridge notebook (DC MS 2), so that he must, by then, have felt quite pleased with it. In 1797 Coleridge would read the poem and allude to it in 'The Ancient Mariner',[39] and in 1799 Wordsworth returned to it when composing the spots of time passage for the two-part *Prelude*. In 1815 he published a brief extract with his collected poems, which was all that would come to public notice until 1940.[40] While it would always remain an incoherent, episodic and fragmentary work, 'The Vale of Esthwaite' can only have increased in significance with the passage of time.

[39]   Coleridge drew on the 'Vale' in 'The Ancient Mariner' and therefore must have had access to DC MS 3 between July and November 1797; see '*The Ancient Mariner.* A Wordsworthian Source', *N&Q* 38 (1991) 301.
[40]   'Extract from the conclusion of a Poem, Composed upon leaving School', to be found in *PW* i 2.

2

'In black Helvellyn's inmost womb'

'And the dead friend is present in his shade.'
(Notebook jotting, DC MS 2)

The emotional trauma of July 1787 brought to light powerful currents in Wordsworth's psyche that had previously exerted their influence, but without his knowing precisely what they were or how they worked. In that respect 'The Vale of Esthwaite' is a divided work in that it contains poetry which looks towards the crisis of the summer while remaining innocent of it, as well as a markedly more mature verse that refers back to that crisis, and could not have been written without it.

Even if one goes back to 1786, when he composed 'The Dog – An Idyllium', it is possible to find traces of the anxieties and aspirations that were to precipitate the breakthrough of the following year. In some respects it would be hard to conceive of a quirkier, less obviously Wordsworthian poem. Its position in its manuscript indicates that it was probably composed in 1786, although Landon and Curtis prefer 1787–8[1] – either way, years before Wordsworth first met Coleridge.[2] It adapts the elegiac mode of *Lycidas* for a putative lament for Ann Tyson's 'rough Terrier of the hills':

> Where were ye nymphs when the remorseless deep
> Clos'd o'er your little favourite's hapless head
> For neither did ye mark with solemn dread
> In Derwent's rocky woods the white Moon's beam
> Pace like a Druid o'er the haunted steep
> Nor in Winander's stream
> Then did ye swim with sportive smile
> From fairy-templ'd isle to isle

---

[1] See Cornell *Early Poems* 397.
[2] Woof suggests a date between 22 August and 1 September 1795; see Woof Ph.D. 13–18.

Which hear her far off ditty sweet
Yet feel not ev'n the milkmaid's feet
What tho' he still was by my side
When lurking near I there have seen
Your faces white your tresses green
Like water lillies floating on the tide
He saw not bark'd not he was still
As the soft moonbeam sleeping on the hill
Or when ah! cruel maids ye stretch'd him stiff and chill.

(ll. 1–17)

Up to this point Wordsworth pursues the trajectory suggested by Milton, but his concluding lines turn elsewhere. Abandoning the elegiac, he moves smartly out of the present into a vividly recollected past:

If while I gazed to Nature blind
On the calm Ocean of my mind
Some new created Image rose
In full grown beauty at its birth
Lovely as Venus from the sea
Then while my glad hand sprung to thee
– We were the happiest pair on earth.

(ll. 18–24)

Gazing across 'the calm Ocean of my mind', oblivious to the charms of nature, a 'new created Image' rises out of (for want of a better word) the unconscious, assuming an ideal shape – not that of the goddess Venus, but of Wordsworth's drowned dog. With the words, 'while my glad hand sprung to thee', he returns, like Venus from the waters' depths, to be assimilated by the poet's touch into the world of the living. The optimism so often associated with the *annus mirabilis* of 1797–8 is triumphantly present in verse composed over a decade before. And lest we are in doubt as to the nature of what he is describing, Wordsworth alludes to Lyttelton's *Monody to the Memory of a Lady Lately Deceased* – 'We were the happiest pair of human kind!'[3] The implied comparison with Adam and Eve manages to suggest not merely that he and his dog are as well matched as the Lytteltons, but that they have entered a prelapsarian realm. In Classical terms, a vision of beauty allows him, figuratively speaking, to descend into the underworld and bring back his Eurydice from the dead. But the Orphean parallel begs the question. Ann Tyson's dog did not drown in 1786, and was still barking in 1788. Why, then, should the

---

[3]   Line 252.

16-year-old Wordsworth have equated imaginative vision with redemption from death? Why was he concerned with death at all?

Wordsworth's imagination, even in childhood, was intensely self-reflexive. In *The Thirteen-Book Prelude* the creative mind becomes, famously, a 'breathing-place' in the mist seen from the top of Snowdon; in a passage from 'The Vale of Esthwaite' written prior to the crisis of July 1787 it is located within the subterranean depths of the Lake District, when he is led by a spectre-guide beneath Helvellyn:

> He wav'd again we enter'd slow
> A narrow passage damp and low
> The mountain seem'd to nod on high
> Shriek'd loud then groan'd a hollow sigh
> And on we journey'd man[y] a mile
> While all was black as night the while . . . .
> Now as we wandered through the gloom
> In black Helvellyn's inmost womb
> The Spectre made a solemn stand
> Slow round my head thrice waved his [hand]
> And cleaved mine ears then swept his [lyre]
> That shriek'd terrific, shrill an[d] [dire]
> Shudder'd the fiend. The vault a[lo]ng
> Echoed the loud and dismal song.
>
> ('The Vale of Esthwaite' 232–7, 242–9)

This ritualized exchange retains a degree of obscurity. The three waves of the spectre's hand carry the same inscrutable logic as Aeneas' three attempts to embrace his dead father, Anchises, when he descends into the underworld in the *Aeneid* Book VI.[4] If, like Aeneas, Wordsworth is attempting to pass beyond materiality, it is significant that he does so 'In black Helvellyn's inmost womb'. Even at the age of 17 Wordsworth had an unerring sense of the weight of language, and could hardly have been unaware that the implications of the word 'womb' lent Helvellyn an unavoidably maternal quality. Licence may be found in Dryden's translation of the *Georgics*, where Aristaeus pursues the shape-changing Proteus to his home 'Within a Mountain's hollow Womb . . . conceal'd from Human Eyes'.[5] Here the shelter helps Aristaeus control the most slippery of gods; the young Wordsworth is similarly guarded during the ceremony he witnesses. In both cases, the protagonist is granted a revelation: a journey into the past in Dryden discloses the misery Aristaeus has caused

---

[4] *Aeneid* vi 700–2.
[5] Dryden, *Georgics* iv 603–4.

Orpheus by his rape of Eurydice (the reason why the gods have in turn struck
down Aristaeus' bees); in Wordsworth's poem it offers him a vision of the
Battle of Dunmail Raise, a pivotal moment in Cumbrian history when in the
tenth century Dunmail, last King of Cumbria, was defeated by the Saxon
King Edmund. Edmund is thought to have put out the eyes of Dunmail's two
sons.

> I saw the Ghosts and heard the yell
> Of every Briton [   ] who fell
> When Edmund deaf to horror's cries
> Trod out the royal Brothers' eyes
> With dismal yell and savage scowl
> While Terror shapeless rides my soul,
> Full oft together are we hurl'd
> Far Far amid the shadowy world –
> [And since that hour the world unknown
> The world of shades is all my own]
>
> (ll. 263–71)

The eighteenth-century couplet manner can fool us into thinking this conventional and unadventurous, but it is strange poetry for anyone to be writing, let alone someone in their seventeenth year. Wordsworth's passage into
the depths of mother earth has taken him beyond the limits of time and space,
beyond materiality, to confront the world of 'shadows'. There's something
Gothic about the 'shadowy world' which is, for the moment, the most sophisticated way Wordsworth can find of articulating his preoccupation with death.
A year before, Helen Maria Williams had published her popular poem, 'Part
of an Irregular Fragment, found in a Dark Passage of the Tower', which fea-
tured visions of deceased monarchs such as Richard III and Edward V.
Wordsworth almost certainly read it,[6] and would have been intrigued to find
that there, 'Yon bloody phantom waves his hand, / And beckons me to deeper
gloom.'[7] Williams' aim is partly to scare, partly to make the implicitly republican argument that the Tower has been the site of some of the bloodiest
crimes in English history. Wordsworth's poem is more personal. Without commenting directly on its implications, he has first described an underworld descent into Helvellyn's womb. This is highly suggestive; as Mircea Eliade puts
it, 'The mother did no more than bring to completion the creation of the
Earth-Mother: and, at death, the great desire was to return to the Earth-

---

6   WR i 149.
7   Helen Maria Williams, *Poems* (2 vols, London, 1786), ii 37.

Mother, to be interred in the native soil.'[8] On some level the underworld journey is inextricable from that 'great desire', and the vision of the battle confirms an engagement with some of those who have already been interred within the landscape into which Wordsworth has taken us.

None of this is flagged by the poet: it is imaged, figured, described, but not explicated. Wordsworth is aware of some need, some urge, but does no more than frame it within inherited models. If those models have any value, it is to suggest that access to the 'world of shades' is granted so that the dead may be revisited if not reclaimed – just as in 'The Dog' a visionary experience enabled him to retrieve his drowned companion. But these are hints, no more. It is as if Wordsworth was unsure of where the poetry was taking him, though he must have had his suspicions. All the same, the parallels are consistent in their suggestiveness. It was within a mountain's 'womb' that Aristaeus received the wisdom that enabled him to bring his bees back to life; Orpheus too wished to return Eurydice to life. Both episodes speak powerfully of the desire to resuscitate the dead through the power of primitive, elemental forces in nature. It is evidence of Wordsworth's ability to surprise us, even in his juvenile work, that this story culminates not with the retrieval of a person or dog, but with the vision of the Battle of Dunmail Raise. One senses that he is feeling his way towards a fuller understanding, and that as a step towards reaching into the underworld, he had first to establish his closeness to the Burkean quality of Terror:

> Full oft together are we hurl'd
> Far Far amid the shadowy world –
> [And since that hour the world unknown
> The world of shades is all my own]

It is sometimes suggested that Wordsworth needed Coleridge before he could think or write in the way he does in *The Prelude*. Here, twelve years before the first version of that poem, Wordsworth discusses the 'ministry' of fear and its effects on him. In some respects this is a more compelling account than that in *The Prelude*, because its composition is contemporary with the events described there; it is a report from the front line. And what it tells us is remarkable: he has been 'hurl'd' with Terror into the world of the dead, and since 'that hour' he has possessed for himself – or has been possessed by – 'The world of shades'. There is a sophistication here that belies its author's youth. In straightforward emotional terms, Wordsworth is looking for a way of dis-

---

[8] Quoted in J. R. Watson, 'Lucy and the Earth-Mother', *EIC* 27 (1977) 187–202, p. 195.

cussing his inner state, and sees Terror as having conducted him towards some kind of underworld. And what is this Terror? The poetry seems to indicate that it is external to him; like Milton's Death it is 'shapeless' and 'rides' his soul. It is what De Quincey would call the dark interpreter, and is roughly equivalent to Anchises in Virgil. But in the context of Wordsworth's emotional life, it's not external at all. The literary models dictate that the clumsy personification manifest itself as a distinct entity; in fact, he's talking about his inner world. It is the part of his personality that has become attuned to, or even welcoming of, fear, charged with the task of mediating with the dead. Gothicism was useful to him primarily as a means of discussing psychological process.

This passage appears in the notebook containing 'The Vale of Esthwaite' immediately before the stubs that precede the early version of the waiting for the horses. It was among the last things he wrote prior to the events of July 1787. Given the importance of those events, and their impact on him, one might expect them to have inspired an early version of *The Prelude* – or at least for his poetry to have reflected the various insights to which they led. But there is nothing schematic about artistic process. Writers tend not to be predictable – not if they're any good. In any case, that Wordsworth failed immediately to write the great autobiographical poem of the day isn't wholly surprising; such subjects were not regarded as fit for poetry in 1787. Nor was he sure of how to assess the autobiographical sections of the 'Vale'; it is notable that when he came to make fair-copy extracts from the poem during his first term at Cambridge, he did no work on the waiting for the horses. His obvious satisfaction with the more formal, eighteenth-century passages which display his technical abilities suggest that he may have been abashed by its overtly confessional character.

Wordsworth seems to have found it difficult to begin writing at Cambridge. When he got going, he would produce a considerable quantity of material, but his preoccupation with fair copying of the 'Vale' suggests, initially at least, creative exhaustion. When he did begin, he turned to translation as a vehicle for his talents. Virgil's account of Orpheus and Eurydice would have had obvious appeal: it re-enacted the trauma of grief, but with the hope of restitution. By embedding it within a tale of retrieval (that of Aristaeus and his bees), Virgil had given it a cheerful complexion, an effect intensified by the pantheism that pervades his view of the natural world. However, Wordsworth dispenses with the story of Aristaeus and concentrates entirely on the Orpheus legend. Were it to have been a straightforward translation, it would have been an unmitigated tale of loss; this rendering was anything but straightforward, however. No fair copy of the work appears to have survived, although rough drafts show that he was drawn to Virgil's account of Orpheus' grief:

> He wandering far along the lonely main
> Sooth'd with the hollow shell his sickly pain
> Thee, thee dear wife he sung forlorn
> From morn to eve – and thee from eve to morn.[9]

Wordsworth's distinctiveness is evident in that word 'lonely', which tells us that the natural world empathizes with Orpheus' plight. This looks forward to the pantheist sensibility of 1798, where all nature seems to be implicated in Orpheus' emotions. That argument is supported by Wordsworth's fidelity to Virgil's repeated 'te'; correctly punctuated, the lines should read: '"Thee, thee, dear wife!" he sung forlorn / From morn to eve – and "Thee!" from eve to morn.' He takes particular care to carry the insistent rhythms of Virgil's text into his rendering:

> ipse cava solans aegrum testudine amorem
> te, dulcis coniunx, te solo in litore secum,
> te veniente die, te decedente canebat.
>
> (*Georgics* iv 464–6)

Wordsworth follows Virgil in giving emphasis to that important monosyllable by placing it both at the beginning and in mid-line. In his mature work repetition is consciously acknowledged as a means of enabling 'impassioned feelings' to declare the 'deficiencies of language' by clinging to 'the same words, or words of the same character'.[10] The Virgilian translations were composed a decade before 'The Thorn', but he is already aware of the effectiveness of tautology as a means of expressing an emotional intensity found jointly in nature and the bereaved Orpheus. As the translation proceeds, his tears become a lyric outpouring for the failure to return the dead to the material world:

> For seven long moons he sat by Strymon's desert side
> He wept unceasing to the hollow tide
> While overhead while still he wept and sung
> Aerial rocks in shaggy prospect hung –
> Meek grew the tigers when in Caverns hoar
> He sung his tale of sorrow o'er and o'er.
> The solemn oaks – at the magic song
> Had ears to joy – and slowly mov'd along

[9]   Cornell *Early Poems* 638.
[10] Cornell *Lyrical Ballads* 351.

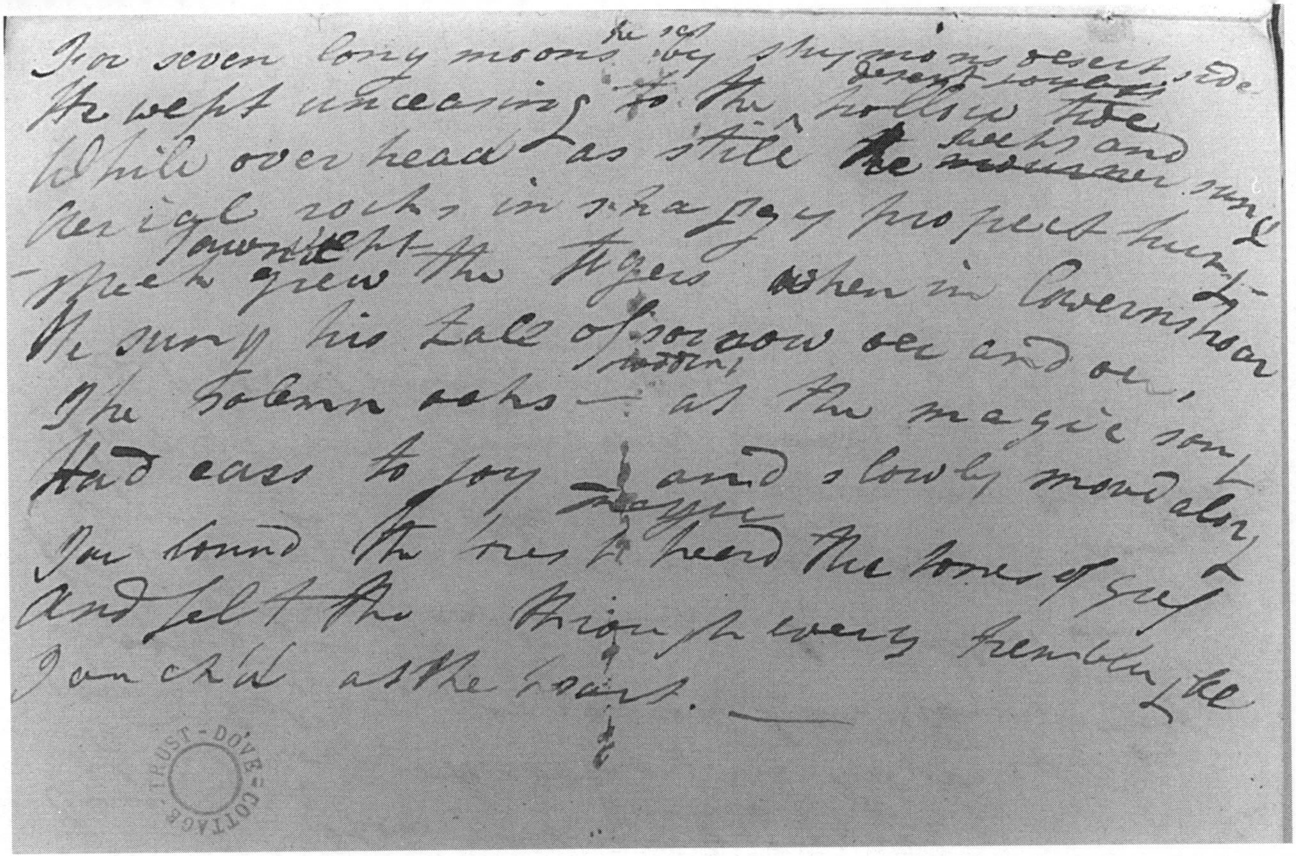

Figure 3. DC MS 5, 15r. 'Orpheus and Eurydice': 'For seven long moons by strymons desert side': Orpheus laments Eurydice among the tigers and the oaks, translated at Cambridge, c.1788.

Far round the forest heard the tones of grief
And felt the [   ] through every trembling le[af]
Touch'd at the heart.–[11]

Like Dryden, Wordsworth had an acute sensitivity to the nuances of the Latin, and strives to 'make Virgil speak such English as he would himself have spoken, if he had been born in England, and in this present age'.[12] As part of that strategy of domestication he expands 'sub antris' so that the 'Aerial rocks' become mountains, and Orpheus becomes a Lake District swain. The assimilation of the Classical context into his native landscape is revealing. Wordsworth had begun the process a year before when the same myth had informed the descent beneath Helvellyn's womb; to that extent the Virgilian translations refer back to that episode rather than the more recently composed waiting for the horses, which would tend to support the view that he was unsure whether or not its explicitly autobiographical ambitions had been a false step. Not until late 1798 would he have the confidence to return to that line of development. All the same, the poetry inspired by the delayed mourning of 1787 had made Wordsworth conscious of how profoundly affected he had been by his father's death, and although for the moment he would not explore the confessional seam opened up by it, that revelation could not help but shape his future work.

There is something knowing about the translations of 1788. Even Wordsworth's relocation of the story to Cumbria is calculated; it is licensed by Dryden, and is elemental to an increasing awareness that elements in his own life had a mythic dimension. Years later a Cambridge contemporary testified: 'The only time, indeed, that I have a clear recollection of having met him, I remember his speaking very highly in praise of the beauties of the North: with a warmth indeed which, at that time, appeared to me hardly short of enthusiasm.'[13] The enthusiasm testifies to the formation of a literary personality by which the landscape of the Lakes had become the setting for dramas that illustrated the shifting development of the spirit. It is not surprising, therefore, that instead of writing an early version of *The Prelude* Wordsworth does the next best thing, fully appropriating his Classical source, and adding passages designed to amplify his unique vision of the landscape:

[11]   Cornell *Early Poems* 646; see figure 3 overleaf.
[12]   'Dedication of the Aeneis', *Essays of John Dryden*, ed. W. P. Ker (Oxford: Clarendon Press, 1900), ii 228.
[13]   'Peregrinator', *Gentleman's Magazine* 64 (1794) 252.

Far round the forest heard the tones of grief
And felt the [   ] through every trembling le[af]
Touch'd at the heart. –

These lines look forward to the pantheism of 1798 in their portrayal of a natural world exquisitely sensitive to the aggrieved Orpheus. Perhaps they were inspired by John Martyn's commentary to Virgil, in front of Wordsworth as he worked, which suggests that 'The poplar is judiciously chosen by the Poet . . . because the leaves of this tree, trembling with the least breath of air, make a sort of melancholy rustling.'[14] Its effect is that in his recasting of Virgil, the qualities implied by the 'womb' of Helvellyn – protectiveness, security, emotional restoration – are supplied, at least partially, by natural forces. Other details tend to support this reading: 'The solemn oaks – at the magic song / Had ears to joy' alludes to Milton's invocation to Urania, where an account of his own isolation, 'fallen on evil days . . . with dangers compassed round', compares the dangers he faced with

> that wild rout that tore the Thracian bard
> In Rhodopè, where woods and rocks had ears
> To rapture, till the savage clamour drowned
> Both harp and voice . . .
>
> (*Paradise Lost* vii 34–7)

These lines were so important to Wordsworth at Cambridge that he copied into one of his notebooks the phrase, 'When Woods and rocks had ears to rapture'.[15] He would allude again to Milton's invocation, most memorably in the Prospectus to 'The Recluse'; in that case his aim, as Jonathan Wordsworth puts it, would be to use 'a comparable grandeur of style to evoke a purpose comparably grand'.[16] Lucy Newlyn goes on to suggest that Wordsworth meant to displace Milton, 'and with him the whole of Christian tradition'.[17] If there is any measuring up going on in the Virgilian translations twelve years before, it is a good deal less obvious. On one level Wordsworth is keenly preoccupied with poetic vocation: in her letter to Jane Pollard of July 1787 Dorothy had

---

[14]   John Martyn, *The Georgicks of Virgil* (3rd edn, London, 1750), p. 481. As Professor of Botany at Cambridge, 1732–68, Martyn wrote with authority on Virgil's flora. I am grateful to Sandra Raphael for this observation. Wordsworth also mentions poplars at *Evening Walk* 230.
[15]   DC MS 2, 105v; see the photograph at Cornell *Early Poems* 140.
[16]   *Borders of Vision* 109.
[17]   Paradise Lost *and the Romantic Reader* (Oxford: Clarendon Press, 1993), p. 238.

noted his intention to be a lawyer[18] (a choice of profession no doubt influenced by the suit which their guardians would bring against Lord Lonsdale in
January 1788), and by April 1790 that had turned into a desire to take orders.[19] At the time he translates Virgil he is still unsure as to whether poetry is
his chosen path; indeed, he was under financial pressure from his guardians to
follow a more remunerative calling. But the woods and rocks enraptured by
Orpheus' lament are important for another reason: the solemn oaks that 'Had
ears to joy' return us to a prelapsarian sympathy between man and nature.
And that heightened sympathy is evidence of Orpheus' ultimate victory.

Wordsworth's view of nature diverges increasingly from that of Virgil, who
spends little time on Orpheus' death. Martyn translates as follows: 'The
Ciconian dames enraged at his neglect of them, tore the young man in pieces,
even at the sacred rites of the gods, and nocturnal orgies of Bacchus, and
scattered over the wide plains his limbs.'[20] Working on these uninformative
details, Wordsworth expands the story quite significantly:

> Still of his dear lost partner did he plain
> Giv'n to his arms from Death but giv'n in vain
> For which sad dearer office coldly spurn'd
> The Fell Ciconian Matrons inly burn'd
> [   ] to Bacchus as they paid
> Nocturnal orgies in the midnight shade
> Him mourning still the savage [maenads] found
> And strew'd his mangled limbs the plai[ns] around
> The head when from its neck of marble torn
> Was down the Oeagrian Hebrus slowly borne
> Then too upon the voice and faltering tongue
> Euridice in dying accents hung
> Ah poor Euridice it feebly cried
> All round Euridice the [moaning banks reply'd]
> From [s]till small voices heard on every side.[21]

Richard F. Thomas, one of Virgil's more recent editors, has described the
original as 'ill-motivated';[22] Wordsworth's version is more considered. He
relocates it 'in the midnight shade' and reorders events drastically. After the

[18] *EY* 3.
[19] *EY* 29.
[20] John Martyn, *The Georgicks of Virgil* (3rd edn, London, 1750), pp. 482–4.
[21] Cornell *Early Poems* 644.
[22] See Virgil, *Georgics* ed. Richard F. Thomas (2 vols, Cambridge: Cambridge University
Press, 1988), ii 234.

Ciconian matrons become aware of Orpheus' grief, grow jealous, and the orgies take place, Wordsworth adds 'Him mourning still', keeping our attention on his protagonist. But the master-stroke is reserved for the final line – again Wordsworth's invention.[23] As far as Virgil is concerned, Orpheus' tale is over, but Wordsworth gives the legend a twist. Just as it seems that the hero is defeated, the still small voices tell us that, like Eurydice, he has been incorporated into the natural world that shares his woes. The voices are biblical, of course,[24] but in Wordsworth's translation they are neither divine nor a mere echo of Orpheus. They belong to the living things that shared his sufferings, which have inherited his energies. Immediately after the recollection of his father's death in the final section of the 'Vale', Wordsworth had remarked that 'A still voice whispers to my breast / I soon shall be with them that rest.'[25] As in the Orpheus translation, the still (and presumably silent) voice allows the guilt of the survivor – whether Orpheus or the young poet himself – to be assuaged, for Wordsworth's guilt at failing to mourn his father at the time of his death is offset by the prospect of one day joining him.

Wordsworth's Orpheus is not the hapless victim portrayed by Virgil; fostered by an empathizing, natural force, he, like the narrator of the 'Vale', is redeemed from isolation by a protective influence that speaks with a still small voice. Virgil goes on to explain how Aristaeus propitiated the gods and brought his bees back to life, but the rough drafts indicate that Wordsworth went no further than Orpheus' death. He was less interested in the means by which the pagan universe was returned to harmony than in the integration of psychology and the natural world.

This is not autobiographical, or at least not explicitly. But the translation does follow the pattern established in the final section of the 'Vale', which argued energetically for the consolatory power of nature, friends and family. And although in Virgil Orpheus is bereft, in Wordsworth's translation he is not: the 'moaning banks' echo his grief-stricken cries and the natural world is 'Touch'd at the heart'. Orpheus' solace is that the dying lament uttered by the 'voice and faltering tongue' of his decapitated head survives him. By the same token the poet of the 'Vale', after the crisis of July 1787, had been reassured first by the thought that he will soon follow his father into the grave and secondly by contemplating the obsequies performed by his schoolfriend John Fleming. 'Then may one kind an[d] pious friend / Assiduous o'er my body bend,' he writes, imagining himself in the grave with Fleming standing over him:

---

[23] See my 'Wordsworth's *Orpheus and Eurydice*: The Unpublished Final Line', *N&Q* 38 (1991) 301–2.
[24] I Kings 19:12.
[25] Lines 302–3.

Ah! may my weary body sleep
In peace beneath a green grass heap
In church-yard such at death of day
As heard the pensive sighs of Gray
And if the Children loitering round
Should e'er disturb the holy ground
Come [   ] come with pensive pace
The violated sod replace
And what would ev'n in death be dear
Ah pour upon the spot a tear.

('The Vale of Esthwaite' 314–23)

Placed in the position occupied in fact by his deceased parents, the poet trans-
fers the pain of grief, and guilt of the survivor, to Fleming – fugitive emotions
that in turn precipitate the tear Fleming sheds at his dead friend's grave. After
the events of summer 1787 it must have seemed to him that grief was not
destructive; here and in the Orpheus translations it is evidence of creativity
and imagination. In literary terms he is looking back to the lachrymose epitaph at the end of Gray's *Elegy*, and forward to his own 'There was a boy',
with its silent memorial of the nameless protagonist. Inextricably related to
the process by which the dead are symbolically redeemed, grief is proof of
their continuing life as an inspirational force: 'without the belief in immortality . . . neither monuments nor epitaphs, in affectionate or laudatory com-
memoration of the deceased, could have existed in the world.'[26] Though
articulated in the first of the 'Essays upon Epitaphs' in 1810, that conviction
is already to be found in the unfinished epitaph Wordsworth composed in
spring or summer 1788, apparently as an exercise:

> Here rest[s] a maid whose form and mind were so lovely, that [when] Age
> began to prey upon her beauty, heav'n [who saw] so fair a soul in form unwor-
> thy of it, took [a]nd made her what she was before; for immortality was all that
> need be given by[27]

The maid's soul determines the form she is to adopt after death, returning her
to 'what she was before'. As in the 'Essays upon Epitaphs' the young
Wordsworth argues 'that some part of our nature is imperishable',[28] regarding death not as extinction but as restitution. Fleming's pious thoughts at his
friend's graveside effectively endow him with that understanding, and trans-

---

[26] *Prose Works* ii 52.
[27] Cornell *Early Poems* 403.
[28] *Prose Works* ii 50.

form him, for a moment, into a version of the poet; by shedding a tear he mimics the still small voices that echo Orpheus' lament.

A few lines later Wordsworth imagined how as an old man Fleming will recollect the Vale of Esthwaite, 'where first my eyes survey'd / Fair Friendship in th[y] form array'd',[29] and, in the final variation, Fleming turns into the poet's own aged self, looking back on his Hawkshead childhood. In fact, Wordsworth has been discussing himself throughout, assuming different physical forms and crossing temporal barriers, like Proteus in the *Georgics*. Not that the relationship with Fleming is in itself unimportant: the 'Essays upon Epitaphs' insist that 'the wish to be remembered by our friends or kindred after death, or even in absence, is, as we shall discover, a sensation that does not form itself till the social feelings have been developed';[30] similarly, his younger brother Christopher's 1792 'Outline of a Poem' is certain that 'most pleasure may be reaped in social life, among sisters, brothers, children & friends.'[31] As chapter 1 sought to argue, that closeness was one of the benefits of the delayed mourning of summer 1787.

The Orpheus translations of 1788 thus extend the insights of that crisis, positing a world in which grief and loss are not sustained in isolation (as in Virgil), but in which the Lake District landscape performs the protective function of guardian, friend and earth mother. Orpheus' death is no obstacle to this; in death he becomes part of a natural process, gravitating closer to the ideal relationship with the earth mother which in Wordsworth's later poems will be enjoyed by Lucy and the Winander boy. It is tempting to see him as an early version of the Winander boy: both are integrated with the natural world, spiritually and physically. The precise nature of that transaction, its welding together of outer and inner worlds (the very thing that so irritated Blake about the Prospectus to 'The Recluse'),[32] is one of those elements that arose directly out of 'The Vale of Esthwaite'. It is part of the impulse to retrieve the dead, an aspiration consciously understood only with composition of the waiting for the horses episode. Fleming's significance in the section of the 'Vale' composed after July 1787 arises not just from the intense feeling attributed to him after the poet's own envisaged death but from his mediating presence:

[29] Lines 332–3.
[30] *Prose Works* ii 50.
[31] Z. S. Fink, *The Early Wordsworthian Milieu* (Oxford: Clarendon Press, 1958), p. 106.
[32] On Wordsworth's declaration of his theme as being 'How exquisitely the individual Mind . . . to the external World is fitted. – & how exquisitely too . . . The external World is fitted to the Mind,' Blake commented: 'You shall not bring me down to believe such fitting & fitted I know better & Please your Lordship' (*The Complete Poetry and Prose of William Blake*, ed. David V. Erdman, commentary by Harold Bloom (Garden City, NY: Anchor Books, 1982), pp. 666–7).

What from the social chain can tear
This bosom link'd for ever there
Which feels where'er the hand of pain
Touches this heav'n connected chain
Feels quick as thought the electric thrill
Feels it ah me – and shudders still.
While bounteous Heav'n shall Fleming leave
Of Friendship [?what] can me bereave
Till then shall burn the holy flame
Friendship and Fleming are the same.

(ll. 388–97)

Fleming conducts the electric charge that will connect Wordsworth with 'Heav'n'; he is thus a source of power, a muse who forfeits his own uniqueness to confirm that of the poet. His continuing affection is reparation for the poet's grief, and confirms Wordsworth's place in the scheme of things. This is important because of the guilt that underlies the more confessional passages in the poetry of July 1787 – 'I mourn because I mourn'd no more.' That culpability is deeply felt and demands expiation; in the 'Vale' it is achieved through the poet's attachment to his native landscape, sister and best friend. By the time he translated Virgil it has become emblematized in the image of Orpheus' head floating down the Hebrus, its lament echoed by the 'still small voices heard on every side'.

This is the origin of the Wordsworthian vision of the imagination – one I would describe as metamorphic. It is there, in essence, in his favourite poet while at Hawkshead: 'Before I read Virgil I was so strongly attached to Ovid, whose Metamorphoses I read at School, that I was quite in a passion whenever I found him, in books of criticism, placed below Virgil.'[33] In Sandys' translation, which he read in the Hawkshead Grammar School library,[34] Tereus pursues Philomela and Procne with sword drawn, until they

appeare with wings
To cut they ayre: and so they did. One sings
In words; the other neare the house remaines:
And on her brest yet beares her murders staines.
He, swift with griefe and fury, in that space
His person chang'd. Long tufts of feathers grace
His shining crowne; his sword a bill became;
His face all arm'd: whom we a Lapwing name.

(vi 714–21)

---

[33] Fenwick note to 'Ode to Lycoris'; FN 42.
[34] See WR i 108–9.

The transformation of Procne into a swallow, Philomela into a nightingale and Tereus into a lapwing bears out our sense of how things ought to be, for the species of bird, with its accompanying physical attributes, expresses the passions of their human counterparts. Concentrating this episode into a series of nonsense words in *The Waste Land*,[35] Eliot rendered Ovid's characters brutally inarticulate, representatives of the moral and physical degeneration of his modernist dystopia – a remarkably faithful gloss. Transformation in Ovid is entropic, sometimes punitive; Northrop Frye suggested that it was 'an image of what in the Bible is called the fall of man, which traditionally has involved his alienation from nature'.[36] All of which is the precise opposite of the Wordsworthian equivalent. If there is an index of what it meant to be Romantic, this is it. Change, after all, is at the heart of 'The Recluse'. That work was to prophesy a revolution brought about not by physical but spiritual change – a universal brotherhood founded on love of nature. For the Romantics as a whole, change is not degenerative but restorative. This is clearer in Wordsworth's Preface to the first collected edition of his poems in 1815, which defines imaginative power by reference to 'Resolution and Independence'. Wordsworth quotes the passage in which the Leech-Gatherer turns first into a huge stone and then into a sea-beast, 'which on a shelf / Of rock or sand reposeth, there to sun itself' (ll. 69–70), before remarking that

> In these images, the conferring, the abstracting, and the modifying powers of the Imagination, immediately and mediately acting, are all brought into conjunction. The stone is endowed with something of the power of life to approximate it to the sea-beast; and the sea-beast stripped of some of its vital qualities to assimilate it to the stone; which intermediate image is thus treated for the purpose of bringing the original image, that of the stone, to a nearer resemblance to the figure and condition of the aged Man; who is divested of so much of the indications of life and motion as to bring him to the point where the two objects unite and coalesce in just comparison.[37]

Leaving aside the issue of Wordsworth's accuracy as a practical critic,[38] we are to understand that the primary task of the imagination is to 'abstract' the detritus of reality into a more purposive whole. Interfused with stone and sea-beast, the aged man enjoys a unity and a 'justness' inaccessible in the fallen

[35] See *The Waste Land* 202–5.
[36] *The Great Code: The Bible and Literature* (London: Routledge and Kegan Paul, 1982), p. 97.
[37] *Prose Works* iii 33.
[38] This is discussed by Lucy Newlyn, *Coleridge, Wordsworth, and the Language of Allusion* (Oxford: Clarendon Press, 1986), pp. 130–1.

world from which he has come. In opposition to Ovid, therefore, Wordsworthian metamorphosis takes us closer to a prelapsarian order.

In *Prelude* Book VIII, in the midst of a passage both inspired by fragments of his juvenilia and incorporating them, Wordsworth remembered that as a boy, 'I still / At all times had a real solid world / Of images about me.'[39] That 'solid world' is a paradox, for those images existed purely in the imagination. What he means is that, compared with the vividness with which he perceived the ideal, 'reality' faded into the shadows. This is reinforced by the fact that the 'world / Of images' is a source of stability, more so than the things around him: 'I had forms distinct / To steady me.'[40] In September 1806 he was still preoccupied with the intoxicating power of his youthful imagination and discussed it with John Constable, whom he encountered probably at Brathay Hall.[41] Constable later described their conversation to Joseph Farington, who recorded it in his diary:

> Constable remarks upon the high opinion Wordsworth entertains of Himself. He told Constable that while He was a Boy going to Hawkeshead school, His mind was often so possessed with images, so lost in extraordinary conceptions, that He has held by a wall not knowing but He was part of it.[42]

Hugh Sykes Davies has pointed out that the clutch at the wall is 'the outward manifestation of a feeling of identity with it, so that in these moments the normal boundaries between the inner and outer worlds were obliterated'.[43] This precise interpretation inevitably refers us back to the Hawkshead poetry, in which the dissolution of physical separation between self and nature becomes, for the author of the 'Vale', the only way to heal the sense of loss resulting from his parents' deaths. He envisages himself dead (and thus united with them); praises his sister's ability to make up for 'All, all that heav'n has claim'd', and celebrates his best friend for leaving him 'unbereaved'. Together,

---

[39] *Thirteen-Book Prelude* viii 603–5.
[40] Ibid., viii 598–9.
[41] 'Mr Wordsworth had the pleasure of making Mr Constable's acquaintance when he visited this Country long ago,' Wordsworth recalled in 1844 (*LY* iv 553). The meeting took place either at Brathay Hall, then inhabited by the painter John Harden, or at Low Brathay, in which lived Charles and Sophia Lloyd. Constable was in the midst of a two-month tour of the Lakes. See *John Constable's Correspondence* ed. R. B. Beckett (6 vols, Ipswich: Suffolk Records Society, 1961–8), v 74; and J. R. Watson, 'Wordsworth and Constable', *RES* 12 (1962) 361–7.
[42] Farington viii 3164.
[43] *Wordsworth and the Worth of Words* (Cambridge: Cambridge University Press, 1986), p. 174.

these three elements – Dorothy, Fleming and posthumous integration with nature – amount to the same thing: a vehicle by which grief, guilt and isolation may be subsumed into the larger sense of restitution and community. Wordsworth is sometimes said to be a solipsistic, self-absorbed poet, and at times he was; but he was never contemptuous of community. One's place within society was always important to him, and central to the philosophy of 'The Recluse'.

The Wordsworthian imagination is usually appreciated in terms of *The Prelude* and the post-Coleridgean verse. 'The Eolian Harp', 'Reflections on Having Left a Place of Retirement', 'This Lime-Tree Bower my Prison' – most of Coleridge's early verse in fact, creaking under the weight of its unwieldy Berkleian cargo, is often held to be the source of Wordsworth's ideas. No doubt he knew Coleridge's poetry well by 1797, and it exerted a potent influence on him, but only because it articulated truths he already understood. In truth, the aspirations of 'The Recluse' owe more to Wordsworth's pre-Coleridgean work than to Coleridge's pre-Wordsworthian verse; and the emphases on transmutation, immateriality and the sublime, all of which are found in the post-1798 poetry, bespeak a debt to the juvenilia.

It is hard not to be aware of the way in which Wordsworth's self-analysis informs his portrayal of other people – Dorothy, Fleming, Orpheus. There is a sense of its being a continuing struggle, devoted to the formation of a coherent literary and emotional personality. Such questions as his culpability concerning his father's death; his closeness to his sister; his vision of natural sympathy; and the significance of grief – all relate in an immediate and urgent way to himself. This is not always clear because the 'Vale' and the Virgilian translations are so dependent on literary precedent, as preoccupied with the cultivation of technique as with what they have to say. His voice is clearest when the layers of convention are stripped back, as in this rough draft, barely choate, which laments the death of an unnamed woman. Its position in the notebook suggests to me that it was composed in 1786 (although Landon and Curtis prefer 1787–8):

> Now ye meet in the cave
> husband sons and all
> if ye've hands oh make a grave
> for she dies she dies she dies
> She wishes not for a grave
> bear into the salt sea, for
> Where you lie there she will lie,
> Oh bear her into the salt sea
> If you wish her peace [?oh] bear
> Bear her to the salt sea bear

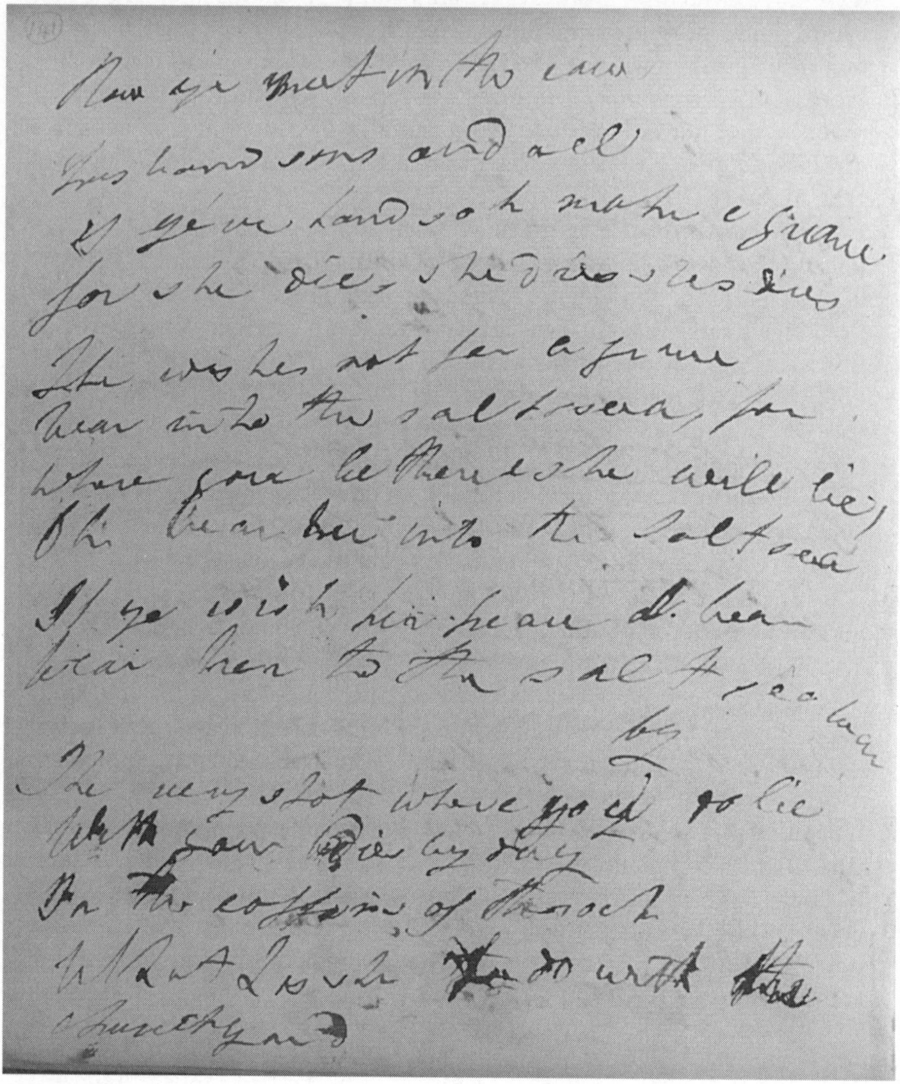

Figure 4. DC MS 2, 106v. 'Now ye meet in the cave': the Wordsworthian sense of death at its most elemental. Perhaps composed in 1786, although 1787–8 is advanced by Landon and Curtis.

Bear her to the salt sea bear
[   ] by
The very spot where you do lie
With your [?wives] by day
In the coffins of the rock
What has she [to] do with the churchyard

Shifting, unfinished, the draft catches the Wordsworthian sense of death at its most elemental. The gravediggers are the woman's husbands and sons, who must scrape the earth away with their bare hands. Like them, the narrator seems to be grappling physically with the sense and substance of death; on a practical level there is the problem of how and where she is to be buried, which raises the question of laying her spirit to rest. Neither is fully resolved, and the grave undergoes a series of transformations – from earth to sea, and finally to rock. More strikingly, the poem provides an analogue for the descent beneath Helvellyn, for it describes an encounter with a father-figure in another cave; the insistence of the lament, and the urgent knowledge that she must be buried in the sea 'If you wish her peace', hints at guilt. There may even be cause for thinking that this poem is about Wordsworth's reaction to his mother's death; if so, it is the one place where he approaches that subject.

As is consistent with the verse composed before the crisis of July 1787, none of this seems to be fully understood by the poet himself. Of all the juvenile fragments, this is the one in which the fight to come to terms with overwhelming emotion is most obvious. There is something very primitive about it. It feels pagan, setting the rituals of death in a brutally unadorned setting, in terms of a lament that might have been spoken by someone like Orpheus: 'What has she [to] do with the churchyard.' On a technical level, it reminds us that Wordsworth is already aware of the power of tautology to embody 'impassioned feelings': 'for she dies she dies she dies.'

Wordsworth's struggle to deal with the emotions arising out of a period of intense mourning as reflected in this early, fragmentary draft, is suggestively analogous to a dream reported by Melanie Klein. The comparison takes on added force from the fact that although she attributed it to one of her patients, recent research shows that Klein experienced it herself as she mourned her dead son: 'She was flying with her son, and he disappeared. She felt that this meant his death – that he was drowned. She felt as if she, too, were to be drowned – but then she made an effort and drew away from the danger, back to life.'[44] As in Klein's dream, the narrator of 'Now ye meet in the cave' is

---

[44] 'Mourning and Its Relation to Manic-Depressive States', *The Selected Melanie Klein*, ed. Juliet Mitchell (Harmondsworth: Penguin, 1986), p. 161. I am grateful to Ronald Britton for directing my attention to Klein.

drawn towards the salt sea of overwhelming grief. But just as the young Wordsworth was afraid of losing himself in the abyss of idealism, the means by which he might retrieve the dead, so Klein pulls back 'from the danger'.

Klein's dream warned her against the destructive power of grief and helped redeem her from it. Aware of the same threat, the young Wordsworth responded differently. As in the 'Vale', death remains one means by which the narrator and his family may be reunited. The dead woman is to be buried in 'The very spot where you do lie', echoing Ruth's declaration of loyalty to her mother-in-law Naomi: 'Where thou diest, will I die, and there will I be buried: the Lord do so to me, and more also, if ought but death part thee and me.'[45] 'Now ye meet in the cave' differs from the Lucy poems in suggesting that the close relationship with nature enjoyed by the dead mother does not separate her from the narrator; on the contrary, 'husband sons and all' will also be buried in the coffins of the rock. Likewise, as we have seen, the 'Vale' finds its resolution in the narrator's contemplation of his death and the responses of those he will leave behind him. Although 'Now ye meet in the cave' seeks a natural harmony, it isn't completely realized: hence the conditional 'If you wish her peace . . .' What the poet seems to offer is the shamanistic promise that enduring guilt and grief may be at least partly exorcized by a natural order. The voice of the poem lays claim to a primitive wisdom by which nature is comprehended as capable of incorporating the dead and, in some sense, resurrecting them.

In this draft, as in other poems composed during these years, Wordsworth attempts to address emotions that remain obscure. His last memory of his mother is unrevealing: 'My last impression was having a glimpse of her on passing the door of her bedroom during her last illness, when she was reclining in her easy chair.'[46] The indefiniteness of Wordsworth's language – 'impression', 'glimpse' – indicates that the recollection is on the verge of dissolution. Perhaps this is not surprising: he is concerned less with Ann Wordsworth's physical reality than with her surrogate, the natural force which admitted him to its most secret recesses.

In this context Wordsworth's first published poem, the 'Sonnet on Seeing Miss Helen Maria Williams Weep at a Tale of Distress', takes on unexpected importance. It was composed by March 1787, a few months before the emotional crisis of summer 1787:

> She wept. – Life's purple tide began to flow
> In languid streams through every thrilling vein;
> Dim were my swimming eyes – my pulse beat slow,
> And my full heart was swell'd to dear delicious pain.

---

[45]   Ruth 1:17.
[46]   *Prose Works* iii 372.

Life left my loaded heart, and closing eye;
A sigh recall'd the wanderer to my breast;
Dear was the pause of life, and dear the sigh
That call'd the wanderer home, and home to rest.

That tear proclaims – in thee each virtue dwells,
And bright will shine in misery's midnight hour;
As the soft star of dewy evening tells
What radiant fires were drown'd by day's malignant pow'r,
That only wait the darkness of the night
To chear the wand'ring wretch with hospitable light.[47]

The situation is fictional: he was not to meet Helen Maria Williams until
1820. As James Averill has shown, sonnets addressed to Helen Maria Williams
became fashionable in the wake of her popular two-volume *Poems* (1786).[48]
But Wordsworth goes about his task in a distinctive manner for, having set up
the poem's inciting incident – 'She wept' – he turns to himself and his own
visionary state. In 'Tintern Abbey' he was to describe the 'sensations sweet'
associated with the memory of the Wye valley as 'Felt in the blood, and felt
along the heart'; a comparable physicality characterizes his response to Miss
Williams' grief. His blood ('purple tide') slows down, running 'In languid
streams' within him, while the pain of grieving is 'dear' and 'delicious' because it presages the moment of imaginative assimilation: 'Life left my loaded
heart, and closing eye; / A sigh recall'd the wanderer to my breast.' In this
'pause of life', the poet is reunited with the dead 'wanderer'. As in his other
poems, the story is one of restoration. And what of Miss Williams? The sonnet
finds her again as the sestet begins – 'That tear proclaims . . .' – only to lose
her once more in a larger cosmic realm of stars and planets. Helen Maria
Williams is significant not on her own account but as a medium between
intense feelings of loss and the assimilation of the individual consciousness
into nature. Despite the ostentatious display of its title, the sonnet could be
about anyone, and in any case its true subject is not the 'She' of line 1.

Most of Wordsworth's extant poetry from the years 1786–7 is about love,
as if he needed to define it or convince himself of its existence. It is no surprise, then, that although Helen Maria Williams lacks physical reality for him,
the sonnet is nonetheless a love poem. The 'pause of life' at its centre is described in terms too physical not to be interpreted as a form of sexual sublima-

---

[47] When published in the *European Magazine*, the poem was signed 'Axiologus', a Greek
transliteration of 'Wordsworth'.
[48] *Wordsworth and the Poetry of Human Suffering* (Ithaca, NY: Cornell University Press,
1980), p. 33.

tion. Even the opening lines echo the eroticism of Langhorne's translation of Bion's 'Death of Adonis', where Venus weeps over her dying lover: 'she saw Life's purple tide, / Stretch'd her fair arms, with trembling voice she cry'd.' Earlier in the same work, Adonis is lamented in distinctly sensual terms:

> Ah! yet behold life's last drops faintly flow,
> In streams of purple o'er those limbs of snow![49]

But there is no Venus to tend the 'swimming eyes' of the speaker of Wordsworth's poem: he is detached and the experiences he describes are solitary. The weeping in the opening line is probably recycled from one of Williams's own lachrymose sonnets. If the speaker of Wordsworth's poem has enjoyed a moment of imaginative sympathy, it is only by contact with a fictional persona.

Even in his best love poetry Wordsworth is acutely conscious of being separated from the object of his affections: 'But she is in her Grave, and oh! / The difference to me'. The pattern is established in the juvenilia, and extends into the great work of his maturity. Unlike Coleridge, who needed to realize the urge to idealize and unify, Wordsworth could be satisfied merely with 'an obscure sense / Of possible sublimity'.[50] Therein lies its attraction as well as its limitations, for throughout his juvenile and mature verse those who are loved and lost remain vague, indistinct, shadowy. Grief and its traumas have preserved them in an ideal world beyond time, where they may be apprehended by glimpses only. Though implicitly present in her son's underworld journey, Ann Wordsworth can never be restored as an independent, physical being; Orpheus' attempt to redeem Eurydice as 'she was before' is, by the same token, doomed. If restitution is possible, it may be found only through such mediating agencies as nature, Dorothy and Fleming. They are essential to the Wordsworthian equation, as they bring the dead within reach; ultimately, when 'The Recluse' was formulated, they would enable paradise to be regained.

[49]   Lines 49–50, 11–12.
[50]   *The Thirteen-Book Prelude* ii 336–7.

3

'Charg'd by magic'

Though now the visionary scenes appear
Like the faint traces of a vanisht dream.
(John Langhorne, *Elegy II* 7–8)

So densely allusive is the texture of Wordsworth's early poetry that critics find
it hard not to explain its sophistication by reference to other writers. It would
be tempting, for instance, to suggest that by 1789 he was aware of the climax
of Marvell's 'Upon Appleton House':

> LXXXII
> But now away my Hooks, my Quills,
> And Angles, idle Utensils.
> The *young Maria* walks to night:
> Hide trifling Youth thy Pleasures slight.
> 'Twere shame that such judicious Eyes
> Should with such Toyes a Man surprize;
> *She* that already is the *Law*
> Of all her *Sex,* her *Age's Aw.*

> LXXXIII
> See how loose Nature, in respect
> To her, it self doth recollect;
> And every thing so whisht and fine,
> Starts forth with to its *Bonne Mine.*
> The *Sun* himself, of *Her* aware,
> Seems to descend with greater Care;
> And lest *She* see him go to Bed;
> In blushing Clouds conceales his Head.

> LXXXIV
> So when the Shadows laid asleep
> From underneath these Banks do creep,
> And on the River as it flows
> With *Eben Shuts* begin to close;
> The modest *Halcyon* comes in sight,
> Flying betwixt the Day and Night;

And such an horror calm and dumb,
Admiring Nature does benum.

LXXXV
The viscous Air, wheres'ere She fly,
Follows and sucks her Azure dy;
The gellying Stream compacts below,
If it might fix her shadow so;
The stupid Fishes hang, as plain
As *Flies* in *Chrystal* overt'ane;
And Men the silent *Scene* assist,
Charm'd with the *Saphir-winged Mist.*

LXXXVI
Maria such, and so doth hush
The *World,* and through the *Ev'ning* rush.
No new-born *Comet* such a Train
Draws through the Skie, nor Star new-slain.
For streight those giddy Rockets fail,
Which from the putrid Earth exhale,
But by her *Flames,* in *Heaven* try'd,
Nature is wholly vitrifi'd.

In the upside-down world of Nun Appleton, to which Lord General Fairfax had retired at a decisive moment in his nation's history (1650), the ordering influence of his daughter Mary (to whom Marvell was tutor) required the help of a few divine scene-shifters. Not that there is anything intrinsically funny about the idea of order which, in Marvell's crepuscular fantasy, crystallizes for a moment in a sudden apprehension of purity: 'But by her *Flames,* in *Heaven* try'd, / *Nature* is wholly vitrifi'd.' Self-consciously artificial perhaps, but there is no doubting the seriousness of what is being said. Against the upheaval to which Fairfax had borne witness – the civil war, the execution of Charles I (of which he disapproved) and the political machinations of the commonwealth (which had led to his withdrawal from public life)[1] – Marvell places a transcendent vision of harmony. The contrivance is deliberate; we are to be mindful that the world is so debased that only through a conscious effort could its redemption be envisaged. His emphasis on her innocence is all the more poignant in the light of Mary's fate: she was married to the second Duke of Buckingham (Dryden's Zimri) in 1657. Buckingham's motives were entirely venal, as the

---

[1] Lord General Fairfax, commander-in-chief of the Parliamentary army (and effectively the most powerful man in the country) had resigned in protest over the proposed invasion of Scotland in 1650.

union provided the means by which he could recover lands confiscated by the Protectorate. All the same, restitution is the possibility held out to us, however transient it may be. Marvell's thinking, even within its historical context, looks forward to the imaginative redemption anticipated by the author of 'The Recluse'. In 1798 Wordsworth would propose that a similarly enhanced perception of the world had the power to bring about the political and social revolution for which the radicals had campaigned in the early 1790s.

Marvell was certainly known to Wordsworth by May 1802, when he was praised for his republican sympathies alongside such like-minded souls as Algernon Sydney and James Harrington:[2]

> These Moralists could act and comprehend:
> They knew how genuine glory was put on;
> Taught us how rightfully a nation shone
> In splendor: what strength was, that would not bend
> But in magnanimous meekness.
>
> ('Great men have been among us' 5–9)

It is as a 'Moralist' that Wordsworth celebrates Marvell – someone capable of distinguishing 'genuine glory' from mere show, and teaching their country that strength lies in 'magnanimous meekness'. The importance of morality to Wordsworth's valuing of the past is not always given its proper emphasis. Post-1798, he is at pains to emphasize the ethical aspect of imaginative power. This is because 'The Recluse' will argue that nature can improve the conduct of human beings towards each other – hence, for instance, the utilitarian aspect of such figures as the Old Cumberland Beggar.[3]

Wordsworth's first reading of Marvell may be traced to 1795[4] – well in time to influence the thinking behind 'The Recluse' and shape the poetry that followed.[5] That doesn't explain, however, why verse written before that seems touched by his presence, most notably the finale of *An Evening Walk*, composed while Wordsworth was at Cambridge in 1789:

[2] On the larger question of Wordsworth's relationship to the English republicans see, among others, Z. S. Fink, 'Wordsworth and the English Republican Tradition', *JEGP* 47 (1948) 107–26.
[3] For the utilitarian interpretation, see A. D. Nuttall, *A Common Sky* (London: Chatto and Windus, 1974), pp. 130ff., which David Bromwich counters in his analysis, *Disowned by Memory* 30–43.
[4] See my 'Wordsworth's Reading of Marvell', *N&Q* NS 40 (1993) 41–2.
[5] This is discussed by Frederick Burwick, 'What the mower does to the meadow: action and reflection in Wordsworth and Marvell', *Milton, the Metaphysicals, and Romanticism*, ed. Lisa Low and Anthony John Harding (Cambridge: Cambridge University Press, 1994), pp. 172–84.

Now with religious awe the farewel light
Blends with the solemn colouring of the night;
Mid groves of clouds that crest the mountain's brow,
And round the West's proud lodge their shadows throw,
Like Una shining on her gloomy way,
The half seen form of Twilight roams astray;
Thence, from three paly loopholes mild and small,
Slow lights upon the lake's still bosom fall,
Beyond the mountain's giant reach that hides
In deep determin'd gloom his subject tides.
– Mid the dark steeps repose the shadowy streams,
As touch'd with dawning moonlight's hoary gleams,
Long streaks of fairy light the wave illume
With bordering lines of intervening gloom,
Soft o'er the surface creep the lustres pale
Tracking with silvering path the changeful gale.
– 'Tis restless magic all; at once the bright
Breaks on the shade, the shade upon the light,
Fair spirits are abroad; in sportive chase
Brushing with lucid wands the water's face,
While music stealing round the glimmering deeps
Charms the tall circle of th' enchanted steeps.
– As thro' th'astonish'd woods the notes ascend,
The mountain streams their rising song suspend;
Below Eve's listening Star, the sheep walk stills
It's drowsy tinklings on th'attentive hills;
The milkmaid stops her ballad, and her pail
Stays its low murmur in th'unbreathing vale;
No night-duck clamours for his wilder'd mate,
Aw'd, while below the Genii hold their state.
– The pomp is fled, and mute the wondrous strains,
No wrack of all the pageant scene remains,
So vanish those fair Shadows, human Joys,
But Death alone their vain regret destroys.

(*An Evening Walk* 329–62)

Wordsworth's 'pageant scene' is as theatrical as the climax of 'Upon Appleton House': why, if not to emphasize contrivance, describe lights projected through the 'three paly loopholes' in the clouds, the sourceless music accompanying the spectacle, or allude to *The Tempest*?[6] But there is an important distinction to be drawn. In Marvell the natural world is suspended in a kind of vacuum,

---

[6] Line 360 alludes to *The Tempest* IV i 155–6: 'And, like this insubstantial pageant faded, / Leave not a rack behind.'

'an horror calm and dumb', so that, for instance, 'The stupid Fishes hang, as plain / As *Flies* in *Chrystal* overt'ane.' It is static, a tableau. Nature, as Marvell points out, is 'vitrify'd' – a frozen, passive witness to Mary's purity of spirit. Wordsworth's landscape is also 'enchanted' but the magic that plays across it is 'restless': the spirits skating across the lake's surface are its emanations. Unlike Marvell's, it is animistic. Wordsworth would never have described it, or anything in it, as 'stupid', numb or dumb. It shimmers with power and intensity, eloquent and vigorous like the rocks in the 'Recluse' drafts of 1798 that speak 'The ghostly language of the ancient earth'.[7] It was essential to the philosophy of 'The Recluse' that nature be instinct with life, a medium between man and cosmic forces beyond, capable of changing whoever it touched. The 'Fair spirits' of *An Evening Walk* may be a cumbersome eighteenth-century device deriving from Pope's sylphs,[8] but they were the only means by which he could have described that activity. Coleridge would help him find other words in 1798, but the concepts are already present here. If *An Evening Walk* (though written a decade prior to the *annus mirabilis*) contains much that is distinctive to 'The Recluse', including elements that, though akin to those in earlier writers such as Marvell, do not have an obvious literary source, where did it all come from?

By the time he was worrying about his failure to write 'The Recluse' Wordsworth had mythologized his Cambridge years into a period of low achievement. In Book III of the *Five-Book Prelude* he recalled having 'Read lazily in lazy books'[9] and compared himself with the floating island of Esthwaite ('Unsound, of spongy texture'),[10] but says little about his writing. Extant manuscripts suggest that, whatever his protestations, he was far from idle. He kept in practice by translating Virgil, a project that led directly to the composition of *An Evening Walk* (drafts for both works appear in the same notebook). During this period, 1787–9, the first two years of his undergraduate career, he also worked on a number of shorter poems, including a series of sonnets. Much of his creative and emotional energies were poured into these brief, discrete utterances. They reflect the influence of numerous writers, but the voice is always distinctively Wordsworth's.[11]

---

[7] Cornell *Ruined Cottage* 371.

[8] There are several Popean echoes; for instance, the 'lucid wands' in Wordsworth are borrowed from Ariel's 'Azure Wand' (*Rape of the Lock* ii 72).

[9] Line 258.

[10] Line 342.

[11] See my 'Wordsworth's Reading of Bowles', *N&Q* 36 (1989) 165–7. Paul Bauschatz has also discussed Bowles' influence on the Cambridge sonnets; see 'Coleridge, Wordsworth, and Bowles', *Style* 27 (Spring 1993) 17–40.

When slow from pensive twilight's latest gleams
'O'er the dark mountain-top descends the ray'
That stains with crimson tinge the water grey
And still, I listen while the dells and streams
And vanish'd woods a lulling murmur make;
As Vesper first begins to twinkle bright
And on the dark hillside the cottage light,
With long reflexion streams across the lake. –
The lonely grey-duck, darkling on his way,
Quaakes clamourous – deep the measur'd strokes rebound
Of unseen oar parting with hollow sound
While the slow curfew shuts the eye of day –
Sooth'd by the stilly scene with many a sigh
Heaves the full heart nor knows for whom, or why –

As in the climactic episode of *An Evening Walk*, this sonnet describes an experience that occurs just after the sun has disappeared and darkness has descended. Wordsworth is listening to the 'lulling murmur' of the streams and woods, an almost human sound lent numinous possibility by the fact that its source has 'vanish'd'. Ensuing lines describe other sounds whose sources must be inferred: the oar is 'unseen', as is the lonely duck which, like the nightingale in Milton's Eden, 'Sings darkling'.[12] Other literary nightingales come to mind: 'I cannot see what flowers are at my feet, / Nor what soft incense hangs upon the boughs.'[13] Keats' poem was three decades in the future, but in both cases the denial of one sense stimulates others, and encourages a concentration on the invisible. In this case the drama is emotional. His senses on the stretch, Wordsworth feels obscurely moved by nature, 'Sooth'd by the stilly scene'. Gray is clearly an important literary model, whose 'Elegy' provided the same mood of twilight repose, along with some of the details mentioned by Wordsworth, not least a curfew that tolls the knell of passing day.[14]

At the same time, Wordsworth is conscious of the work of another admirer of the famous 'Elegy', William Lisle Bowles, whose sonnets enjoyed tremendous popularity from 1789 onwards. In this case, Wordsworth has his eye on the diction and manner of Bowles' 'Sonnet Written at Tinemouth, Northumberland, after a tempestuous voyage':

[12] *Paradise Lost* iii 39.
[13] Keats, 'Ode to a Nightingale' 41–2.
[14] Angus Easson mentions other instances of Gray's influence on Wordsworth's early writing, 'Gray and Wordsworth', *Thomas Gray: Contemporary Essays*, ed. W. B. Hutchings and William Ruddick (Liverpool: Liverpool University Press, 1993), pp. 205–23.

As slow I climb the cliff's ascending side,
Much musing on the track of terror past,
When o'er the dark wave rode the howling blast,
Pleas'd I look back, and view the tranquil tide,
That laves the pebbled shore; and now the beam
Of evening smiles on the grey battlement,
And yon forsaken tow'r that time has rent: –
The lifted oar far off with silver gleam
Is touch'd, and hush'd billows seem to sleep!
Soothed by the scene, even thus on sorrow's breast
A kindred stillness steals, and bids her rest;
Whilst sad airs *stilly* sigh along the deep,
Like melodies which mourn upon the lyre,
Wak'd by the breeze, and as they mourn, expire.[15]

This is the language of sensibility, whereby words are not always commensurate with the emotions they describe. Wordsworth may have borrowed Bowles' language for a time, but it would have no permanent impact on him. Much more impressive to his way of thinking was Bowles' ability to ventilate the emotional interior of his poems. The 'kindred stillness' precipitates a psychological shift: the soothing of his 'sorrow'. From a twentieth-century perspective that may seem unexceptional, but Bowles was unusual in attributing such power to nature. Charlotte Smith, the success of whose *Elegiac Sonnets* had enhanced the vogue for sonneteering from the moment of their first outing in 1786, was an expert at describing a melancholic absorption in nature, but without the mitigating shift in mood.[16] Bowles, by contrast, describes a modulation in temper which he attributes to his surroundings. Of course, he writes from a picturesque tradition with a comparatively superficial interest in nature. He is neither a deist nor a pantheist, and makes no religious claim for the 'kindred stillness' that descends on the sorrowing breast. All the same, his portrayal of nature licenses a more powerful one, culminating in the 'sensations sweet' which the remembered 'forms of beauty' on the banks of the Wye would bring to the weary, city-dwelling poet of 'Tintern Abbey'.

With that in mind 'When slow from pensive twilight's latest gleams', at first glance an uninspired imitation, becomes increasingly redolent of mature Wordsworth. He does not downplay the 'stilly' sigh of the breeze, as Bowles

---

[15]   My italics. Quotations from Bowles are taken from the second edition of his sonnets, *Sonnets written chiefly on Picturesque Spots during a Tour* (Bath, 1789), as it seems to have had most impact on Wordsworth. There is every reason to think that Wordsworth also knew the first edition, *Fourteen Sonnets* (Bath, 1789). See *WR* i 18.
[16]   For Wordsworth's early enthusiasm for Smith's poetry see *WR* i 127–8.

does, but foregrounds it: 'Sooth'd by the stilly scene with many a sigh /
Heaves the full heart . . .' As in *An Evening Walk*, the magic of the scene is
dependent on the deep calm that attends the twilit landscape. Such dramatic
heightening of the effects described by Bowles increases our sense that the
outside world can act as a catalyst of emotional response. Everything is sucked
into an inner drama – even the twilight in line 1 is 'pensive', and the 'parting'
oar with its 'hollow' beat in line 11 is related to the mood of valediction.
Nothing could be further removed from the Gothic episodes of 'The Vale of
Esthwaite', written two years before. In conscious rejection of such 'extraordinary incident',[17] Wordsworth had begun to cultivate the aesthetic that would
underpin the *Lyrical Ballads* and 'The Recluse'. To a large extent, his skill
resides in an ability to infuse external objects with emotion. There is a bashful-
ness about it, a desire to address his feelings without appearing in an obvious
way to be doing so. And it is a testament to his precocious understanding of
psychology that he writes persuasively of being moved to tears without knowing 'for whom or why'. In other words, this poem is about displacement –
effectively another screen memory. The tears are precipitated by something
which appears to have nothing to do with their actual cause, to which some
incidental detail has attached them. Many decades later Tennyson would discuss the same subject in a lyric written, coincidentally, at Tintern Abbey: 'Tears,
idle tears, I know not what they mean . . .'

As he continued to compose sonnets at Cambridge Wordsworth developed
the aesthetic of transcendental style. Indeed, it is significant that on arrival at
Alfoxden he reviewed his juvenilia with Coleridge, so as to confirm that powerful sense of having been destined to compose 'The Recluse'. In the course
of these rereadings, Coleridge cannibalized a number of early Wordsworthian
drafts for hybrids of his own, published in the *Morning Post*,[18] and Wordsworth
converted a Cambridge sonnet, 'How rich in front with twilight's tinge impressed', into two of the poems published in *Lyrical Ballads* (1798): 'Remembrance of Collins' and 'Lines written while sailing in a boat at evening'.
The original sonnet, known to us only from a rough, unfinished draft in the
Racedown notebook (see figure 5 opposite), describes a light effect which he
later recalled having seen 'during a solitary walk on the banks of the Cam'.[19]

---

[17] Preface to *Lyrical Ballads*, *Prose Works* i 128.
[18] Among the Hawkshead poems Coleridge published 'Lewti' and 'Lines imitated from
Catullus'; see R. S. Woof, 'Wordsworth's Poetry and Stuart's Newspapers: 1797–1803',
Studies in Bibliography 15 (1962) 149–89.
[19] *FN* 36.

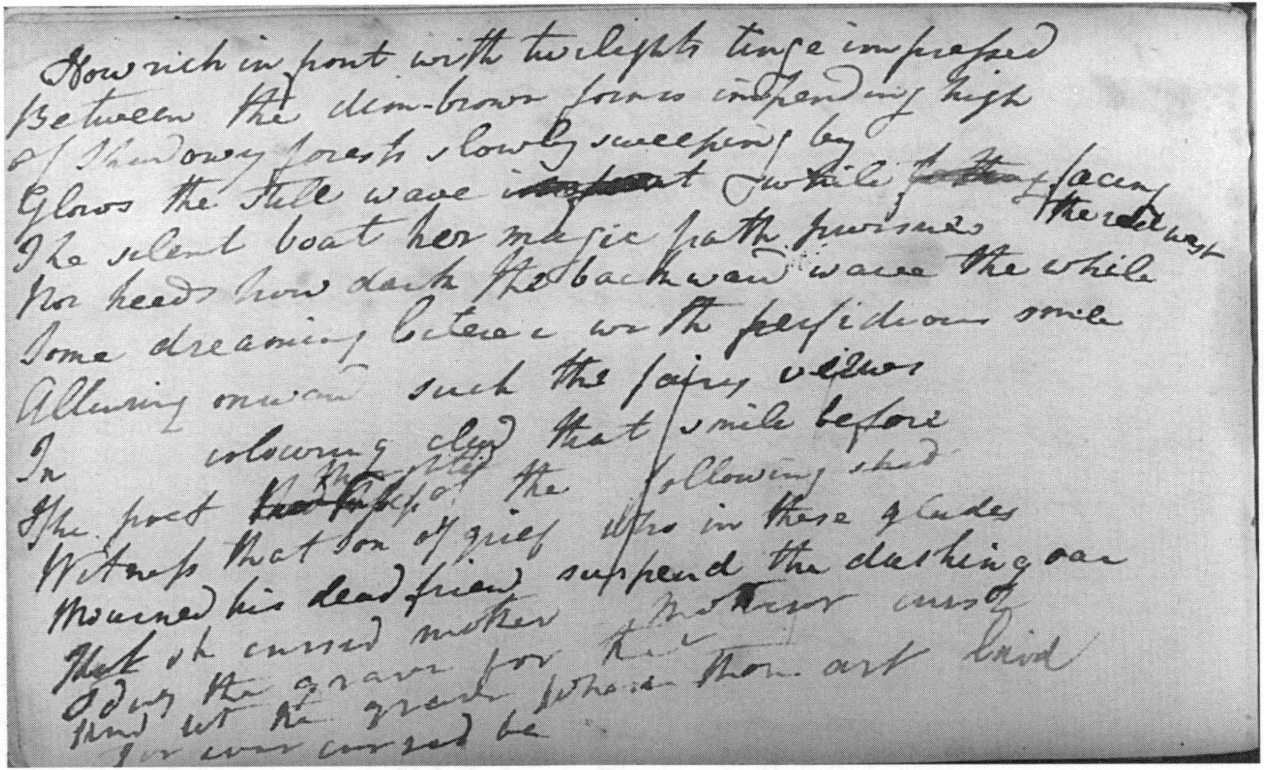

Figure 5. DC MS 11, 48v. 'How rich in front with twilights tinge impressed': one of Wordsworth's Cambridge sonnets, a source for 'Written on the Thames near Richmond', published in *Lyrical Ballads* (1798).

How rich in front with twilight's tinge impressed
Between the dim-brown forms impending high
Of [s]hadowy forests slowly sweeping by
Glows the still wave, while facing the red west
The silent boat her magic path pursues
Nor heeds how dark the backward wave the while
Some dreaming loiterer with perfidious smile
[Alluring onward such the fairy views
In [   ] colouring clad that smile before
The poet [thoughtless] of the following shad[?es];
Witness that son of grief who in these glades
Mourned his dead friend, suspend the dashing oar
That

Like the climax of *An Evening Walk*, this is set at twilight, a few moments after the sun has disappeared. A boat (presumably a punt) glides westward down the Cam towards the afterglow, pursued by the shades of night; on the riverbank a 'dreaming loiterer', 'The poet', stands watching. As in mature Wordsworth, its diction holds the key to the poem's internal drama. 'How rich in front . . . Glows the still wave': Landon and Curtis do not punctuate their texts, partly because Wordsworth did not. Had he published them at the time of their composition the printer, or a judicious copy-editor, would have pointed them on his behalf. The blandness of the transcription should not stop us from hearing the tone of that opening cadence. It is awestruck, and the correct emphasis demands an exclamation mark. It is sufficient to tell us that, as the poem begins, its author is in the midst of a visionary experience not unlike the one at the climax of *An Evening Walk*. Everything is heightened accordingly: the wave is uncannily 'still', while the tinge of the twilight sky is 'impressed' between the silhouetted trees, as if the ochrous radiance had not merely penetrated the eye but marked itself indelibly on the poet's brain.

At this pitch, Wordsworth's imagery and language do for the poetic evocation of landscape what Turner did in paint; dispensing with the nymphs, dryads and pastoral fixtures bequeathed by Spenser and Milton, he substitutes imaginative intensity for neo-classicism. The painterly construction of the scene is deliberate; a copy of Daniel Webb's *Inquiry into the Beauties of Painting*, a standard text for artists of the mid-eighteenth century, was owned by Wordsworth at Cambridge.[20] But his originality lies in the knowledge, which he shared with Turner, that it was possible to create an aesthetic equal to the darkness visible of the sublime. These intimations accumulate as the sonnet proceeds: though in motion the boat is 'silent', navigated by 'magic' towards

[20]   *WR* i 144.

'fairy views'. By implication we too are being swept, with the perceiving intelligence of the poet, toward some otherworldly destination.

A shift of focus is essential if the vision is to be given context. So far we have perceived it through the disembodied viewpoint of the omniscient narrator; in lines that follow Wordsworth identifies himself as the figure in the landscape, observing this haunting scene from the riverbank.

> Nor heeds how dark the backward wave the while
> Some dreaming loiterer with perfidious smile
> [Alluring onward such the fairy views
> In [   ] colouring clad that smile before
> The poet [thoughtless] of the following shad[?es];
> Witness that son of grief who in these glades
> Mourned his dead friend, suspend the dashing oar
> That
>
> (ll. 6–13)

The lack of punctuation hardly makes for ease of reading, but if as I suspect there should be a semicolon after 'loiterer' in line 7, the 'perfidious smile' must belong to the 'fairy views', which lure the poet further along the riverbank. As in the vision of the Battle of Dunmail Raise in the 'Vale', when terror hag-like 'rode' his soul, there is a sinister aspect to all this: 'Many times while going to school have I grasped at a wall or tree to recall myself from this abyss of idealism to the reality. At that time I was afraid of such processes.'[21] That fear drove Wordsworth to summon himself back 'to the reality' almost by reflex, a habit so integral to his thinking that by June 1798 Coleridge described it as giving 'a something corporeal, a *matter-of-fact-ness*, a clinging to the palpable, or often to the petty, [to] his poetry'.[22] Although by then Coleridge had relinquished his own poetic ambitions, having nominated Wordsworth as the poet of 'The Recluse', this was a shrewd admonition. The possessed poet of *Kubla Khan* (a poem which it is worth remembering was written initially for a readership consisting of Wordsworth and Dorothy), whose flashing eyes and floating hair terrifies everyone who sees him, amplifies that cautionary voice, suggesting that only he who has drunk the milk of paradise and surrendered wholly to its effects could compose 'The Recluse'. Coleridge knew from the start that Wordsworth was detained from such mad raptures, and for years continued to monitor his increasing tendency to retreat into the

---

[21]   *FN* 61. There are other accounts of this process, which are discussed by Hugh Sykes Davies, *Wordsworth and the Worth of Words* (Cambridge: Cambridge University Press, 1986), pp. 173–4.
[22]   'My First Acquaintance with Poets', Wu ix 104.

arms of the women he gathered round him. It was something he despised in him, antithetical to the visionary spirit behind 'The Recluse'. Typical of this is a letter to Thomas Poole of 14 October 1803, which notes that Wordsworth 'has made a Beginning to his Recluse', before going on to attack his 'Indolence' and 'Self-involution':

> I saw him more & more benetted in hypochondriacal Fancies, living wholly among *Devotees* – having every the minutest Thing, almost his very Eating & Drinking, done for him by his Sister, or Wife – & I trembled, lest a Film should rise, and thicken on his moral Eye.[23]

Given Coleridge's own chronic inability to manage his time efficiently, one can only marvel at the irony of his lecturing someone else on the topic – in this case someone who had by this time composed much great poetry in his presence. No wonder he exhorted Poole to 'be so good as to destroy this Letter'. But the larger argument is clear. He had *not* been detained; he had gone off the rails at Cambridge, been to prostitutes, got drunk, become addicted to opium, and continued to indulge himself for the rest of his life. He was also profoundly religious, with a sound sense of his own sinful past.

So what does Coleridge mean when he expresses fear that 'a Film should rise, and thicken on his moral Eye'? He is talking about the need for the 'Recluse' poet to remain close to life as it is lived, close to the edge. He fears that Wordsworth is becoming too closeted, too insulated from sinful reality to be able to confront it in his poetry and discuss its transformation. The film that could obscure Wordsworth's vision is likely, in other words, to blind him to the exemplary morality that 'The Recluse' was to expound. This emerges again in the letter to Wordsworth of 30 May 1815, in response to Wordsworth's request that he send him his 'remarks on the Poems, and also upon the Excursion'.[24] Coleridge there emphasizes repeatedly the need for *The Recluse* to engage with the 'Fall . . . as a fact . . . the reality of which is attested by Experience & Conscience'.[25] His fear, since at least 1803 and probably before, was that Wordsworth would forget what it was like to carry with oneself the knowledge of having fallen from grace.

There is a considerable body of critical literature arguing that by 1798 there were a number of skeletons in Wordsworth's closet. Suggestions range from involvement with prostitutes at Cambridge[26] to the notion that he was complicit

---

[23]   Griggs ii 1012–13.
[24]   *MY* ii 238. Wordsworth had already heard from mutual friends, most notably Lady Beaumont, that Coleridge did not much like *The Excursion*.
[25]   Griggs iv 575.
[26]   See Johnston 127–33.

in nefarious acts in revolutionary France. Wordsworth may have felt guilty about something he said or did during his youth, but if so it is remarkable that neither Coleridge nor anyone close to him, including any member of his family, wrote or otherwise recorded anything about it. Unlike, of course, the one crime we know did cause him pain: his abandonment of Annette Vallon and his French daughter Caroline in 1792. (This was certainly known to Coleridge, because he wrote a poem about it in 1802.)[27]

How intriguing, then, that in a sonnet written nearly a decade before the *annus mirabilis* Wordsworth was already attaching a moral charge to imaginative vision: the smile which lures the riverside walker towards the 'fairy views' is 'perfidious'. Those who wish to place him in harm's way might read it as the smile of a prostitute; the more literary-minded as that of the serpent in Paradise. However we construe it, it turns inner vision into temptation. Wordsworth is again recalling Bowles, whose 'Sonnet on leaving a village in Scotland' places Caledonian beauty-spots in a similar light:

> Yet still your brightest images shall smile,
> To charm the lingering stranger, and beguile
> His way . . .

> (ll. 10–12)

Lost travellers throng eighteenth-century verse from Thomson's *Seasons* to Erasmus Darwin's *The Loves of the Plants*; Bowles serves up a literary cliché meant to adorn his picturesque view of Scotland. It may be unfair to make the comparison, but Wordsworth goes one better, using the smiling 'images' as a vehicle for the psychological undercurrents that make his poetry more sophisticated. The darkness of 'the backward wave' – that is, the water behind the punt; the '[s]hadowy forests'; and the 'shad[?es]' that pursue the dreaming loiterer along the bank, are equally ominous, deepening the note of apprehension implicit in the alluring but perfidious smile. The mood is one of anticipation – but of what, or whom?

Being '[thoughtless] of the following shad[?es]', Wordsworth is unaware of the night sky behind him – though 'shade' can also mean ghost, the sense in which it is used in 'The Vale of Esthwaite', parts of which he had recently been revising and, in all likelihood, reciting to his Cambridge contemporaries. Nor is that the only intimation of mortality in the fragment. As it draws to its conclusion we are enjoined to 'Witness that son of grief who in these glades / Mourned his dead friend, suspend the dashing oar . . .' To Wordsworth and those who may have read this sonnet when it was first composed, the most

---

[27] 'Spots in the Sun', for which see pp. 177–8 below.

obvious thing about that command was its allusion to Collins's *Ode Occasion'd by the Death of Mr Thomson*, set not in Cambridge but on the banks of the Thames near Richmond (Collins and Thomson had lived close to each other, and shared the same circle of friends, for at least a year before the latter's death):

> Remembrance oft shall haunt the Shore
> When Thames in Summer-wreaths is drest,
> And oft suspend the dashing Oar
> To bid his gentle Spirit rest!
>
> (ll. 13–16)

What in Collins is a respectful gesture, a mark of one man's affection for another, is invoked by Wordsworth for quite different motives. As far as Collins is concerned, Thomson is quite definitely deceased, won't be returning, and the best he can do is grant him the tribute of remembrance. His *Ode* is genuinely bereft. In Wordsworth's sonnet the dead are not in any sense absent; they are understood to be close by, in the trees and waters, just as they had infused 'The Vale of Esthwaite', from the site of the Battle of Dunmail Raise to the desolate ridge above Borwick Lodge where he waited for the horses in 1783. It may only have been a matter of months before composing this sonnet that he had translated Virgil's *Georgics*, in which Orpheus is described 'treading on the edge of day' and, in an alternative reading, 'on the very brink of day'.[28] Both phrases adapt Virgil's 'luce sub ipsa'[29] to Wordsworth's evolving mythology by which the visionary state opened up by the abyss of idealism gave renewed access to that twilight zone between the world of the living and that of the dead. Indeed, Orpheus' story documents that process in meticulous detail.

It is frustrating that 'How rich in front' survives only as a fragment, but the substance of its concluding lines may be conjectured from a rough draft of 'Remembrance of Collins' to which they contributed, dating from 1797:

> But let remembrance now suspend
> For him suspend the dashing [oar]
> And pray that never muses friend
> May know his chilling sorrows sore
> How dark how still the only sound
> The dripping of [the] oar suspend[ed][30]

---

[28]   See Cornell *Early Poems* 640–1. Landon and Curtis read 'brink' as 'brind' (which makes no sense) or 'bound' (which does); 'brink' is what Wordsworth has written.
[29]   *Georgics* iv 490.

This expresses a similar sense of resolve; his vision concluded, the poet returns from the contemplation of fairy views to the real solid world of objects, water dripping from the end of an oar. Something else has altered; the sonnet is about suppressed grief. If the dead inhere in his surroundings, Wordsworth doesn't want to join them. By admitting the allurements of the 'red west' and then returning to earth, he has symbolically discharged his grief without surrendering to it. So it is that 'never muses friend / May know his chilling sorrows sore'. The poem re-enacts the delayed grieving of summer 1787 so as to affirm its setting to rights the 'mighty debt' of grief owed to his dead parents. In a very real sense the poetry of 1789 finds Wordsworth taking stock.

The demands of the sonnet – that most rigorous and contained of models – seems to have suited his desire to explore his attitude towards the dead two years after the crisis of summer 1787. A third Cambridge sonnet, 'On the [   ] village Silence sets her seal', bears this out. In substantially revised form it was published in the *Morning Post*, 13 February 1802, as 'Sonnet. Written at Evening', and was later included in further revised form in *Poems in Two Volumes* (1807) under the title, 'Written in very early Youth'.

> On the [   ] village Silence sets her seal,
> And in the glimmering vale the last lights die;
> The kine, obscurely seen, before me lie
> Round the dim horse that crops his later meal
> Scarce heard. A timely slumber seems to steal
> O'er vale and mountain: now, while ear and eye
> Alone are vacant, a strange harmony,
> Home-felt and home-created, seems to heal
> That grief for which my senses still supply
> Fresh food. [For never but when Memory
> Is hush'd, am I at peace:] my friends, restrain
> Those busy cares that must renew my pain;
> Go rear the [sensitive] plant – quick shall it feel
> The fond officious touch, and droop again.[31]

---

[30] My transcription, from DC MS 2, 13v; photograph at Cornell *Early Poems* 37, transcription at Cornell *Lyrical Ballads* 275.

[31] On this occasion I have abandoned the Cornell edition and resorted to my own text. For entirely understandable reasons the Cornell editors have preserved the two substantial gaps in the manuscript at lines 10–11 and 13 (see figure 6 overleaf). Though defensible from a scholarly perspective this makes the poem so incoherent as to be virtually incomprehensible. I have filled lines 10–11 from the *Morning Post*, supplying square brackets to

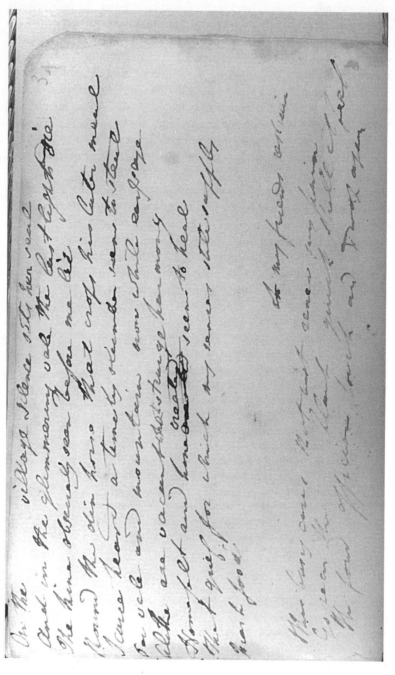

Figure 6. DC MS 11, 49r. 'On the [   ] village Silence sets her seal': another Cambridge sonnet, better known in revised form as 'Written in very early Youth'. Though dated by its author to 1786 it was more probably composed in 1788.

Later versions begin with the famous line, 'Calm is all nature as a resting wheel' – an improvement that shows what energy Wordsworth could put into his revisions, which are not invariably for the worse.[32] (Indeed, De Quincey thought well enough of it to borrow it in 'Levana and Our Ladies of Sorrow', and comment at some length on the fact in a footnote.)[33] It manages to articulate, in a way the undergraduate poet could not, what lies at the heart of the twilight scene. Once again, the poem is set immediately after the sun has disappeared, so that we are dealing with a moment out of the glare of the day, beyond the ceaseless flow of chronological time. By returning constantly to that limbo betwixt night and day, Wordsworth thought of himself as writing the same poem. In a sense, the Cambridge sonnets amount to a single, evolving meditation on the same experience. As in 'How rich in front' the last of the sun's light glimmers in the sky, leaving the animals 'obscure' and 'dim'. Everything is reduced to its minimum; even the horse's chewing is 'Scarce heard' in the impending darkness.[34] The poem places us at the very margins of perception, the edges of verifiable reality.

At the moment when his senses are least to be trusted, 'A timely slumber seems to steal' across 'vale and mountain'. What is that haunting slumber? Wordsworth would not forget it, and in a lyric composed a decade later, re-cast it as a fearful vision of anticipated loss: 'A slumber did my spirit seal.' That first line also incorporates some of the rhythms and diction of this one: 'On the [   ] village Silence sets her seal'. By reading from the later poem back to the sonnet, we may surmise that the Silence, and its attendant slumber, give the poet access once again to the world of shades. In that sense it can be no coincidence that Wordsworth has returned us, by way of 'vale and mountain', to the Lake District; wherever this sonnet was composed, it harks back to the same landscape of the Orpheus translations on which he had worked the previous year. In other words, it not only recapitulates the myth of loss and grieving formulated in 'The Vale of Esthwaite' but locates its action in the same place.

In the next line the ear and eye 'Alone are vacant' – another anticipation of the great poetry to come when, for instance, 'in vacant or in pensive mood'

---

indicate the additions, and offer 'sensitive' at line 13 as a conjectural reading. The *Morning Post* text identifies the plant as the 'shrunk Mimosa', commonly known as the sensitive plant. While at it, I have also punctuated for sense.

[32]   David Bromwich makes the same point about the 1842 text of *The Borderers*, *Disowned by Memory* 45.

[33]   Masson xiii 363.

[34]   Editors usually attribute this detail to the influence of Anne Finch, Countess of Winchelsea (see for instance Cornell *Early Poems* 682), though it is surely something Wordsworth would have experienced for himself.

the daffodils 'flash upon that inward eye / Which is the bliss of solitude'.[35] This is a vacancy full of significance, which is to recur throughout his poetry (most notably in 'There was a boy'). It is a kind of paradox, as becomes clear from this explication, attributed to Wordsworth by De Quincey in 1839:

> I have remarked, from my earliest days, that if, under any circumstances, the attention is energetically braced up to an act of steady observation, or of steady expectation, then, if this intense condition of vigilance should suddenly relax, at that moment any beautiful, any impressively visual object, or collection of objects, falling upon the eye, is carried to the heart with a power not known under other circumstances.[36]

Nearly three decades had passed since these words were spoken (they date from about 1810–11), but De Quincey places them within quotation marks, and they must carry the weight of documentary fact. The observation stems 'from my earliest days', which refers us back to Hawkshead if not to Cockermouth; it is certainly something Wordsworth would have understood by the time he reached Cambridge. What he is discussing has little to do with vacancy as we use the word. As he has been doing in his poetry from 1786 onwards, Wordsworth is attempting to analyse his own habits of mind. He is aware, in retrospect, of times when the senses are baffled – as in the case of the Cambridge sonnets, by darkness. Their initial reaction is to strain, attempting to perceive what is no longer visible, or to hear those things that have fallen silent ('steady observation . . . steady expectation'). Tired and frustrated at last, the mind is compelled to 'relax', at which point 'any beautiful, any impressively visual object, or collection of objects, falling upon the eye, is carried to the heart with a power not known under other circumstances'. Once again, he is talking about access – the 'power' that inheres in natural objects, and reconnects us with our most profound feelings.

Wordsworth's explanation is at once revealing and diffident. Although he spells out a sequence of events repeated elsewhere, he is reluctant to say too much about them. Indeed, the carrying to the heart of 'any impressively visual object, or collection of objects' sounds almost mechanistic, anticlimactic. Perhaps Wordsworth didn't really want to talk to De Quincey about these things – and he seems in any case to have been wary of him, perhaps sensing about him something not to his taste. (From the very beginning of their relationship Wordsworth was prone to address De Quincey with 'coldness', and in his second letter counsels him to remain 'chaste' in the face of the 'frantic and

---

[35] 'I wandered lonely as a cloud' 14–15.
[36] *De Quincey as Critic*, ed. John E. Jordan (London: Routledge and Kegan Paul, 1973), p. 442.

dissolute' ways of Oxford life.)[37] So it is not altogether surprising if his explanation poses more questions than it answers. It refuses to say what 'power' consists of, where it comes from, and what the emotional constituent of the experience is likely to be.[38] His observations are readily applicable to a number of poems by him and Coleridge – the blessing of the water-snakes in 'The Ancient Mariner'; the climbing of Snowdon in *The Prelude*; the sudden, unexpected vision of the cathedral dome in 'St Paul's'. He often thinks of the sensory fatigue that precedes these experiences in terms of a larger emotional mood. In 'St Paul's' he is 'Press'd with conflicting thoughts of love and fear'[39] (for Coleridge); in 'Daffodils' he wanders 'lonely as a cloud'. As in the last section of 'The Vale of Esthwaite', imaginative vision carries in its wake an emotional freight; the 'fairy views' and 'strange harmony' are inextricably caught up with the continuing need to exorcize grief. Not that the wounds left by his parents' deaths are unhealed; in Dorothy, he had written, 'I fondly view / All, all that heav'n has claim'd in you.'[40] His poetry is one of restitution. Like Seamus Heaney in his translation of *Philoctetes*, Wordsworth believed in 'miracles / And cures and healing wells'.[41]

This Cambridge sonnet illustrates the process. Wordsworth thinks of the frustration of the senses in the darkening light as precipitating 'a timely slumber' that steals over them, a state leading directly to 'a strange harmony, / Home-felt and home-created'. That harmony is paradoxical: it comes from the depths of the mind while appearing 'strange'. Whatever its source, it 'seems to heal / That grief for which my senses still supply / Fresh food'. There is an explicit connection between the poet's perceptions and the turbulent feelings merely hinted at in the other sonnets. Sights and sounds of which he is dimly aware in the gloom speak of loss, but give way to a harmony which, like the 'fairy views' of the previous poem, implicitly restore what has been taken.

The poem's conclusion is an address to the poet's friends to abstain from 'busy cares' that will renew memories of the dead:

> [For never but when Memory
> Is hush'd, am I at peace:] my friends, restrain
> Those busy cares that must renew my pain;
> Go rear the [sensitive] plant – quick shall it feel
> The fond officious touch, and droop again.

[37] See *EY* 401, 454.
[38] W. J. B. Owen compares Wordsworth's explications in both the Preface to *Lyrical Ballads* and De Quincey's account, and finds that the theory does 'agree with the event'; see 'A Sense of the Infinite', *WC* 21 (1990) 18–27, p. 23.
[39] 'St Paul's' 1.
[40] Ibid. 386–7.
[41] Seamus Heaney, *The Cure at Troy* (London: Faber and Faber, 1990), p. 77.

Wordsworth's diffidence has come to the fore. He doesn't want his emotions to be attended to. It is a side of his personality always present, whether in the stoicism of 'The Vale of Esthwaite' or his teasing manner towards De Quincey. Unusually, it here becomes the subject of his poetry. As Landon and Curtis show, these lines allude to a number of eighteenth-century poems about grief that make the same point; Cuthbert Shaw had written, in *To the Memory of a Young Lady*,

> Forbear, my fond officious friends, forebear
> To wound my ears with the sad tales you tell.[42]

These lines were probably known to him, and others besides, but Wordsworth is no less sincere for that. It can be no accident that his self-portrayals characteristically show him alone: he wanders 'lonely as a cloud' by the shores of Ullswater, and is in a 'lonely place'[43] when he encounters the leech-gatherer, even though on both occasions he was with Dorothy. By eliding her presence he plays into the hands of those who would argue that their relationship was in some way exploitative. But Wordsworth is using a concept that describes something to which he was prone in the company of others – 'in lonely rooms, and mid the din / Of towns and cities'.[44] Surrounded by the bustle of the metropolis, the rooms are not at all lonely though their inhabitant, the young poet, is. It is likely, in fact, that his equivocal attitude towards the city is related to the heightened susceptibility he felt there to these emotions.

But they are not exclusive to the city. They can descend anywhere, at any time, whether he is on his own or not. This loneliness is akin to the feeling of abandonment that he and Dorothy had experienced in July 1787 when they renewed their grieving for their parents in Penrith. And throughout his work he discusses its recurrence. The connection between adult depression and childhood loss has long been recognized by psychoanalysts, but few readers have thought it central to Wordsworth's poetry.[45] I would not want to suggest that he was suffering from some kind of pathological condition, nor would I wish to say that it amounted to anything like the feelings of genuine despair suffered by Coleridge. But how could his adult temperament have been unaffected by early loss? I am reminded of the American novelist William Styron, who has courageously described the course taken by his depression in vivid detail, tracing it to

---

[42]   See Cornell *Early Poems* 682.
[43]   'Resolution and Independence' 52.
[44]   'Tintern Abbey' 26–7.
[45]   See, for instance John Bowlby, *Attachment and Loss, Volume III: Loss, Sadness and Depression* (Harmondsworth: Penguin, 1981), pp. 32–7.

the death of my mother when I was thirteen; this disorder and early sorrow – the death or disappearance of a parent, especially a mother, before or during puberty – appears repeatedly in the literature on depression as a trauma sometimes likely to create nearly irreparable emotional havoc. The danger is especially apparent if the young person is affected by what has been termed 'incomplete mourning' – has, in effect, been unable to achieve the catharsis of grief, and so carries within himself through later years an insufferable burden of which rage and guilt, and not only dammed-up sorrow, are a part, and become the potential seeds of self-destruction.[46]

Styron's case is different in degree but not in kind; I'm not persuaded that Wordsworth was ever a serious candidate for suicide. But his mourning was 'incomplete' in 1783, and probably only partially expiated in summer 1787. Although he suffered no serious mental disorder in later life, the evidence indicates that he did carry a 'burden of rage and guilt' that occasionally led to depressive episodes, exacerbated by events in his personal life. Separation from Annette and their child in 1792; the drowning of John Wordsworth in 1805; the deaths of Catherine and Thomas Wordsworth in 1812; and that of Dora in 1847 – each initiated bouts which in all likelihood stemmed from his initial response to his parents' deaths, particularly that of his father when he was 13.

Depression, as Styron reveals, is paralysing, but that paralysis was not Wordsworth's problem, at least for the first thirty years of his life. It is a testimony to his psychological poise that he was able to analyse his responses so thoughtfully in 'The Vale of Esthwaite', and then draw on them in subsequent poems. No doubt Dorothy was instrumental in enabling him to do this – but if they understood each other (as I'm sure they did), they were reluctant to lay their feelings open to the scrutiny of others. This was entirely understandable under the circumstances; the harsh judgements so widespread today about those with depressive illnesses were more common in the late eighteenth century, when no psychopharmacological therapies were available for the treatment of 'melancholia' (from which Charles and Mary Lamb were certainly sufferers).

This very English diffidence uncharacteristically becomes Wordsworth's subject in the closing lines of this third Cambridge sonnet, where his 'busy friends' are told to desist from attempting to allay his 'pain'. It marks a turning-point in his artistic development: henceforth he will submerge his emotions beneath the surfaces of things, preferring to allow them to colour the manner in which the world is perceived. Mediated through the alchemy of

---

[46] William Styron, *Darkness Visible: A Memoir of Madness* (London: Jonathan Cape, 1991), pp. 79–80.

verse, they are usually withheld from direct analysis. In 1798 he would say that we 'murder to dissect'[47] – a further glance at the 'fond officious touch'. This sonnet of 1789 is one of those moments at which he presents his grief to view and acknowledges it as a form of sustenance. The 'busy cares' of the onlooker are unhelpful because they serve not just to renew his pain but to defuse its power. The drooping flower in the final line speaks of a failure of creativity, the price of too much emotional display.

This is the most obvious reason for Wordsworth's notorious disinclination to publish. He was loath to lay himself bare. Much of the writing he concealed from view approached these matters more directly than was usual – most notably *The Prelude* in all its forms (published posthumously, 1850). Even when memorializing his brother John in verse his grief is mediated through Sir George Beaumont's painting of Piel Castle and the figure of Nelson, but remains out of direct view. Only in that way could it retain its power. This helps explain Wordsworth's increasing reticence towards De Quincey, whom he may have sensed had a talent for murdering to dissect.[48]

The conclusion of *An Evening Walk* assimilates the lessons of the Hawkshead verse and Cambridge sonnets; in that respect it could be regarded as Wordsworth's first mature work. Here is the passage with which this chapter began, but this time I take my text from the manuscript. In this form it reads as originally drafted, over three years before publication, shortly after completion of the sonnets I have just discussed. Equivalent lines in the 1793 text are given in square brackets on the left; manuscript references are given for those with access to the facsimiles in the Cornell edition:

---

[47] 'The Tables Turned' 28.

[48] De Quincey remains one of the most astute, if somewhat biased, critics of Wordsworth. It is interesting to find him declaring, in a letter of 17 January 1835 to his publisher, William Tait, that he was preoccupied with Wordsworth's ideas to the neglect of biographical materials:

> I therefore who might from Coleridge have learned every particular about Wordsworth's life, have felt so exclusive concern about his mind and intellectual being, and should have been so ashamed that any friendship for him and his family could be supposed to stand upon any other than the purest intellectual interest, that I threw away my opportunities almost unconscious of their existence.
>
> (Quoted Robert Woof, *Thomas De Quincey: An English Opium-Eater 1785–1859* (Grasmere: Trustees of Dove Cottage, 1985), p. 69)

There were various sources of tension between Wordsworth and De Quincey. Margaret Simpson came high on the list, followed by De Quincey's overenthusiastic felling of the ash tree and hedges in the Dove Cottage garden in 1811 (see Sara Hutchinson's letter to Mary Monkhouse, 3 December 1811, in Woof, *De Quincey*, 71).

[DC MS 7, 3r]
                                awe
         Now with religious Touch the farewell light
[330]   Blends with the solemn colouring night

[DC MS 7, 4r]
         – Mid groves of clouds that crest the mountains brow
                                wests
         And round the days proud lodge their shadows throw
                                shining on her sombrous
         Like Una lost and pensive on her way
                                the
         The half-seen form of Twilight roams, astray
[335]   Thence from three lilac loop-holes mild & small
         Pale lights upon the lakes still bosom fall

[DC MS 7, 3r]
         Beyond the mountains stretch of shade that hides
                                subject
         In deep determind gloom, his midway tides

[DC MS 7, 4r]
         Mid the dark steeps repose the shadowy streams
[340]   As touch'd with dawning moonlights hoary gleams
         Long streaks of fairy light the wave illume
         With bordering lines of intervening gloom

[DC MS 7, 3v]
[351]   As stealing thro' the woods the notes ascend
         The mountain streams their rising song suspend
         Below Eve's listening star the sheep walk stills
                distant
         Its drowsy tinklings on th' unbreathing hills
[355]   The milkmaid stops her ballad and her pail
         Stays its low murmur in the hollow vale
         No night-duck clamours for his wilder'd mate
         Aw'd [?below] the Genii hold their state
         – The Shades are fled, and mute the wondrous strains
[360]   No rack of all the pageant Scene remains
         So vanish those fair shadows human joys
         Yet not their vain regret which death alone destroys[49]

---

[49] My transcription; facsimiles at Cornell *Evening Walk* 105–11 and see figure 7 overleaf.
It has not been necessary for my purposes to present overwritten readings.

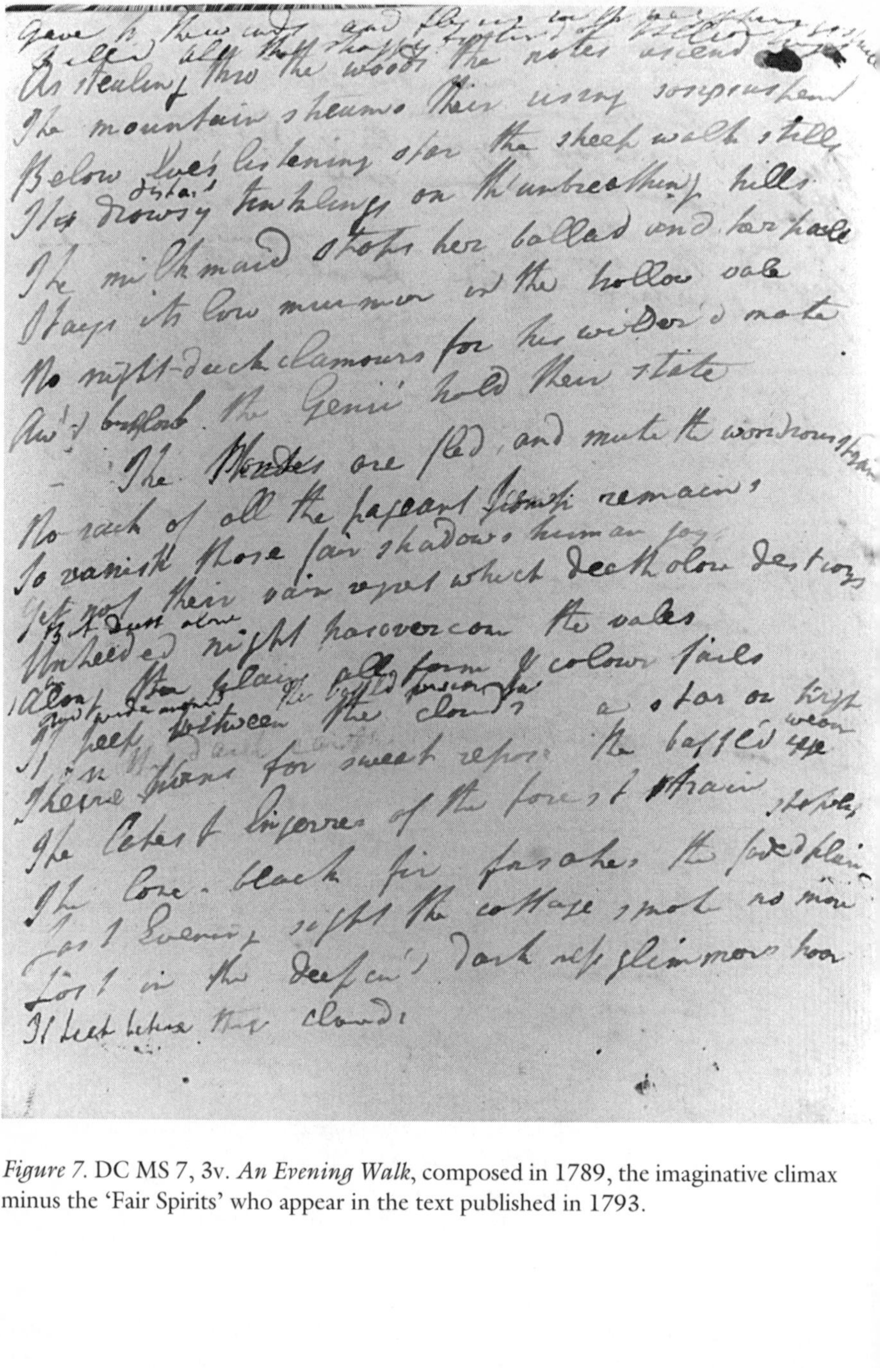

Figure 7. DC MS 7, 3v. *An Evening Walk*, composed in 1789, the imaginative climax minus the 'Fair Spirits' who appear in the text published in 1793.

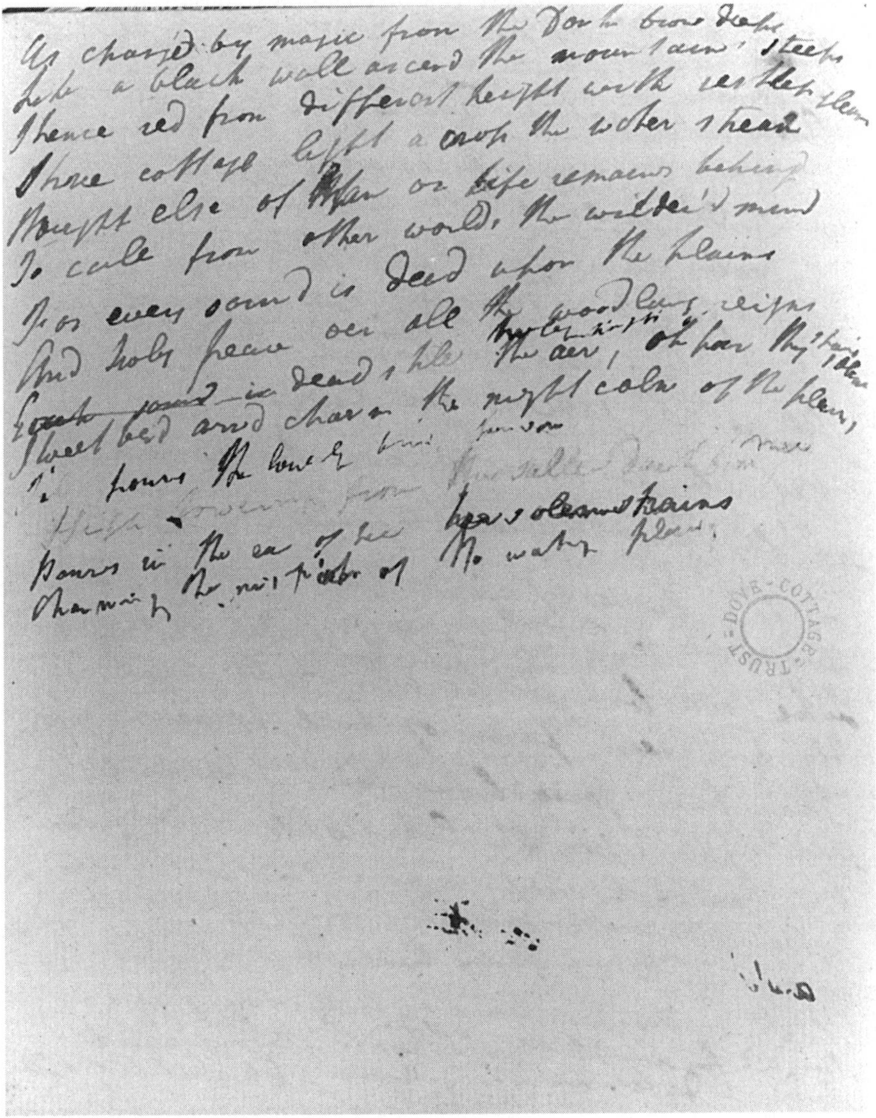

Figure 8. DC MS 7, 4v. *An Evening Walk,* draft of 1789. 'As charg'd by magic . . .': a line dropped from the published text of 1793.

The most obvious difference between the draft and the published text is that it lacks lines 343–50, which described the antics of the 'Fair Spirits'. The notebook is incomplete, and it may be that those lines were drafted in 1789 and have been lost. But I doubt it. My conjecture is that Wordsworth's sylphs were added close to publication, partly to establish his claims as the inheritor of Pope's mantle. Whenever they were composed, the verse in their absence is less cluttered, less artificial, closer in mood to the Cambridge sonnets. Other details recall the shorter poems: here, light twice 'touches' the landscape – at line 340 (as in 1793), and at 329 (revised to 'awe' in the later text). That 'touch' is full of numinous possibility. And in a jotting towards lines 371–2, immediately adjacent to this passage in the manuscript, he wrote:

> As charg'd by magic from the Dark brow deeps
> Like a black wall ascend the mountains steeps[50]

That inspired phrase, 'charg'd by magic', which recalls the 'magic path' pursued by the boat in 'How rich in front', may seem crude in comparison with the poetry Wordsworth was to write in the late 1790s, but it confirms our sense of a landscape 'far more deeply interfused'.

Perhaps the most revealing difference between the 1789 and 1793 versions of this passage comes in line 359, where the published text tells us that 'The pomp is fled', and the manuscript says, 'The Shades are fled'. As in the sonnets, Wordsworth dares to figure the insubstantial not out of fashion but out of an irresistible need to confront the ghosts of his past. Breaking upon the darkness of the underworld, he is compelled, by the terms of his private mythology, to return them, as Orpheus attempted to return Eurydice, to daylight. This is what transcendental style means to him. The vision of innocence at the end of 'Upon Appleton House' makes no such claim. It is fanciful, a vision of glorious possibility made all the more poignant by the effort so conspicuously invested in it. All the same, Wordsworth probably didn't read it until 1795 at the earliest, and perhaps not until much later.

---

[50] See Cornell *Evening Walk* 112–13. Averill's reading is 'chang'd by magic' but Wordsworth wrote 'charg'd', as is clear from the facsimile (see figure 8 overleaf).

4

The world is poisoned at the heart

The principles of moderate men are branded with the name of Republicanism: they must either expose themselves to the penalties of a
præmunire, or be ranked by the alarmists among the herd of the sedi-
tious.

(Joshua Lucock Wilkinson, *Political Facts* (1793), p. 130)

In *Descriptive Sketches* (1793) Wordsworth described an event that had taken
place the previous year but which he had not witnessed:

> The cloister startles at the gleam of arms,
> And Blasphemy the shuddering fane alarms . . .
>
> (ll. 60–1)

The sacking of the monastery of the Grande Chartreuse took place in May
1792, two years after his visit there in August 1790, but it seems to have made
quite an impact on him. Sixteen years later he returned to it in 'The Tuft of
Primroses':

> Alas for what I see, the flash of arms,
> O sorrow! and yon military glare,
> And hark those voices! let us hide in gloom
> Profoundest of St Bruno's wood, these sighs,
> These whispers that pursue, or meet me, whence
> [   ] are they but a common [   ]
> From the two Sister Streams of Life and Death;
> Or are they by the parting Genius sent,
> Unheard till now, and to be heard no more?
>
> (ll. 517–24)

In all probability Wordsworth and Robert Jones were among the last visitors
received by the Carthusian monks of the monastery. Mary Moorman observes
that 'There can be no doubt that in August 1790 there was no "flash of arms"

anywhere near the Chartreuse,'[1] though Reed suggests that Wordsworth may have seen 'some soldiers who were in the neighbourhood for other than official reasons and later attached some significance to them'.[2] The events which Wordsworth envisages, when they did occur, were momentous. Four hundred soldiers were quartered at the monastery for five months, treating the buildings and the monks with contempt. In October 1792 the monks were either expelled, imprisoned, deported, or executed. Wordsworth may not have seen this but nonetheless chose to describe it. The 'whispers' that pursue him at first seem to be those of the soldiers who are to pillage the monastery, but their association with the 'Sister Streams of Life and Death' turn them into something more like the 'low breathings' that pursue the young boy in *The Prelude*.

When composing *The Thirteen-Book Prelude* in 1805 Wordsworth mentioned in passing his stay at the Chartreuse, and the 'awful Solitude' of the place.[3] He did not say anything about the revolutionary army, or any other military activity there. However, when revising *The Prelude* in 1818–20, he incorporated a rewritten version of the Chartreuse passage from 'The Tuft of Primroses',[4] describing

> Arms flashing and a military glare
> Of riotous men commissioned to expel
> With senseless rapine.
>
> (C-stage text, vi 434–6)

Wordsworth again rewrites history so as to testify to a military presence absent at the time of his visit. This survived into the *Fourteen-Book Prelude* published in 1850[5] and stimulated the interest of Matthew Arnold, who visited the monastery during his honeymoon in September 1851. His poetic memorial of his visit, 'Stanzas from the Grande Chartreuse', was published in 1855.

These literary portrayals have their roots in an eighteenth-century landscape tradition well known to Wordsworth and Arnold. Thomas Gray's letters had been familiar to Wordsworth ever since he read Mason's edition of the works as a schoolboy;[6] in a letter of 16 November 1739 to Richard West, Gray described the Chartreuse in glowing terms:

---

[1] Moorman i 136.
[2] Reed i 103n11.
[3] *The Thirteen-Book Prelude* vi 424.
[4] See Cornell *13–Book Prelude* ii 995–7.
[5] *The Fourteen-Book Prelude* vi 421–89. The relevant passage can be found on pp. 152–5 of the 1850 edition.
[6] *WR* i 70.

In our little journey up to the Grande Chartreuse, I do not remember to have
gone ten paces without an exclamation, that there was no restraining: Not a
precipice, not a torrent, not a cliff, but is pregnant with religion and poetry.
There are certain scenes that would awe an atheist into belief, without other
argument. One need not have a very fantastic imagination to see spirits there at
noonday: You have Death perpetually before your eyes, only so far removed, as
to compose the mind without frighting it.[7]

William Ruddick observed the way in which this description offers 'one of the
classic definitions of the Sublime, almost twenty years before Burke's *Origin
of our Ideas of the Sublime and the Beautiful* (1757)'.[8] Against the alienated
stance that Gray tends to adopt in his poetry, the letter presents the Chartreuse as a natural temple, a deist's paradise. This is clearer in his 'Alcaic Ode'
to the Chartreuse (for which Wordsworth later expressed admiration),[9] which
was copied into the album of the monastery in 1741 (the album was destroyed during the Revolution):

> Praesentiorem & conspicimus Deum
> Per invias rupes, fera per juga,
> Clivosque praeruptos, sonantes
> Inter aquas, nemorumque noctem . . .[10]

The Latin text is more pious than the letter, but makes much the same point,
turning the landscape of the Chartreuse into a hallowed place. Gray's descriptions promoted the Chartreuse as a tourist attraction as soon as they were
published in 1775, and three years later it received a visit from William Beckford.
Beckford described it in *Dreams, Waking Thoughts and Incidents* (1783), which
was withdrawn shortly before publication by Joseph Johnson. Ten years later
Johnson published *An Evening Walk* and *Descriptive Sketches*, and if he retained a copy of Beckford's work may have shown it to Wordsworth.[11] Beckford

---

[7] *The Works of Mr Gray*, ed. William Mason (York, 1775), pp. 66–7.
[8] 'Thomas Gray's Travel Writing', *Thomas Gray: Contemporary Essays*, ed. W. B. Hutchings
and William Ruddick (Liverpool: Liverpool University Press, 1993), pp. 126–45, p. 129.
[9] Unexpectedly, in *Kendal and Windermere Railway* (1844): 'In a noble strain also does
the Poet Gray address, in a Latin Ode, the *Religio loci* at the Grande Chartruise' (*Prose
Works* iii 342).
[10] *Works*, ed. Mason, p. 117. Lonsdale translates as follows: 'we perceive God closer to us
among pathless rocks, wild ridges and precipitous ravines, and in the thundering of waters
and the darkness of the woods . . .' (*The Poems of Thomas Gray, William Collins, Oliver
Goldsmith* (London: Longman, 1969), p. 317).
[11] Copies were given to Madame de Staël, Samuel Henley and Alexander Cozens, and it
was read by Samuel Rogers, Thomas Moore and John Mitford, among others. The chances

described himself led by the sight of crosses placed on the tops of alpine rocks to a prospect which 'no voice need have declared . . . holy ground, for every part of it is stamped with such a sublimity of character, as would alone be sufficient to impress the idea'[12] – a recension of the sentiments expressed by Gray.

By the time Wordsworth and Jones visited the Chartreuse they would have known how earlier visitors had reacted and apparently they were not disappointed. Although the letter he addressed to Dorothy from there does not survive, that of September 1790 recalled 'contemplating, with increased pleasure its wonderful scenery' and praised 'the almost uninterrupted succession of sublime and beautiful objects which have passed before my eyes during . . . the last month'.[13] When in 1820 he returned to the continent with Dorothy and Mary he refused them permission to go there 'with the irrevocable decree that no Female is to tread on that sacred ground'.[14]

What was it that the Chartreuse represented? And why claim to have witnessed its sacking – an event that occurred in his absence? Born in early August 1769, Joshua Lucock Wilkinson was eight months older than Wordsworth.[15] The two men knew each other from early childhood. In 1745 Wilkinson's maternal grandfather had built the large house in Cockermouth High Street where the Wordsworths were brought up; William and Joshua were probably in the same class at Cockermouth Grammar School. During the early 1790s Wilkinson pursued a legal career in London, entering a solicitor's office at Gray's Inn as a clerk in January 1791 alongside Richard Wordsworth. By 1792 they were sharing lodgings at Staple Inn, at the junction of Holborn and High Holborn, to which William headed on his return from France in December. In September he had written to Richard:

> I look forward to the time of seeing you Wilkinson and my other friends with pleasure. I am very happy you have got into Chambers, as I shall perhaps be obliged to stay a few weeks in town about my publication you will I hope with Wilkinson's permission find me a place for a bed. Give Wilkinson my best Complts I have apologies to make for not having written to him, as also to almost all my other friends.[16]

of a copy having been retained by Johnson are high. Just five copies are known to survive today.

[12]   *Dreams, Waking Thoughts and Incidents*, ed. Robert Gemmett (Rutherford, NJ: Farleigh Dickinson University Press, 1971), p. 267.

[13]   *EY* 32–3.

[14]   *LY* i 176.

[15]   Wilkinson was christened on 9 August at St Nicholas' church, Liverpool.

[16]   *EY* 81.

Unfortunately none of Wordsworth's letters to Wilkinson have survived (if indeed any were ever written), but the fact that they might have been in contact during Wordsworth's stay in France is indicative of the strength of their friendship and shared interests. Both had toured the continent and were fervent in their support of the French Revolution (unlike, I suspect, Richard). They would have had much to discuss; in particular, Wilkinson would have been eager to hear of Wordsworth's experiences among the revolutionaries. For his part, Wordsworth would have known that Wilkinson had toured the continent in 1791 with an itinerary close to that followed by him in 1790. Wilkinson would have been eager to hear of Wordsworth's exploits as he was busily planning another tour of the continent on which he would embark in August. They are bound to have exchanged tales, and Wilkinson would have shown his old friend his journal, parts of which would be published as *The Wanderer* in 1795. He there records that when he visited the Grande Chartreuse 'a guard of a serjeant, and twelve men' had been summoned to protect the monks against 'some ungodly peasants, who seditiously presumed that men were equal':

> On one side of the building, the monk was offering up his fervent, and incessant prayers to heaven, with many a pious and devout ejaculation against the obstinate perverseness and irreligion of the times; on the other side the soldiers were playing at cards, cursing and swearing, by *Sacré Dieu!* at the holy fathers, who, passing from their prayers, condescended to utter *comment vous en vat?* upon the reprobate copartners of the sacred mansion.[17]

Although Wilkinson's tone suggests that he was on the side of the peasants rather than on that of the monks, it is clear that he did witness soldiers in occupation, and the beginning of the events related in *Descriptive Sketches*. It is almost certainly Wilkinson's account of the desecration, rather than his own memories, that Wordsworth was recalling when he described the impact of revolution on the Chartreuse.

Wordsworth's reason for returning to London from France in late 1792 was to get *An Evening Walk* and *Descriptive Sketches* into print; he needed money for Annette and Caroline, and his only means of generating it was by his pen. It is reasonable to conjecture that after talking to Wilkinson about the Chartreuse he inserted into his fair copy of *Descriptive Sketches* 26 lines describing its sacking. If my conjecture is correct, and *Descriptive Sketches* 53–79 were composed on Wordsworth's return to London in late 1792, possibly to replace an earlier description of the Chartreuse, they would have been among

[17] Joshua Lucock Wilkinson, *The Wanderer* (2 vols, London, 1795), i 154.

the last lines to be written for the poem before its publication in January 1793.

> Ev'n now I sigh at hoary Chartreuse' doom
> Weeping beneath his chill of mountain gloom.
> Where now is fled that Power whose frown severe
> Tam'd 'sober Reason' till she crouch'd in fear?
> That breath'd a death-like peace these woods around . . .
>
> (ll. 53–7)

'Ev'n now' marks a Wordsworthian 'jump' in time, from the tour of 1790 to the present of December 1792/January 1793.[18] He is now able to lament the monastery's fate in the light of what he had heard from Wilkinson. If he follows Gray in sanctifying the landscape he does so in a very characteristic manner. On the surface the idiom is that of the Cambridge poetry. The 'death-like peace' conducts us back to the banks of the Cam in 'How rich in front', or to the Lake District in 'On the [   ] village', where the landscapes had provided the locations for the playing-out of a cycle of loss and retrieval. Any reader acquainted with his work (such as Dorothy) would be primed to read the landscape of the Chartreuse in the same way. In the background there was Burke, who described the sublime as a power that 'anticipates our reasonings, and hurries us on by an irresistible force'; it created a 'state of the soul, in which all its motions are suspended, with some degree of horror'.[19]

But the expected completion of that pattern is thwarted. Instead of imaginative vision granted through 'fairy views' or 'Fair Spirits', Wordsworth describes 'Blasphemy':

> The cloister startles at the gleam of arms,
> And Blasphemy the shuddering fane alarms;
> Nod the cloud-piercing pines their troubl'd heads,
> Spires, rocks, and lawns, a browner night o'erspreads.
> Strong terror checks the female peasant's sighs,
> And start th' astonish'd shades at female eyes.
>
> (ll. 60–5)

Again, the practised reader of Wordsworth would have recognized the significance of the 'browner night', the twilight that descends upon the Chartreuse – which in the Cambridge poetry was the prelude to imaginative 'harmony'.

---

18 Cf. the jump in 'The Vale of Esthwaite', discussed on pp. 6–7 above.
19 Edmund Burke, *A Philosophical Enquiry into the Origins of our Ideas of the Sublime and Beautiful*, ed. J. T. Boulton (2nd edn, Oxford: Blackwell, 1987), p. 57.

That is not how things turn out here. Wordsworth would have assumed on the part of his readers an awareness that the Carthusians were a very strict order; they wore hair shirts and lived solitary lives, praying and studying in their cells, gathering only for worship. Besides taking vows of chastity, they abstained from eating meat and on Fridays consumed only bread and water. Given such austerity, what happens is all the worse: the cloisters are filled with blaspheming soldiers and prostitutes ('female eyes').

Wordsworth cannot have approved, but he is thinking less as a Christian than as a pagan. The Hawkshead and Cambridge poetry argued for a world in which nature is spiritually charged; you don't need to subscribe to conventional Christian theism to believe in that. The 'Blasphemy' in the monastery, while no doubt a bad thing, would have been overshadowed by the disapprobatory nodding of the 'cloud-piercing pines'. To Wordsworth the Chartreuse was freighted with a more than purely Christian significance. In February 1805 Coleridge copied into his notebook a brief verse that may have been given him by Wordsworth:

> C'est ici que la Mort et que la Verité
> Elevant leur flambeux terribles;
> C'est de cette demeure au monde inaccessible
> Que l'on passe à l'Eternité.[20]

This 'Inscription over the Chartreux' is held by Coleridge to prove that had France been 'a freer . . . and a protestant Nation, and a Milton had been born in it, the French Language would not have precluded the Production of a Paradise Lost, tho' it might perhaps that of an Hamlet or a Lear'. Wordsworth would have regarded it more highly for turning the Chartreuse into the gateway to eternal life. At the same time it fits neatly into the idiosyncratic, pagan system established in the Hawkshead and Cambridge verse. Throughout those poems too, he postulated the existence of a realm between sublunary reality and the world of the dead – a kind of underworld. If that is the context from which the 'astonish'd shades' of line 65 have come, they have been cruelly marginalized. And that is why the desecration of the Grande Chartreuse really matters to Wordsworth. Unfortunately it is not known what happened to him and Jones when they stayed there on 4 and 5 August, partly because his accounts of their stay are consistently revised in the light of Wilkinson's journal. Whatever he experienced, the place was sacred as the concrete manifestation of his private mythology, and its violation must have seemed like the breaking of a sacred trust.

---

[20] *Notebooks* ii 2431 f. 7. 'Here it is that Death and Truth raise their awful torches. It is from this retreat inaccessible to the world that one passes to Eternal Life.'

The potential that once inhered in the natural world is in this episode compromised:

> The cross with hideous laughter Demons mock,
> By angels planted on the aëreal rock.
> The 'parting Genius' sighs with hollow breath
> Along the mystic streams of Life and Death.
>
> (*Descriptive Sketches* 70–3)

In a footnote Wordsworth explains that these lines allude 'to crosses seen on the tops of the spiry rocks of the Chartreuse, which have every appearance of being inaccessible', and that the Guiers Vif and the Guiers Mort are 'Names of rivers at the Chartreuse'. Their inaccessibility is their point; like the dead, they are beyond reach. Even in his mature work Wordsworth is only to be given intimations, 'an obscure sense of possible sublimity'. Here he is denied even that, as the cross is subjected to mockery. The language suggests a parallel with the persecution of Jesus, but any straightforwardly religious notion we may bring to the poetry is queried by the allusion in line 72. Milton's 'On the Morning of Christ's Nativity' describes the collapse of paganism at Christ's birth: 'The parting genius is with sighing sent.'[21] In Wordsworth's poem it is not so much paganism that is under attack, but that unconventional way of thinking peculiar to him, established in the poetry of his last seven years. The genius that once guaranteed access to the mystic streams of Life and Death had been dammed up.

What I call 'betrayal' was present from the start of Wordsworth's career. His parents were taken from him and, whatever the consolations he found in his sister and friends, nothing could be done to reverse that. Their deaths must at times have felt like abandonment. That in turn would have generated feelings of resentment and guilt that could not be stifled. It is in that context that I would place the suggestion of the early poetry that he was somehow complicit in his father's death, which surfaces during the summer of 1787, when delayed mourning took place in Penrith due partly to unsympathetic treatment from the Cooksons. The continuing evolution of a psychological subtext in Wordsworth's Cambridge poetry – one designed to reclaim the dead through nature – takes place against the odds. It should correctly be understood as having been a struggle, an epic task of wish-fulfilment that culminated with 'The Recluse' in the midst of a complex pagan psychomachia. His implied culpability in the waiting for the horses episode of the 'Vale', and the inevitable loss sustained by Orpheus in the Virgil translations, run counter

---

[21]   Line 186.

to the claims to which the poetry aspires, containing within them seeds of doubt.

Those cross-currents do not express themselves fully until late 1792 or early 1793 when Wordsworth composed the Chartreuse passage at the last moment for *Descriptive Sketches.* This is all the more subversive in a work that contains its fair share of transcendental style; for instance, at lines 492–519 Wordsworth describes a morning in the Alps which is a precursor of the *Prelude* ascent of Snowdon,[22] and lines 536–53 relate the mystic experiences of a Swiss peasant:

> Uncertain thro' his fierce uncultur'd soul
> Like lighted tempests troubled transports roll;
> To viewless realms his Spirit towers amain,
> Beyond the senses and their little reign.
>
> (ll. 546–9)

This was composed *before* the Chartreuse passage – months before.[23] The Chartreuse description is special not just because it undercuts the aspirations of the earlier poetry, but because it was probably the last thing to be written before *Descriptive Sketches* was put to bed. The thwarting of those expectations is doubly unexpected, as the agency by which it is wrought is that of the Revolutionary army which, as a radical, Wordsworth might have been expected to support. Indeed the poem as a whole had been written to promote Revolutionary ideas. Its concluding lines describe the violence and destruction of revolution in wholly laudatory terms:

> Yet, yet rejoice, tho' Pride's perverted ire
> Rouze Hell's own aid, and wrap thy hills in fire.
> Lo! from th' innocuous flames, a lovely birth!
> With it's own Virtues springs another earth . . .
>
> (ll. 780–3)

The forces of counter-revolutionary 'Pride' may summon the flames of hell, but they cannot stifle freedom and justice. 'The Recluse' demands to be seen in this light. Though often framed as Coleridge's idea, Wordsworth writes about earthly regeneration as early as 1793, when he turns the 'flames' of warfare into a vision of millenarian rebirth: 'And I saw a new heaven and a new earth: for the first heaven and the first earth were passed

---

[22] The influence is discussed *Borders of Vision* 310–12.
[23] Birdsall says that 'most of the drafting of the poem was done between early December 1791 and the fall of 1792' (Cornell *Descriptive Sketches* 8).

away.'[24] It is as the inhabitant of such a brave new world that Wordsworth advises us at line 803 to 'Look up for sign of havoc, Fire, and Sword.' But the portrayal of 'Blasphemy' in the cloisters of the Chartreuse is also in the background; the same 'Fire, and Sword' are to blame for its sacking.

This confusion is reflected in the poem's mixture of styles. It contains examples of the Thomson-derived landscape poetry characteristic of earlier years alongside passages full of eighteenth-century poetic diction illustrating contemporary incident. Into the latter category fall passages equivalent in their crude energy to political caricature or agitprop – uncharacteristic shades of Wordsworth also to be seen in the final stanzas of 'Salisbury Plain' (1793), 'The Convict' (1795) and 'Imitation of Juvenal, Satire VIII' (1795). The tension is evidence of strain between artistic vocation and necessity.

What was his state of mind during December 1792 and January 1793 while preparing his work for the press? Wordsworth must have felt that his life had reached a crisis. He was under intense pressure from his family to get a job and earn his keep. His Uncle William Cookson had offered him a curacy in Harwich, but by July 1793 the offer had been withdrawn, probably out of disapproval at Annette and Caroline.[25] In the meantime he was concerned for their welfare and desperate to return to them. Such was his anxiety that his friends feared for him; as De Quincey rather gloatingly recorded: 'Every night they played at cards with him, as the best mode of beguiling his sense of distress.'[26] He had everything invested in *An Evening Walk* and *Descriptive Sketches*, and the wait for publication on 29 January 1793 would have felt interminable. He was counting the days until he could sail back to France with a full purse. This imperative caused him to consider a number of money-making schemes; for one thing, Dorothy told De Quincey, her brother 'had all but resolved . . . to take pupils'.[27] Fortunately this came to nothing. Another idea was to write a pot-boiler – a notion that resurfaced in 1797 when he composed 'A Somersetshire Tragedy'. As on that occasion, the initial impetus came from someone else[28] – in this case, Joshua Lucock Wilkinson. That much can be conjectured from *The Wanderer*, where Wilkinson records:

[24]   Revelation 21:1.
[25]   As Johnston notes, Annette's Catholicism would also have disqualified him, though I suspect that was the least of Wordsworth's crimes in the opinion of his relatives; see Johnston 333.
[26]   'Lake Reminiscences, From 1807 to 1830. No. III. – William Wordsworth – *Continued*', *Tait's Edinburgh Magazine* 6 (April 1839) 246–54, p. 248.
[27]   Ibid.
[28]   For details see in the first instance Cornell *Lyrical Ballads* 459, which lists the critical and scholarly literature.

I flattered myself with the hope of being permitted to insert a woeful tale of the loves of a chevalier near Blois, and a young bourgeoise, his consequent imprisonment and insanity, the barbarous rigour of his noble father, the blessed effect of *Lettres de cachet*, and the mild controul of the ancient government; but as the gentleman, who is possessed of the facts, intends to throw the substance into the stile of a novel, the public will receive it in a much more finished form, than if curtailed and despoiled of its numerous circumstances, to suit the varied and detached method of the Wanderer.[29]

Though published in 1795, this refers us back to Wordsworth's London residence in 1792–3. At that moment it seems that, having read the story of Antoine Augustin Thomas du Fossé in Helen Maria Williams' *Letters written in France* (1790), Wilkinson told Wordsworth of his decision to fictionalize it. Wordsworth (Wilkinson's 'gentleman') had probably read Williams' volume soon after publication[30] and would have remembered the du Fossé story immediately, as it occupies nearly a third of the book. Recognizing the potential of the idea, he persuaded Wilkinson to let him write the novel instead. Williams' *Letters* had gone through eight printings in 1790 partly on the strength of the du Fossé story, which appealed to the popular taste for sentimental romances. A novelization would surely succeed.

Wilkinson makes an interesting slip that supports the identification of the 'gentleman' with Wordsworth. Contrary to what he says, Blois is not the location of Williams' story, which is set in Rouen: it was, however, where Annette Vallon lived. The error is understandable and Wordsworth must have noticed a number of other parallels between himself and du Fossé.[31] Most obviously, given his situation in late 1792, there was the painful separation of du Fossé from his wife and child – something Wordsworth was experiencing at first hand. And the treacheries of du Fossé's father, the Baron, which included luring him home and throwing him in prison, must have recalled the petty tyrannies of his guardians. He would not write this novel, but the narrative would provide the basis for that of Vaudracour and Julia.

The main reason why he was detained from writing fiction is that events overtook him. On 21 January 1793 the head of Louis XVI was cut off and held up to the crowds at the foot of the guillotine in Paris. Wordsworth's poems were published on 29 January, and on 1 February the National Convention declared war on George III and William of Orange. Within less than a fortnight of Louis' death, France was at war with Prussia, Piedmont, Spain, Holland, the Austrian Empire and Britain. The consequences were

---

[29] Joshua Lucock Wilkinson, *The Wanderer* (2 vols, London, 1795), ii 205–6.
[30] *WR* i 150.
[31] It is recounted by Shaver (ibid.) and Johnston 284.

far-reaching. Just at the moment when Wordsworth might have considered returning to Annette, travel to France had become much trickier, and anyone attempting it would come under suspicion of spying by both sides. Circumstances would compel him to stay put (at least for the moment); it was what he must have feared most.

How did he react? Angrily. It is an index of his state of mind that his next piece of writing was a political pamphlet, 'A Letter to the Bishop of Llandaff . . . by a Republican'. This ostentatious self-description knowingly demonizes its author. 'Republican' was the hate word of the moment, like 'communist' in 1950s America.[32] The debate had been less polarized when in 1790 Richard Price's *Discourse on the Love of our Country* had initiated a pamphlet war which had occasioned works by Burke, Paine and Wollstonecraft, among others. Wordsworth's contribution probably dates from early February 1793,[33] and it was a potent one. At a moment when events in France had made the British government paranoid about the outbreak of revolution at home, Wordsworth wrote in favour of regicide and violent change in general. His immediate inspiration was a recantation of radicalism by Richard Watson, Bishop of Llandaff, in a hastily composed appendix to a sermon published on 30 January, but there is reason to think that the stress Wordsworth was under at that moment predisposed him to a degree of intemperance:

> In France royalty is no more; the person of the last anointed is no more also, and I flatter myself I am not alone, even in this kingdom, when I wish that it may please the almighty neither by the hands of his priests nor his nobles (I allude to a striking passage of Racine) to raise his posterity to the rank of his ancestors and reillume the torch of extinguished David.[34]

Wordsworth was in no position to reinstate the Bourbon succession even if he *had* wished to do so. But he knows that, and is telling us this because it gives him the occasion to remind his readers that 'In France royalty is no more.' That phrase is an act of provocation. And lest we are in doubt, the allusion to Racine's *Athalie*, which he probably read during his stay in France, is particularly apposite. After the death of Ahaziah, her son, Athaliah usurped the throne and reigned for seven years in the course of which she massacred all the members of the royal house of Judah except Joash. Thanks to a successful uprising,

---

[32]   Owen and Smyser provide examples, *Prose Works* i 50.

[33]   Reed suggests a conjectural date of June (Reed i 142) but I don't see why Wordsworth would have waited so long; it is more likely that the 'Letter' was composed shortly after publication of Watson's *Sermon*, when Wordsworth would have been incensed by its contents.

[34]   *Prose Works* i 33.

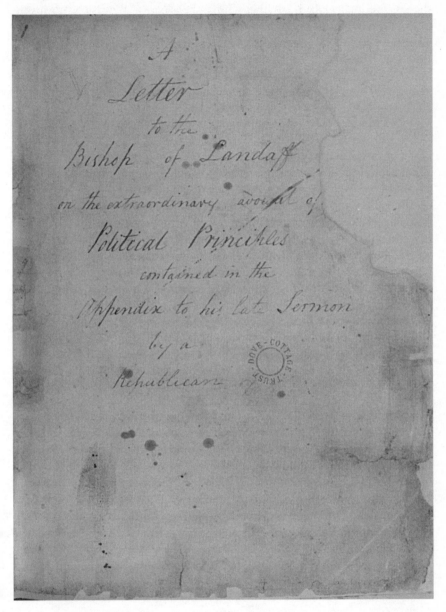

Figure 9. DC MS 8, title-page. 'A Letter to the Bishop of Llandaff . . . by a Republican' – the kind of self-styling that cannot have endeared Wordsworth to his uncle, the Revd William Cookson, Canon of Windsor. Incidentally, the hand that composed this title-page was not Wordsworth's. It remains unidentified.

she was eventually killed. In other words, she is part of Wordsworth's justification for republicanism. To him, monarchs are invariably tyrannical, and the
execution of Louis is greeted as a sign of things to come. In the speech to
which Wordsworth refers, Racine writes:

> Pour forth, my God, on Her and on her Priest,
> That dark'ning and infatuating Spirit,
> Which constantly foreruns the Fall of Kings![35]

None of this would have gone down well with Pitt's government, which was
at that moment ill-disposed to humour rabble-rousers. Godwin's *Political
Justice* narrowly missed prosecution when discussed by the cabinet on 25 May,
on the grounds that, as Pitt declared, 'a three guinea book could never do
much harm amongst those who had not three shillings to spare.'[36] This was
not the only reason for giving it the benefit of the doubt. Godwin's work
seemed detached from current events, and was framed as a work of philosophy. Even if its sympathies were with the French, it did not explicitly advocate
king-killing. Wordsworth's 'Letter' by comparison was inflammatory:

> What! have you so little knowledge of the nature of man as to be ignorant, that
> a time of revolution is not the season of true Liberty. Alas! the obstinacy &
> perversion of men is such that she is too often obliged to borrow the very arms
> of despotism to overthrow him, and in order to reign in peace must establish
> herself by violence.[37]

This would have struck Pitt and his ministers as treasonable had they read it,
and it was as well for Wordsworth that it remained in manuscript. If, as seems
likely, he showed it to Joseph Johnson, he would have been counselled against
publication, as the government would have shown scant mercy for either of
them. (Despite whatever caution Johnson may have shown here, he would in
1798 be tried merely for selling a pamphlet by Gilbert Wakefield – a reply to
the same Bishop of Llandaff's *Address to the People of Great Britain* (1798) –
which resulted in his being found guilty and incarcerated for six months at the
King's Bench.)[38]

The 'Letter' is an attention-grabber. It invites disapproval, goading us with

---

[35]   Racine, *Athaliah*, trans. William Duncombe (2nd edn, London, 1726), I ii 134–6.
[36]   Don Locke, *A Fantasy of Reason: The Life and Thought of William Godwin* (London:
Routledge and Kegan Paul, 1980), p. 60.
[37]   *Prose Works* i 33.
[38]   For details see Leslie F. Chard II, 'Joseph Johnson: Father of the Book Trade', *BNYPL*
79 (1975) 51–82, pp. 70–3.

repeated sniping at the established order. It is an unconcealed attempt to offend. It is also the utterance of an outsider, an extremist, someone on the fringes who wishes to identify themselves as such. Given that it was written with publication in view, it is also a profoundly courageous, self-destructive document. Wordsworth felt emotionally wedded to the destiny of France – more so than to that of his own country – and in large measure the 'Letter' is a refutation of Englishness. He must have felt that he had nothing to lose: the poems gained him scant reward and return to Annette was precluded by the political situation. Why shouldn't he write and publish what he believed?

This was not merely a personal matter. Europe was living through an extraordinary moment in its history. The execution of Louis enacted a collective myth that had been hanging over it since that of Charles I in January 1649. It had haunted the House of Hanover throughout the eighteenth century, and provided a continuing counterweight to absolutism. To some extent it was foreshadowed in the du Fossé story, in which after years of conflict the tyrannical Baron eventually died, leaving the oppressed du Fossé and his family to inherit his wealth. In her recounting of the narrative, Williams left no doubt as to its correct interpretation, commenting after the Baron's death that 'the overthrow of the antient government would have been a sufficient punishment to him for all his cruelty. . . . The idea of liberty being extended to the lower ranks, while, at the same time, tyranny was deprived of its privileges, he would have found insupportable.'[39] This is the death of the father as political liberation – a feelgood fable for revolutionaries. No one could have overlooked its value as propaganda, least of all Wordsworth. Perhaps he wanted to fictionalize that story, but a good reason not to bother, at least at that moment, was that recent history tracked the same emotional path much more effectively.

On this occasion the personal and the public converged in a startling manner. Had he killed John Wordsworth Sr through his impatience as he waited for the horses on the ridge above Borwick Lodge in December 1783? Painful though it was, that was as nothing next to the 'Letter to the Bishop of Llandaff', where the figure of Oedipus returns to Wordsworth's writing as the persona adopted by the poet. The apologist for regicide, he takes up the Oedipal mantle on behalf of his nation, justifying Louis' execution: think of the 'murders' committed by the *ancien régime*, he says to Watson, 'and you will not want consolation under any depression your spirits may feel at the contrast exhibited by Louis on the most splendid throne of the universe, and Louis alone in the tower of the Temple or on the scaffold.'[40] By implication, the prompt

---

[39]   Helen Maria Williams, *Letters written in France* (London, 1790), p. 193.
[40]   *Prose Works* i 32.

dispatch of George III was just as necessary. There are other father-figures in the 'Letter': Edmund Burke, influential as a Whig MP, whose 'philosophic lamentation over the extinction of Chivalry'[41] (a mocking reference to his *Reflections on the Revolution in France*) placed him among the earliest of the former radical sympathizers to side with the forces of conservatism. Wordsworth writes him off as an 'infatuated moralist!'[42] He returns to Burke several times in the course of the 'Letter', on the last observing that Watson has 'partaken of Mr Burke's intoxicating bowl'.[43] And Watson himself, by aligning himself with the government, had in Wordsworth's eyes cast his lot with the forces of authority and corruption. In the very first paragraph he suggests that Watson has 'at last fallen, through one of the numerous trap-doors, into the tide of contempt to be swept down to the ocean of oblivion'.[44] The image is that of a man falling through the opening at the base of a scaffold.

Wordsworth writes passionately against Burke and Watson because they had so publicly deserted the radical cause. And the essence of his own situation, as he saw it, was that opposition to the government had been so successfully quashed as to leave him in the minority, if not alone. A weight of tyrannical authority hangs over the 'Letter', like the guardians who loom large in the background to the concluding section of 'The Vale of Esthwaite' – a weight predicated by the energetically pro-revolutionary stance of its author. He perceived himself as a tragic hero, compelled by circumstances to act as he did, alone. No doubt his personal situation made him feel solitary and compelled, but the intensity of the writing can be explained at least in part by a melodramatized self-image. It was a necessary and important stage in his artistic development.

But this is not all. Wordsworth did not merely borrow this surprisingly resonant myth with all its contemporary fictional and historical layers; he compounded it with another. The Chartreuse passage in *Descriptive Sketches* is important because it refutes the visionary optimism of the Cambridge poetry, surrendering it to the 'Blasphemy' of the Revolution. It is about betrayal. If he was not fully aware of that, his proposed novel took a similar tack. The repeated deceptions of the Baron to thwart the wishes of his son, which culminate in du Fossé's imprisonment, mean that treachery is its dominant motif. In the same way, Wordsworth saw Burke and Watson as traitors to the 'brotherhood of man'. Unfortunately that knife cut both ways. If he had spent the last eighteen months in a country with which Britain was now at war, was

---

[41] *Prose Works* i 35.
[42] *Prose Works* i 36.
[43] *Prose Works* i 49.
[44] *Prose Works* i 31.

a fluent speaker of its language and had a French family, what did that make him? What was he, moreover, if, having fathered a child, he deserted it and the woman who had given it birth?

The outbreak of war in February 1793 left him little choice. Thanks to a bizarre convergence of historical, political and personal factors, Wordsworth's self-image at that moment is a composite made out of the figures of Oedipus and the betrayer. If he thought himself alone, he was wrong. There was another author who at this moment was thinking along similar lines: William Godwin. His *Caleb Williams*, published in May 1794, created a character who pursues the Oedipal task of destroying a father-figure – the flawed tyrant-killer turned tyrant, Ferdinando Falkland – while betraying his own sense of justice. It is a story of self-destruction and self-recrimination. In the climactic courtroom scene Williams declares that, although he has exposed Falkland, he has debased himself:

> I came hither to curse, but I remain to bless. I came to accuse, but am compelled to applaud. I proclaim to all the world that Mr Falkland is a man worthy of affection and kindness, and that I am myself the basest and most odious of mankind! Never will I forgive myself the iniquity of this day. The memory will always haunt me, and embitter every hour of my existence.[45]

Godwin writes as a radical who has intuited through the writing of his fiction that the destruction of the tyrant is self-defeating, as it makes the revolutionary as vicious and degraded as the power he deposes. *Caleb Williams* is a fable by a revolutionary sympathizer with the imaginative insight to realize the futility of violent action. At its core is a conundrum: that the tyrant and his victim are interdependent. Falkland and Williams are locked in a kind of dysfunctional love affair that renders Williams' victory hollow. Wordsworth probably read this classic novel soon after its first publication and would certainly have known it by February 1795, when he began a series of frequent meetings with Godwin.[46] It would crystallize much that was already evident in his thinking; like Williams, the Sailor of 'Adventures on Salisbury Plain' (1795), and Mortimer, the protagonist of *The Borderers* (1797–9), would suffer guilt by their actions and come to realise how self-defeating they had been.

But this lay in the future. In spring 1793, with *An Evening Walk* and *Descriptive Sketches* in print, and the 'Letter to the Bishop' in manuscript but unpublishable, Wordsworth found himself stranded in London. Having

---

[45] *Caleb Williams*, ed. David McCracken (Oxford: Oxford University Press, 1982), p. 323.
[46] See *WR* i 66.

arrived in late December the previous year, he would remain there probably until July. What was he doing? What was going on in his head? It is hard to say, because the 'Letter' seems to have been the last serious piece of writing he produced before going on a walking tour of the Isle of Wight and south-west England with William Calvert. His continuing anxiety, no doubt aggravated by the war, is hinted at in the 'Advertisement' for *Guilt and Sorrow* in 1842:

> During the latter part of the summer of 1793, having passed a month in the Isle of Wight, in view of the fleet which was then preparing for sea off Portsmouth at the commencement of the war, I left the place with melancholy forebodings. The American war was still fresh in memory. The struggle which was beginning, and which many thought would be brought to a speedy close by the irresistible arms of Great Britain being added to those of the allies, I was assured in my own mind would be of long continuance, and productive of distress and misery beyond all possible calculation. This conviction was pressed upon me by having been a witness, during a long residence in revolutionary France, of the spirit which prevailed in that country.[47]

This public statement alludes to the anxieties troubling Wordsworth without revealing them to view. As well as being a witness, he had participated in the spirit that 'prevailed' in revolutionary France, and must have continued to experience feelings of intense distress on behalf of Annette and Caroline. The phrase 'melancholy forebodings' can hardly do justice to his emotions as he watched the fleet preparing for battle. It is not surprising that he remembered this nearly fifty years later, because the experience inspired a poem, probably the first he had drafted since the Chartreuse passage in late December or early January. It was composed on the Isle of Wight, perhaps in the neighbourhood of Ryde:

> How sweet the walk along the woody steep
> When all the summer seas are charmed to sleep
> – While on the distant sands the tide retires
> Its last faint murmur on the ears expires
> The setting sun [   ] his growing round
> On the low promontory's purple bound
> For many a league a line of gold extend[s]
> Now lessened half his glancing disc de[scends]

(ll. 1–8)

Wordsworth returns to the couplet manner of the poems he had published earlier that year, and the loco-descriptive mode developed in the Cambridge son-

---

[47] Cornell *Salisbury Plain* 215–17.

nets. Its opening line, which echoes the exclamatory 'How rich in front', warns us that as the poem begins we are already in the midst of a visionary experience, characterized by a moment of stillness and repose. As in those earlier works, this poem is set at the end of the day. He has long outgrown the Bowlesian manner of the sonnets, so such words as 'stilly' are not to be found here; instead he exploits the language to create the impression that nature is at rest – the tide 'retires' and its last sound 'expires'. The stage is prepared for a reprise of the Wordsworthian descent into the underworld, and in the lines that follow he tells us that 'O'er earth o'er air and oce[an] [   ] / Tranquillity extends . . .'[48] Though fragmentary, enough survives for us to hear behind it echoes of the pantheist undertones of the Virgilian translations and foreshadowings of the great poetry of 1798. The expected resolution, however, is denied.

> But hark from yon proud fleet in peal profound
> Thunders the sunset cannon; at the sound
> The star of life appears to set in blood
> Old ocean shudders in offended mood
> Deepening with moral gloom his angry flood.
>
>   (ll. 15–19)

As in the description of the Chartreuse, Wordsworth describes an act of des-ecration. The transcendent moment of unity which seems to enclose the natural world is suddenly disrupted by cannon fire. The language he uses to describe the 'proud fleet' is reminiscent of Milton's simile when describing Satan on his way to the gates of hell: 'As when far off at sea a fleet descried / Hangs in the clouds'.[49] The British navy is an equally sinister force, but there is nothing celestial about it. It ravages the mood of repose to which the poetry had been working, and brings harbingers of apocalypse – the reddening star of life and shuddering ocean. As so often in this poetry, the scene is morally charged; the assumption is that the natural world is alive, affronted and oppressed by im-pending conflict. And where does Wordsworth stand in relation to all this? He is an onlooker, impotent to prevent it, aware that Annette and Caroline are separated from him, on the other side of the Channel, in the land which is about to receive the combined aggression of Europe. Well might the Solent express 'moral gloom'; it bears witness to Wordsworth's stranded ineffective-ness, which must have felt like betrayal. The denial of the spiritual resolution promised by the beauty of the sunset is an act of treachery that speaks of 'distress and misery beyond all possible calculation'.

---

[48]   'How sweet the walk' 13–14.
[49]   *Paradise Lost* ii 636–7.

5

'Their life is hidden with God'

Coleridge's arrival at Racedown Lodge on 5 June 1797 marked the beginning of one of the most important years in Wordsworth's life. Wordsworth recalled many years later that 'he did not keep to the high road, but leapt over a gate and bounded down the pathless field, by which he cut off an angle.[1] We both [that is, he and Dorothy] retain the liveliest possible image of his appearance at that moment.'[2] With that momentous arrival, Wordsworth acquired a new audience for two works in progress – *The Borderers* and 'The Ruined Cottage'.

The Borderers was inspired partly by repeated visits to the Covent Garden and Drury Lane theatres during his stay in London, February–August 1795. By October 1796 he was 'ardent in the composition of a tragedy',[3] and had nearly finished a first draft by 27 February 1797.[4] Coleridge arrived on 5 June, read 'The Ruined Cottage' immediately, after tea recited two and a half acts of his own play *Osorio*, and the next day listened to Wordsworth's reading of *The Borderers*.[5] He would have heard a work which represented the culmination of the various elements in the poetry of 1792–3. It is about damnation, full of multiple acts of deception.[6] The initial one, and the inciting incident of the play, years before the stage action takes place, is that of Rivers by the crew of the ship with which he sailed to Syria. He was tricked by them into aban-

---

[1] A photograph of the site of this leap, which includes the gate, may be found in Tom Mayberry, *Coleridge and Wordsworth in the West Country* (Stroud: Alan Sutton, 1992), p. 84.
[2] *LY* iv 719. The welcome at Racedown seems to have made an impact on Coleridge too; he recalled it in a letter of February 1804 to the Wordsworths (Griggs ii 1060).
[3] *EY* 172.
[4] *EY* 177.
[5] *EY* 189.
[6] I am partly indebted for this reading to David Bromwich, 'Revolutionary Justice and Wordsworth's *Borderers*', *Raritan* 13 (Winter 1994) 1–24.

doning the captain to die alone on a desert island;[7] as he observes, 'I had been betrayed.'[8] That experience changed him forever, but instead of filling him with guilt and humiliation, it had the obverse effect of turning him into a kind of *Übermensch*, no longer bounded by human laws, or even those of time and space:

> I seemed a being who had passed alone
> Beyond the visible barriers of the world
> And travelled into things to come.
>
> (IV ii 143–5)

Rivers is a kind of demonic visionary, charged with the task of drawing others into this power-crazed lawlessness. It was his good fortune, as a member of the gang of outlawed borderers led by the 23-year-old Mortimer, to have him save his life – a deed for which he 'hates' him, regarding gratitude as 'a heavy burthen / To a proud soul'.[9] In order to get back at him, Rivers tells him that an old blind man, Herbert, is plotting against him, the only solution being murder. After much soul-searching Mortimer leads Herbert onto a heath where he is abandoned without food or drink. Before he leaves him to the mercy of the elements, Mortimer has a crisis of conscience, aware that he is 'blind! old! alone! betray'd!'[10] All the same, he does not change his course, and goes. When he discovers Rivers' deception, Mortimer accuses him: 'Monster, you have betray'd me.'[11] Discovered on the heath in the throes of death by Robert, a cottager, Herbert is not saved because Robert is frightened of being implicated in his death. When they hear of Herbert's fate, Robert in turn observes to his wife, Margaret, 'We are betrayed!'[12]

---

[7] This story was based partly on Fletcher Christian's mutiny on the *Bounty* in 1789. Wordsworth had known Christian at Cockermouth Grammar School, where they had been contemporaries. While at Racedown Wordsworth read a bogus account of the mutiny, said to be by Christian, in the *Weekly Entertainer* 28 (26 September 1796) 255–6, where the alleged author goes to some lengths to exonerate Bligh from blame – indicating, for instance, that Christian had organized the mutiny while drunk, and adding: 'It is but justice . . . that I should acquit Captain Bligh in the most unequivocal manner, of having contributed in the smallest degree to the promotion of our conspiracy, by any harsh or ungentlemanlike conduct on his part' (p. 255). Some element of the narrative (perhaps the reference to alcohol) alerted Wordsworth to its falseness, and he wrote to the *Weekly Entertainer* to say so (see *EY* 171 and n).
[8] *The Borderers* IV ii 70. All quotations from the 1797–9 text in Cornell *Borderers*.
[9] Ibid. I i 9–10.
[10] Ibid. II iii 203.
[11] Ibid. IV ii 182.
[12] Ibid. IV iii 96.

The play brings to its fullest expression Wordsworth's interest in the figure of the traitor. In this world, human nature is seen to be innately given to deception; as Mortimer observes, 'The world is poisoned at the heart.'[13] Mortimer starts out as a virtuous man who for all his goodness discovers the seeds of evil within. This rich vein of thought draws on Wordsworth's own experience in obvious ways. The sense of having in some way let his father down had overshadowed the awakening of grief in summer 1787, and continued to preoccupy his subsequent poetry. With his abandonment of Annette and their child in 1792 the sense of having betrayed those closest to him can only have intensified.

There are occasions in Wordsworth's life when the books at his disposal seem to have informed his thinking in a coherent and consistent manner. This is one of them. The Racedown Lodge library included a copy of Machiavelli's *Discourses* in Edward Dacres' 1674 translation;[14] in chapter 42 Dacres renders: 'It is remarkable also . . . how easily men are corrupted, so that they make themselves become of a quite contrary nature, though at first good, and well brought up.'[15] The conundrum that corruption is somehow inherent in our psychology, waiting to be awakened, was precisely what Wordsworth would find himself discussing in *The Borderers*. This sentiment finds an echo in Jean-Baptiste Louvet's *Narrative of the Dangers to which I have been exposed*, which Wordsworth read in late 1795, where Louvet counsels the youth of Paris to 'Be equally on your guard against rushing headlong too soon upon obstacles, and in going in quest of them where they do not exist.'[16] This is in the context of arguing that, 'When the ignorant and misguided multitude reigns, crimes are as numerous as masters.'[17] With these statements in mind, it is hard not to see *The Borderers* as providing a clever analogy for the events of the Revolution. Whether or not it was in preparation for writing a play, he settled down to reacquaint himself with some of the comedies he had either read or seen on the London stage, among them Farquhar's *The Beaux' Stratagem*. The world of Restoration drama would have been particularly instructive given that, as Charles Lamb would point out, 'Judged morally, every character in these plays – the few exceptions are mistakes – is alike essentially vain and worthless.'[18] In

---

[13]   Ibid. II iii 344.
[14]   *WR* i 91–2.
[15]   *Machiavel's Discourses upon the First Decade of T. Lucius*, trans. Edward Dacres (2nd edn, London, 1674), p. 139. See *WR* i 91–2.
[16]   Jean-Baptiste Louvet de Couvray, *Narrative of the Dangers to which I have been exposed, since the 31st of May, 1795* (London, 1795), pp. vi-vii. It was published by Joseph Johnson. See *WR* i 89.
[17]   Ibid., p. 70.
[18]   *Charles Lamb as Critic*, ed. Roy Park (London: Routledge and Kegan Paul, 1980), p. 64.

Farquhar's play Cherry remarks, though as a joke, that in order to obtain his mistress a lover must 'adore the Person that betrays him, he must bribe the Chambermaid that betrays him, and court the Footman that laughs at him. . . . he must treat his Enemies with Respect, his Friends with Indifference, and all the World with Contempt.'[19] It was the sort of mixed-up value system that would contribute to the confusions of *The Borderers*. This is not merely a question of tracing Wordsworth's sources, most of which are accounted for by the Cornell editor;[20] I'm thinking rather of the books that informed his thinking about guilt on a more general level. It was something that would continue to preoccupy him at Alfoxden as he created such characters as Martha Ray and Peter Bell. Joseph Fawcett's *The Art of War*, which he read in spring or summer 1795, contains a portrait of a murderer after committing his crime:

> He is 'afraid to think on what he has done;'
> That 'twere undone, is his devoutest wish.
> Of heaven and earth he feels himself accurst.
>
> (ll. 1032–4)

Although he may have read these lines two years before starting work on *The Borderers*, they stayed with him, and that sense of feeling oneself 'accurst' went straight into Mortimer at the end of the play, as he announces that he will wander the earth, an outcast of the universe.[21] The sense of being personally damned is present also in Schiller's *The Robbers*, when Charles de Moor exclaims: 'I alone the outcast – the prodigal son! – Of all the children of his mercy, I alone rejected. (*Starting back with horror.*) The companion of murderers – of viperous fiends – bound down, enchained to guilt and horror!'[22]

There is another element to Wordsworth's play not readily to be found in his reading: the Oedipus figure. In a subplot, Mortimer is in love with Matilda, Herbert's daughter, who, Rivers claims, Herbert is about to 'sell' to the debauched Earl Clifford. The destruction of Herbert is therefore doubly self-defeating because it means that Mortimer's relationship with Matilda is destroyed. Mortimer is forced to take responsibility for the death of a man who in effect is his future father-in-law.

One of the play's oddities lies in the way it portrays evil. Rivers' argument is

[19] George Farquhar, *The Beaux' Stratagem* (London, 1707), Act 2, p. 19. See *WR* i 57.
[20] See also Robert Osborn, 'Meaningful Obscurity: The Antecedents and Character of Rivers', *Bicentenary Wordsworth Studies*, ed. Jonathan Wordsworth (Ithaca, NY: Cornell University Press, 1970), pp. 393–424.
[21] See *The Borderers* (1797–9) V iii 264–75.
[22] Friedrich Schiller, *The Robbers*, trans. Alexander Fraser Tytler (London, 1792), pp. 110–11. The play is clearly a source for Wordsworth's drama; see *WR* i 121.

that he is giving Mortimer an education – 'this youth may live / To thank me for this service!'[23] The insight he offers is that compassion and pity are of no use to the proud.[24] Essentially, Rivers advocates ruthlessness and contempt for anyone who displays Christian virtues or obeys the law. Wordsworth was sufficiently intrigued by Rivers to write a commentary on him at the same time as the 1797 version of the play. Having been 'betrayed into a great crime' he is morally confused, seeking good in evil and evil in good. But he also sought relief from two sources, 'action and meditation'.[25] His meditative side makes him a perverse precursor of the Wordsworthian visionary.

It is significant that Rivers is also a rationalist – persuading Mortimer to kill Herbert, he tells him that 'This is an act of justice,' and later, "tis an act of reason'[26] – an element of his character that, as a number of critics have observed, turns the play into a critique of Godwinism. And of course, the revolutionary of character of Rivers, with his intoxicated advocacy of 'action', also turns the play into a commentary on the failed French revolution. *The Borderers* is, in that light, a refutation of the position adopted in the 'Letter to the Bishop', as David Bromwich has pointed out.[27] But I would emphasize the fact that Wordsworth writes the play out of emotional truths that have begun to appear in his work by 1793, and that for all its obvious relevance to Godwinian philosophy and Robespierre, it remains in certain respects a deeply personal work. The component parts of Rivers' character are present in Wordsworth's writing from the Hawkshead period onwards. The apprehension of being implicated in the death of his father is present in 'The Vale of Esthwaite', while the figure of betrayal came to play an important role in the poetry of late 1792 onwards. Behind all this lies a weight of grief. Herbert observes of Mortimer that he 'had some grief which pressed upon him',[28] and the motif of the traitor and his repeated calumnies is seen by Wordsworth as part of a twisted response to guilt. Part of Rivers' motivation, Wordsworth reasons, arises from the fact that 'the exhibition of his own powers [is] . . . almost identified with the extinction of those painful feelings which attend the recollection of his guilt.'[29] Like the Cambridge poetry, *The Borderers* is

---

23 Ibid. II iii 235–6.
24 Ibid. III v 74ff.
25 Cornell *Borderers* 62–3.
26 *The Borderers* II i 57, 81.
27 Bromwich observes: 'If, as seems to me likely, *The Borderers* is a more exacting allegory of his mental life at that time than *The Prelude* or *The Excursion*, one may surmise that the play served him as a delayed apology' (*A Choice of Inheritance* (Cambridge, Mass.: Harvard University Press, 1989), p. 64).
28 *The Borderers* III iii 2.
29 Ibid 63.

partly about the need to purge intense emotion. No wonder Thomas Harris, manager of Covent Garden theatre, felt that Rivers' 'metaphysical obscurity'[30] rendered the play unstageable.[31]

On the surface, the other work that confronted Coleridge when he visited Wordsworth at Racedown in June 1797 was quite distinct in its concerns. 'The Ruined Cottage' told a story of relentless suffering. It was a pathetic tale that concluded with the death of Margaret, a war widow. But it deals with emotions not so different from those in *The Borderers*. In fact, there are numerous similarities, besides the fact that Margaret and Robert (the couple in 'The Ruined Cottage') are also names of characters in the play. For one thing, Margaret's reaction to her husband's departure for the war is to grieve; as the Pedlar observes:

> Once again
> I turned towards the garden gate and saw
> More plainly still that poverty and grief
> Were now come nearer to her . . .
>   ('The Ruined Cottage' MS B, 450–3)

That powerful emotion remains undischarged and its repression causes Margaret to become unhinged. Depressed, she sits for hours on the bench staring into the distance – a psychological touch that impressed Coleridge sufficiently for him to copy out the relevant lines in a letter to John Prior Estlin.[32] What both works have in common is that they sketch people deranged by intense emotion. Rivers' perverted sense of justice and truth stems from guilt; as Wordsworth pointed out in his Preface to *The Borderers*, the experience of committing crime turns Rivers into 'a moral sceptic' and thence, 'pressed by the recollection of his guilt, he seeks relief from two sources, action & meditation.'[33] In 'The Ruined Cottage' Margaret's abandonment and grief derange her. Arguably, they share a sense of betrayal. The theme which runs through *The Borderers* is matched in 'The Ruined Cottage' by the ruthlessness with which Margaret's family is torn apart by socio-political forces beyond her control.

Examination of these works at Racedown famously persuaded Coleridge that their author was 'a great man', as he told Estlin on 10 June

---

[30]   *EY* 197n.
[31]   It is possible that the play was rejected also by Sheridan, although the evidence for it has not been followed up by scholars; see R. S. Woof, 'Coleridge and Thomasina Dennis', *University of Toronto Quarterly* 32 (1962) 36–54, p. 45.
[32]   Griggs i 327–8.
[33]   *Prose Works* i 76.

1797.[34] And when the Wordsworths were ushered to Alfoxden House one of the inaugural events of the *annus mirabilis* was a reading of *The Borderers* in its grounds to an audience that included Coleridge and Tom Poole.[35] For his part, Wordsworth must have been favourably impressed by Coleridge's *Osorio*, or at least the two and a half acts which were made available to him, as they dealt with similar themes.[36] It opens with the lament of Maria who, like Margaret in 'The Ruined Cottage', is waiting for her lover, Albert, to return from the Spanish civil wars against the Moors. Suspecting her fidelity to him, Albert returns incognito, hoping that 'She is no traitress!'[37] A misunderstanding lends support to the suspicion that she has fallen in love with his younger brother Osorio, but at the end of the Act he still hopes that

> I shall meet her where no evil is,
> No treachery, no cup dash'd from the lips!

(I i 369–70)

Coleridge's interest in treachery had been present from the start of work on *Osorio*. As Robert Woof points out,[38] it had begun with a jotting on the subject in Coleridge's notebooks:

> The Treachery of Renneburg, a Tragedy –
> Vid. Watson's *Hist. Of Phil. 2nd. Vol.* IInd 350
> The assassination of the Prince of Orange –
> Gaspar Anastro, a Spanish Banker of ruined circumstances, a man of hard heart, cunning but a coward – prevails on John Jauregui, a young Biscayan, of a thoughtful melancholy disposition, deeply superstitious –
>
> (*Notebooks* i 210)

None of these have much to do with *Osorio*, except for the fact that they return to the theme of betrayal. Again, Woof was the first to observe that the treachery of Renneburg and Coleridge's play most resemble each other in being morality plays, both of which conclude with the protagonist being lamented by those he has betrayed.[39] Clearly, Wordsworth and Coleridge had similar interests and were thinking along similar lines even before they began

---

[34] Griggs i 327.

[35] Griggs i 332.

[36] The play was complete by October, although the bulk of it – some 1500 lines – was in draft by 10 May.

[37] *Osorio* I i 274. In the absence of the relevant volume in the Collected Coleridge, I am compelled to use the text provided by E. H. Coleridge in the Clarendon edition.

[38] Woof Ph.D. 70.

[39] Ibid. 72.

to read each other's work in summer 1797.[40] Wordsworth must have noticed the resemblances between the two dramas, for he encouraged his new friend in his work, as Coleridge proudly reported to Estlin.[41] Furthermore, for a short while they considered publishing their dramatic works in a joint volume.[42] A central parallel in their preoccupations lies in a sensitivity to the nuances of human psychology. Even in the shorter verse composed by Wordsworth at Racedown, he made the workings of the human mind his subject. In 'The Baker's Cart' he described a poor woman similar to Margaret whose extreme poverty had made her mind 'Sick and extravagant'.[43] In 'A Somersetshire Tragedy' there appears an idiot girl[44] whose face 'bespake a weak and witless soul / Which none could think worthwhile to teach or to controul';[45] while the speaker of 'Incipient Madness' is compelled by grief:

> There is a mood,
> A settled temper of the heart, when grief,
> Become an instinct, fastening on all things
> That promise food, doth like a sucking babe
> Create it where it is not.

(ll. 7–11)

That word 'instinct' turns the speaker's feelings into a compulsion, constantly regenerating itself. What marks these lines out as mature is their embodiment of the psychological truth that grief is part of an uncontrollable process. Characteristic of them, and much of Wordsworth's writing during the Racedown period, is a preoccupation with mental disarray,[46] in particular that of people who cannot exert conscious control over patterns that have come to dominate them. Rigorous self-analysis had revealed to Wordsworth some of the reasons why people surrendered to involuntary habit.

This is certainly the case with Margaret in 'The Ruined Cottage', and she is sufficiently self-aware to know it:

---

[40] This is also explored by Johnston 539–40.

[41] Griggs i 326.

[42] See Joseph Cottle, *Reminiscences of Samuel Taylor Coleridge and Robert Southey* (London, 1847): 'I offered Mr Coleridge and Mr Wordsworth thirty guineas each, as proposed, for their two tragedies; but which, after some hesitation, was declined, from the hope of introducing one, or both, on the stage' (p. 167).

[43] Line 21.

[44] If Wordsworth had followed the facts on which this story was based, her name would have been Jenny.

[45] One of the two fragments of the poem that survive; see Cornell *Lyrical Ballads* 317.

[46] Johnston regards the speaker of the poem as pathological; see Johnston, *Recluse* 34.

> I have slept
> Weeping, and weeping I have waked; my tears
> Have flowed as if my body were not such
> As others are, and I could never die.
>
>   ('The Ruined Cottage' MS B, 407–10)

Grief so transforms her as to make her seem immortal, susceptible to torment even in sleep. Once again the emphasis is on the individual's inability to dictate terms to the mind. The subterranean forces of grief and abandonment are consistently more powerful than what Wordsworth in his Preface to *Lyrical Ballads* calls the 'conscious will', and his insight into them was one reason why Coleridge recognized his friend's genius.

This was one of the most important pieces of wisdom Wordsworth brought to the *annus mirabilis*. Coleridge understood it in philosophical rather than psychological terms – as necessitarianism, mediated to him most notably through Hartley's writings on the compelled action of 'vibratiuncles'. He quickly understood how fundamental this was to Wordsworth's thinking; as he told Poole in 1804, 'W, you know, was even to Extravagance a Necessitarian.'[47] Prior to June 1797 both were well acquainted with the notion that certain mental processes were predestined, but it may have taken Wordsworth's advocacy for Coleridge to understand just how crucial it was to 'The Recluse'. It shows up in the first poem Coleridge composed after the Wordsworths moved to Alfoxden, 'This Lime-Tree Bower my Prison', where, without conscious premeditation,

>   A Delight
> Comes sudden on my heart, and I am glad
> As I myself were there![48]

And in 'The Ancient Mariner' the mariner's second glance at the water-snakes triggers another unwilled response: 'A spring of love gusht from my heart, / And I bless'd them unaware.'[49] In this light it is reasonable to interpret a similar image, the 'mighty Fountain' of 'Kubla Khan',[50] as symbolic of the potential for love within the human heart, waiting perpetually for release. Coleridge's use of this Wordsworthian insight was peculiarly positive in its

---

[47] Griggs ii 1037.

[48] From the earliest version of the poem in Coleridge's letter to Southey, 17 July 1797; Griggs i 335.

[49] Lines 276–7; I refer to the text in Cornell *Lyrical Ballads*.

[50] Line 19 of the Crewe manuscript text, as given by Beer in his Everyman edition.

implications, and necessarily so. For the purposes of 'The Recluse' it was essential to argue that human beings were potentially loving and well-disposed towards each other, and that only outside circumstances denied them the brotherhood to which, innately and unconsciously, they aspired. By contrast, Wordsworth's Racedown poetry discussed in a more negative context our unconscious reactions to grief and hardship – usually in the form of depression, insanity and mental imbalance. The shift of vision is expressed in a passage from *Osorio* which Coleridge published in *Lyrical Ballads* (1798) as 'The Dungeon':

> With other ministrations thou, O nature!
> Healest thy wandering and distempered child:
> Thou pourest on him thy soft influences,
> Thy sunny hues, fair forms, and breathing sweets,
> Thy melodies of woods, and winds, and waters,
> Till he relent, and can no more endure
> To be a jarring and a dissonant thing,
> Amid this general dance and minstrelsy;
> But, bursting into tears, wins back his way,
> His angry spirit healed and harmonized
> By the benignant touch of love and beauty.
>
> (ll. 20–30)

This is Coleridge writing under Wordsworth's influence. He would not have placed such emphasis on nature prior to June 1797. It is effective not for its subscription to the nature-loving creed of Wordsworth, but for its account of alienation, the state in which the individual becomes 'a jarring and a dissonant thing'. Nor does it stop at that; the man breaks into tears as he returns to a renewed sense of belonging, 'healed and harmonized' by nature. It brings together the conflicting currents of thought in Wordsworth's poetry before and after June 1797. On the one hand the world is poisoned at the heart, so thoroughly 'distempered' that even the virtuous seem compelled to commit acts of cruelty and vice; on the other, mankind is redeemed by 'the benignant touch of love and beauty'. It is a tension that will resurface in Wordsworth's poetry with interesting results.

Wordsworth's distinctive preoccupations in the Alfoxden poetry can be seen in 'Goody Blake and Harry Gill', where another involuntary mental process inflicts on Harry Gill eternal punishment for his persecution of Goody Blake. Where this poem differs from 'The Ancient Mariner' or 'Kubla Khan' is that it is grounded in medical pathology. Wordsworth's source is a textbook, Erasmus Darwin's *Zoönomia* (1794–6), which cites Goody Blake's curse and its effects as an example of 'Mutable Madness. Where the patients are liable to mistake ideas of sensation for those from irritation, that is, im-

aginations for realities'.[51] Unlike Coleridge's poems, this one grounds the
strange events at its heart in recorded history – and scientific history at that.
Wordsworth says so in the 'Advertisement': 'The tale of Goody Blake and
Harry Gill is founded on a well-authenticated fact which happened in War-
wickshire.'[52] It is interesting to find some of the periodicals which reprinted
the poem placing great emphasis on this point. The *Ipswich Magazine* even
prefaced it with a moral essay exhorting farmers to turn a blind eye to 'the
depredations daily committed on the hedges in the neighbourhood':

> Should there be one more rigorous than the rest, let him attend to the poetical
> story inserted in page 115 of this magazine, and tremble at the fate of farmer
> Gill, who was about to prosecute a poor old woman for a similar offence. The
> thing is a fact, and told by one of the first physicians of the present day, as having
> happened in the south of England, and which has, a short time since, been
> turned by a lyric poet into that excellent ballad.[53]

It's not that magazine editors were sermonizing fools, nor would I argue that
this poem reveals Wordsworth's tendency to cling to the palpable: what's
important about it, both for the editor of the *Ipswich Magazine* and for
Wordsworth, is that it contextualizes the workings of the mind, however extraordinary, within a recognizably real world in which poor people literally
struggled for survival. In that respect it seems very much like a Racedown
poem, for while resident in Dorset the Wordsworths witnessed that struggle
on a daily basis: 'The peasants are miserably poor,' Dorothy wrote in 1795,
observing that they lived in cottages made of wood and clay. Nor were the
Wordsworths exempt from the obligation to keep themselves warm. In March
1796 Wordsworth told Wrangham that 'I have been engaged an hour and a
half this morning in hewing wood and rooting up hedges, and I think it no
bad employment to feel "the penalty of Adam" in this way.'[54] But if 'Goody
Blake and Harry Gill' may be thought of as a Racedown poem, in the sense
that it enshrines some of the experiences they had there, it is utterly different
from anything Wordsworth actually wrote there. Why? In the early 'Ruined
Cottage', 'The Borderers' and the shorter works, suffering and hardship were
seen to be both inevitable and unrelieved; by contrast 'Goody Blake and Harry
Gill' posits a self-correcting process which protects the weak and poverty-
stricken in society, and for that reason is optimistic in its implications. This is
not, notably, the same world of folklore as that in which such writers as James

---

[51]   Quoted Cornell *Lyrical Ballads* 344.
[52]   *Prose Works* i 117.
[53]   *Ipswich Magazine* (April 1799) 105.
[54]   *EY* 168.

Hogg thrived, where God would intervene directly to save peasant folk from the injustices of the laird or from bogus clerics; in Wordsworth's universe redemption comes from qualities that inhere in the individual mind, to which Darwin's case study is adduced as evidence.

Just how optimistic Wordsworth felt about the potential of the mind can be seen in 'The Idiot Boy'. This may be one of his most misunderstood works, partly because of confusion surrounding the figure of Johnny Foy. Wordsworth's first description of him on his pony begs the question in stark terms:

> There is no need of boot or spur,
> There is no need of whip or wand,
> For Johnny has his holly-bough,
> And with a hurly-burly now
> He shakes the green bough in his hand.
>
> (ll. 57–61)

That 'green bough' of holly is one of those properties that defies precise translation into words, like the branch of wilding held by Matthew in 'The Two April Mornings'. But for anyone used to Wordsworth's classical allusions it is reminiscent of the golden bough that protected Aeneas on his journey to the underworld. Its effect is to elevate Johnny to the level of classical hero, though in purely dramatic terms it is expressive of his excitement, his 'hurly-burly': Wordsworth is trying to describe his inner world, and the bough provides a bridge between him and us. At the same time, with Aeneas in our minds, it is impossible not to be reminded of Orpheus and Eurydice, whose underworld journey resonates throughout so much of Wordsworth's poetry prior to 1798. If so, it is by way of contrast, because Johnny's story is not one of loss.

The moment at which Betty sends her son into the night is a crucial one in terms of the poem's drama.

> And Betty's most especial charge,
> Was, 'Johnny! Johnny! mind that you
> Come home again, nor stop at all,
> Come home again, whate'er befal,
> My Johnny do, I pray you do.'
>
> To this did Johnny answer make
> Both with his head, and with his hand,
> And proudly shook the bridle too,
> And then! his words were not a few,
> Which Betty well could understand.

And now that Johnny is just going,
Though Betty's in a mighty flurry,
She gently pats the pony's side
On which her idiot boy must ride,
And seems no longer in a hurry.

But when the pony moved his legs,
Oh! then for the poor idiot boy!
For joy he cannot hold the bridle,
For joy his head and heels are idle,
He's idle all for very joy.

And while the pony moves his legs,
In Johnny's left-hand you may see,
The green bough's motionless and dead;
The moon that shines above his head
Is not more still and mute than he.

                                      (ll. 67–91)

Coleridge had contemplated the individual as 'a jarring and a dissonant thing', but there is nothing of this about Johnny Foy. His mongolism is no obstacle to his place in the world: 'And then! his words were not a few, / Which Betty well could understand.' 'Words' is a euphemism: we know Johnny's articulation to be imperfect. But Wordsworth's implication is clear: although Johnny's speech is beyond reach of the untrained ear, Betty's love for her son gives her access to his every word. As Wordsworth says in the Preface, the poem is meant to trace 'the maternal passion through many of its more subtle windings'.[55] The suffering of the figure in 'The Dungeon' was caused by alienation from 'love and beauty'; Johnny Foy, by contrast, is surrounded by it.

Southey's well-known review of Lyrical Ballads begins by attacking 'The Idiot Boy' as resembling 'a Flemish picture in the worthlessness of its design and the excellence of its execution', while misrepresenting the poem in its account of the narrative: '[Betty] therefore puts him upon her poney, at eight o'clock in the evening, gives him proper directions, and returns to take care of her sick neighbour.'[56] Southey does not mention Betty's ability to understand her son because, as far as he is concerned, Johnny is devoid of psychological complexity. In private Southey remarked, 'tho the Idiot Boy is sadly dilated, it is very well done,'[57] a much more balanced assessment, prompting the

---

55 Prose Works i 126.
56 Critical Review 24 (1798) 197–204, pp. 200, 198.
57 Letter to Wynn, 17 December 1798; Curry i 177.

suggestion that his need to criticize it publicly is symptomatic of anxiety. No doubt it was; in June 1798 he had published his own poem about an 'idiot' called Ned whose love for his mother was such that he dug up her corpse after its burial, took it home and seated it by the hearth.[58] Ned is introduced as 'A thing of idiot mind' and never rises above that level. He is stripped of dignity, true to the way in which mongols were regarded at the time. Nor, for that matter, is there any trace in his poem of the affection and humour to be found in Wordsworth's treatment of Betty and the pony. Even today, despite political correctness, mongols remain somehow other, excluded from most people's daily experience. The discomfort westerners have often felt in their presence takes us to the heart of the problem that has always dogged 'The Idiot Boy'. It comes unstuck if Johnny Foy is in any respect seen to be inferior, on an intellectual or spiritual level, to the other characters: Wordsworth grants his feelings the same intensity as those of his mother. In so doing, he knew that he was challenging some deeply ingrained prejudices. John Wilson, one of his earliest admirers, wrote to Wordsworth on this very point, saying:

> The object of her affection is indeed her son, and in that relation much consists, but then he is represented as totally destitute of any attachment towards her; the state of his mind is represented as perfectly deplorable, and, in short, to me it appears almost unnatural that a person in a state of complete idiotism should excite the warmest feelings of attachment in the breast even of his mother. This much I know, that among all the people ever I knew to have read this poem, I never met one who did not rise rather displeased from the perusal of it, and the only cause I could assign for it was the one now mentioned.[59]

Wordsworth would not have wished Johnny to be seen as 'deplorable'. Even the term 'idiotism' is hardly justified by his portrayal, and I'm inclined to read even the poem's title ironically. Wilson understands it not in terms of what Wordsworth actually says but of his preconceived notions. That is what Wordsworth meant when he told Wilson that

> the loathing and disgust which many people have at the sight of an Idiot, is a feeling which, though having som[e] foundation in human nature is not neces-

[58] See the texts in Kenneth Curry, *The Contributions of Robert Southey to the Morning Post* (Tuscaloosa: University of Alabama Press, 1984), pp. 68–9, and my *Romanticism: An Anthology* (2nd edn, Oxford: Blackwell, 1998), pp. 562–4. Southey's poem is discussed by B. R. McElderry Jr., 'Southey, and Wordsworth's "The Idiot Boy"', *N&Q* 200 (1955) 490–1; see also Geoffrey Carnall, 'The Idiot Boy', *N&Q* 201 (1956) 81–2.
[59] Mary Gordon, *'Christopher North': A Memoir of John Wilson* (2 vols, Edinburgh, 1862), i 46.

sarily attached to it in any vi[rtuous?] degree, but is owing, in a great measure to a false delicacy, and, if I [may] say it without rudeness, a certain want of comprehensiveness of think[ing] and feeling.[60]

By implication it is Wilson who has been guilty of a false delicacy, and a 'want' (or lack) of thought and feeling. A central aim of 'The Idiot Boy' is to break through that so as to demonstrate that the underclass of beggars, peasants and vagrants that throng the pages of *Lyrical Ballads* is no less sensitive than the higher orders. As Wordsworth remarked of 'The Brothers' and 'Michael', they 'were written with a view to shew that men who do not wear fine cloaths can feel deeply'.[61] But the ambition is not purely political; it is also psychological. Johnny Foy's idiotism is significant because it is subject to constant redefinition. This is an idiot who communicates faultlessly with those who love him most, and who is dignified by the language with which he is described:

> But when the pony moved his legs,
> Oh! then for the poor idiot boy!
> For joy he cannot hold the bridle,
> For joy his head and heels are idle,
> He's idle all for very joy.
>
> And while the pony moves his legs,
> In Johnny's left hand you may see,
> The green bough's motionless and dead;
> The moon that shines above his head
> Is not more still and mute than he.
>
> (ll. 82–91)

The simplicity of the verse is evidence of Wordsworth's formal mastery, and tends to beguile readers into believing his intentions to be uncomplicated. As for its language, there is at first sight nothing here that could give rise to the suspicion that Wordsworth is doing anything more than narrate. Its full significance emerges only when seen in the context of *Lyrical Ballads* as a whole. For instance, in 'Lines written at a small distance from my house', Wordsworth exhorts Dorothy to join him in Holford Dell, 'for this one day / We'll give to idleness.' Instead of the moral disapprobation normally associated with it, Wordsworth makes idleness the prerequisite for the exalted state in which one experiences the love which flows 'From earth to man, from man to earth'. It

---

[60]   *EY* 356.
[61]   *EY* 315.

becomes a code word for the inward suspension that precedes a vision of the natural world. But there is another word in these stanzas from 'The Idiot Boy' which Wordsworth seeks to emphasize: 'For joy he cannot hold the bridle, / For joy his head and heels are idle.' On the simplest level, 'joy' denotes Johnny's happiness at the prospect of unrestrained freedom. But as with 'idleness', other usages in the 1798 poetry lend it more exalted shades of meaning. That February, Wordsworth had written that the Pedlar 'saw one life, and felt that it was joy'[62] – connecting the emotion firmly with a mystic apprehension of the natural world. And in 'Tintern Abbey' Wordsworth described 'the joy / Of elevated thoughts' in his account of the transcendental apprehension of the spirit

> that impels
> All thinking things, all objects of all thought,
> And rolls through all things.
>
> (ll. 101–3)

The idleness and joy experienced by Johnny as he moves out of the poem and into the night point to his centrality in the Wordsworthian cosmos.

There are further clues to be found in Wordsworth's perverse celebration of his own incompetence:

> Oh reader! now that I might tell
> What Johnny and his horse are doing!
> What they've been doing all this time,
> Oh could I put it into rhyme,
> A most delightful tale pursuing!
>
> Perhaps, and no unlikely thought!
> He with his pony now doth roam
> The cliffs and peaks so high that are,
> To lay his hands upon a star,
> And in his pocket bring it home.
>
> Perhaps he's turned himself about,
> His face unto his horse's tail,
> And still and mute, in wonder lost,
> All like a silent horseman-ghost,
> He travels on along the vale.

[62] 'The Pedlar' 218.

And now, perhaps, he's hunting sheep,
A fierce and dreadful hunter he!
Yon valley, that's so trim and green,
In five months' time, should he be seen,
A desart wilderness will be.

Perhaps, with head and heels on fire,
And like the very soul of evil,
He's galloping away, away,
And so he'll gallop on for aye,
The bane of all that dread the devil.

I to the muses have been bound,
These fourteen years, by strong indentures;
Oh gentle muses! let me tell
But half of what to him befel,
For sure he met with strange adventures.

Oh gentle muses! is this kind?
Why will ye thus my suit repel?
Why of your further aid bereave me?
And can ye thus unfriended leave me?
Ye muses! whom I love so well.

(ll. 322–56)

We are ill-advised to regard Wordsworth's proclaimed failure as anything but tactical. Their convenience as objects of blame lies mainly in the fact that the muses do little more than act as vectors for something more immediate and urgent, communicated by stealth. Wordsworth uses a similar technique in 'The Thorn', written supposedly in the persona of a retired sea-captain with an unhealthy curiosity in other people's business. He too fails to relate a co-herent story, although his excuse is different. He's obtuse – seeing, but not understanding, what is before him. The narrator of 'The Idiot Boy' both sees and understands, but lacks the technical skill to convey it. The effect is the same in both cases, however: the narrator's inability to do his work shifts the interpretive responsibility to his audience.

These repeatedly ditched opportunities for resolution serve to raise questions in the reader's mind. And if we are confused, that feeling is only compounded by the parody of Gothicism in the inspired portrait of Johnny as a phantom horseman (influenced no doubt by Bürger's 'Lenora').[63] For Johnny

---

[63]   See Mary Jacobus, *Tradition and Experiment in Wordsworth's Lyrical Ballads 1798* (Oxford: Clarendon Press, 1976), pp. 250–61, 277–83.

to have laid his hands upon a star is, we know, impossible, except insofar as intensely spiritual experiences may be described in similar terms. Take, for instance, the opening stanzas of Henry Vaughan's 'The Night':

> Through that pure *Virgin-shrine,*
> That sacred veil drawn o'er thy glorious noon
> That men might look and live as glow-worms shine,
> And face the moon:
> Wise *Nicodemus* saw such light
> As made him know his God by night.
>
> Most blessed believer he!
> Who in that land of darkness and blind eyes
> Thy long expected healing wings could see,
> When thou didst rise,
> And what can never more be done,
> Did at mid-night speak with the Sun!
>
>   (ll. 1–12)

The arch manner of Wordsworth's poem makes comparison with Vaughan seem pompous and unwarranted; after all, Vaughan's ambitions appear much more elevated. Moreover, it is virtually certain that when he composed 'The Idiot Boy' Wordsworth had not read Vaughan, nor is it clear that he ever did so.[64] But Johnny's final speech – a response to Betty's enquiry about where he has been – sounds, at least to me, evocative of Vaughan: 'The cocks did crow to-whoo to-whoo, / And the sun did shine so cold.' The image of the sun shining coldly upon the earth makes a kind of inverted sense; in a slightly patronizing way, we may be inclined to suggest that it's just Johnny's way of talking about moonshine. But the similarities with Vaughan are more suggestive. His reference to the 'glorious noon' of night closely anticipates Johnny's statement, and, as Alan Rudrum has pointed out, there is an analogue in the writings of the German mystic Jacob Boehme: 'there is a wonderful time coming, but because it beginneth in the night, there are many that shall not see it, by reason of their sleep and drunkenness: yet the Sun will shine on the Children at Midnight.'[65] Boehme notes that the 'Children' are those of 'Sophia,

---

[64]   See John T. Shawcross, 'Kidnapping the Poets: the Romantics and Henry Vaughan', *Milton, the Metaphysicals, and Romanticism,* ed. Lisa Low and Anthony John Harding (Cambridge: Cambridge University Press, 1994), pp. 185–203, and *WR* ii 263–4.
[65]   From Boehme's *The Three Principles of the Divine Essence* (1648), as quoted in *Henry Vaughan: The Complete Poems,* ed. Alan Rudrum (Harmondsworth: Penguin, 1976), p. 627.

or the Divine Wisdom' – tending to confirm the suggestion that he, like Vaughan, has in mind a moment of profound vision.

Could this be anything other than a parallel to what Johnny Foy attempts to describe? The contexts are surely distinct. Vaughan and Boehme are explicitly devotional; Wordsworth is not. But if he was unfamiliar with Vaughan, Wordsworth had probably read Boehme, or at least heard about his ideas from Coleridge. In 1817 Coleridge told Tieck that there were ideas about light and sound that 'Before my visit to Germany in September, 1798, I had adopted (probably from Behmen's Aurora, which I had *conjured over* at School).'[66] Coleridge's enthusiasm was ongoing; he projected some work on Boehme in a 1796 notebook entry. In that context it is not fanciful to propose that the paradoxical interplay between sun and moon, heat and cold, darkness and light, blindness and spiritual enlightenment, to be found in both Vaughan and Boehme, is an element also in Johnny Foy's concluding remarks. At the very least his words, which seem like nonsense, may be an attempt to articulate his sense of the sublime. That is confirmed by his 'joy' as he sets off at the beginning of the poem – one that, at the time it was written in spring 1798, had specifically pantheist associations for both Wordsworth and Coleridge.

If, during his absence, Johnny experienced an ecstasy of some kind, Wordsworth had good reason not to say so explicitly. Besides his readers' prejudices, there was the matter of literary taste. In 1798 it would have been questionable for a poet writing in the ballad form to have described a quasi-religious event, let alone one attributed to a mongol child. No poet, however skilled, could have carried it off without offending late eighteenth-century sensibilities. Wordsworth was at the peak of his powers, but his declared inability to do justice to Johnny's experience may not be entirely feigned. In terms of the 1798 poetry Johnny's 'idiotism' places him in a permanent Wordsworthian state of grace, a mystic consciousness that knows no end. Far from being retarded, he has ascended to the highest level of existence available to him. There is more than a hint of this in Wordsworth's admonition to John Wilson: 'I have often applied to Idiots, in my own mind, that sublime expression of scripture that, *"their life is hidden with God."* They are worshipped, probably from a feeling of this sort, in several parts of the East.'[67] The 'sublime expression' in Wordsworth's mind is Ephesians 3:9 where Paul writes that he has been ordained to help 'all men see what is the fellowship of

---

[66] Quoted CC *Marginalia* i 554. Boehme's influence on Wordsworth is discussed by Newton P. Stallknecht, *Strange Seas of Thought* (Bloomington: Indiana University Press, 1958).

[67] *EY* 357.

the mystery, which from the beginning of the world hath been hid in God, who created all things by Jesus Christ'. The allusion and the sacredness it imparts to the consciousness of mongoloids is crucial to how we interpret this poem. Johnny Foy has been privileged to become part of the fellowship of the mystery.

Wordsworth was taking a very different attitude towards human suffering from that evident in the Racedown verse. Here is a character who by rights should be a suffering, tormented figure, like Margaret in 'The Ruined Cottage' or the 'weak and witless soul' of 'A Somersetshire Tragedy'. The recurrent emotions of grief which torment them even in sleep are the cause of insanity. But despite being a mongol, Johnny is eminently sane. Though unable to communicate in language everyone can understand, he has visionary powers that enable him to live more intensely in his new-found freedom than most people could ever imagine: 'He's idle all for very joy.' Riding into the night, he ascends to the heavens and plucks a star from the sky, chases sheep across the fields, and becomes for a moment the horseman-devil of popular myth. He is the ultimate Wordsworthian visionary. A psychological process that causes infinite grief to Margaret provides Johnny with unending pleasure. It is not that Wordsworth had lost interest in suffering and political oppression, but that the psychological insights which in the Racedown verse were the source of continuing unhappiness have in 1798 become the source of something quite different: redemption.

This was evident from the moment Wordsworth began writing in January 1798. 'A Night-Piece' and 'The Discharged Soldier' both feature episodes in which the mind's compulsive tendencies regenerate the exhausted or depressed visionary. The 'musing [man]' whose eyes are bent to earth at the beginning of the first poem is 'startled' by the 'instantaneous light' that hits the ground before him. Glancing skywards, he is treated to a near-psychedelic display as the moon and stars 'Drive' through the night sky: 'How fast they wheel away! / Yet vanish not!'[68] It isn't so; the moon and stars aren't in motion. But the mind thinks they are, and, fooled by an optical illusion, is betrayed into quiescence. The point is that such experiences, where the mind surrenders completely, are restorative. At the beginning of 'The Discharged Soldier' the confusion of the road's surface with 'another stream' has a tranquillizing effect on the poet. He is by his own admission 'worn out by toil', but finds himself irresistibly soothed,

> My body from the stillness drinking in
> A restoration like the calm of sleep
> But sweeter far.
>
> (ll. 22–4)

---

[68] Lines 15–16.

It is impossible not to hear in that concluding phrase an echo of Michael's valediction to Adam and Eve as they are ushered out of Eden:

> then wilt thou not be loath
> To leave this Paradise, but shalt possess
> A paradise within thee, happier far.

> (*Paradise Lost* xii 585–7)

Where for Adam and Eve that inner paradise had been prospective, the Wordsworthian experience is retrospective. It is already claimed, and promises future power. In 'Tintern Abbey' the 'tranquil restoration' of his body and mind by the memory of the 'forms of beauty'[69] seen on the banks of the Wye years before have the same 'fructifying virtue' as the spots of time in the two-part *Prelude*.[70] All along the line, the incorporation of 'forms of beauty' into the mental economy of Wordsworth's protagonists, such as Johnny Foy, is involuntary. In 'The Pedlar' Wordsworth states that the '*active* power' to fasten images upon the brain – that is, the conscious ability – develops only after the mind has been shaped by experiences beyond its control:

> In such communion, not from terror free,
> While yet a child and long before his time,
> He had perceived the presence and the power
> Of greatness, and deep feelings had impressed
> Great objects on his mind with portraiture
> And colour so distinct that on his mind
> They lay like substances, and almost seemed
> To haunt the bodily sense.

> (ll. 27–34)

This 'communion' – implicitly a religious process – which occurs before a time when the child has gained the sophistication to censor or manipulate the sense-impressions made upon him, consists of a physical moulding of the mind by outside forces, its 'impressing'. Those forces are sublime, associated with terror and greatness, and intensely visual ('portraiture / And colour'). The metaphor Wordsworth selects is that of an artist depicting a landscape; it implies the existence of some external force capable of shaping the very constitution of the individual consciousness. In this Wordsworth is partly consistent with the psychological theories of Godwin, who had noted in the first edition

---

[69] 'Tintern Abbey' 23–31.
[70] *The Two-Part Prelude* ii 288–90.

of *Political Justice* that 'All our knowledge, all our ideas, every thing we possess as intelligent beings, comes from impression.' He goes on: 'The actions and dispositions of men . . . flow entirely from the operation of circumstances and events acting upon a faculty of receiving sensible impressions'.[71] The distinction to be made is that by 'intelligent being' Godwin means rational, and therefore dispassionate; Wordsworth on the other hand makes the 'impressing' of the mind the occasion for its being made sensible of deep feeling.

This conceit, which represents an extension of the ideas found in the pre-1798 poetry, was essential to 'The Recluse'. The epic poem that, in describing the psychological processes that would lead to universal brotherhood, would help bring about the millennium, was formulated in 1797–8 as the crowning ambition of Wordsworth's poetic career. Coleridge arrived at Racedown in June 1797 with the subject very much on his mind. He was to have written it himself, as a poem called 'The Brook', in around 1796–7, when it would no doubt have looked something like 'Religious Musings',[72] and it was almost certainly one of the first things he broached to Wordsworth at Racedown. Only a few months before he had written to Joseph Cottle about his intention to devote at least the next twenty years of his life to an epic poem.[73] 'The Recluse' would always remain his brainchild rather than Wordsworth's, and for that reason eluded Wordsworth's genius. Whatever else *The Borderers* and 'The Ruined Cottage' revealed to Coleridge in June 1797, it was clear to him from the outset that Wordsworth's understanding of human psychology qualified him to inherit his millenarian epic. Whenever he discussed it, Coleridge always emphasized this element of the poem. In the letter to Wordsworth of May 1815, explaining his disappointment with *The Excursion*, he was very clear about that:

> I supposed you first to have meditated the faculties of Man in the abstract, in their correspondence with his Sphere of action, and first, in the Feeling, Touch, and Taste, then in the Eye, & last in the Ear, to have laid a solid and immoveable foundation for the Edifice by removing the sandy Sophisms of Locke, and the Mechanic Dogmatists, and demonstrating that the Senses were living growths and developements of the Mind & Spirit in a much juster as well as higher sense, than the mind can be said to be formed by the Senses –.[74]

---

[71] *Political Justice* (London, 1793), i 95, 111.
[72] See CC *Biographia* i 196. Coleridge's remarks are corroborated by Wordsworth in *The River Duddon.*
[73] Griggs i 320–1.
[74] Griggs iv 574.

Who could be so hard-hearted, reading this letter, as not to feel sympathy for Wordsworth? After all, he had every reason to claim that he had already done this in 'The Pedlar' and then in *The Prelude*. But Coleridge had the advantage; 'The Recluse' was an ideal, unrealizable by any earthly hand. What marks it out as an impossibility is that the 'whole state of man and society' which it described would have to be 'illustrative of a redemptive process in operation, showing how this idea reconciled all the anomalies, and promised future glory and restoration'.[75] It was, in short, to have been no less than the catalyst for the regaining of paradise.

In Coleridge's mind it may have resembled William Gilbert's bizarre and incomprehensible poem, *The Hurricane*. Coleridge and Southey had known the Antiguan poet in Bristol, and Coleridge had published part of *The Hurricane* in *The Watchman*.[76] Southey described it as 'a strange poem with still stranger notes, written by a man of brilliant genius and polished manners who is deranged'.[77] For all its peculiarities, *The Hurricane* is one of those compelling works that emerged from the ferment of creative activity in dissenting circles in the 1790s, which has much to say about its author's sense of millenarian expectation (not unlike 'Religious Musings'). Coleridge thought well enough of it to show it to Wordsworth during the *annus mirabilis*, and he in turn never forgot one of Gilbert's unusual prose notes, which he noted down and reprinted in *The Excursion*, describing it as 'one of the finest passages of modern English Prose'.[78]

But the examples of 'Religious Musings' and *The Hurricane* were of dubious value. They were too eccentric to provide the kind of intellectual regimen demanded by an epic such as 'The Recluse', and it is hardly surprising that, halfway through work on the five-book *Prelude* in March 1804, Wordsworth wrote to Coleridge, then in London *en route* for the Mediterranean: 'I am very anxious to have your notes for the Recluse. I cannot say how much importance I attach to this, if it should please God that I survive you, I should reproach myself for ever in writing the work if I had neglected to procure this help.'[79] No amount of commentary or guidance from Coleridge could have helped him complete the work. 'The Recluse' had already become an ideal inextricably intertwined with the ups and downs of the thwarted love affair between him and Coleridge. Indeed, it became an index of the tensions between them; in October 1803, for instance, Coleridge wrote to Poole to say

---

[75] CC *Table Talk* ii 177.
[76] CC *Watchman* 350–1.
[77] Curry i 120. Gilbert was also a bit of an astrologist (Curry i 149).
[78] See *The Excursion* (1814), pp. 427–8; *PW* v 422–3. See also *WR* i 63.
[79] *EY* 452.

that Wordsworth 'has made a beginning to his Recluse', adding that he feels 'hostility' towards the *Lyrical Ballads* and the 'multitude of small Poems' which Wordsworth had recently been composing.[80]

Coleridge's retrospective argument for 'The Recluse', articulated in the letter of 1815, is clear as to the relation between the senses and the mind. The senses are 'living growths and developements of the Mind & Spirit in a much juster as well as higher sense, than the mind can be said to be formed by the Senses'. He reiterated this in July 1832, over seventeen years later, when he told Henry Nelson Coleridge that Wordsworth should have published the thirteen-Book *Prelude* when he completed it, adding that 'The Recluse' was to have treated 'man as man – a subject of eye, ear, touch, taste, in contact with external nature – informing the senses from the mind and not compounding a mind out of the senses'.[81] The philosophical emphasis in both accounts prioritizes imaginative process in the manner one would expect of a disciple of Berkeley and Hartley – entirely consistent with his writings of the 1790s. As early as the 'Lecture on the Slave-Trade', delivered in June 1795, Coleridge had declared that the acquisition of what he then called 'intellectual aliment' was the primary end of the mind.

> To develope the powers of the Creator is our proper employment – and to imitate Creativeness by combination our most exalted and self-satisfying Delight. But we are progressive and must not rest content with present Blessings. Our Almighty Parent hath therefore given to us Imagination that stimulates to the attainment of *real* excellence by the contemplation of splendid Possibilities that still revives the dying motive within us, and fixing our eye on the glittering Summits that rise one above the other in Alpine endlessness still urges us up the ascent of Being, amusing the ruggedness of the road with the beauty and grandeur of the ever-widening Prospect.[82]

What is significant about this statement is that it is the aspiration towards splendid possibilities that compels the eye up the ascent of being. The sense of sight (and by implication the other four) is given impetus and ambition by pre-existent longings within. In effect, it is imagination which, according to Coleridge, creates and develops the senses as instruments of spiritual engagement: 'To develope the powers of the Creator is our proper employment.' As Ian Wylie points out, this elevation of the mind as creative of the senses and their functions is indebted to Erasmus Darwin's theory that it was implicated

---

[80] Griggs ii 1012–13.
[81] CC *Table Talk* i 307.
[82] CC *Lectures 1795* 235.

in the physical reproduction of the species.[83] It was literally creative of other human beings, and spiritually regenerative, allowing us to climb the 'ascent of Being' towards our maker. The emphasis on that power must have been known to Wordsworth, whether through his reading or discussion with Coleridge.

For the purposes of 'The Recluse', Wordsworth's most important single piece of writing in 1798 was 'Not Useless do I Deem', composed as part of a draft conclusion to the revised 'Ruined Cottage', and intended to be spoken by the Pedlar. It won immediate approval from Coleridge, who quoted its first eighteen lines in a letter to his brother George, *c*.10 March 1798:

> Not useless do I deem
> These shadowy Sympathies with things that hold
> An inarticulate Language: for the Man
> Once taught to love such objects, as excite
> No vengeance & no hatred, needs must feel
> The Joy of that pure principle of Love
> So deeply, that, unsatisfied with aught
> Less pure & exquisite, he cannot chuse
> But seek for objects of a kindred Love
> In fellow-natures, & a kindred Joy.
> Accordingly, he by degrees perceives
> His feelings of aversion softened down,
> A holy tenderness pervade his frame!
> His sanity of reason not impair'd,
> Say rather that his thoughts now flowing clear,
> From a clear fountain flowing, he looks round –
> He seeks for Good & finds the Good he seeks.[84]

It is not easy to guess what George Coleridge, always concerned for his wayward brother, would have made of this. It was probably designed to reassure, coming as it does shortly after a declaration by Coleridge that he has 'snapped my squeaking baby-trumpet of Sedition & the fragments lie scattered in the lumber-room of Penitence'.

The fragment is significant because of its acceptance of the psychological schema that Coleridge reiterated in later accounts of 'The Recluse'. As in 'A Night-Piece', 'The Discharged Soldier' and 'Tintern Abbey', the effect is restorative. Natural 'things' speak to the individual of love and in return he is compelled to 'seek for objects of a kindred Love / In fellow-natures, & a

---

[83] Ian Wylie, *Young Coleridge and the Philosophers of Nature* (Oxford: Clarendon Press, 1989), p. 138.
[84] Griggs i 397–8.

kindred Joy'. What is so clearly Wordsworthian about the process is its emphasis not so much on sensory perception (although that is the chosen vehicle) as on natural things. Coleridge would be trained by Wordsworth to incorporate nature into his thinking, but it never figured very highly in his programme for 'The Recluse'. For Coleridge, the poem would place its emphasis squarely on the role of the senses in bridging the gap between the individual and God. For Wordsworth, the emphasis was slightly different; natural forms were perceived so as to trigger actions beyond conscious control, whereby affective feelings in them would give life to similar emotions in the perceiving mind, which would in turn be prompted to find like sentiments in others. Love of nature would lead to love of mankind. It was certainly progressive, as Coleridge's comments on the 'ascent of Being' would require, and Wordsworth's mention of the 'holy tenderness' proves that he is thinking about spiritual enlightenment. But this passage isn't primarily religious. God makes a brief appearance at line 18 (convenient for Coleridge as he is appealing to his brother's piety) but there's no sense in which He is instrumental to what takes place; any function He might have had being performed by the 'forms of beauty'. Wordsworth didn't at this stage need God, though He is an occasional presence in the verse.

Coleridge's accounts of Wordsworth at this time are often invoked when discussing the place of God in the Alfoxden poetry. In 1796 he told Thelwall that Wordsworth 'is a Republican & at least a *Semi*-atheist',[85] and in June 1797 told Estlin that Wordsworth 'is more inclined to Christianity than to Theism, simply considered' (by 'Theism' he probably meant deism).[86] In both cases Coleridge tailored his assessment to his reader – as a sceptic[87] Thelwall would have been expected to applaud Wordsworth's semi-atheism; as a Unitarian clergyman Estlin would, accordingly, have approved that the same man was a Christian. Both accounts, though contradictory, contain a grain of truth. It is possible that by the time he consorted with Godwin in February to August 1795 Wordsworth's strongly republican principles had become intertwined with atheism; although it is worth bearing in mind Nicholas Roe's suggestion that Wordsworth may have been present at, and could have suggested, the meeting of the Philomathean Society at which the subject for debate was, as Godwin noted in his diary, 'soldier v. priest' – both early ideas for a career for Wordsworth (though by that time it is almost certain that he was no longer thinking of a life in the

---

[85] Griggs i 216.
[86] Griggs i 327.
[87] Thelwall told Coleridge that Christianity was irrelevant to social reform; see CC *Lectures 1795* p. lxxii.

Church).[88] At all events, there is reason for supposing some religious scepticism on Wordsworth's part during the early to mid 1790s, which alienated him from his uncle, the Revd Dr William Cookson; Farington, for instance, reported that Wordsworth 'for a time had been a great supporter of French principles, which caused a coolness between them'.[89] Among these 'French principles' there might have been a degree of doubt uncongenial to a minister of the established Church, former tutor to the sons of George III, and Canon of St George's Chapel at Windsor Castle. In the 'Letter to the Bishop of Llandaff', Wordsworth had begun with an attack on ministers of the Church of England for having been 'the advocates of slavery civil and religious', and exaggerated Richard Watson's mild reference to the redistribution of Church property in revolutionary France so as to provide himself with a reason for an extended defence of that policy.[90] There is no cause to think that, with his rejection of rationalism, Wordsworth turned from being a sceptic to a devout Christian. No doubt he was capable of uttering semi-atheistic sentiments in 1796 and perhaps even in 1797. All the same, God is an unmistakable presence in the poetry of 1798 – though not in the same overt manner in which He is to be found in the verse of, say, Hannah More. He does not intervene in the Wordsworthian world, nor is close communion with Him seen to be the ultimate end of imaginative thought. Instead of finding 'God', Wordsworth finds 'Good' in others and an inherent 'joy' or 'love' in the natural world. In 'There is an active principle alive in all things', for instance, he is concerned with a 'Spirit' that 'circulates, the soul of all the worlds'.[91] In 'Not useless do I deem' Wordsworth attributes to a 'pure principle of love' found in natural forms the psychological tendency to 'seek for objects of a kindred love / In fellow-natures, and a kindred joy'.[92] There is an unfairness in presuming to stick labels on such beliefs which speak eloquently for themselves. But it does them no violence to suggest that they do not conform to the tenets of conventional Christian thought. In the broadest sense of the word they are theis-

---

[88]   Nicholas Roe, *Wordsworth and Coleridge: The Radical Years* (Oxford: Clarendon Press, 1988), p. 195. See also Roe's '"Atmospheric Air Itself": Medical Science, Politics and Poetry in Thelwall, Coleridge and Wordsworth', in *1798: The Year of the* Lyrical Ballads, ed. Richard Cronin (Houndmills: Macmillan, 1998), pp. 185–202. Roe tells me that Thelwall's lecture on animal vitality (1793) led to accusations of atheism.
[89]   Farington vi 2303.
[90]   *Prose Works* i 31, 34–5.
[91]   'There is an active principle alive in all things' 11. In much-revised form the passage was published as *Excursion* ix 1–52. Although the editors of Cornell *Lyrical Ballads* rightly date the fair copy to the Goslar period, it is consistent with the pantheist poetry of 1798, and may derive from drafts originally composed at Alfoxden.
[92]   'Not useless do I deem' 10–11.

tic, and no doubt would have been congenial to certain dissenting sects – as they were to Coleridge. The low profile maintained by the Christian Deity in these works tempts one to ask whether Wordsworth is in any sense pagan. Quite possibly. But no one-word label quite does him justice. What we can be sure of is that in place of the constant striving for union with an abstract deity, Wordsworth valorizes the softening down of 'feelings of aversion' between people, and their rediscovery of fellowship among themselves.

It was Godwin who had argued in 1793 that 'the moral characters of men originate in their perceptions,'[93] and whose vision of human perfectibility had given rise to Wordsworth's first major poem of social protest, 'Adventures on Salisbury Plain' (1795). Godwin's system never had much appeal for Coleridge, who had little truck with its atheism; but Wordsworth did not completely grow out of it. He imports Godwin's vision of social equality achieved through moral betterment into Coleridge's 'Recluse' scheme. That explains why Wordsworth referred consistently to the poem as designed 'to give pictures of Nature, Man, and Society'.[94] The three elements were interrelated and dependent on each other.

In the course of the *annus mirabilis* Wordsworth had come far. The preoccupation with betrayal and grief that had informed a vision of a poisoned world had taken its inspiration partly from a sophisticated understanding of human psychology. That knowledge gave Wordsworth access, with Coleridge's assistance, to a new aspect of the same theme – the redemptive power of the imagination. As with the shaping of Rivers and the torment of Margaret, psychological forces are understood to operate in a realm beyond consciousness. But where Rivers and Margaret were alienated, the same involuntary mechanisms confirm, in both a political and a cosmic sense, the individual's place in the world. Lest there be any misunderstanding, Wordsworth chose deliberately to write about a mongol so as to bear out the argument that even someone ostensibly removed from human intercourse could enjoy this profoundly spiritual sense of belonging. And when in late January or early February 1798 he came to revise 'The Ruined Cottage' the suffering of its protagonist, which in MS B was the object of the poem, came to be superseded by a quite different resolution. Where social and political injustice had led to misery and death, the new narrative breaks that cycle. Instead the poet-figure, to whom the tale of Margaret has been related, recognizes the grief he feels at her tragedy to be 'impotent'.[95] Grief is stripped of power. It is as if, looking back on the poetry

---

[93]   The title of *Political Justice*, Book I, chapter 3.
[94]   From his first mention of the poem in a letter of 6 March 1798 to James Tobin, *EY* 212.
[95]   'The Ruined Cottage' MS D, 500: 'I blessed her in the impotence of grief.'

he had composed up to this time, Wordsworth understood it to have emerged from the delayed mourning that had so empowered him as a writer in the summer of 1787. That had been valuable, no doubt, but as he revised 'The Ruined Cottage' for 'The Recluse', he realized that the exfoliation of that old skin was to be the first moral lesson of the new epic. Again, the means by which it was taught is a mental response beyond conscious control:

> I well remember that those very plumes,
> Those weeds, and the high spear-grass on that wall,
> By mist and silent rain-drops silver'd o'er,
> As once I passed did to my heart convey
> So still an image of tranquillity,
> So calm and still, and looked so beautiful,
> Amid the uneasy thoughts which filled my mind,
> That what we feel of sorrow and despair
> From ruin and from change, and all the grief
> The passing shews of being leave behind,
> Appeared an idle dream that could not live
> Where meditation was. I turned away
> And walked along my road in happiness.
>
> ('The Ruined Cottage' MS D, 513–25)

It was not that Wordsworth wished to neutralize his painstaking portrayal of Margaret's depression and derangement, nor that the pathos of her situation was being cast aside. But while avoiding either of these possibilities the poetry manages to propose something equally drastic. Instead of making the enshrinement of pain his object – the kind of thing expressed in Orpheus' repeated lamentations in the Cambridge translations – Wordsworth turns to a mental reflex, a habit of mind so customary to the Pedlar that he does not bother to explain it. By its means, the natural forms of the weeds and spear-grass communicate the cosmic awareness that human suffering is no more than an 'idle dream'. That understood, the Pedlar goes on his way 'in happiness'. In view of what Wordsworth has described in the preceding 500-odd lines, you have to remind yourself that there's nothing callous or hard-hearted about this.

The real question is not so much what the poetry means as whether it works. On one hand the tale of Margaret demands that we engage with a story of unmitigated sadness, while on the other we are expected to see eye to eye with a narrator who tells us that it can be resolved into 'tranquillity'. Can the poet have it both ways? It was in an effort to do so that Wordsworth composed the 355 lines of blank verse published in 1969 by Jonathan Wordsworth as 'The Pedlar', which attempts to explain how Armytage became capable of integrating pain and suffering into a redemptive vision. Only in the light of 'The

Pedlar' can MS D maintain its credibility, and perhaps not even then, for many readers still find Armytage's life too idealized, too programmed to persuade. The tension between ideal and reality – a universal throughout the history of ideas – was in this instance a tension between the aspirations of Coleridgean philosophy and Wordsworth's experience of loss. It is no surprise that he found 'The Recluse' impossible to complete; its aspirations cut across the grain of everything he had so far written, and were belied by events in his past. All the same, that tension was productive of some extraordinary poetry, partly because Wordsworth felt so assured of his ability to compose 'The Recluse'. Spring 1798 was, in all probability, the one moment at which the entire thing could have been written. He would spend the rest of his life wondering where all that confidence had gone, and attempting to reconstruct the sublime vision by which it had been informed.

6

'The vital spirit of a perfect form'

Thus have I look'd, nor ceas'd to look, oppress'd
By thoughts of what, and whither, when and how,
Until the shapes before my eyes became
A second-sight procession, such as glides
Over still mountains, or appears in dreams . . .
  (*The Thirteen-Book Prelude*, C-Stage text (1818–20), vii 596–600)

Part I: October 1798–April 1799

In June 1797 the world had been poisoned at the heart; six months later the Pedlar found it bathed 'In gladness and deep joy'.[1] There was something not fully Wordsworthian about the new-felt optimism of the moment, and Wordsworth himself must have sensed that. That's why, having accepted responsibility for writing the great millenarian epic, the poem that would bring the world as we know it to an end, he set about the quite different task of self-analysis in order to define his aims as a poet. In 1800 that ambition would be claimed as elemental to 'The Recluse':

> Possessions have I, wholly, solely mine,
> Something within, which yet is shared by none –
> Not even the nearest to me and most dear –
> Something which power and effort may impart.
> I would impart it; I would spread it wide,
> Immortal in the world which is to come.
>   ('Home at Grasmere' MS B, 897–902)

Wordsworth did not need 'The Recluse' or Coleridge in order to write these lines. The elevation of 'Something within, which yet is shared by none' to the status of an immortal gift to the world had no part in Coleridge's thinking.

---

[1] 'The Pedlar' 99.

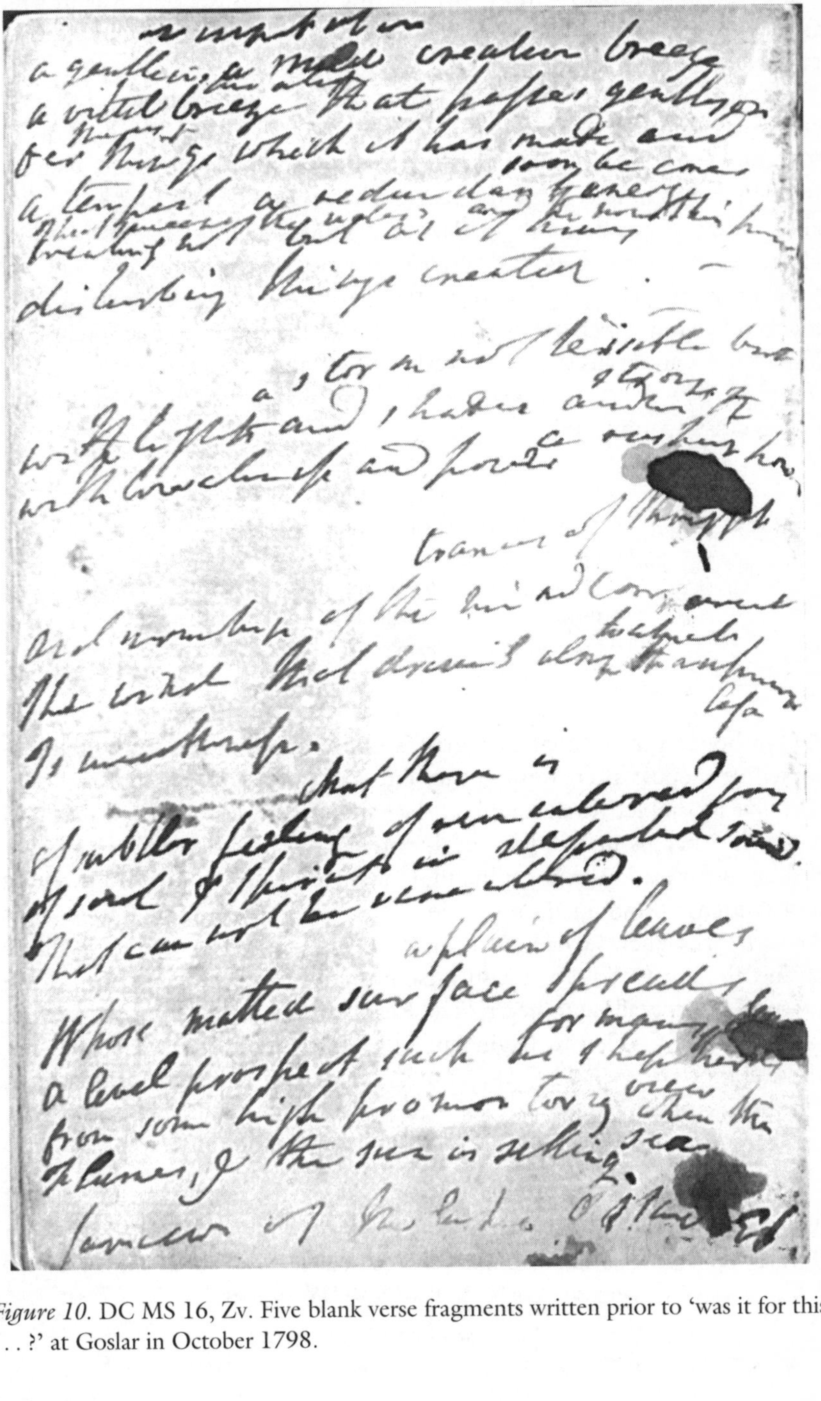

Figure 10. DC MS 16, Zv. Five blank verse fragments written prior to 'was it for this . . . ?' at Goslar in October 1798.

But by 1800 its incorporation into 'The Recluse' was the only way in which that poem could be made viable to its author. Even then, he would struggle to write it.

Having travelled to Germany in autumn 1798, which he believed to be the centre of the intellectual world (the appropriate residence for the poet of 'The Recluse'), Wordsworth there faced a major crisis in his creative life. Detained from fluent commerce with the natives, he was compelled to ask questions about what he was doing there. Anxieties about the future had been evident in the concluding passage of 'Tintern Abbey' where it was feared that 'solitude, or fear, or pain, or grief' might be Dorothy's fate, but in Goslar it was all the more vividly experienced as his inability to get on with 'The Recluse' led him to think about his sense of vocation.[2] Like all artists in such situations, he returned to his roots. In the first instance this related to 'The Recluse' only in being a distraction from it:

> was it for this
> That one, the fairest of all rivers, loved
> To blend his murmurs with my nurse's song
> And from his alder shades and rocky falls
> And from his fords and shallows sent a voice
> To intertwine my dreams . . .
>
> (MS JJ, 22–7)

As can be seen from Stephen Parrish's transcription in the Cornell edition, these lines appear after twenty other lines of blank verse, comprising no less than five incomplete draft fragments (see figure 10 overleaf). Even then, 'was it for this' begins in mid-line, mid-sentence, and continues in a breathless rush, as if frustration at not fulfilling Coleridge's expectations had given way to a sudden, unrestrained outpouring. This is a poet at the peak of his form, someone who knew he had great poetry in him yet, and wanted to pit himself against the greats. So it is not surprising that 'was it for this' at once implies exasperation for failing to begin 'The Recluse', and at the same time provides safe ground on which to begin building his new edifice in verse, as it is a classical topos he would have known from Hawkshead days.[3] For that reason it is the first of many deliberate references back to his poetic roots. So used are

---

[2] These meditations may have been prompted by Wordsworth's reading of the Bible in German. His copy is now at the Wordsworth Library.

[3] It had been used by a host of British authors, including Wordsworth's friend from London days, Francis Wrangham, in *The Destruction of Babylon* 13–16:

> Was it for this those wondrous turrets rose,
> Which taught thy feebled youth a scorn of foes?

we to reading them as the opening lines of the two-part *Prelude* that one has
to remind oneself that at the time he composed them in the same notebook
into which he drafted 'There was a boy' (ostensibly as part of the same endeavour), he had no idea what it was called, or whether it would amount to a
single, discrete work.

He was once more thinking about involuntary mental process. The 'voice'
of the Derwent, having been indistinguishable from the lullabies sung to the
infant poet by his 'nurse', has intertwined his dreams. At the same time he has
abandoned the pantheism of the Alfoxden poetry in favour of a literary neo-
classicism, turning to 'ye beings of the hills / And ye that walk the woods and
open heaths':

> thus from my first day
> Of childhood did ye love to interweave
> The passions
> Not with the mean & vullgar works of man
> But with high objects with eternal things
> With life & nature, purifying thus
> The elements of feiling & of thought
> And sanctifying by such disc[i]pline
> Both pain & fear untill we recognize
> A grandeur in the beatings of the heart.
>
> (MS JJ, 70–9)

Nature's silent, unbidden ministrations are akin to a purification ritual whereby
natural forms cleanse 'the elements of feiling & of thought' and sanctify 'pain
& fear'. If it was ever true that Wordsworth subscribed to a natural religion, it
was now, in October 1798, as he composed these lines. Here he senses, in a
wholly unforced manner, the living, organic power of natural things. It has
little to do with the 'one life' so characteristic of the Coleridge-influenced
verse written earlier that year; they are part of a distinctively Wordsworthian
way of seeing nature.

There are other respects too in which these lines represent a departure from
'The Recluse'. Whenever he spoke of it Coleridge went out of his way to
emphasize the poem's all-encompassing range. In April 1797 he told Cottle

---

For this that earth her mineral stores resigned;
And the wan artist, child of sorrow, pined . . .

If Wordsworth recalled these lines as he began drafting in MS JJ, he may well have thought
of himself as the 'wan artist' of the moment. (Wordsworth is likely to have read the poem in
manuscript, which had been completed in 1795, and was the subject of an enquiry in a
letter to Wrangham of November 1795; see *EY* 159.)

that he would have spent ten years reading in preparation for it and, when he reminded Wordsworth of the encyclopaedic scope of 'The Recluse' in 1815, it was clear that only a highly trained polymath could ever have written it. This was never true of *The Prelude*. No amount of reading could have helped Wordsworth in his pursuit of it, for it was informed less by philosophy than by his own talent for self-analysis. While not hermetic, it was informed largely by memory – just the project for someone trapped in a small town in a foreign country with limited access to books. Dependent to a much larger degree on his inner resources than at Alfoxden, Wordsworth found himself returning both in theme and subject to the creative world he had inhabited prior to June 1797.

At Alfoxden Coleridge had shown him new ways of thinking and bestowed on him a role – that of author of 'The Recluse'. Wordsworth's response should have been to get on with it but instead he found himself questioning it. In fact, the draft in MS JJ is evidence of a profound lack of confidence. That's why it is significant that at the moment he began to write the two-part *Prelude* he had no inkling of what it was to be. He cannot have realized that this was the great project of his life, nor that it would eventually replace 'The Recluse' as his masterwork. So far as he was concerned he was articulating, in some private writing, composed in a very personal manner, a sense of self-doubt. For that reason it is erroneous to present the MS JJ draft as an early version of *The Prelude*.[4] It is not finished and never would be; it is, literally, a draft – and an untitled and fragmentary one at that. Behind the struggle to find the interrogative manner with which it begins there is desperation. It is the same impulse that seeks assurance from the deities of the Lake District – 'Ah not in vain ye spirits of the springs'.

The self-focusing tendency of this writing conveniently placed him beyond Coleridge's reach. Coleridge was easily Wordsworth's superior as a philosopher: he was more widely read, more agile, and had the confidence of a zealot. Humiliatingly, Wordsworth would always look to him for clues as to what 'The Recluse' was supposed to say. And when he failed that test (as was inevitable), Coleridge would reproach him with lectures on 'The Recluse'. Against those demands, the poem on his own life represented a retreat from philosophy to a subject over which he had sovereign command. Implicitly, he seems to have understood that the millenarian scheme devised by Coleridge had been a false step, a deviation from the themes that inspired him in earlier years.

---

[4]   See, for instance, *William Wordsworth: The Prelude: The Four Texts (1798, 1799, 1805, 1850)* ed. Jonathan Wordsworth (London: Penguin, 1995), where it is presented as a poem, 'Was it for this'. Wordsworth more circumspectly presents it as 'A connected sequence of 150 lines' in the Norton *Prelude*, p. 487.

These factors provide a context for his statement in December 1798 that he was 'obliged to write in self-defence'.[5] The ostensible explanation was lack of books, but on another level he was defending himself against the controlling tendencies of Coleridge and the straitjacketing effect of a poem he feared (quite correctly) he could not write. At the time Dorothy copied out the skating scene, 'Nutting', and the boat-stealing episode into a letter for Coleridge in December 1798, the passages in MS JJ were still not thought of as parts of the same work. She refers in passing to 'the mass of what William has written'[6] – indicating that they too were unclear as to its status. It is also evident that they did not wish to tell Coleridge too much about it. He was shown nothing that would reveal what *The Prelude* actually was; 'Nutting' and the skating passage are described as 'scenes', 'some lines', but not 'his poem'. The secret would be kept until October 1799, a year after it had been started. When Coleridge told them of his pleasure at the news, he inadvertently justified their reticence: 'I long to see what you have been doing. O let it be the tail-piece of the "Recluse"! for of nothing but the "Recluse" can I hear patiently.'[7]

It was within this context that Wordsworth returned to the motifs and patterns that had sustained him prior to the Alfoxden year. This is clearest in the three episodes with which the two-part *Prelude* begins, which describe woodcock-snaring, birds'-nesting and boat-stealing. Each returns to an old Wordsworthian haunt: the psychology of guilt.

> Gentle Powers!
> Who give us happiness and call it peace!
> When scudding on from snare to snare I plied
> My anxious visitation, hurrying on,
> Still hurrying hurrying onward, how my heart
> Panted . . .
>
> (*The Two-Part Prelude* i 35–40)

As he understands the part played in his life by feelings of culpability, he sees himself guided by 'Gentle Powers' which act as guardians – 'Retired and seldom recognized, yet kind'.[8] Guilt and trauma have been domesticated, incorporated into a larger schema. And when he talks about other powers which use 'Severer interventions, ministry / More palpable',[9] it is clear that their function is tutelary. They are responsible for rites of passage in which the

---

5   *EY* 236.
6   *EY* 240.
7   Griggs i 538.
8   *The Two-Part Prelude* i 74.
9   *The Two-Part Prelude* i 79–80.

young poet is brought into very close proximity not just with these powers but with life and death. Clearly pagan, unrelated to a Christian God, they are the means by which the natural world shapes the spirit. Wordsworth is thinking not as Coleridge wanted him to, attempting to embark on philosophical disquisitions about millenarian topics; instead his attention is fastened on his psychological growth and the way in which the traumas of early life had shaped him. This was a more personal and private work than 'The Recluse' could ever be, and refers back to the pre-Alfoxden poetry in obvious thematic respects.

By the time Wordsworth got on to the central spots of time in Part I he was consciously reworking motifs from the earlier verse. In the first, the young poet witnesses the dredging of Esthwaite Water for a drowned man.

> Ere I had seen
> Eight summers (and 'twas in the very week
> When I was first transplanted to thy vale,
> Beloved Hawkshead! when thy paths, thy shores
> And brooks were like a dream of novelty
> To my half-infant mind) I chanced to cross
> One of those open fields which, shaped like ears,
> Make green peninsulas on Esthwaite's lake.
> Twilight was coming on, yet through the gloom
> I saw distinctly on the opposite shore
> Beneath a tree and close by the lake side
> A heap of garments, as if left by one
> Who there was bathing: half an hour I watched
> And no one owned them: meanwhile the calm lake
> Grew dark with all the shadows on its breast,
> And now and then a leaping fish disturbed
> The breathless stillness. The succeeding day
> There came a company, and in their boat
> Sounded with iron hooks and with long poles.
> At length the dead man 'mid that beauteous scene
> Of trees, and hills, and water, bolt upright
> Rose with his ghastly face.

(i 258–79)

The heap of clothes on the shore of the lake is a clue surviving from the kind of story in which evidence must be assembled to find answers. *Caleb Williams*, the first modern crime novel, had been published in 1794 and Wordsworth had known its author, William Godwin, very well.[10] 'Adventures on Salisbury

---

[10] See Nicholas Roe, *Wordsworth and Coleridge: The Radical Years* (Oxford: Clarendon Press, 1988), pp. 192–8; *WR* i 66–7.

Plain' and *The Borderers* had both, in different respects, conformed to the aesthetic demands of the whodunnit. But there is something not quite straightforward about the episode, or the way it resolves.

As he descends beneath the 'breast' of the lake, the drowned man figuratively repeats Orpheus' journey with which Wordsworth had been preoccupied a decade before. Subsumed into the 'breathless stillness', the boy seems to have traced his steps, at least in imagination – for it is he whose breathlessness is projected on the landscape as he stares fixedly into the waters before him. In short, the poetry is intent on describing how the scene was perceived and is now remembered, rather than how it actually was. An ostensible interest in the facts of the matter, as suggested by the heap of garments, turns out to be a red herring.

The relation this passage bears to conventional narrative is essentially parodic, for when the denouement comes it is told with what seems to be deliberate incompetence.

> At length the dead man 'mid that beauteous scene
> Of trees, and hills, and water, bolt upright
> Rose with his ghastly face.

The discovery is treated almost with contempt, thrown away in two and a half lines, but in mythic terms it is a stroke of genius, for the man's disruptive re-entry into the world of the living violates the concept of the underworld journey in the most horrible way. It is as if, having made his descent, the man has been vomited back into his proper realm, punished for trespassing into forbidden territory, ruthlessly stripped of life and humanity. Like the hooks and poles that have fetched him from the deep, he has become an object. His face is 'ghastly' and therefore, by a shift of vowel, 'ghostly'. There is something chimerical about him, and it may be no accident that a verbal echo recalls the dragon in Sandys' translation of Ovid, which Wordsworth had known since Hawkshead days, who '*bolt-upright* his monstrous length displaies / More than half-way, and all the woods survaies'.[11] The more frightening the better, from Wordsworth's point of view. It is for this very reason – the fear it inspires in the onlooker – that the memory can be claimed as educative; it 'impressed my mind / With images'.[12] Those sublime, uncontrollable emotions help bury them in the seedbed of the imagination. They are preserved there in an Esthwaite more vivid than its real-life counterpart. In that interior realm the lake is uncannily humanized; the stillness is 'breathless'; the man, who we are

---

[11]   George Sandys, *Ovid's Metamorphoses Englished* (Oxford, 1632), iii 45–6.
[12]   *The Two-Part Prelude* i 283–4.

assured is dead, rises 'bolt upright' from the depths, coarsely mimicking the ways of the living. As the boy stares into the void, everything undergoes change.

Coleridge could take some credit for the poetry Wordsworth composed at Alfoxden, but nothing he had to say could have helped Wordsworth write with greater conviction or authority than he does here. Wordsworth has returned to the matter and style of his Hawkshead and Cambridge verse. The true precursor of the drowned man of Esthwaite is 'The Dog – An Idyllium', probably composed in 1786, and discussed in chapter 2 above (see pp. 20–2). It is a mock elegy for an animal by no means deceased at the time of composition, and takes an unexpected turn in its concluding lines:

> If while I gazed to Nature blind
> On the calm Ocean of my mind
> Some new created Image rose
> In full grown beauty at its birth
> Lovely as Venus from the sea
> Then while my glad hand sprung to thee
> – We were the happiest pair on earth.

Wordsworth conducts us from the exterior reality – the 'remorseless deep' into which the dog has disappeared – into 'the calm Ocean of my mind', out of which the 'new created Image' rises up, 'Lovely as Venus from the sea'. The dog's fate is neither here nor there; what matters is its continuing existence in the mind. Likewise, for all the questions begged by the man's clothes – the possibility of foul play, misadventure and the rest – what matters to Wordsworth is not the working through of narrative possibility, but that the man lives on as a memory

> to which in following years
> Far other feelings were attached, with forms
> That yet exist with independent life
> And, like their archetypes, know no decay.

(i 284–7)

He will enjoy immortality though of an unexpected kind. As an image to which intense emotions have been 'attached' he has achieved permanence as the inspiration for great verse. He enjoys an afterlife in the perpetual present of the imagination, mediated through Wordsworth's mind and those of his readers.

In the second spot of time Wordsworth's younger self becomes separated from his grandparents' servant, 'honest James', who was escorting him home from school.

I remember well
('Tis of an early season that I speak,
The twilight of rememberable life)
While I was yet an urchin, one who scarce
Could hold a bridle, with ambitious hopes
I mounted, and we rode towards the hills;
We were a pair of horsemen: honest James
Was with me, my encourager and guide.
We had not travelled long ere some mischance
Disjoined me from my comrade, and through fear
Dismounting, down the rough and stony moor
I led my horse and, stumbling on, at length
Came to a bottom where in former times
A man, the murderer of his wife, was hung
In irons; mouldered was the gibbet mast,
The bones were gone, the iron and the wood,
Only a long green ridge of turf remained
Whose shape was like a grave. I left the spot,
And, reascending the bare slope, I saw
A naked pool that lay beneath the hills,
The beacon on the summit, and more near
A girl who bore a pitcher on her head
And seemed with difficult steps to force her way
Against the blowing wind. It was in truth
An ordinary sight but I should need
Colours and words that are unknown to man
To paint the visionary dreariness
Which, while I looked all round for my lost guide,
Did, at that time, invest the naked pool,
The beacon on the lonely eminence,
The woman and her garments vexed and tossed
By the strong wind.

(i 296–327)

Again, the motif of the underworld descent resonates with the classical models that preoccupied Wordsworth a decade before. This time we are to be disappointed, like the boy:

          . . . mouldered was the gibbet-mast,
          The bones were gone, the iron and the wood,
          Only a long green ridge of turf remained
          Whose shape was like a grave.

The turf was *like* a grave – which is not to say that it was one. The gibbet, bones and iron have vanished too. They tell us everything about the boy's anxieties, but nothing of what was actually before him. In fact, the valley-bottom into which the young boy thought he had wandered was Cowdrake Quarry, east of Penrith; Thomas Nicholson was hanged in 1767 on nearby Red Hill for having murdered Thomas Parker, a butcher. But Nicholson's gibbet had not 'mouldered down' in 1775, and a 5-year-old could not have ridden that far. As in the drowned man episode, expectations are being teased. At first we are offered spooks, but the props required to bear out such fears are conspicuously absent.

It is in the belief that he has seen a grave (as opposed to an innocent ridge of turf) that he climbs the valley to see nothing out of the ordinary – a girl with a pitcher, the Penrith beacon, a pool of water – all infused with an intensity that haunts him. The objects are in no way peculiar ('It was in truth / An ordinary sight'), but the manner in which they are perceived – and, later, described – is.

> . . . I should need
> Colours and words that are unknown to man
> To paint the visionary dreariness
> Which, while I looked all round for my lost guide,
> Did, at that time, invest the naked pool,
> The beacon on the lonely eminence,
> The woman and her garments vexed and tossed
> By the strong wind.

As with the 'breast' of the calm lake, natural objects mysteriously acquire human qualities: the pool is 'naked', the eminence 'lonely'. If their vulnerability reminds us of the boy's desperation in being separated from honest James, it is worth bearing in mind that the poet states that it was not him but James who was lost: 'while I looked all round for my *lost* guide'. Though alienated from his surroundings, the boy has arrived in a landscape that has the familiarity of dreams, full of features that seem to embody his state of mind. They are, in a sense, produced by it. Like the landscape of nightmare, this is a world that seems more solid than reality. He may have emerged from the valley, but the boy has returned from the underworld with possessions 'wholly, solely mine'.

Wordsworth signals possession through tautology. The technique is analogous to the literal repetition found in the juvenilia where Orpheus had lamented Eurydice.

> He wandering far along the lonely main
> Sooth'd with the hollow shell his sickly pain
> Thee, thee dear wife he sung forlorn
> From morn to eve – and thee from eve to morn.[13]

---

[13]   Cornell *Early Poems* 638.

Orpheus too is signalling emotional (if not physical) possession through tautology; as Wordsworth noted in his Note to 'The Thorn': 'now every man must know that an attempt is rarely made to communicate impassioned feelings without something of an accompanying consciousness of the inadequateness of our own powers, or the deficiencies of language. During such efforts there will be a craving in the mind, and as long as it is unsatisfied the Speaker will cling to the same words, or words of the same character.'[14] With characteristic shrewdness he has singled out the hinge on which each spot of time turns: an unsatisfied craving in the mind.

Repetition need not be exclusively verbal. When he began work on 'The Ruined Cottage' in 1797 Wordsworth started not at the opening but with its conclusion, where the Pedlar describes Margaret's increasing depression at the disappearance of her husband and the deaths of her children:

> I have heard, my Friend,
> That in that broken arbour she would sit
> The idle length of half a sabbath day,
> There – where you see the toadstool's lazy head –
> And when a dog passed by she still would quit
> The shade and look abroad. On this old Bench
> For hours she sate, and evermore her eye
> Was busy in the distance, shaping things
> Which made her heart beat quick.
> ('The Ruined Cottage' MS B, 485–93)

Like Orpheus, Margaret is engaged in an imaginative act, as her mind shapes what she sees in the far distance in the hope that it might be her long-lost husband. The solecism is deliberate and effective: though her eye has not detached itself from the rest of her body to travel to the far horizon it might have done, so irresistible is the craving for what has been taken from her. The repetition is not precisely verbal because it is internalized. Like Orpheus, she laments Robert inwardly; like the boy by Esthwaite Water, she is drawn into the breathless stillness of an imagined reality generated by intense emotion. The slave of yearnings that cannot be satisfied, her mind is fixated on a single object and treads the same mental territory over and over again. (Margaret literally traces the same path 'through many a day / Of the warm summer'.)[15] Perhaps a better name for it would be 'second sight'.[16] The 'calm ocean of the

14 Cornell *Lyrical Ballads* 351.
15 'The Ruined Cottage' MS B, 495–6.
16 I allude to the passage from the C-stage text of the *Thirteen-Book Prelude*, vii 596–600 quoted as the epigraph to this chapter. The concept of the second-sight procession, which

mind' into which the 16-year-old poet had 'gazed' in the hope of seeing his dog is another example.

There is tautology in the second spot of time too, for Wordsworth describes the 'ordinary sight' twice: once at lines 314–19, and then, having said that he would need 'Colours and words that are unknown to man' to describe the 'visionary dreariness', again at lines 324–7. That second glance is subtly different from the first. The beacon which had been situated on the 'summit' is now on a 'lonely eminence' and the 'girl who bore a pitcher on her head' changed into a 'woman and her garments vexed and tossed / By the strong wind'. Repetition is introduced so as to disclose 'impassioned feelings' that have become attached to these images and cause them to assume a life of their own. Without authorial commentary, however, it is hard to be certain as to the part played by these forces. The third spot of time brings the argument into focus.

It returns us to 19 December 1783, when the young poet waited for horses to take him and his brothers from Hawkshead Grammar School to Cockermouth.

> . . . 'twas a day
> Stormy, and rough, and wild, and on the grass
> I sate, half-sheltered by a naked wall;
> Upon my right hand was a single sheep,
> A whistling hawthorn on my left, and there,
> Those two companions at my side, I watched
> With eyes intensely straining as the mist
> Gave intermitting prospects of the wood
> And plain beneath. Ere I to school returned
> That dreary time, ere I had been ten days
> A dweller in my Father's house, he died,
> And I and my two Brothers, orphans then,
> Followed his body to the grave.
>
> (i 341–53)

As in earlier episodes, it is with the act of perception that Wordsworth is concerned: 'I watched / With eyes intensely straining.' The verse is expertly manipulated; the run-on line, stresses on 'watched' and 'eyes', and that compelling phrase, 'intensely straining', leave us in no doubt of the boy's attentive

goes back to Wordsworth's earliest poetry, has been discussed by W. J. B. Owen, '"A Second-Sight Procession" in Wordsworth's London', *N&Q* 16 (1969) 49–50. Owen glosses 'second-sight' as 'visionary'. See also Wordsworth's 'When in my bed I lay', Cornell *Lyrical Ballads* 316.

peering into those 'intermitting prospects'. As before, an undeviating fixation has become the correlative of tautology as the mind draws shapes out of ether. Wordsworth again thwarts narrative expectation which logically might lead us to think that something is about to happen. Instead there is a hiatus as the poetry throws away in five lines what might have provided a narrative climax:

> Ere I to school returned
> That dreary time, ere I had been ten days
> A dweller in my Father's house, he died,
> And I and my two Brothers, orphans then,
> Followed his body to the grave.

These lines are more precise that those in 'The Vale of Esthwaite' which describe the same thing. There, the father's death and the boy's return were conflated; he had gone back to 'sorrow o'er a Father's bier'. Here, Wordsworth takes care to point out that John Wordsworth died ten days after his arrival. And that phrase, 'orphans then', is casually dropped in at the end of the line, as if it hardly signifies. In one sense it doesn't because the episode is concerned less with linear narrative than with memory and imagination:

> The event
> With all the sorrow which it brought appeared
> A chastisement, and when I called to mind
> That day so lately passed when from the crag
> I looked in such anxiety of hope,
> With trite reflections of morality
> Yet with the deepest passion I bowed low
> To God, who thus corrected my desires . . .
>
> (ll. 353–60)

As I suggested in chapter 1, the 'Vale' constructs a fiction of reproach whereby grief in the present (1787) is held to expiate a feeling of culpability at not having mourned his father sufficiently in 1783. *The Prelude* is characteristically more detailed and in some ways more complex. Here the tautological impulses of the mind, its peering into the ether, are invoked as evidence against the boy's troubled conscience. It turns his father's death into divine punishment for the 'trite reflections of morality' and the 'anxiety of hope', about which we have not previously heard. These rash judgements, which work against the poet, turn him into his father's murderer. This goes a good deal further than the poetry of 1787; Wordsworth probably could not have taken that extra step had he not explored guilt and the figure of the betrayer in works written subsequently.

It is significant that, in the *Prelude* version, there is an ironic element not present in 1787. This is understandable given that the boy's perspective, which in 1787 had been little different from that of three and a half years before, is by 1799 over a decade in the past. By presenting his point of view so faithfully the poetry quite deliberately presents a judgement which the reader knows to be unfair. In so doing it prompts us to ask what lies behind it. It seems to me that the rash judgement so accurately described here derives from feelings of anger. In 1787 Wordsworth felt angry at his father's death, and angry at his own failure fully to understand its significance at the time. Looking back on those feelings, the adult poet implicitly comments on the belief system that led his boyhood self to feel culpability when in truth he was innocent.

As the passage moves towards its conclusion, it draws these strands together into another extended tautology:

> And afterwards the wind, and sleety rain,
> And all the business of the elements,
> The single sheep, and the one blasted tree,
> And the bleak music of that old stone wall,
> The noise of wood and water, and the mist
> Which on the line of each of those two roads
> Advanced in such indisputable shapes,
> All these were spectacles and sounds to which
> I often would repair, and thence would drink
> As at a fountain, and I do not doubt
> That in this later time when storm and rain
> Beat on my roof at midnight, or by day
> When I am in the woods, unknown to me
> The workings of my spirit thence are brought.
>
> (i 361–74)

The 'blasted tree' is a more powerfully symbolic natural object than the hawthorn bush; the 'naked wall' has become the source of a 'bleak music'; and most evocatively the mist has matured into 'indisputable shapes' which take on a momentum of their own, advancing along each fork in the road. Critics have found powerfully evocative literary analogues for what is going on here. Jonathan Wordsworth writes of the echo of the 'questionable shape'[17] of the ghost in *Hamlet*,[18] while Gordon Thomas points out that the convergence of the three roads north of Borwick Lodge mirrors the location at which Oedipus' father, Laius, was killed – in Sophocles' treatment (which Wordsworth

---

[17] *Hamlet* I iv 43.
[18] See *Borders of Vision* 63; also Jonathan Bate, *Shakespeare and the English Romantic Imagination* (Oxford: Clarendon Press, 1986), p. 116.

read at Cambridge),[19] 'where three roads meet'.[20] Both refer us to the theme
first mooted in July 1787: unexpiated guilt. In 'The Vale of Esthwaite' the
poet's attention had turned to the inability or failure to mourn his father
adequately at the time of his death; by 1798 that has become a more mythic
construction – that the boy had in some inscrutable way colluded with the
forces that brought his father to his fate. Although Hamlet and Oedipus provide literary authority for it, Wordsworth's own past writing establishes the
potency of the myth beyond question. Over the last decade he has returned
again and again to the themes of betrayal and guilt, and the casting of himself
in the role of betrayer represents its culmination.

One further surprise lies in store. The expectation of a story has resulted in
a tautologous memory that shows the poet acting out a myth of his own
creation. That is extraordinary enough; but it is then compared with a fountain from which he takes refreshment.

> . . . and I do not doubt
> That in this later time when storm and rain
> Beat on my roof at midnight, or by day
> When I am in the woods, unknown to me
> The workings of my spirit thence are brought.

The poetry makes a chronological leap at line 371, when Wordsworth moves
from an after-recollection of the episode (which could have occurred at any
time subsequent to 1783) to the present of December 1798, as he hears the
wind and rain outside his lodgings at Goslar. The weather provides an associative connection between past and present, and takes us beyond that to a spiritual realm. Such memories as his father's demise and the circumstances which
surrounded it are explicitly presented as evidence of subconscious mental activity: 'unknown to me / The workings of my spirit thence are brought.'

That Part I is so accomplished should not blind us to the fact that it draws
heavily on the insights of the juvenilia. It is a deliberate attempt to re-establish
contact with the motifs and ideas that had inspired Wordsworth at Hawkshead
and Cambridge, and from which he probably felt distanced. 'The Recluse'
would demand a prodigious range of knowledge and theoretical skill – things
Wordsworth conspicuously didn't have, and which gave away the fact that it
had been designed by and for Coleridge. Unable to get on with it, the only
way for Wordsworth to assure himself of his vocation was to write a poem of

---

[19]   WR i 129.
[20]   Gordon Thomas, '"Orphans Then": Death in the *Two-Part Prelude*', *CLB* NS 96 (October 1996) 157–73.

his own design. Before he could begin Part II, he would subject his friendship with Coleridge, and its strange fruit, to close scrutiny.

Between Parts I and II: April–May 1799

Wordsworth might be expected to have shown Part I to Coleridge but did not; only in early October was Coleridge informed of it, and even then it was not made clear whether or not it was part of 'The Recluse'. This must have been deliberate, and is explicable by reference to the fact that the poem (which still had no title) had no part in Coleridge's scheme. Coleridge, the self-appointed monitor of Wordsworth's creative life, would not have approved of it. The lack of title therefore had a tactical significance; as long as it had none it could be taken for potential 'Recluse' material even if it was not.

As he concluded Part I, prior to 21 April 1799, Wordsworth found himself appealing hopefully for the friendly eye of the conveniently absent Coleridge. By this time he knew that the draft that had begun with the phrase, 'was it for this', was a long poem that would have further sections:

> Nor will it seem to thee, my Friend, so prompt
> In sympathy, that I have lengthened out
> With fond and feeble tongue a tedious tale.
> Meanwhile my hope has been that I might fetch
> Reproaches from my former years, whose power
> May spur me on, in manhood now mature,
> To honourable toil.

(ll. 447–53)

It is wishful of Wordsworth to characterize Coleridge as 'prompt / In sympathy'. No doubt Coleridge was supportive, but Wordsworth desperately needed to assure himself of the fact. The possibility that he has done nothing but drag out a tale described as 'fond', 'feeble' and tedious' is rather more persuasive, stemming as it does from the failure to begin work on 'The Recluse' (that, after all, had been the origin of the two-Part *Prelude* in the first place). In view of that, Coleridge might be thought likely to espouse a more critical view of the *Prelude*. How odd, then, that it is 'former years' rather than Coleridge which are held to reproach him, spurring him on to the 'honourable toil' of 'The Recluse'. Wordsworth has it the wrong way round, as is often the case with wishful thinkers: Coleridge was the one most likely to reproach him, and effectively did so when he first heard about *The Prelude*; whereas Wordsworth's 'former years' provided the encouragement he needed to continue the poem which it was his destiny to write. The confusion is understandable: it is what Wordsworth wanted to believe.

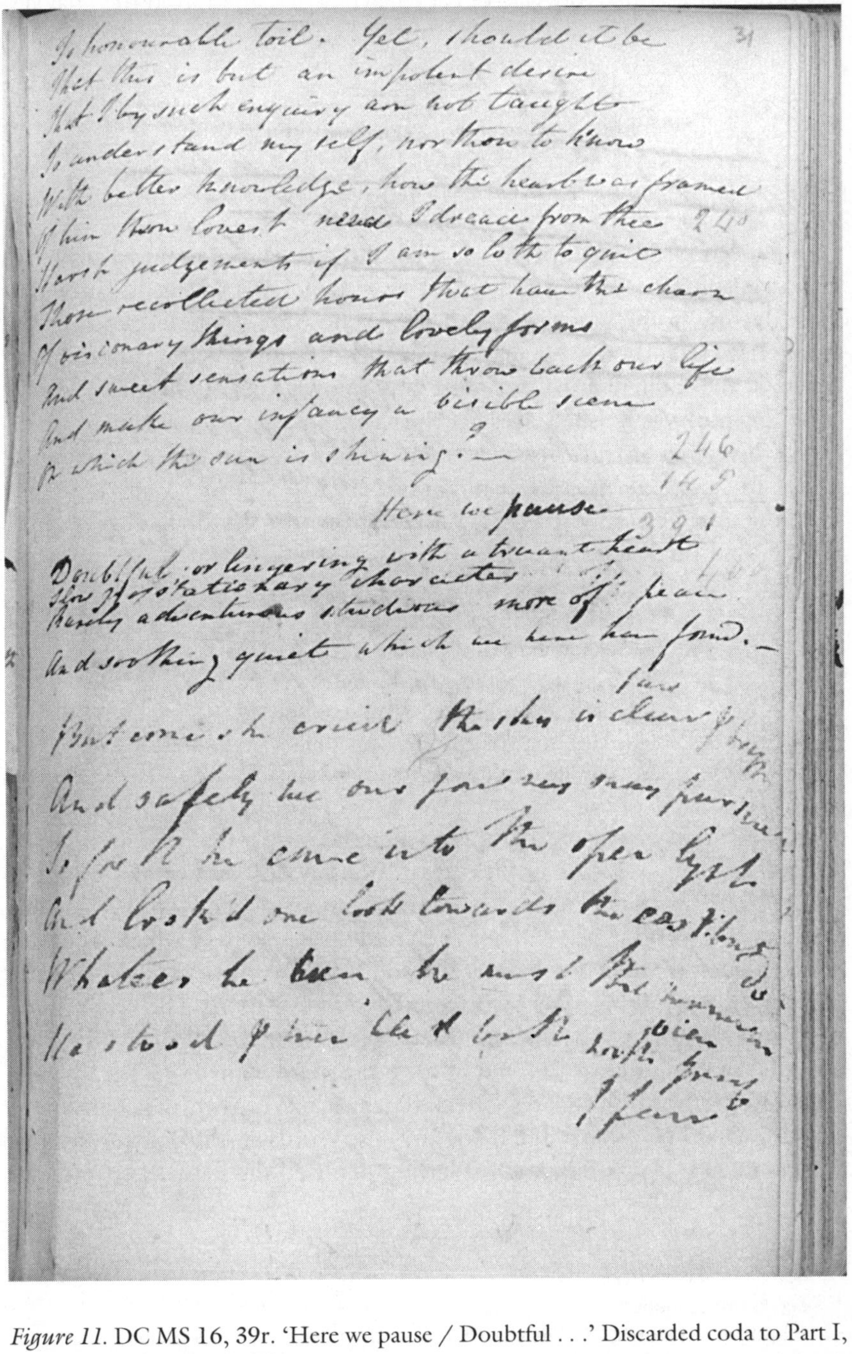
Is honourable toil. Yet, should it be
That this is but an impotent desire
That I by such enquiry am not taught
To understand myself, nor thou to know
With better knowledge how the heart was framed
Of him thou lovest, need I dread from thee
Harsh judgements if I am so loth to quit
Those recollected hours that have the charm
Of visionary things and lovely forms
And sweet sensations that throw back our life
And make our infancy a visible scene
On which the sun is shining? —

Here we pause
Doubtful or lingering with a truant heart
Slow & stationary character
Rarely adventurous studious more of peace
And soothing quiet which we here have found. —

Figure 11. DC MS 16, 39r. 'Here we pause / Doubtful . . .' Discarded coda to Part I, composed in late April 1799.

In the manuscript Wordsworth added a coda discarded from the final version:

> Here we pause
> Doubtful; or lingering with a truant heart
> Rarely adventurous studious more of peace
> And soothing quiet which we here have found. – [21]

Pausing 'Doubtful' was not a good sign. He was uneasy about what he had embarked on, and the possibility that he was literally playing 'truant' from 'The Recluse' was a very real one. That was how the sympathetic Coleridge would have seen things. He may have wished for the 'peace / And soothing quiet' of the fulfilled artist but must have known he wouldn't have it until 'The Recluse' was finished. Despite their wish to assert the serenity of fulfilment, these lines are full of anxiety about the uneasy situation of thanking his absent friend for a sympathy he might not grant.

At the time he composed these lines Wordsworth also drafted an opening for the '2nd Part' of the poem:

> Friend of my heart & Genius we had reach'd
> A small green island which I was well pleased
> To pass not lightly by for though I felt
> Strength unabated yet I seem'd to need
> Thy cheering voice or ere I could pursue
> My voyage, resting else for ever there[22]

Wordsworth may have aborted this opening because it declared his insecurities too openly; as Jonathan Wordsworth observes, it 'shows the extent to which Wordsworth depended on Coleridge's approval of his work'.[23] I would go further. Coleridge had still not been told of the poem of which they were part, and would not be for another six months. How, then, could he offer his 'cheering voice' before Wordsworth embarked on Part II? The very suggestion must have made Wordsworth feel guilt, and may have thrown into question that opening phrase, 'Friend of my heart'. How much of a friend could Coleridge be, however well respected his genius, if Wordsworth was unable to tell him what he was writing? It was not just Wordsworth's insecurities that were speaking; it was the sense of having betrayed the trust that Coleridge

---

[21] See figure 11 overleaf.
[22] See figure 12 opposite.
[23] William Wordsworth, *The Prelude: The Four Texts (1798, 1799, 1805, 1850)*, ed. Jonathan Wordsworth (London: Penguin, 1995), p. 549.

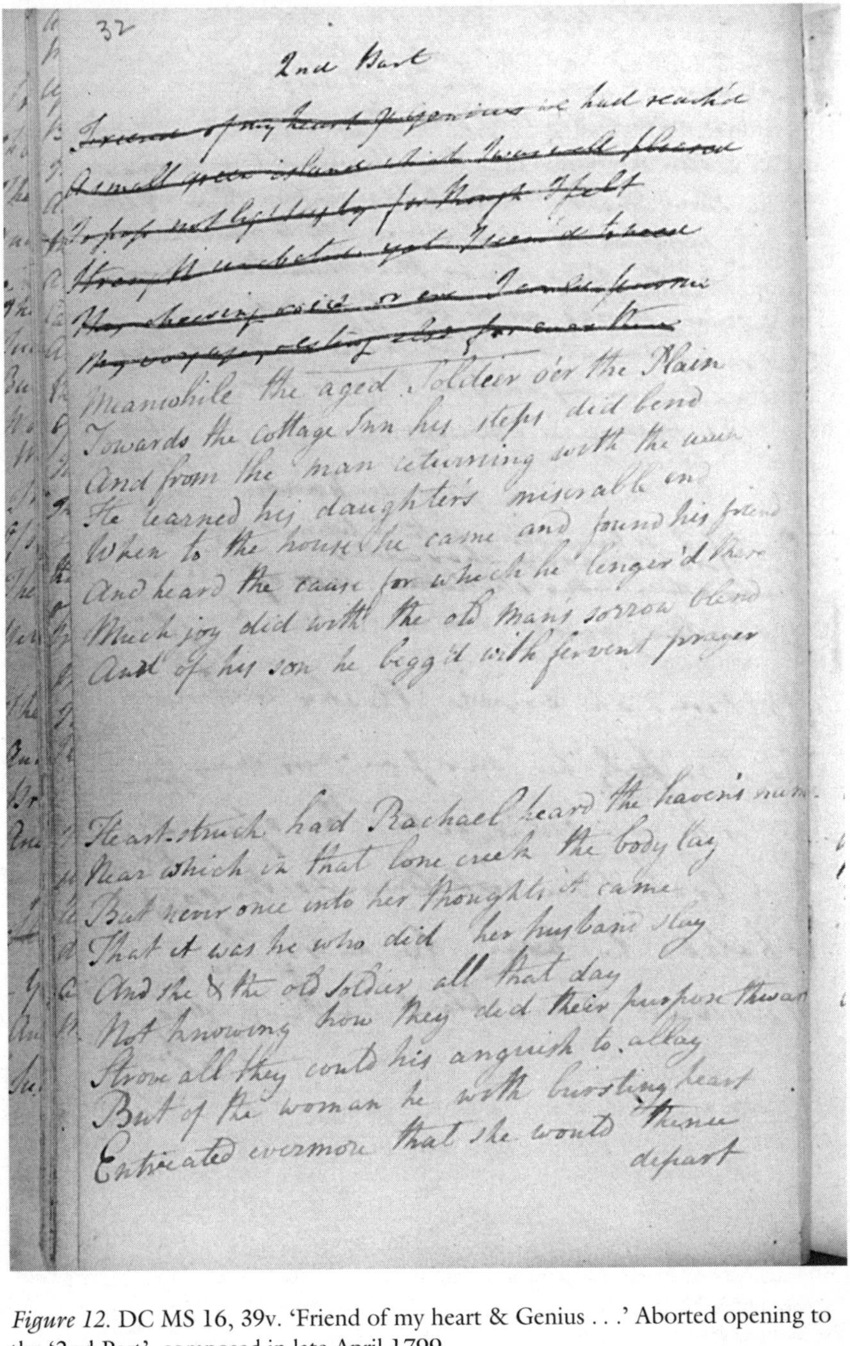
32

2nd Part

~~Friend of my heart & genius we had reach'd~~
~~A small green island which [illegible]~~
~~To pass not lightly by for though I felt~~
~~[illegible]~~
~~[illegible]~~
~~[illegible]~~

Meanwhile the aged Soldier o'er the Plain
Towards the cottage Inn his steps did bend
And from the man returning with the wain
He learned his daughter's miserable end
When to the house he came and found his friend
And heard the cause for which he linger'd there
Much joy did with the old man's sorrow blend
And of his son he begg'd with fervent prayer

Heart-struck had Rachael heard the heaven's [illegible]
Near which in that lone creek the body lay
But never once into her thoughts it came
That it was he who did her husband slay
And she & the old Soldier all that day
Not knowing how they did their purpose thwart
Strove all they could his anguish to allay
But of the woman he with bursting heart
Entreated evermore that she would thence depart

Figure 12. DC MS 16, 39v. 'Friend of my heart & Genius . . .' Aborted opening to the '2nd Part', composed in late April 1799.

had placed in him. No wonder these lines are crossed out in the manuscript. Indeed, the poem very nearly foundered at this point. Coleridge's presumed disapproval must have felt stiflingly inevitable, to the point that when they met in April 1799 knowledge of *The Prelude* was kept from him.

Their meeting was a strange affair which, given what we know about it, has attracted surprisingly little comment.[24] Both men were in a peculiar state. Coleridge had heard about Berkeley Coleridge's death only weeks before, and had recently begun writing the series of passionate letters to his wife inspired by a potent mixture of grief and guilt. The Wordsworths were exhausted after a depressing and draining winter. For his part Wordsworth had done a good deal of writing, including some of the finest he would ever accomplish – but he did not at that moment tell Coleridge about it. The manuscripts reveal that by the time they met he knew he had completed the first part of a long poem, and that would have made it hard for him to keep his counsel. These tensions alone would have accounted for Coleridge's perception of Wordsworth and Dorothy as 'melancholy and hypp'd'. But this was a euphemism. Coleridge's obstinate refusal to join the Wordsworths in the Lake District drove William to tears: he twice told Poole that 'W. was affected to tears, very much affected.'[25] In fact Wordsworth was wrestling with complex emotions: he must have felt that 'The Recluse' was slipping from his grasp.

The meeting was difficult, to say the least. Coleridge reacted to Wordsworth's insistent desire to settle in Cumbria by arguing that Wordsworth was too retiring:

> My many weaknesses are of some advantage to me; they unite me more with the great mass of my fellow-beings – but dear Wordsworth appears to me to have hurtfully segregated & isolated his Being / Doubtless, his delights are more deep and sublime; / but he has likewise more hours, that prey on his flesh & blood. – [26]

This criticism, which surfaces here for the first time, would be repeated as an explanation as to why Wordsworth failed to compose 'The Recluse'. Coleridge believed that its author had to be a man who suffered with the mass of sinful humanity, sharing in its weaknesses and sorrows; the trouble with Wordsworth was that he placed himself above all that and was in danger of turning into a snob. This is what Coleridge was getting at when in October 1803 he at-

---

[24]   Mary Moorman and Kenneth Johnston discuss it in passing: see Moorman i 434–6; Johnston 664–5.
[25]   Griggs i 491.
[26]   Griggs i 490–1.

tacked Wordsworth's 'Self-involution': 'I trembled, lest a Film should rise, and thicken on his moral Eye.'[27] As Wordsworth became more alienated from the mass of suffering, sinful humanity, he became less capable of relating to those instincts and urges which had to be accounted for by 'The Recluse'.

This disquiet communicated itself to Wordsworth and began immediately to distort his work. 'Home at Grasmere', Part First, Book First of *The Recluse*, which he composed on arrival in Grasmere in early 1800, seems to have been framed as a response to Coleridge's arguments. Over half of it consists of lengthy self-justification in which Wordsworth tries to persuade the reader that he is capable of sympathizing with every peasant and dog in the neighbourhood; he begins with

> That Shepherd's voice, it may have reached mine ear
> Debased and under prophanation, made
> An organ for the sounds articulate
> Of ribaldry and blasphemy and wrath,
> Where drunkenness hath kindled senseless frays
> ('Home at Grasmere' MS B, 423–7)

and ranges as far as

> the small grey Horse that bears
> The paralytic Man; I know the ass
> On which the Cripple in the Quarry maimed
> Rides to and fro: I know them and their ways.
> The famous Sheep-dog, first in all the vale,
> Though yet to me a Stranger, will not be
> A Stranger long; nor will the blind Man's Guide,
> Meek and neglected thing, of no renown.
> ('Home at Grasmere' MS B, 725–32)

The reason why the second half of 'Home at Grasmere' doesn't work is that Wordsworth's desperation to prove his goodwill towards these humble creatures gives away the absence of genuine kinship between them. When he tries to convince us that he is one of them, the tone of Miltonic grandeur collapses into bathos. It wasn't something he would have been led to write had he not been the author of 'The Recluse'.

Shortly after his arrival in Sockburn in May,[28] Wordsworth drafted four

---

[27] Griggs ii 1013.
[28] Parrish gives no date for them (although they must have been composed by October 1799); de Selincourt suggested 1798–1800; in the Norton *Prelude* Jonathan Wordsworth

blank verse fragments, apparently for *The Prelude*, which show how depressed the meeting in Göttingen had left him.

> nor had my voice
> Been silent often times had I burst forth
> In verse which with a strong and random light
> Touching an object in its prominent parts
> Created a memorial which to me
> Was all sufficient and to my own mind
> Recalling the whole picture seemed to speak
> An universal language: Scattering thus
> In passion many a desultory sound
> I deemed that I had adequately cloathed
> Meanings at which I hardly hinted thoughts
> And forms of which I scarcely had produced
> A monument and arbitrary sign

Between this fragment and the next, de Selincourt suggested, the argument requires a connecting thought along the lines of: 'When I reviewed this random and desultory verse I saw its worthlessness, and came to realize that an artist reveals his true power only . . .'[29]

> In that considerate and laborious work
> That patience which admitting no neglect
> By slow creation doth impart[30] to speach
> Outline & substance even till it has give[n]
> A function kindred to organic power
> The vital spirit of a perfect form[31]

Wordsworth is preoccupied with aesthetic questions, and particularly with false steps taken in the past. Why? Because he is anxious about the worth of the extensive blank verse drafts written in Goslar, which still have no title. In the first fragment he recalls that some of his poetry, which 'seemed to speak / An universal language', satisfied him at the time of its composition. That

suggested *c.* February 1799, but in *The Borders of Vision* revised that to summer 1799. The most likely moment of composition is summer 1799, after composition of Part I and prior to serious work on Part II.

[29] See OET *Prelude* lvi.

[30] This actually reads 'imparts' in the manuscript, the result of a revision earlier in the line.

[31] These transcriptions are taken from the manuscript page reproduced in figure 13 opposite, though my readings differ slightly from those given by Parrish at Cornell 1799 *Prelude* 162–3.

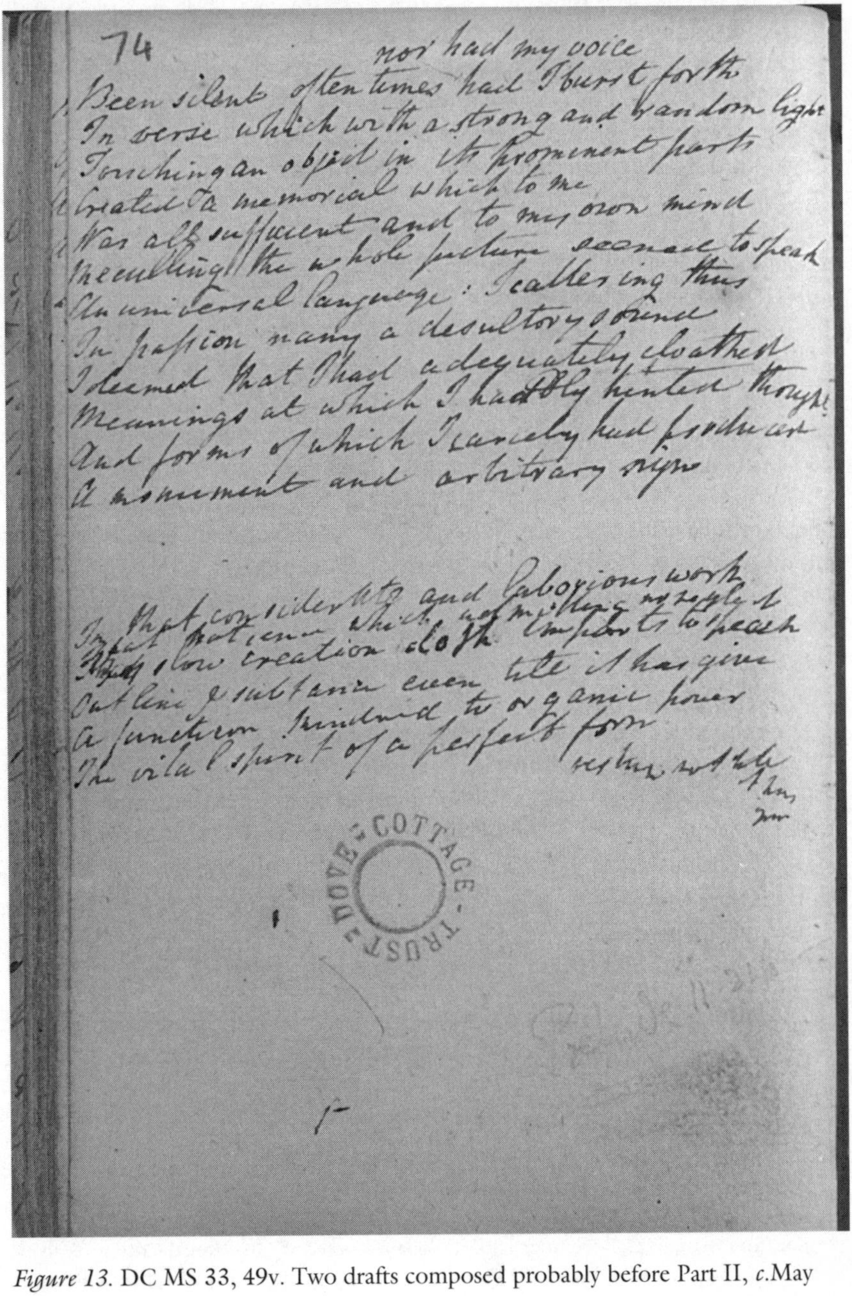

74

           nor had my voice

Been silent, often times had I burst forth
In verse which with a strong and random light
Touching an object in its prominent parts
Created a memorial which to me
Was all sufficient and to my own mind
Recalling the whole picture seemed to speak
An universal language: Scattering thus
In passion many a desultory sound
I deemed that I had adequately cloathed
Meanings at which I had but hinted though
And forms of which I scarcely had produced
A monument and arbitrary sign

In that considerate and laborious work
that ... which ... ... to speak
slow creation doth ... ...
Outline & substance even till it has given
A function kindred to organic power
The vital spirit of a perfect form

Figure 13. DC MS 33, 49v. Two drafts composed probably before Part II, *c.*May 1799.

'universal language' is important because 'The Recluse' was supposed to be capable of addressing humanity as a whole; it is a statement of policy that predates the claim that language be 'an incarnation of the thought'[32] (in the *Essays Upon Epitaphs*) by over a decade. However, the fragment castigates him for believing he had written in such a language. The poetry he had hoped was written in this egalitarian style was in fact 'desultory' and 'inadequate'.[33] This criticism can apply only to the verse in which we know him to have aspired to a 'universal language' – most notably, the blank verse expressly composed for 'The Recluse' in 1798: 'The Ruined Cottage', 'The Pedlar', 'The Discharged Soldier', 'Not useless do I Deem', 'There is an active principle' and the other 'Recluse' fragments.[34] Feelings of dissatisfaction with those materials had been growing. MS D of 'The Ruined Cottage' was composed in Goslar not later than February 1799 concurrently with Part I of the two-part *Prelude*; comparison was unavoidable. Wordsworth would remain unhappy with 'The Ruined Cottage' and set about it again in 1801–2 when, according to Dorothy, it made him ill.[35] The Grasmere journal entries make it perfectly clear that any effort spent on that poem and 'The Pedlar' was liable to tire and sicken their author because, as Dorothy puts it, 'though Wm could find fault with no one part of it – it was uninteresting & must be altered. Poor William!'[36] To judge by the fragments postdating the encounter with Coleridge in April 1799, Wordsworth was already nauseous at the thought of 'The Recluse' and what he had written towards it.

   The second fragment projects an idealized 'Recluse', a 'considerate and laborious work' in which 'substance' is given to language in much the same way that 'deep feelings' had in 1798 impressed themselves so distinctly on the Pedlar that they lay on his mind 'like substances, and almost seemed / To haunt the bodily sense'.[37] Wordsworth wanted to give his reader the same experience as that attributed to the Pedlar in his visionary state. But it goes further in anticipating a concept usually held to be Coleridge's as described in the eighth of his Shakespeare lectures delivered in London, 22 or 29 December 1812:

---

[32]   *Prose Works* ii 84–5.
[33]   See also Finch 158.
[34]   A number of these are presented by Butler and Green among the 'Other Poems Composed between 1797 and 1800', Cornell *Lyrical Ballads* 271ff.
[35]   See, for instance, 23 December 1801: 'William worked at The Ruined Cottage & made himself very ill' (*Grasmere Journals* 52); also see the entries listed by Butler, Cornell *Ruined Cottage* 24–5.
[36]   *Grasmere Journals* 63.
[37]   'The Pedlar' 30–4.

The form is mechanic when on any given material we impress a predetermined form, not necessarily arising out of the properties of the material – as when to a mass of wet clay we give whatever shape we wish it to retain when hardened – The organic form on the other hand is innate, it shapes as it developes itself from within, and the fullness of its development is one & the same with the perfection of its outward Form.[38]

Compare with this Wordsworth's belief in 'A function kindred to organic power / The vital spirit of a perfect form', and it becomes clear that both men are talking about the same thing. They are agreed on an aesthetic in which the work assumes a form which emerges from within – innate, vital and, to that extent, 'perfect'. As is well known, Coleridge is indebted to Schlegel for his remarks, and offers them in the context of a defence of Shakespeare against Voltaire's famous attack. The context of Wordsworth's fragment is more intriguing. He has just been criticizing himself for verse which he now deplores, and is by contrast hoping to write something possessed of qualities that will validate his high ambitions – 'organic power', 'perfect form'. As criticism of 'The Ruined Cottage' and 'The Pedlar' this was astute. There was a strong argument for saying that they were not coherent: form had been imposed upon them; different parts had been composed at different times, grafted on each other in a 'mechanic' rather than 'organic' manner. In March 1798 they had been combined to make a single work of over 900 lines, as Dorothy reported to Mary Hutchinson.[39] As she presented this outsize narrative to her friend, Dorothy hints at its unwieldiness: 'The Pedlar's character now makes a very, certainly the *most*, considerable part of the poem.' The problem of what to do with these two very different works was partly the cause of Wordsworth's self-recrimination in summer 1799.

    Still preoccupied with guilt at working on something clearly not related to 'The Recluse' and not telling Coleridge about it, he turned immediately to the facing page of the notebook and drafted a third and fourth fragment:

> I knew not then
> What fate was mine nor that the day would come
> When after-loathings, damps of discontent[40]
> Returning ever like the obstinate pains
> Of an uneasy spirit, with a force
> Inexorable would from hour to hour
> For ever summon my exhausted mind

[38] CC *Literature* i 495.
[39] *EY* 199.
[40] This line is not punctuated in the MS, but some pointing is necessary, however minimal, if it is to be understood.

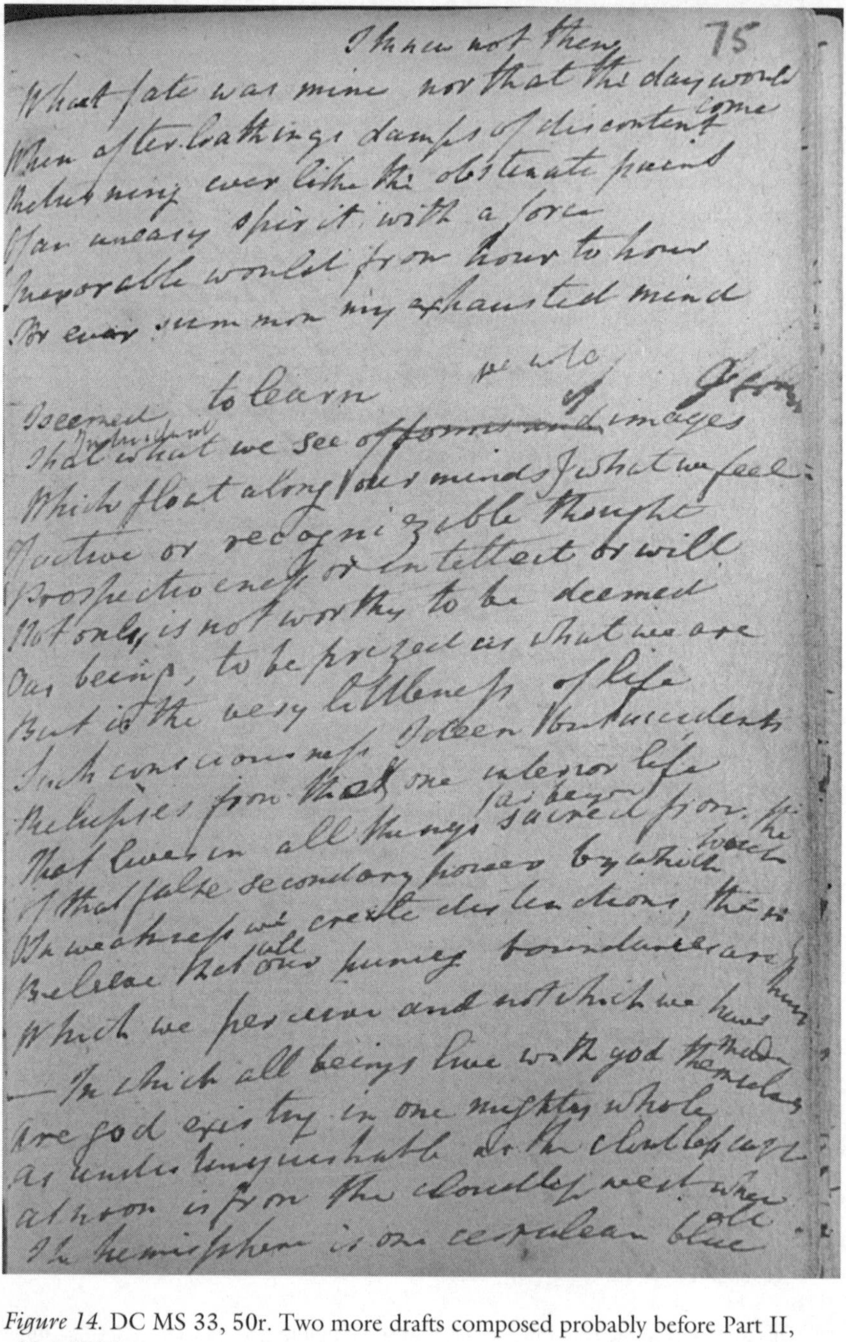

Figure 14. DC MS 33, 50r. Two more drafts composed probably before Part II, c.May 1799.

Leaving a gap of no more than a line, he continued:

> I seemed to learn
> That what we see of forms and images
> Which float along our minds & what we feel
> Of active or recognizable thought
> Prospectiveness or intellect or will
> Not only is not worthy to be deemed
> Our being, to be prized as what we are
> But is the very littleness of life
> Such consciousness I deem but accidents
> Relapses from that one interior life
> That lives in all things sacred from the touch
> Of that false secondary power by which
> In weakness we create distinctions, then
> Believe that all our puny boundaries are things
> Which we perceive and not which we have made
> – In which all beings live with god themselves
> Are god existing in one mighty whole
> As undistinguishable as the cloudless east
> At noon is from the cloudless west when all
> The hemisphere is one cerulean blue[41]

The harsh criticisms attached to the 'Recluse' drafts of 1798 in the first fragment return here; and if we think of him as referring to 'The Ruined Cottage'
and 'The Pedlar', which in 1801–2 would make him ill with anxiety, these
comments make perfect sense. Exhaustion is one of the symptoms that dogged
him whenever he returned to them (the Grasmere journals entries listed by
Butler establish that beyond question),[42] as mentioned in the last line of the
third fragment. The spiritual unease he felt as he contemplated them was
entirely understandable – these were parts of a work that lacked the 'vital
spirit' of organic form. Whatever else the autobiographical drafts of 1798–9
had shown him, he knew that they came from within; that they had the vital
qualities absent from the 'Recluse' poetry.

The last fragment was to contribute directly to the two-part *Prelude* (Part
II, lines 251–4). Again, Wordsworth is distinguishing false from true vision.
The false is characterized by its relation to 'will' and 'intellect'; it is 'little', to
do with 'distinctions', 'puny boundaries' devised in the abstract. The distinction being drawn is that between Coleridgean pantheism and Wordsworth's

---

[41] See figure 14 opposite.
[42] See Cornell *Ruined Cottage* 24–5.

belief in the immanent divinity of natural forms. Wordsworth regards a faith based on philosophical analysis as a relapse from

> that one interior life
> That lives in all things . . .
> In which all beings live with god themselves
> Are god existing in one mighty whole
> As undistinguishable as the cloudless east
> At noon is from the cloudless west when all
> The hemisphere is one cerulean blue

It may sound like pantheism, but Coleridge would not have been content with that concluding image. The 'one interior life' ratifies Wordsworth's vision – as resistant to analysis as the cerulean blue of the sky. To that extent this is the most acute commentary Wordsworth could have provided for the two-part *Prelude* as it was in that poem that he sought to shake himself free of 'that false secondary power' which had driven Coleridge to intellectualize his beliefs; through the spiritual archaeology of *The Prelude* he would convey himself back to the 'interior life' which had always informed his poetry, from Hawkshead days onwards. Having articulated that for himself, he was able to begin Part II. He turned to another notebook and began to write.

Part II: May–December 1799

Wordsworth came from the unhappy encounter with Coleridge in April 1799 to the security of the Hutchinson estate at Sockburn where in May he began Part II, completing most of it by the time Coleridge came to visit on 26 October. The fragments expressing dissatisfaction with the 'Recluse' seem to have exorcized his discomfiture in part and confirmed him in the knowledge that the autobiographical verse he had begun at Goslar was worth pursuing. No doubt Dorothy and Mary helped in this, as indicated by the fact that they fair-copied much of Part II.[43] (It is likely that the heavy accountant's paper from which the manuscript was constructed was provided by Mary.)

It originally began with five lines now lost, continuing with line 46 of the final version, 'We ran a boisterous race . . .'[44] As at the beginning of Part I, Wordsworth is preoccupied with psychological process, as he reflects on the fact that

---

[43]   MS RV; see Cornell *1799 Prelude* 167.
[44]   See Cornell *1799 Prelude* 170–1.

> the beauteous scenes
> Of nature were collaterally attached
> To every scheme of holiday delight
> And every boyish sport, less grateful else
> And languidly pursued.
>
> (ll. 49–53)

Wordsworth's use of the term 'collateral' shows that he has just been rereading the end of Part I, where he had written of how Nature used 'collateral interest' as a means of peopling his mind with 'forms, or beautiful or grand'.[45] Now he asks himself how the mind comes consciously to value natural beauty for its own sake. His answer is that in the first place it was an unnoticed 'attachment' to childhood experience; in that way it unconsciously entered his soul and came to be integral to his mental constitution. An involuntary response is being traced to its origins. As he writes, Wordsworth cannot but be aware that this is a reflex not shared by Coleridge; Coleridge valued it – as the blessings of the 'last rook' in 'This Lime-Tree Bower' and the water-snakes in 'The Ancient Mariner' were designed to prove – and had accommodated the scheme of 'The Recluse' to it. But its foregrounding at this moment is symptomatic of the way in which Wordsworth is again concerned with defining those 'Possessions . . . wholly, solely mine' in opposition to the Coleridge-designed agenda for 'The Recluse'.

As if uneasy about this, the poetry as originally composed gave way immediately to a series of spots of time devoted to expounding the ministry of beauty. Wordsworth must have had 'The Vale of Esthwaite' before him as he worked, because one of them, envisaging his deathbed recollection of the Lakes, is developed from a passage in the earlier poem. Again, he is concerned with marking out territory over which he considered himself sovereign. As he continued, his ambivalence about Coleridge was becoming clearer. Reviewing the blank verse fragments he had been composing just before starting on Part II, he incorporated them in a curious way. The last had criticized the visionary manner of the Alfoxden verse as drawing on a

> false secondary power by which
> In weakness we create distinctions, then
> Believe that all our puny boundaries are things
> Which we perceive and not which we have made . . .

First and foremost, these lines had been criticism of a cerebral manner which he now found untrue to his innermost convictions. By the time he

---

[45] *The Two-Part Prelude* i 376–8.

incorporated them into the fair copy of Part II, their context had become
markedly different:

> Thou my Friend art one
> More deeply read in thy own thoughts no slave
> Of that false secondary power by which
> In weakness we create distinctions then
> Believe our puny boundaries are things
> Which we perceive & not which we have made[46]

Wordsworth has just asked 'who shall parcel out / His intellect by geometric
rules / Split like a province into round & square',[47] and now seeks to elucidate his notions of unproductive, over-rationalized thought. In the earlier
fragment this way of thinking was characterized as 'the very littleness of life'.
So it is here, but in this draft it is quite differently conceived. It occurs in a
sentence not about Wordsworth, or the literary mode he adopted in 1798, or
indeed his way of thinking at any time – but about Coleridge, the 'Friend' still
unaware that Wordsworth is playing truant from 'The Recluse'. Ostensibly it
appears to exonerate Coleridge from the charge of parcelling out his intellect
or being susceptible to the 'false secondary power'; but upon closer examination Wordsworth's tone and language reveal other implications.

Why should he invoke Coleridge? After all, the aim of the passage is to
discuss a misleading way of seeing the world. There's no obvious cause for
dragging him into it. Nor, for that matter, is any reason adduced for bearing
out the argument that Coleridge *isn't* guilty of this form of speciousness; it's
simply asserted. It would be naive to take all this at face value. The only way in
which this can make sense is if one attends to the anxiety underlying the verse.
As so often in Wordsworth, tones of doctrinal certainty – 'Thou my Friend art
one / More deeply read in thy own thoughts no slave . . .' – are expressive of
doubt. It is almost impossible not to read these lines ironically. Parcelling up
the mind, creating distinctions, and believing in the ultimate truth of 'puny
boundaries' were habits long associated with his friend.

Wordsworth had probably realized that the false ways of thinking and seeing which had been dismissed in the earlier fragment, and which he wanted to
criticize here, were traceable to Coleridge. If he could not admit it consciously,
the only reason for mentioning Coleridge was to associate him with the kind
of deluded thought he wanted to condemn. As the passage continues in the

[46] MS RV; for facsimile see Cornell *1799 Prelude* 186. In my transcription I have accepted
Wordsworth's deletions and alternative readings (when accompanied by deletion), aiming
to present the draft as it stood on completion.
[47] Cornell *1799 Prelude* 185.

fair copy it proceeds to bear out the ambivalence with which he regarded Coleridge:

> If to thee my Friend
> The unity of [   ] hath been revealed
> Then wilt thou doubt with me less aptly skill'd
> Than many are to class the cabinet
> Of their sensations & in voluble phrase
> Run through the history and birth of each
> As of a single independent thing.[48]

Once again, the manuscript is more revealing than the final version, which begins: 'To thee, unblinded by these outward shews, / The unity of all has been revealed.' Through revision they would be turned into a celebration of Coleridge's Unitarianism, and the justification for excluding him from the influence of that 'false secondary power'. But the manuscript is embarrassingly conditional about all this: 'If to thee my Friend / The unity of [   ] hath been revealed'. Here Wordsworth is far from certain that Coleridge has been granted the Unitarian vision that will be his main defence in the final text. Nor is there any reassurance to be found in the gap in the manuscript after 'unity of' – 'unity of what?' it seems to ask. The last of the fragmentary drafts composed immediately prior to Part II had concluded with a comparison of their beliefs, finding Coleridge's to be flawed by dependence on intellect, and his own to be guaranteed by its 'interior life'. The effect is to bring into question the nature of the revelation to which Coleridge laid claim.

Coleridge's relation to this poetry is increasingly problematic. He doesn't know of its existence, believes that Wordsworth is writing a completely different work which notably blends philosophy (a cerebral discipline) with poetry, and can exert no sway over the inner world from which it takes its inspiration (wholly, solely Wordsworth's). Moreover, he is seen by implication to have been responsible for the false consciousness that gave rise to the 'Recluse' poetry of 1798, now denounced as 'desultory' and 'inadequate'. Coleridge needed a stronger defence than Wordsworth was capable of offering here. Perhaps, on a conscious level, Wordsworth had intended to exempt him from blame; instead he has implicitly associated him with 'that false secondary power by which / In weakness we create distinctions', and questions the validity of the Unitarian convictions of which Coleridge claimed himself apprised. The quotation concludes with reference to Wordsworth himself,

---

[48]   Cornell *1799 Prelude* 186.

less aptly skill'd
Than many are to class the cabinet
Of their sensations & in voluble phrase
Run through the history and birth of each
As of a single independent thing.

This is deliberately ironic; the 'skill' Wordsworth cannot claim for himself is an extension of the 'false secondary power' which Coleridge by implication does have. On the surface, Coleridge is allied with him in not being able to catalogue 'sensation' but in fact he is more correctly understood to be a lost soul, damned to wander in a morass of bogus abstraction, divorced forever from the true, unified vision he sought. In context, the fair copy draft is an indictment of Coleridge, doubtless the product of suppressed anger.

Wordsworth had reason to feel aggrieved. At their last meeting in Göttingen Coleridge had accused him of having 'hurtfully segregated & isolated his Being',[49] partly as justification for refusing the invitation to relocate to the Lakes. He had then boasted to Poole of Wordsworth's tearful response. Coleridge must have appeared obstinate in rejecting the proposal to go to Cumbria, and then returning to England, as he did in mid-July, and not visiting the Wordsworths. Grief on Wordsworth's part would have given way to irritation. The fragments of April-May articulate 'after-loathings' for the 'Recluse' verse, and doubts about the direction in which they had taken him. His present trajectory, by contrast, had been productive of some of his finest work to date. Had he been thinking about this, he would have been hard put not to resent the burden of having to write a poem that would theorize about 'distinctions', 'boundaries', 'sensations', and so forth – an exercise that in the context of his present work must have seemed meretricious to say the least. Wordsworth and Coleridge appear not to have been in communication while Part II was being composed, not suprisingly; when Wordsworth did write, in early September, it was to reveal (as Coleridge reported to Poole) that 'he is ill — & seems not happy . . . he renounces Alfoxden altogether.'[50] The letter to which Coleridge refers has not survived, but there is reason to think that Wordsworth's unhappiness went deeper than he suspected, and that his renunciation of Alfoxden extended not merely to an intention not to reside there, but to the work he had produced there under Coleridge's influence.

These lines are of particular importance because they are the preamble to the set-piece of Part II, the infant babe passage. It was not possible for Wordsworth to compose it without thinking of Coleridge and his reaction to

---

[49]   Griggs i 491.
[50]   Griggs i 527.

the death of baby Berkeley, which had occurred on 10 February 1799. The April meeting in Göttingen had taken place only weeks after Coleridge received the tragic news, and we can be sure that it was discussed with the Wordsworths; on 4 July Dorothy told Poole that 'When we were at Göttingen he received a letter from Mrs. Coleridge by which we had the pleasure of hearing that she and dear little Hartley were well. Poor Berkeley! I was much grieved to hear of his death.'[51] Given their own experience of bereavement, the Wordsworths would have been intrigued by Coleridge's reaction to the news. In the same letter in which he recorded Wordsworth's grief at his refusal to relocate to Cumbria, Coleridge told Poole that

> There are moments in which I have such a power of Life within me, such a conceit of it, I mean – that I lay the Blame of my Child's Death to my absence – not *intellectually*; but I have a strange sort of sensation, as if while I was present, none could die whom I intensely loved – and doubtless *it* was no absurd idea of your's that there may be unions & connections out of the visible world.[52]

At first, one is prepared to be struck by the weight of grief one expects to underlie these remarks – and there are no grounds for doubting Coleridge's love for his child; but on close inspection it is difficult not to feel surprised – shocked, even – by their sheer self-centredness. For these remarks are concerned less with grief than with Coleridge's sense of his own connectedness with the cosmos. His son's death is the occasion to affirm his own 'power of Life'. All of which is consistent with the letter Coleridge had written to Poole a month before on 6 April, which had seen Berkeley's life as something that continued despite his physical demise: 'It was *life* — ! it was a particle of *Being* — ! it was *Power*! — & *how could* it perish — ?'[53]

All this underpins Wordsworth's first poetic account of the early beginnings of imaginative power. Again I quote from the fair copy rather than the final version, presenting deleted readings in square brackets:

> Bless'd the infant babe
> (For with my best conjectures I would trace
> The progress of our Being) blest the Babe
> Nurs'd in his Mother's arms the Babe who sleeps
> Upon his Mother's breast who when his soul
> Claims manifest kindred with an earthly soul
> Doth gather passion from his Mother's eye.

51 *EY* 266.
52 Griggs i 490.
53 Griggs i 479.

Such feelings pass into his torpid life
Like an awakening breeze and hence his min[d]
Even in the first trial of its powers
Is prompt and [active *del. to*] wakeful – eager to combine
In one appearance all the elements
And parts of the same object else detach'd
And loth to coalesce. Thus day by day
Subjected to the discipline of love
His organs and recipient faculties
Are quicken'd are more vigourous his mind spreads
Tenacious of the forms which it receives.
In one beloved presence nay, and more
In that most apprehensive habitude
And those sensations which have been derived
From [   ] beloved presence there exists
A virtue which irradiates and exalts
All objects through all intercourse of sense.
No outcast He [abandon'd *del. to*] bewilder'd & depress'd
Along his infant veins are interfused
The gravitation & the filial bond
Of Nature that connect him with the world.
Emphatically such a Being lives
An inmate of this *active* universe.
From Nature largely he receives nor so
Is satisfied but largely gives again
For feeling has to him imparted strength
And powerful in all sentiments of grief
Of exultation fear & joy his mind
Even as an agent of the one great mind
Creates, creator & receiver both
[Working but in the spirit of the works *deleted*]
Which it beholds.[54]

Though Coleridgean in having Berkeley as its inspiration, the infant babe is profoundly Wordsworthian in that his first action on assuming consciousness is to 'gather passion from his Mother's eye'. For Wordsworth, emotion is central. In Godwinian thought the rationalizing faculty had flourished at the expense of emotion, and refusal to accept that had led Wordsworth to reject it. Wordsworth sees the child's emotional development as the initiating event of its intellectual life. To him, the emotions are what will enable the individual to become a reasoning being. He would have found support for this in Erasmus

---

[54] Cornell *1799 Prelude* 187–91.

Darwin's account of babyhood in his medical textbook, *Zöonomia*, which pointed out that the force that enables the baby's senses to develop 'is love'.[55] This extends the argument put forth in the preceding lines because it is pitched against those who exalt the analytical faculties above the emotions.

It was to make this point that Wordsworth composed the passage. In every other respect it doesn't belong here. The first 200 lines of Part II are devoted to describing encounters with natural beauty during his Hawkshead years, and he should logically have proceeded to the next stage in his development. Instead he turns back to a far earlier moment. This can only partly be attributed to Berkeley Coleridge; that was something of which he had been aware since beginning work on Part II, and he could easily have written about it before now. In fact, the real inspiration for the infant babe passage was a rereading of the four fragments written prior to Part II – which expressed dissatisfaction with the 'Recluse' drafts of 1798 and their lack of organic form, and brought into focus a simmering resentment at being shackled to an aesthetic manner, and a project, which were burdensome. Having composed the lines claiming that Coleridge was not enslaved to that 'false secondary power by which / In weakness we create distinctions' (a proposition undermined by the poetry), Wordsworth proceeded to compose the infant babe passage which explained in greater detail how he and Coleridge were distinct.

For Wordsworth, his creative abilities were traceable to the love of his mother in infancy, when he found the irradiating and exalting influence of her 'beloved presence' productive of imaginative power. Against that idealized upbringing (which Wordsworth appropriates as his own) there are those who are 'bewilder'd & depress'd' – or, in the deleted reading, 'abandon'd'. Deprived of parental affection they experience alienation from their surroundings and society. It was no coincidence that this was the self-constructed myth Coleridge had spun about himself. He was the one who had described his feelings of isolation in the lime-tree bower, the cosmic alienation of the ancient mariner and the violation of the innocent Christabel. These stories concern estrangement from the 'discipline of love' such that each character is in a manner marked by it. In 'Frost at Midnight' Coleridge had portrayed his boyhood as a period of dislocation, when he was divorced from nature or familial love. He had found compensation by blessing infant Hartley with the Wordsworthian childhood by 'lakes and sandy shores' withheld from him. Now, in Part II of the poem which pointedly dispensed with the grandiose pretensions of 'The Recluse', Wordsworth found the converse of the imaginatively gifted, chosen soul of the infant babe to be his old friend who had declared his unwillingness to settle in the Lake District.

[55] *Zöonomia* (2 vols, London, 1794–6), i 145–6. It had provided the source for 'Goody Blake and Harry Gill'.

At their last meeting Coleridge had accused Wordsworth of having 'hurt-fully segregated & isolated his Being' partly because of his intention to settle in the Lake District;[56] the infant babe is a rebuke to that. The babe, notice-ably, has 'interfused' through his 'infant veins'

> The gravitation & the filial bond
> Of Nature that connect him with the world.

He is moreover 'An inmate of this *active* universe'. Wordsworth's response to Coleridge's disapprobation is to idealize his own infancy as a time when his status as a cosmic seer and fully socialized being was beyond doubt. In so doing he answers the charge that he was losing touch with social realities. The extent to which the babe is Wordsworthian is indicated by the fact that he is 'powerful in all sentiments of grief' – the peculiarly Wordsworthian experi-ence that had fuelled so much of the pre-Alfoxden verse. Even before he has acquired life-experience, the babe is imbued with an awareness of that dis-tinctly Wordsworthian emotion that will provide so much inspiration for fu-ture years, and connect him with those possessions that were wholly, solely his.

Wordsworth was working on this passage when he heard that Coleridge was attempting once more to rent Alfoxden House for him and Dorothy. His response to this news was to write to Coleridge to say (as Coleridge reported) that 'he renounces Alfoxden altogether.'[57] It was true. The infant babe pas-sage, Part II, the four blank verse fragments, and indeed all of the two-part *Prelude* thus far composed were an effective renunciation of Alfoxden. In-stead of writing the great millenarian work devised for him Wordsworth had returned to his creative roots and the lines of thought that inspired him before his association with Coleridge. He perhaps hoped that Coleridge would un-derstand that he wished to be rid of 'The Recluse' so as to return to the sources that had produced *The Borderers* and the early version of 'The Ruined Cottage'. The pressure he was under to continue with 'The Recluse' was prob-ably one of the causes of his feelings of illness at this moment; Dorothy re-corded on 3 September that 'he is sadly troubled with a pain in his side.'[58]

Coleridge was having none of this. He responded with a reminder that further work on 'The Recluse' was long overdue, and proposed that Wordsworth write an additional work related to it:

[56]   Griggs i 491.
[57]   Griggs i 527.
[58]   *EY* 270.

I am anxiously eager to have you steadily employed on 'The Recluse' . . . My dear friend, I do entreat you to go on with 'The Recluse;' and I wish you would write a poem, in blank verse, addressed to those, who, in consequence of the complete failure of the French Revolution, have thrown up all hopes of the amelioration of mankind, and are sinking into an almost epicurean selfishness, disguising the same under the soft titles of domestic attachment and contempt for visionary *philosophes*. It would do great good, and might form a part of 'The Recluse,' for in my present mood I am wholly against the publication of any small poems.[59]

This is usually cited as the inspiration for the passage towards the end of Part II which laments 'these times of fear . . . when good men / On every side fall off we know not how' (ll. 478–82).[60] But those lines cannot have been written for *at least* another two months. Wordsworth was distinctly not inspired – at least not immediately – by Coleridge's exhortations.

Given his renunciation of Alfoxden and all that implied, how might we expect Wordsworth to have interpreted Coleridge's letter? Coleridge begins by exhorting him to become 'steadily employed' on a poem he cannot write, and compounds this with the invention of a second, related project designed to attack the 'epicurean selfishness' of those who have retreated from their former radicalism into 'domestic attachment and contempt for visionary *philosophes*'. The apostasy of James Mackintosh in his lectures of February–June 1799 is usually invoked to justify Coleridge's concerns, but this cannot explain the references to 'epicurean selfishness' or 'domestic attachment'; Coleridge clearly has something else in mind.

Domestic attachment was something of a sore point in Coleridge's own life; he had just confessed in a letter to Poole that he felt guilty at Berkeley's death partly because he was separated from his family, and his letters to Sara are full of expressions of devotion intended to compensate for that. He was uncomfortably aware when the Wordsworths passed through Göttingen in April of how 'they burn with such impatience to return to their native Country, they who are all to each other.'[61] It is impossible not to be aware of his envy; they enjoyed the kind of ideal relationship from which he felt excluded. In his letter to Sara of 23 April he observes that for him 'every thing pleasant & every thing valuable, & every thing dear to me [is] at a distance.'[62] In early December 1798, while Wordsworth was composing Part I of the two-part *Prelude*, he had written a hexameter poem which concluded:

---

59 Ibid.
60 See Norton *Prelude* 26n9; *Borders of Vision* 104–5.
61 Griggs i 484.
62 Ibid.

William, my head and my heart! dear William and dear Dorothea!
You have all in each other; but I am lonely, and want you!

('Hexameters' 35–6)

Festering envy had given way to feelings of exclusion and, during the April meeting, outright rejection of Wordsworth's plan to settle in the Lake District. In this light Coleridge's suggestion that Wordsworth compose a new blank verse poem directed against those who have retreated from their early radicalism into 'epicurean selfishness' and 'domestic attachment' is double-edged: it points the finger at Wordsworth himself. This is consistent with the fact that Coleridge told Poole in his letter of 6 May that Wordsworth had 'hurtfully segregated & isolated his Being', adding that 'he has likewise more hours, that prey on his flesh & blood.'[63] In advising Wordsworth to turn his attentions towards the dangers of 'domestic attachment' he may have hoped that he would take the hint, and realize that his own way of life was flawed and likely to detain him from 'The Recluse'. This was Coleridge's real fear, and would resurface in 1803 when he criticized Wordsworth's 'having every the minutest Thing, almost his very Eating & Drinking, done for him by his Sister, or Wife'.[64] Just in case Wordsworth suspected Coleridge of sarcasm, Coleridge added the reference to 'contempt for visionary *philosophes*'. Of course, there was a good deal of such contempt around as there always is, and according to Hazlitt (who attended his lectures) Mackintosh reserved his most splenetic utterances for 'our visionary sceptics and Utopian philosophers'.[65] At the same time, that contempt was something Wordsworth could be depended on to deplore. In that way it would sugar the pill, and might help warn him against the character flaws that would disqualify him from composing 'The Recluse'.

If this is a correct reading of Coleridge's letter (which unfortunately survives only in this fragment), it provides a useful indication of the distance between the two men at this moment. Coleridge was still unaware of *The Prelude*, still hopeful that Wordsworth might emerge as the author of 'The Recluse', but harboured doubts about his ability to do so. Besides anything else, his own domestic strife made him more jealous than ever of the retired domesticity that characterized Wordsworth's life. For his part, Wordsworth was going through a very difficult period. Since the *annus mirabilis* had finished he had written nothing towards 'The Recluse' and the consequent anxiety was causing him psychosomatic pains. In truth, he had no reason to fret;

[63] Griggs i 491.
[64] Griggs ii 1013.
[65] Wu vii 155.

despite not having continued with 'The Recluse' he had written a substantial volume of poetry that drew him back to lines of thought he had been following prior to June 1797. Its quality was such as to make the 'Recluse' verse seem inadequate, and the highly intellectualized approach it would require specious and insincere. And here, in response to a serious attempt to signal this to Coleridge, was another exhortation to get on with 'The Recluse', and an invitation to write an additional work denouncing the direction which his own life had taken. Wordsworth's irritation with Coleridge would have been further stoked by this correspondence; he would have realized that the time was fast approaching when he must be told about *The Prelude*.

The manuscript suggests that progress on Part II became difficult at this time – not surprisingly under the circumstances. Unable to see how to continue with it – the infant babe was, he must have known, out of sequence – Wordsworth recycled a draft of 1798 in which the Pedlar was described listening to the 'ghostly language of the ancient earth'. This led into a newly composed passage about John Fleming, 'a friend / Then passionately loved', perhaps inspired by the address to him in 'The Vale of Esthwaite'.[66] Again, I quote from the manuscript rather than the final version:

> With heart how full
> Will he peruse these lines this page perhaps
> A blank to other men, for many years
> Have since flowed in between us, and our minds
> Both silent to each other, at this time
> We live as if those hours had never been.[67]

It is impossible to read this without being acutely conscious that Fleming, whom Wordsworth had not seen for many years, is being privileged over Coleridge. It is he who is imagined perusing these lines, and he who will fully understand them – 'perhaps / A blank to other men' (namely Coleridge). Not only that, but Coleridge is necessarily excluded from their long-term friendship, a point Wordsworth is at pains to emphasize: although he and Fleming are now virtual strangers, they are said to be as close as ever. None of which, conspicuously, could be said of Wordsworth and Coleridge, who had known each other for a comparatively short time, and who despite being separated for months had grown apart.

The address to Fleming thus serves a dual purpose. It places Wordsworth back in touch with his roots, both creatively (via 'The Vale of Esthwaite') and

---

[66]   See p. 13 above.
[67]   Cornell *1799 Prelude* 197.

spiritually. Secondly, it puts Coleridge in his place. Despite his proprietorial attitude towards Wordsworth, Coleridge hasn't known him for long, and doesn't understand this important poetry half as well as his old schoolfriend.

At around the time he composed these lines Wordsworth wrote to Coleridge, having taken the decision that he could no longer withhold news of this auto-biographical work. But what was he to say? Their rapidly diverging views of Wordsworth's future can only have been exacerbated by embarrassment about the fact that Coleridge had been in England since mid-July, for two and a half months, and made almost no effort to get in touch. Instead he had renewed his acquaintance with his old chum Southey, whom he embraced in Lime Street in Stowey when they were reunited. Coleridge was attempting to find an alternative focus for his intellectual sympathies. Wordsworth would have sensed this whether or not he knew about the renewed friendship with Southey, and was accordingly guarded in written exchanges. From Coleridge's reply to Wordsworth, which survives only in part, it is clear that Wordsworth revealed only that he was at work on something addressed to him, without mentioning its relation (if any) to 'The Recluse'. This drew forth a response, dated 12 October, that should not have surprised him:

> I long to see what you have been doing. O let it be the tail-piece of 'The Rec-luse!' for of nothing but 'The Recluse' can I hear patiently. That it is to be addressed to me makes me more desirous that it should not be a poem of itself. To be addressed, as a beloved man, by a thinker, at the close of such a poem as 'The Recluse,' a poem *non unius populi*, is the only event, I believe, capable of inciting in me an hour's vanity – vanity, nay, it is too good a feeling to be so called; it would indeed be a self-elevation produced *ab extra*.[68]

These congratulations are covert warnings. What they imply is that Coleridge doesn't want to know about anything but 'The Recluse'; that any other work is by definition so trivial that it is not worth telling him about; and that he has no wish to be addressed in any other context. That Latin tag, *non unius populi* (not of one people), puts the rest of English literature in its parochial place; 'The Recluse' is special because it will aspire to a universality denied to other works – including autobiographical ones. These congratulations are anything but congratulatory. Coleridge would only have written in this way had he suspected the worst – that Wordsworth was playing hookey, dissipating his energies on other projects, and expiating his feelings of guilt by addressing them to him. He was more than capable of sending his regards ironically, and in that light his letter makes perfect sense.

---

[68]   Griggs i 538.

Wordsworth knew he was being pressurized, and cannot have been molli-fied by being called 'a thinker' – he knew that was not his gift. It was Coleridge who had been reading Kant and Schelling in the original German. He, on the contrary, was writing his new poem – nothing to do with 'The Recluse' – in order to shake off the Coleridge-designed model of the philosopher-poet, and remind himself of where his real strengths lay. In all likelihood Wordsworth would have resented Coleridge's letter, and felt more confirmed than ever in his ambitions for the work on which he was engaged.

If he did feel irritated, it would not have made it any easier for him to write poetry. The manuscript indicates that progress at this moment was tentative. He was compelled again to cannibalize 'The Pedlar', using some overtly pan-theist lines to describe his sense of the 'one life'. These were the lines which had celebrated the heightened awareness in which the Pedlar had sensed the 'sentiment of being spread / O'er all that moves, and all that seemeth still' – from one of the climactic episodes of the poem. Having incorporated that pantheistic episode into his text, he turned immediately to another notebook and continued Part II with another earlier draft written just a few months before, which functions as a commentary on the Pedlar's reattributed ecstasy:

> By such communion I was early taught
> That what we see of forms and images
> Which float along our minds and what we feel
> Of active or recognizable thought
> Prospectiveness intelligence or will
> Not only is not worthy to be deemed
> Our being, to be prized as what we are
> But is the very littleness of life
> Such consciousnesses seemed but accidents
> Relapses from the one interior life
> Which is in all things from that unity
> In which all beings live with god, are lost
> In god & nature in one mighty whole
> As undistinguishable as the cloudless east
> At noon is from the cloudless west, when all
> The hemisphere is one cerulean blue[69]

This is, of course, a revised version of the fourth of the fragments written soon after the April meeting at Göttingen. Were any final proof needed of Wordsworth's rejection of the Coleridge-influenced poetry of 1798, this is it. It places that verse and the way of thinking it represented in a

[69] Cornell *1799 Prelude* 207–9.

context of inadequacy when compared with the more profound spiritual commitment he felt to the landscape of his birth. Significantly, this passage would not survive into the final version. It must have given Wordsworth pause, for he continued with a passage that expresses, within a conditional phrasing, an underlying insecurity stemming once again from anxiety about Coleridge:

> If this be error and another faith
> Find easier access to the pious mind
> Yet were I grossly destitute of all
> Those human sentiments which make this earth
> So dear . . .[70]

No doubt to the eyes of a pious Unitarian such as Coleridge his preferences would seem erroneous, perhaps pagan. But as the sentence continues it reiterates Wordsworth's true allegiance:

> . . . if I should fail with grateful voice
> To speak of you, ye mountains! & ye lakes
> And sounding cataracts, ye mists and winds
> That dwell among the hills where I was born . . .[71]

This had been the underlying aim of the two-part *Prelude* from the start. The *annus mirabilis* had produced some important writing, and marked the beginning of his most productive period as a poet. But it also brought things that came between Wordsworth and the sources of his considerable power as a poet – the ambition to philosophize (something for which he knew he was not well adapted) and the burden of writing 'The Recluse'. The quite different autobiographical poem on which he had been working for the best part of a year without Coleridge's knowledge had been his way of reminding himself why he had become a poet in the first place, and reorienting himself in terms of his innermost resources. In the course of its writing he had nearly reached the point at which it was possible to relinquish the burden of 'The Recluse' for ever, and in these lines he effectively does so.

Wordsworth would compose no more before, as Parrish puts it, 'the presence of Coleridge once more fell across *The Prelude*.'[72] Coleridge arrived at Sockburn farm on 26 October. He had been in England for three months, associating closely with Southey, corresponding spasmodically with the Wordsworths. Their artistic differences aside, William and Dorothy would

---

[70] Cornell *1799 Prelude* 209.
[71] Ibid.
[72] Cornell *1799 Prelude* 30.

have felt hurt and neglected. All the more so, given that Coleridge was consorting with the very man whose attack upon *Lyrical Ballads* in the *Critical Review* was felt by Wordsworth to have been unhelpful, to say the least. As Wordsworth had complained to Cottle in a letter of 27 May,

> He knew that I published those poems for money & money alone. He knew that money was of importance to me. If he could not conscientiously have spoken differently of the volume, in common delicacy he ought to have declined the task of reviewing it.[73]

And this was the man with whom Coleridge was making common cause. What's more, the letters to Cottle prove that when Coleridge did eventually visit the Wordsworths, it was a last-minute decision. There is nothing in the letters that passed between Wordsworth and Cottle to indicate that Coleridge was expected. That of 2 September, which gives Cottle directions, makes *no mention* of Coleridge; it is assumed that Cottle would be travelling singly.[74] And in truth Coleridge had not intended to visit the Wordsworths. We know that he left Nether Stowey for Bristol 'in search of his travelling chests';[75] had he not found them there he would have travelled to London in search of them, so he told his wife. However, while in Bristol he visited Cottle on 22 October, and discovered that he was on the verge of leaving for Sockburn on the strength of an invitation extended by the Wordsworths.

This was a pivotal moment in literary history. Coleridge was as aware as the Wordsworths of the growing tensions in their relationship. He knew that Cottle would report having bumped into him as he was about to depart, and that failure to accompany him might be construed as confirming the break. He would have asked himself what was the cost. He would lose 'The Recluse', and that was no small thing. He had abandoned his own poetic ambitions so as to leave the field clear for Wordsworth and had no intention of allowing that poem, which was in large part his, to die. That was the best reason he had for deciding – on the spur of the moment, without having time to write a note to his wife to tell her of his change of plan – to board the coach with Cottle and make the journey north. His wife still did not know his whereabouts by 2 November, and he did not write to her until December.[76] Travelling with

---

[73] Butler *JEGP* 145.
[74] Butler *JEGP* 150.
[75] This information comes in a letter from Sara Coleridge to Mrs George Coleridge, 2 November 1799, when she still didn't know where her husband had gone; see Molly Lefebure, *The Bondage of Love: A Life of Mrs Samuel Taylor Coleridge* (London: Gollancz, 1988), p. 123.
[76] Griggs i 542n1.

Cottle probably also had the advantage, as Mary Moorman has suggested, of saving Coleridge money.

Biographers have tended to accept Coleridge's explanation as to why he decided at such short notice to travel north[77] – as he told Southey, 'I was called up to the North by alarming accounts of Wordsworth's Health.'[78] Well, perhaps. But there must have been other motives for him to have dropped everything in order to see a friend he had studiously avoided for the last three months. This is the reason mentioned in every surviving fragment of correspondence between them at this period: Coleridge's determination that 'The Recluse' be composed. It is confirmed by Wordsworth's conduct during and after Coleridge's visit. Had he failed to make the journey, the consequence would have been predictable. In the autumn of 1799 Wordsworth came closer than ever again to abandoning 'The Recluse'; perhaps he had already resolved to do so by the time Coleridge arrived. To have remained true to such a decision would have emancipated Wordsworth from an impossible task that would warp his creative life for the next three decades. Instead Coleridge made a surprise visit to Sockburn and turned Wordsworth's thoughts back, however reluctantly, to the great millenarian epic of the age.

The visit was symbolic on other levels too. It was plainly conciliatory, signalling acceptance in principle that Coleridge's relocation to the Lakes might after all be a possibility. And it was understood as such by Wordsworth, who conducted Coleridge and Cottle on a tour of the Lakes.

Coleridge's arrival was a surprise for everyone concerned, most of all the Wordsworths. It was no doubt the cause of rejoicing. Hours after being reunited with them, and meeting the Hutchinsons for the first time, Coleridge recorded in his notebook: '– Few moments in life so interesting as those of an affectionate reception from those who have heard of you yet are strangers to your person.'[79] This was the occasion of his first meeting with Sara Hutchinson, a relationship that would prove harrowing for both of them. Little wonder that it was December before Coleridge got round to telling his wife where he had gone. Wordsworth took Cottle and Coleridge to Greta Bridge the next day;[80] Cottle departed for the south on the 30th, leaving Coleridge and

---

[77] See Moorman i 447; Richard Holmes, *Coleridge: Early Visions* (London: Hodder and Stoughton, 1989), p. 246; Johnston 682.

[78] Griggs i 545.

[79] *Notebooks* i 493.

[80] James A. Butler says that Wordsworth returned as 'an ambivalent tourist':

> The three travelers – two on foot, flanking the mare Lily, ridden by Cottle with his rheumatic 'Legs hugely muffled up' – must have looked like some satirical drawing of tourists, in the manner of Thomas Rowlandson's depiction of the picturesque Dr

Wordsworth to embark on a two and a half week walking tour. During this tour Coleridge received a letter from Daniel Stuart, offering him work as a journalist in London, an invitation Coleridge decided to accept. A week later they found themselves in Eusemere at the house of the anti-slavery campaigner Thomas Clarkson, whose wife Catherine described them in a letter to her friend Priscilla Lloyd:

> I must tell you that we [had] a visit from Coleridge and W. Wordsworth. They spent a whole day with us. C was in high spirits and talked a good deal. W was more reserved, but there was neither hauteur nor moroseness in his reserve. He has a fine commanding figure, is rather handsome, and looks as if he was born to be a great prince or a great general. He seems very fond of C, laughing at all his jokes and taking all opportunities of shewing him off . . .[81]

It is an intriguing description. By this point they had no doubt made up their differences and it had been agreed that Coleridge would return south to take up his post as a journalist while the Wordsworths would move to Grasmere. It follows that Coleridge would by now have known about the autobiographical verses Wordsworth had been writing, and probably heard them read by their author. How had Wordsworth chosen to justify the time and energy he had spent on them? It is hard to be sure, but there could not have been any attempt to claim them as part of 'The Recluse'. What we can surmise is that an agreement was reached: Coleridge graciously accepted the dedication of the autobiographical verses to himself on condition that Wordsworth start work on 'The Recluse' as soon as possible.[82]

Instead of travelling south immediately, Coleridge returned with Wordsworth to Sockburn, where he reacquainted himself with Sara Hutchinson, whom he now knew he loved. Reconciliation inspired Wordsworth to complete the poem which over the summer and early autumn had shown signs of faltering. He tactfully acceded to Coleridge's earlier request to 'write a poem, in blank verse, addressed to those, who, in consequence of the complete failure of the French Revolution, have thrown up all hopes of the amelioration of mankind' by adding some concluding lines, which condemned the

---

Syntax. Coleridge entered into his notebook a mocking comment about a 'pikteresk Toor' (*Notebooks* i 508), the kind of journey that the three of them now undertook.

('Tourist or Native Son: Wordsworth's Homecomings of 1799–1800', *Nineteenth-Century Literature* 51 (1996) 1–15, p. 2)

[81]   Letter in the possession of Jonathan Wordsworth, quoted *Borders of Vision* 101.

[82]   John Finch agrees that there is 'no doubt that Coleridge received the new poem favorably' (Finch 172).

'falling off' of good men 'in this time / Of dereliction and dismay'.[83] Finally the poem turned explicitly to Coleridge to bestow a parting blessing on him as he began the journey to London. At the same time Wordsworth removed the fragment which had commented deprecatingly on the Pedlar's ecstasy and brought the second part to an end. It was only now, as Wordsworth concluded this work, that it became what it would always be – the poem *to* Coleridge. It had certainly not begun as that, and most of it had been written in defiance of him and without his knowledge. But as he concluded, their reconciliation, and feelings of guilt at not having written 'The Recluse', drove Wordsworth to cast the poem in his mind as a tribute to Coleridge.[84]

Stephen Gill has written that 'The *1799 Prelude* is a major achievement,'[85] and so it is – though in aesthetic terms, it is somewhat mixed. Part I must be one of the most impressive single passages of poetry Wordsworth was ever to write. The case has been made – and it remains arguable – that the 1799 text of the spots of time is superior to subsequent ones.[86] At any event, the disposal of the material in Part I is a work of genius, and singles out the two-part *Prelude* as a special work in the canon. Most of all, it succeeded in bringing Wordsworth back into very close contact with the powerful emotional currents that had shaped his inner world since 1786. He knew himself to be the poet of grief, guilt and betrayal, and as he worked on Part I he may have begun to think seriously about further works concerned with those themes.

Part II begins impressively, and at its heart stands the great set-piece of the infant babe. But thereafter it is a less persuasive performance.[87] The obvious anachronism seems to send it off course; the verse falters, and Wordsworth is forced to reuse passages composed in 1798 which espoused pantheist views he no longer held. To that extent insincerity may be its greatest flaw. There were other problems which injured it – not least guilt at not disclosing the poem to Coleridge, the effects of pressure to work on 'The Recluse', and a growing sense of irritation and resentment for being put under such pressure. It is certainly significant that this major work of Wordsworth's maturity was written largely out of Coleridge's sight, kept secret during most of its compo-

---

[83]   The other gesture towards Coleridge's request, as Robert Woof has pointed out, was to preface *Lyrical Ballads* (1800) with a motto, 'Quam nihil ad genium, Papianae, tuum!' ('How little to your taste, O lawyers!'), a reference presumably to Mackintosh.

[84]   John Finch observes: 'If this poem had started as a digression from the main work of *The Recluse*, it had fed back into it' (Finch 172).

[85]   Gill 169.

[86]   *Borders of Vision* 270–6.

[87]   Many readers of the poem may feel this judgement to be unnecessarily harsh. I draw some encouragement from Johnston's admission that the second half of Part II is problematic; Johnston, *Recluse* 73.

sition. It was an achievement, but one that resulted from an intense struggle on Wordsworth's part to resist pressure to compose 'The Recluse'.

In that sense the two-part *Prelude* is not entirely successful. Wordsworth very nearly achieved his aim of detaching himself from Coleridge's influence, and almost certainly would have done so had Coleridge not decided, on the spur of the moment, to travel north with Cottle. But for Coleridge's intuitive understanding that the only way of guaranteeing the future of 'The Recluse' was to renew contact, the course of Wordsworth's career would have been utterly different. From that perspective the shift of gear detectable in the closing sections of Part II and the final blessing upon Coleridge are the ultimate betrayal – a betrayal of those 'possessions wholly, solely mine' which would have ensured Wordsworth's independent vision as a poet. As it was, he decided in late 1799 to enslave himself to a vision that was not his, and pay homage to a millenarian philosophy that in truth he did not understand. But it was willingly done, on the strength of a confidence generated by a new understanding between him and Coleridge. As he wrote, in an unsent draft of a letter written to Coleridge on Christmas Eve 1799, 'My dear Friend, we talk of you perpetually, and for me I see you everywhere.'[88] For all that, he would never complete 'The Recluse', would suffer from a growing sense of frustration, and an increasing feeling that he had failed to exploit his natural inheritance. His one stab at publishing 'Recluse' verse, *The Excursion*, which announced in its Preface the intention of publishing at least another two parts of 'The Recluse', precipitated a fire-storm of abuse, not least from Francis Jeffrey, who made it the occasion of one of the worst reviews of any Romantic publication. By Coleridge, who might have been expected to hail it as a great epic work, it was greeted with disappointment, and gave rise to the ambivalent defence of Wordsworth in *Biographia Literaria*. Although it won limited appreciation from such contemporaries such as Keats, to others it revealed that Wordsworth was a slave to the dominant ideology of the day,[89] and for years would be a byword for literary pomposity, apostasy, egotism,[90] even lunacy. All that lay in the future, but it might not have happened had not Coleridge made the sudden decision to travel north with Joseph Cottle in late October 1799. Another couple of weeks or even days, and it might have been otherwise.

---

[88] *EY* 679.
[89] Mary Shelley, *The Journals of Mary Shelley 1814–1844*, ed. Paula R. Feldman and Diana Scott-Kilvert (2 vols, Oxford: Clarendon Press, 1987), i 25.
[90] Even in the more favourable text of his review, in *The Examiner*, Hazlitt observes that 'It is as if there were nothing but himself and the universe' (Wu ii 327).

In the short term the most important result of Coleridge's decision to travel north was what Wordsworth did next. As soon as he moved into Dove Cottage at the end of 1799 he bowed his head to the yoke and composed the Prospectus to 'The Recluse', followed in the spring by a number of passages towards Book First, Part First of the poem, entitled 'Home at Grasmere'.

7

'Serious musing and self-reproach'

Coleridge's removal to Greta Hall in Keswick on 24 July 1800 was almost certainly motivated by the knowledge that Wordsworth needed policing if he was to continue with 'The Recluse'. From this point of view Coleridge's return northwards was a mixed blessing, and regarded as such by mutual acquaintances. The Wedgwoods were opposed to it, and Tom Wedgwood made a doom-laden prophecy concerning Wordsworth.[1] In February Poole cautioned Coleridge against it and received a stiff riposte: on 31 March 1800 Coleridge defended himself from the charge of 'prostration in regard to Wordsworth' by hailing him as 'a greater poet than any since Milton'.[2] Besides bearing out Poole's argument, this was an index of the high hopes Coleridge entertained for 'The Recluse'. He continued to order Wordsworth to work from his London office, where he was employed by the *Morning Post* from January to March 1800. In February 1800 he wrote to tell him, 'I grieve that "The Recluse" sleeps.'[3] It was the same treatment he had doled out for much of the previous year. Though gratified to be thought Milton's successor, Wordsworth cannot have been pleased that the blackmail continued; the pressure must have been intolerable. All the same, by the time Coleridge made his first ever visit to Dove Cottage on 6 April Wordsworth had accumulated a good quantity of blank verse for 'The Recluse', including the Prospectus and much (if not all) of 'Home at Grasmere'.[4]

Given this kind of progress Wordsworth would be expected to continue

---

[1] By 1812 Coleridge felt it to have been fulfilled (Griggs iii 438). The letter to Poole of 31 March 1800 is clearly a response to a warning from Poole against the move; see Griggs i 584–5.

[2] Griggs i 584.

[3] Griggs i 575.

[4] It is not easy to be sure how much. The Cornell editor suggests that some of 'Home at Grasmere' was composed; Jonathan Wordsworth suggests all.

but surprisingly did the opposite, setting it aside, not to return to it for an-other six years. Why? The only plausible explanation is that he did not feel satisfied with it. It contained some good poetry, but did not finally bear out the high ambitions planned for it. As time passed he came to see that it was not 'philosophical' enough – and Coleridge would not have been slow to point this out. Recent critics have elaborated on this: John Finch notes that it was a 'literal and particularized' work;[5] for Jonathan Wordsworth the poem fails 'to move beyond the personal';[6] Kenneth R. Johnston suggests that 'the identification of the master-poem with the master's life was too quick and insufficiently mediated';[7] to Paul Hamilton, the poem is a failed pastoral idyll.[8] Something of these criticisms would, I suspect, have been anticipated by Wordsworth even as he abandoned it in early April; they would have been brought into focus by the thought of having to show it to Coleridge. In fact, he seems to have made a deliberate decision not to do so.[9] He hadn't shown the two-part *Prelude* to him for nearly a year after beginning work on it, and had he been in any way fearful of Coleridge's opinion of 'Home at Grasmere' would have kept it from him. Accordingly, there is no mention of it in Coleridge's letters or notebooks. Wordsworth did refer to 'Home at Gras-mere' in a letter to De Quincey in 1804, unrevealingly, as 'one Book' of 'a moral and Philosophical Poem',[10] but did not show it to him either.

Prior to Coleridge's arrival in Grasmere Wordsworth devised an excuse for not going on with 'The Recluse': *Lyrical Ballads* volume two. He argued that it was a five-finger exercise for 'The Recluse' in that both projects shared an interest in redefining the pastoral. When announcing the project to Southey Coleridge not surprisingly gave this some emphasis: 'Wordsworth publishes a second Volume of Lyrical Ballads, & Pastorals. He meditates a novel – & so do I.'[11] (The novel would have been another good reason for not getting on with 'Home at Grasmere'.) In MS R of 'Home at Grasmere' Wordsworth wrote feelingly of this quest:

> Is there not
> An art a music & a stream of words
> That shall be like the acknowledgd voice of Life

[5] Finch 194.
[6] *Borders of Vision* 139.
[7] Johnston, *Recluse* 94.
[8] Paul Hamilton, *Wordsworth* (Brighton: Harvester, 1986), p. 78.
[9] James A. Butler and Beth Darlington concur that there is no positive evidence that Coleridge ever saw the poem.
[10] *EY* 454.
[11] Ibid.

Shall speak of what is done among the fields
Done truly there or felt of solid good
And real evil yet be sweet withal
More grateful more harmonious than the breath
The idle breath of sweetest pipe attuned
To pastoral fancies?[12]

The manuscript shows that Wordsworth originally wrote: 'more harmonious than the breath / The idle breath of *pastoral* pipe attuned / To pastoral fancies' (my italics). Scholars disagree over whether these lines were composed by the time Coleridge arrived in Grasmere in April 1800;[13] they could have been, and it would make sense if they were. They relate intriguingly to the fragments written shortly after the unsatisfactory meeting in Göttingen a year before, which dealt with the problem of writing poetry that would enshrine 'The vital spirit of a perfect form'. Wordsworth's answer to that question was to redefine the aims of 'The Recluse', shifting its focus away from the 'false secondary power by which / In weakness we create distinctions' – the cerebral, intellectualizing activity he wasn't very good at – towards 'The idle breath of pastoral pipe attuned / To pastoral fancies'. Coleridge appeared to have no qualms about this, as indicated by the fact that when he read 'The Brothers' to Humphry Davy in May 1800 he described it as 'that beautiful Poem'.[14] From Wordsworth's perspective *Lyrical Ballads* had the dual virtue of being both a legitimate distraction from 'The Recluse' and an adjunct to it. It would certainly discourage Coleridge from pestering him.

There was another reason for bringing *Lyrical Ballads* forward as a priority: it was collaborative. Given the tensions of the past six months, it may have seemed like a good way of sealing their friendship. The outcome of this was more momentous than either could have guessed.

Coleridge left Grasmere for Bristol on 4 May, where he arranged for *Lyrical Ballads* to be printed by Biggs and Cottle and proofread by Humphry Davy, then at the Pneumatic Institute at Clifton. Longman would publish. He decided to settle in the Lakes and returned to Grasmere with Sara Coleridge and Hartley on 29 June, prior to the move to Keswick on 24 July. During their stay at Dove Cottage something strange happened to Wordsworth. He

---

[12] Quoted from the manuscript; for a facsimile see Cornell *Home at Grasmere* 149.
[13] Darlington is doubtful (see Cornell *Home at Grasmere* 11); Jonathan Wordsworth argues that the poem was largely complete by early April 1800, pointing out that MS R is 'Wordsworth's chief rough-notebook of 1800' (*Borders of Vision* 390); Butler and Green appear to agree with Jonathan Wordsworth (Cornell *Lyrical Ballads* 26–7).
[14] Griggs i 611. Coleridge is writing in late July, remembering a reading that must have taken place in May.

fell ill. On the day he moved into Greta Hall Coleridge reported to Poole that Wordsworth 'is well, unless when he uses any effort of mind – then he feels a pain in his left side, which threatens to interdict all species of composition to him'.[15] And in a letter to James Webbe Tobin the following day Coleridge reported that Wordsworth 'was tolerably well, and meditates more than his side permits him even to attempt'.[16] Meditation was an appropriate non-writing pastime for the poet of 'The Recluse', and no doubt thought to be compensation for its continuing delay. Not untypically Coleridge reported on 17 September that 'Wordsworth's Health is but *so so*';[17] on 22 September Wordsworth was 'not well enough to submit to the drudgery' of revising *The Borderers* (a condition that would have precluded work on 'The Recluse');[18] at the end of the month 'Wordsworth's health declines constantly';[19] and on 4 October Coleridge was so afraid for him that he made a mercy dash to Grasmere. Even at this stage he was suspicious. On 25 July he told Humphry Davy that 'W. Wordsworth is such a lazy fellow that I bemire myself by making promises for him.'[20] Was his friend's problem illness or laziness? Whatever it was, it can be no accident that Wordsworth now had the ideal excuse for going no further with 'Home at Grasmere' (as would have been expected had he shown it to Coleridge in April).

In the meantime various inducements were held out to Coleridge to keep him occupied now that negotiations with Biggs, Cottle and Longman were concluded. It was agreed that he would contribute at least two poems to the new volume of *Lyrical Ballads*: one of them was *Christabel*, which he was expected to finish within the next few months. The second arose out of a walk round Grasmere lake with Dorothy and William during July, when they had an encounter with a local peasant. It led them to christen the rocky outcrop where it took place 'Point Rash-Judgement'. Coleridge commemorated it in his notebook with a brief entry: 'Poor fellow at a distance idle? in this haytime when wages are so high? Come near – thin, pale, can scarce speak – or throw out his fishing rod.'[21] This was the sketch for a poem which could, it was agreed, take its place as one of the 'Poems on the Naming of Places'.

Coleridge was also given the task of writing a Preface for the new edition. As the Preface would be a work of theory it was natural that he should write it. However, for whatever reason, Coleridge backed out. Instead it was agreed,

---

[15] Griggs i 608.
[16] Griggs i 608, 613.
[17] Griggs i 623.
[18] Griggs i 624.
[19] Griggs i 627.
[20] Griggs i 611.
[21] *Notebooks* i 761.

on a walk to the deserted quarry in Grasmere, that Wordsworth would write it. Coleridge later admitted that 'the f[irst pass]ages were indeed partly taken from notes of mine / for it was at first intended, that the Preface should be written by me.'[22] In later years Wordsworth would recall that he 'never cared a straw about the theory – & the Preface was written at the request of Mr Coleridge out of sheer good nature'.[23] The passing on of the job to Wordsworth was symptomatic of the power shift that was taking place in the relationship. While away Coleridge had been able to pressure him to write 'The Recluse'; now he was being assigned specific compositions for volume two, and deferring to Wordsworth when asked to write the Preface. To compound whatever awkwardness this may have generated, Wordsworth put Coleridge to work on corrections for volume one.

At this point Wordsworth's hostility towards 'The Ancient Mariner' came to the fore. In June 1799 he told Cottle that it 'has upon the whole been an injury to the volume' on account of the 'old words and the strangeness of it', promising that in a second edition it would be replaced by 'some little things which would be more likely to suit the common taste'.[24] He was correct in citing it as the cause of some of the harsher reviews,[25] but could not bring himself to eliminate it completely, fearing that it would be too obvious an expression of hostility. Instead he did something which in some respects was more wounding. He set Coleridge the task of removing the 'old words' and some of the 'strangeness' from it, and moved it from its place at the beginning of volume one to twenty-third in order. Coleridge copied out the 'corrections' to 'The Ancient Mariner' in a fair hand and sent them to the printers in mid-July.[26] This could hardly have felt like anything but a humiliation.

It was probably a relief for everyone when the Coleridges moved out of Dove Cottage and into Greta Hall on 24 July. By that point Wordsworth had been given the task of writing the Preface and most of the poems in volume two, and Coleridge had yet to finish *Christabel* and write 'Point Rash-Judgement'. The projected date of publication was early October.

It was not to be. The main problem was *Christabel*. At first all seemed well. Part I was with Biggs and Cottle by mid-September,[27] and at the end of the month an early draft of the Preface to *Lyrical Ballads* attributed it to 'a Friend'. At this point its inclusion seemed assured, as Coleridge reported to Daniel

---

[22] Griggs ii 811.
[23] Little 62n101.
[24] *EY* 264.
[25] See Cornell *Lyrical Ballads* 22.
[26] Griggs i 598–602.
[27] *EY* 302.

Stuart: 'Wordsworth's health declines constantly – in a few days his Poems will be published, with a long poem of mine. Of course, you will procure them. The Preface contains our joint opinions on Poetry.'[28] The implication is that *Christabel* would stand alongside the Preface as evidence of the partnership that might still culminate in 'The Recluse', despite Wordsworth's fluctuating health.

Two things happened to change this, the first in late September. Still unappeased, Wordsworth's dislike of 'The Ancient Mariner' led him to compose a written attack on it masquerading as a note, which he posted to the printer of *Lyrical Ballads,* instructing that it be appended to the poem.[29] It lists its 'great defects', claiming on that account that Coleridge had requested it to be 'suppressed', but that Wordsworth had argued for its inclusion, on which account 'such Readers as may have been pleased with this poem . . . owe their pleasure in some sort to me.'[30] Composition of this note seems to have exerted a tremendous strain on Wordsworth as it coincided with a precipitous decline in his health. On Saturday 4 October, just after it was sent to the printer, Coleridge was summoned to Grasmere to attend him.

Christabel Part II was read to the Wordsworths on Coleridge's arrival, when according to Dorothy's journal they were 'exceedingly delighted' with it, and derived 'increasing pleasure' from it the next day. This changed abruptly. On 6 October Dorothy made a stark entry in her diary: 'Determined not to print Christabel with the LB.' In justifying this Wordsworth presented a number of arguments which Coleridge reiterated in a letter to Davy of 9 October:

> The Christabel was running up to 1300 lines – and was so much admired by Wordsworth, that he thought it indelicate to print two Volumes with *his name* in which so much of another man's was included – & which was of more consequence – the poem was in direct opposition to the very purpose for which the Lyrical Ballads were published – viz – an experiment to see how far those passions, which alone can give any value to extraordinary Incidents, were capable of interesting, in & for themselves, in the incidents of common Life. —— We mean to publish the Christabel therefore with a long Blank Verse Poem of Wordsworth's entitled the Pedlar . . .[31]

This last promise was an empty one. Wordsworth must have known how hurtful it would be to exclude *Christabel* from the volume, and the promise of publishing it with 'The Pedlar' was a transparent attempt to buy Coleridge off. As

---

[28]   Griggs i 627.
[29]   *EY* 303.
[30]   Cornell *Lyrical Ballads* 791.
[31]   Griggs i 631.

nothing more was said about it, it was probably never likely. Not surprisingly, either; the publication of *Christabel* with 'The Pedlar' would have made no more sense in thematic terms than its appearance with the *Lyrical Ballads*. Curiously, it was not the extent of Coleridge's poem (1300 lines was a projected length, as the text extended at this moment to just over 600) that was held to be the problem so much as its position within a work which Wordsworth had claimed as his own – in spite of the fact that volume one now contained no less than five poems by Coleridge. Nor, apparently, was Wordsworth much bothered by the fact that the poem was still incomplete.

But it is the suggestion that *Christabel* would have been out of place in a volume about emotions and their role in 'the incidents of common Life' that really begs the question of what the Wordsworths thought of the poem. Dorothy's journal is little help, but in a letter of 18 December to Longman and Rees Wordsworth was explicit:

> A Poem of Mr Coleridge's was to have concluded the Volumes; but upon mature deliberation I found that the Style of this Poem was so discordant from my own that it could not be printed along with my poems with any propriety.[32]

This makes perfect sense if Wordsworth is seen to have established a field of interest, and a way of working, before he met Coleridge; by June 1797 he had made himself the poet of grief, guilt, betrayal, injustice, and their psychological hinterland. The two-Part *Prelude* had brought him back into contact with that resource, and he would have seen the writing of 'The Brothers' and 'Michael' as of a piece with it. *Christabel* would have seemed eccentric by comparison. Its rejection was as much to do with Wordsworth's desire for self-definition as a literary personality as with the artistic coherence of *Lyrical Ballads*. That Wordsworth understood this is indicated by the fact that a few days after expelling *Christabel* from its pages he revised the Preface so as to omit a crucial phrase he had earlier written about himself and Coleridge: 'our opinions on the subject of poetry do almost entirely coincide.'[33]

As a further means of salving his conscience Wordsworth reminded Coleridge of 'Point Rash-Judgement'; that would be more in keeping with the rest of the volume, but would have to be complete by the time he returned to Grasmere in two weeks' time. On either 6 or 7 October Wordsworth accordingly wrote to the printer to make a further alteration to the Preface. Instead of the sentence mentioning *Christabel*, he substituted the following remark: 'It is proper to inform the Reader that the Poems entitled the ancient Mariner, the

---

[32] *EY* 309.
[33] *EY* 304–5. The phrase was eventually reinstated in the third paragraph of the Preface.

Foster Mother's Tale, the Nightingale, the Dungeon, and Love, are written by a friend, who has also furnished me with a few of those Poems in the second volume, which are classed under the title of "Poems on the Naming of Places."'[34] By now Wordsworth had already composed 'To M.H.' and 'To Joanna'; Coleridge, who had worked so hard towards volume two, would still appear in it with a work based on a Wordsworthian theme.

This double humiliation hit Coleridge hard. He had rushed to Grasmere on account of his friend's health, and within a few days had been first applauded for *Christabel* before seeing it cancelled from *Lyrical Ballads*. During that period he had also, presumably, endorsed Wordsworth's 'note' to 'The Ancient Mariner'. It is hard to avoid the conclusion that Wordsworth's ill health had been psychosomatic, evidence of a guilty struggle to deal with hostile feelings towards Coleridge and his influence. The sops of future joint publication and the possible inclusion in *Lyrical Ballads* of another poem yet to be written can only have compounded the blow. Coleridge left Dove Cottage the day after Wordsworth had announced his decision, and when he wrote to Davy on 9 October two days later was still in shock: 'I was right glad, glad with a *Stagger* of the Heart, to see your writing again.'[35] It is the utterance of a depressed man. In the same letter he told Davy, 'I think very differently of CHRISTABEL. — I would rather have written Ruth, and Nature's Lady ['Three years she grew in sun and shower'] than a million such poems.'[36] Like many depressed people he engaged in self-destructive activity, as when on 11 October he climbed Carrock Fell in bad weather and almost broke his neck. Two days later he told Godwin that the investment of time and energy in *Christabel* had set him 'fearfully back in my *bread-and-beef* occupations'[37] (by which he meant his journalism). The subtext of this was that newspaper work did pay, whereas the labour invested in *Christabel* would not result in the reward of seeing it in print.

Others have commented perceptively on this. Richard Holmes is right to say that 'Wordsworth, from a position of apparent weakness, had ruthlessly come to dominate the terms of the collaboration.'[38] Stephen Gill describes Wordsworth's treatment of Coleridge as 'unfeeling'.[39] So far as I know, no one has yet pointed out that the effect on Coleridge was a reiteration, in worse form, of the fate that had befallen Wordsworth during the harsh winter of 1798–9, when he found himself in Goslar incapable of writing 'The

[34]   Ibid.
[35]   Griggs i 630.
[36]   Griggs i 631–2.
[37]   Griggs i 635.
[38]   *Early Visions* 285.
[39]   Gill 187.

Recluse'. Not that Wordsworth thought of it in that way. The point is that these events had their roots not in *Christabel* or, come to that, in the pressure Coleridge was under to produce copy. But they were intricately intertwined with 'The Recluse' and its derailing of Wordsworth's career.

Catherine Clarkson's account of them during the walking tour of late 1799, immediately after their reconciliation, describes Coleridge 'in high spirits' and Wordsworth as 'more reserved'. So he would have been. He knew how destructive Coleridge's 'encouragement' could be. He could not have forgotten the chivvying letters about 'The Recluse', a campaign that would not cease with Coleridge's departure for London in December 1799. Coleridge's return to the Lakes, accompanied by continuing urgings to go on with 'The Recluse', would have revived the feelings that had stifled him in Goslar, and which were now almost certainly the cause of his psychosomatic illness. Coleridge had become, literally, a thorn in his side.

In *Lyrical Ballads* Wordsworth had a project he could make his own, and it was no accident that in eliminating *Christabel* from it – a lengthy, very different kind of poem – he would preserve the distinctive identity of the work. He was understandably ambitious to create his own literary personality. For too long he had been labouring in Coleridge's shadow, and 'The Recluse' was in fundamental respects not his project. As he said in the fragments composed in the wake of the Göttingen meeting in April 1799, he was afraid of falling into the trap of creating a 'desultory' and inadequate verse which would cause him 'after-loathings, damps of discontent'. He was 30. It was time to establish his own voice. Coleridge left Dove Cottage at 11a.m. on 7 October with orders to produce 'Point Rash-Judgement': it must have been an empowering experience for Wordsworth. He had been laid low by the stress of having Coleridge in the vicinity and the guilt of not writing the poem he had set him; now the tables were turned. Had Coleridge seen 'Home at Grasmere'? Probably not. Wordsworth knew that he would probably have pointed out its defects. Anxiety about Coleridge's opinion had now translated itself into a ruthless act of self-assertion.

How conscious of this Wordsworth was is hard to say, but the politics of the situation could not have been lost on him. Its most significant result was that he was now back in touch with his creative roots. When surveying the course of his career he could look back on the Hawkshead and Cambridge poems as having established a range of subject-matter he continued to mine, beside which the 'Recluse' verse of early 1798 must have seemed like a departure – one inspired largely by Coleridge. It may even have seemed like a mistake.

That this came as a shock to Coleridge points to the fact that Wordsworth had been repressing his feelings. The reconciliation of late 1799, which had taken Wordsworth by surprise, had probably not led to a full outpouring of his confused emotions – as in 1783, when his father died, and he had not fully expiated his grief. The ensuing months had given him scant opportunity to speak openly about them with Coleridge. By October 1800 he probably felt angry – at the requisition of his poetic abilities in the service of someone else's ambition; at himself for falling into the same trap a second time with the failed 'Home at Grasmere'; and most of all with Coleridge for following him up to the Lake District so as to plead the cause of 'The Recluse'. In darker moments it may have seemed to Wordsworth that *Lyrical Ballads* was an uneasy compromise devised to make the kind of poetry he really wanted to write more palatable to his tormentor. Under the circumstances it would have been amazing had he not been angry. The problem was that he seems to have preferred to paper over their differences rather than speak honestly about them. Given their continuing close contact that was not wise; as Blake had observed in 'A Poison Tree',

> I was angry with my friend;
> I told my wrath, my wrath did end.
> I was angry with my foe:
> I told it not, my wrath did grow.

(ll. 1–4)

It ends with the figure of Blake's foe 'outstretchd beneath the tree'. Coleridge's cutting-down began with the decision not to include *Christabel*. It was, besides anything else, an angry decision, although this was a less unhealthy way to express it than to turn it against himself as Wordsworth had been doing up to now.

On 6 or 7 October Wordsworth expected Coleridge to write some of the poems on the naming of places, one of which was to have been 'Point Rash-Judgment'; Coleridge went home to Keswick on the 7th, and would return to Grasmere on the 22nd (with a copy of the poem, it was hoped). However, on 10 October Dorothy recorded, 'William sat up after me writing Point Rash judgment,'[40] and on 13 October she wrote, 'I copied poems on the naming of places,' indicating that the remainder were by then complete. At the most only three days can have passed between the agreement that Coleridge would write the poem and its composition by Wordsworth. On 17 October Dorothy made another stark entry in her journal: 'Coleridge had done nothing for the LB.'[41] In a painfully self-aware notebook entry dated 30 October Coleridge wrote: 'He knew not what to do – something, he felt, must be done – he rose,

---

[40]   *Grasmere Journals* 26.
[41]   *Grasmere Journals* 27.

drew his writing-desk suddenly before him – sate down, took the pen – & found that he knew not what to do.'[42]

The only explanation for these events that would reflect well on Wordsworth is that on reaching Keswick on 7 October Coleridge realized he could not write the poem and wrote to Wordsworth asking him to do it instead. Such a letter, if ever it existed, has not come to light. It is more likely that Wordsworth pre-empted Coleridge, assumed he would not write the poem, and did it himself in expectation of Coleridge's apologies. If so it would suggest that Wordsworth's anger had not subsided. Still upset with Coleridge and mindful of how far behind *Lyrical Ballads* was, he decided that Coleridge would delay the volume no longer and set about the composition of the poems himself. The 'Poems on the Naming of Places' were in fair copy by 17 October, when Coleridge wrote to the printer with instructions for the half-title that would introduce them – another humiliation.[43] 'Point Rash-Judgement', the poem originally assigned to Coleridge, was thus written by Wordsworth, probably on 10–13 October 1800.

Relations between them would never be the same. At the end of the year Coleridge wrote to their mutual friend Francis Wrangham:

> As to our literary occupations they are still more distant than our residences. – He is a great, a true Poet – I am only a kind of Metaphysician. – He has even now sent off the last sheet of a second Volume of his Lyrical Ballads —.[44]

This downgrading of his talents followed inevitably from the rejection of *Christabel*. Beside Wordsworth's, his poetry felt untrue, fake. Significantly, the *Lyrical Ballads* are now 'his' – indicating that Coleridge felt he no longer had a stake in it. But what he emphasizes most is the distance between them. It is an amplification of what Wordsworth had been feeling for longer – that they were different writers with separate concerns and ways of thinking. This would be understood increasingly as the years passed. It explains the subdued hostility in Coleridge's publication of 'Dejection: An Ode' on Wordsworth's wedding-day, 4 October 1802, and the more obviously aggressive 'Spots in the Sun' a week later:

> My father confessor is strict and holy,
> *Mi fili*, still he cries, *peccare noli*.
> And yet how oft I find the pious man
> At Annette's door, the lovely courtesan!

---

[42]   *Notebooks* i 834.
[43]   Griggs i 637.
[44]   Griggs i 658.

Her soul's deformity the good man wins
And not her charms! he comes to hear her sins!
Good father! I would fain not do thee wrong;
But ah! I fear that they who oft and long
Stand gazing at the sun, to count each spot,
Must sometimes find the sun itself too hot.[45]

For those in the know, this accused Wordsworth of hypocrisy and repressed lust, and refers to Annette Vallon by name. It may have been malicious, but its account of Wordsworth has something to be said for it. The failure to mourn his father fully in 1783 may have left Wordsworth with a tendency to suppress his emotions, particularly when they became unmanageable. His passionate nature had been evident to his mother, who once observed that he 'would be remarkable either for good or for evil. The cause of this was, that I was of a stiff, moody, and violent temper.'[46] That temper was now under strict regulation, something that would be responsible for destroying their friendship. He failed to be completely honest with Coleridge in late 1799, and by the time he rejected *Christabel* the following year it was too late. 'Spots in the Sun' rightly holds Wordsworth guilty of psychological repression and dishonesty, although the *Morning Post* a week after Wordsworth's wedding-day may not have been the most appropriate time or place for such a judgement to be issued.[47]

When on 10 October 1803 Coleridge told Poole that Wordsworth 'has made a beginning to his Recluse' he took the opportunity to trace his previous failure to do so to the fact that 'The habit too of writing such a multitude of small Poems was in this instance hurtful to him.' This was strong stuff and Coleridge didn't stop there. He went on to hail 'The Recluse' as Wordsworth's 'Great Work', suggesting that its relation to the shorter poems was 'what Food is to Famine':

> I have seen enough, positively to give me feelings of hostility towards the plan of several of the Poems in the L. Ballads: & I really consider it as a misfortune, that Wordsworth ever deserted his former mountain Track to wander in Lanes & allies; tho' in the event it may prove to have been a great Benefit to him.[48]

[45]   Published in the *Morning Post*, 11 October 1802.
[46]   *Prose Works* iii 372.
[47]   These turbulent emotions were also part of the poetic dialogue of 1802 – 'Resolution and Independence', the 'Ode', the 'Letter to Sara Hutchinson' and 'Dejection: An Ode'. See on this matter Lucy Newlyn, *Coleridge, Wordsworth, and the Language of Allusion* (Oxford: Clarendon Press, 1986), chapters 3, 4, and 5.
[48]   Griggs ii 1013.

Coleridge's hostility to the *Lyrical Ballads* is entirely understandable. From now on he would undermine it, holding it to be an obstruction to 'The Recluse' (which it designedly was), using its defects as a means of attacking Wordsworth. This culminated in the barbed 'defence' of *Lyrical Ballads* in *Biographia Literaria* chapter 14, particularly Coleridge's attack on the Preface to which he had contributed. The resentment between them was due partly to Coleridge's feeling that the rejection of *Christabel* had destroyed him as a poet; in 1818 he spoke of the Wordsworths' 'cold praise and effective discouragement of every attempt of mine to roll onward in a distinct current of my own – who *admitted* that the Ancient Mariner [and] the Christabel . . . were not without merit, but were abundantly anxious to acquit their judgements of any blindness to the very numerous defects'.[49] This cites as problematic the very thing that Wordsworth must have felt about Coleridge: discouragement of 'every attempt of mine to roll onward in a distinct current of my own'. Coleridge had drawn him away from the path he had been following when at Racedown; in 1800, by demanding that he abandon *Christabel* and produce 'Point Rash-Judgement', Wordsworth had given him a dose of his own medicine.

> No spot but claims the tender tear
> By joy or grief to memory dear . . .
> ('The Vale of Esthwaite' 272–3)

Wordsworth knew by the age of 17 that emotions attached themselves to particular places: it was not something he learned from Coleridge. The 'Poems on the Naming of Places' placed Wordsworth, who had been labouring for too long on a project he could not call his own, back in touch with those feelings and ideas which had nourished him in earlier years. Their governing conceit was Wordsworthian – 'wholly, solely mine'.

As in the 'Vale', the story related in 'Point Rash-Judgement' depends upon a rocky part of the landscape, and begins with an explicit reference to it:

> A narrow girdle of rough stones and crags,
> A rude and natural causeway, interpos'd
> Between the water and a winding slope
> Of copse and thicket, leaves the eastern shore
> Of Grasmere safe in its own privacy.

---

[49]   Griggs i 631n2. Griggs says that this comes from a manuscript in the New York Public Library which at the time of writing has not, I think, been published elsewhere.

> And there, myself and two beloved Friends,
> One calm September morning, ere the mist
> Had altogether yielded to the sun,
> Saunter'd on this retir'd and difficult way.
>
> (ll. 1–9)

It is the sequestered nature of the place that strikes Wordsworth as the poem begins: the narrow girdle of stones, forming a 'natural causeway', is a precarious destination for this 'retir'd and difficult way'. The lingering mist makes it that much more out of the way and mysterious. Our first glance at the landscape turns it into something extraordinary, beyond the everyday, almost a separate realm. (Incidentally, Wordsworth has manipulated historical fact; the encounter must have taken place in July, not September.)

> —— Ill suits the road with one in haste, but we
> Play'd with our time; and, as we stroll'd along,
> It was our occupation to observe
> Such objects as the waves had toss'd ashore,
> Feather, or leaf, or weed, or wither'd bough,
> Each on the other heap'd along the line
> Of the dry wreck.
>
> (ll. 10–16)

Words such as 'toss'd' and 'heap'd' combine with 'Play'd' to emphasize the sense of carelessness, a quality that will be reassessed later.

> And in our vacant mood,
> Not seldom did we stop to watch some tuft
> Of dandelion seed or thistle's beard,
> Which, seeming lifeless half, and half impell'd
> By some internal feeling, skimm'd along
> Close to the surface of the lake that lay
> Asleep in a dead calm, ran closely on
> Along the dead calm lake, now here, now there,
> In all its sportive wanderings all the while
> Making report of an invisible breeze
> That was its wings, its chariot, and its horse,
> Its very playmate and its moving soul.
>
> (ll. 16–27)

Wordsworth's brother John, who came to love this poem, thought these his favourite lines. They signal the fact that their author had completely rejected 'that false secondary power by which / In weakness we create distinctions' – something associated with Coleridge – understanding that philosophy was

not needed to ratify his vision. Accordingly, there is nothing here of the pantheism of the 1798 poetry. Wordsworth has retreated from the cerebral to the
intuitive. As in the preceding lines, the language plays with seeming effortless-
ness on our sense of the numinous. The shores of the lake, and the lake itself,
seem to bear within them an inner existence that reflects the leisure and
'vacancy' of the walkers.

Everything depends on the moment of recognition – one of the simplest
and oldest of narrative devices, a commonplace of myth and legend.
Wordsworth and Coleridge were brought up on such tales, as Coleridge recalled when he wrote to Thomas Poole in October 1797: 'For from my early
reading of Faery Tales, & Genii &c &c – my mind had been habituated *to the
Vast* — & I never regarded *my senses* in any way as the criteria of my belief.
. . . Should children be permitted to read Romances, & Relations of Giants &
Magicians, & Genii? . . . I know no other way of giving the mind a love of
"the Great", & "the Whole".'[50] Everything in the poem thus far has been
tending towards this. From its first line the setting has been undergoing subtle transformation, as the shore has gradually changed into an otherworld.
Wordsworth offers a foretaste of what is to come in those marvellous lines
where the verse's rhythms mimic those of the eye as it passes excitedly from
one plant to another, finally settling on the *Osmunda regalis*, a fern common
in Wordsworth's time, but no longer to be found on the lakeside:

> ———— And often, trifling with a privilege
> Alike indulg'd to all, we paus'd, one now
> And now the other, to point out, perchance
> To pluck, some flower or water-weed, too fair
> Either to be divided from the place
> On which it grew, or to be left alone
> To its own beauty. Many such there are,
> Fair ferns and flowers, and chiefly that tall plant
> So stately, of the Queen Osmunda nam'd,
> Plant lovelier in its own retir'd abode
> On Grasmere's beach, than Naiad by the side
> Of Grecian brook, or Lady of the Mere
> Sole-sitting by the shores of old Romance.
>
> (ll. 28–40)

For a moment the 'shores of old Romance' become those of Grasmere, as the
Lady of the Lake returns – a presiding genius over the transformation we are
to witness. The very name of the *Osmunda regalis* implies metamorphosis – it

---

[50] Griggs i 354.

is a queen turned into a plant, like a character out of Ovid.[51] Its tall, stately
appearance does not merely remind us of a monarch, but foreshadows the
human shape about to appear. Everything is about to change, and the Greek
naiad and the Arthurian Lady of the Lake, introduced into the poem with
their magical associations, confirm that these 'tendencies to shape' are about
to take possession. Wordsworth doesn't need philosophy to persuade; it is all
defiantly unintellectual and works beautifully so long as we read it with the
credulity of a child listening to a fairy-tale.

> —— So fared we that sweet morning: from the fields
> Meanwhile, a noise was heard, the busy mirth
> Of Reapers, Men and Women, Boys and Girls.
> Delighted much to listen to those sounds,
> And in the fashion which I have describ'd
> Feeding unthinking fancies, we advanc'd
> Along the indented shore; when suddenly,
> Through a thin veil of glittering haze, we saw
> Before us on a Point of jutting land
> The tall and upright figure of a Man
> Attir'd in peasant's garb, who stood alone
> Angling beside the margin of the lake.

(ll. 41–52)

The 'busy mirth / Of Reapers, Men and Women, Boys and Girls' recalls the
legends intertwined with the rite and ritual of harvest-time, and summons up
thoughts of the theme of death and rejuvenation invoked by that season. As
the verse progresses, things become stranger. The angler materializes reluctantly, appearing 'Through a thin veil of glittering haze . . . on a Point of
jutting land'. It is a haunting image, incorporating the supernatural with the
everyday. His 'tall and upright figure' echoing the stateliness of the *Osmunda
regalis*, he seems not only kingly but perhaps Christ-like, as if walking on
water. But those initial expectations are about to be undermined.

---

[51] In fact it does not derive its name from any classical source, as C.C.B. explained in
1889:

> There is a legend that a waterman of Loch Fyne hid his wife and daughters under the
> luxuriant foliage of this fern from a sudden raid of the Danes whilst he ferried the invaders
> over the lake, praying meanwhile for the safety of his dear ones, and that one of his daugh-
> ters in after years gave the fern the name of her father, Osmund. ('Osmunda', *N&Q* 7th
> ser. 8 (1889) 87)

Given Wordsworth's text it seems unlikely that he had any inkling of this.

That way we turn'd our steps; nor was it long
Ere making ready comments on the sight
Which then we saw, with one and the same voice
We all cried out, that he must be indeed
An idle man, who thus could lose a day
Of the mid-harvest, when the labourer's hire
Is ample, and some little might be stor'd
Wherewith to chear him in the winter time.

(ll. 53–60)

This is the first test of the reader. The moral judgements made by the narrator
and his friends call into question our own loyalties.

Thus talking of that Peasant we approach'd
Close to the spot where with his rod and line
He stood alone; whereat he turn'd his head
To greet us – and we saw a Man worn down
By sickness, gaunt and lean, with sunken cheeks
And wasted limbs, his legs so long and lean
That for my single self I look'd at them,
Forgetful of the body they sustained. –
The man was using his best skill to gain
A pittance from the dead unfeeling lake
That knew not of his wants.

(ll. 61–72)

In few works does Wordsworth speak so convincingly of the pain of being
human. The peasant turns to greet the voices he hears, perhaps with a smile;
that greeting, given in the face of his plight – all the more desperate not just
because of his own physical state but because of his family's needs – is one of
those poetic images that does a good deal more than play a role in an unfolding drama. 'Then cherish pity, lest you drive an angel from your door,'[52]
Blake had written nearly ten years previously. That line resonates because it
expresses a recognizable fact of life – that we lack the imagination that would
enable us to perceive the world and its inhabitants as they are. This was an
intuition Wordsworth shared, and it is reassuring to find that, on being read
some of Blake's *Songs* by Henry Crabb Robinson in 1812, he is reported to
have been 'pleased with some of them, and considered Blake as having the
elements of poetry a thousand times more than either Byron or Scott'.[53]

[52]   'Holy Thursday' (Innocence) 12.
[53]   Morley i 85.

Wordsworth's encounter with the leech-gatherer took place on 26 September 1800, slightly less than two weeks before this poem was written; that may explain why he set 'Point Rash-Judgement' in September. Like the angler the leech-gatherer appears

> Like one whom I had met with in a dream;
> Or like a Man from some far region sent,
> To give me human strength, and strong admonishment.
> ('Resolution and Independence' 117–19)

Each encounter assumes the clarity of a dream and, as in reverie, the characters deliver their admonitions with an uncanny knowledge of the dreamer's preoccupations. That Wordsworth is thinking along these lines is signalled by the conscious allusion to 'The Discharged Soldier', one of the passages written in 1798 which was to find its way into the *Thirteen-Book Prelude*. Like other solitaries he is encountered unexpectedly, revealed by 'a sudden turning of the road':

> There was in his form
> A meagre stiffness. You might almost think
> That his bones wounded him. His legs were long,
> So long and shapeless that I looked at them
> Forgetful of the body they sustained.
> ('The Discharged Soldier' 43–7)

'Forgetful of the body they sustained': that line, repeated in 'Point Rash-Judgement', emphasizes the odd way in which the lone angler and the discharged soldier are spiritualized by the extremity of their situation. There is something Christ-like about them, and they become almost emblematic of those in desperate need. The apprehension of profound suffering usually has the effect of placing everything else into perspective – and that, to put it blandly, is the effect of the poem. At the moment when the angler's plight registers in our minds the 'idle man' is transfigured by the shock of recognition, and Wordsworth's assumptions exposed for what they were. We, who have identified with his thoughts and judgements, are similarly chastened. The effect is similar to the chastising of the young Wordsworth in the light of his father's death as he recalls his 'trite reflections of morality' when the horses failed to turn up to take him and his brothers home. In both cases a summary judgement is exposed for what it is, and leads to feelings of guilt, even culpability.

If we are attentive to the context suggested by the implied presence of the Lady of the Mere we may be reminded of the Fisher King. In Chrétien de Troyes' twelfth-century poem, *The Story of the Grail*, one of Arthur's knights, Sir Perceval, seeks vainly for somewhere to cross a large river when he meets an old man fishing. The man invites him to his castle for the night where he is dined. At dinner he sees a number of strange things, including a lance that sheds blood, and a bowl. He fails to question the old man about his identity, or to ask about the lance or the bowl. He is told later that the bowl was the holy grail, and is reprimanded for not enquiring after it:

> Had you asked, the wealthy king, so sorely afflicted, would have been cured of his wound and would have held his land in peace, land he will never hold again. And do you know what will befall the king if he is not cured of his wounds, and does not hold his land? Ladies will lose their husbands; hapless maidens will be orphans; many knights will die; and lands will be laid waste. All these ills will result because of you.[54]

Perceval's crimes are compounded by the fact that, as he is told, 'This has happened, know well, because of your sin against your mother, for she died of grief for you.'[55] He is guilty of betrayal – emanating from complicity in his mother's death. Like so many legends, Perceval's has its roots in a traumatic past in which we find ourselves implicated. Wordsworth's encounter is more succinct than Perceval's because, as elsewhere in the *Lyrical Ballads*, he has abandoned traditional narrative structures and telescoped his story, concentrating it into an act of recognition. That should not prevent us from seeing that its consequences are no less devastating for him than for his twelfth-century counterpart.

The Russian film director, Andrey Tarkovsky, wrote of his film, *Mirror*, that it 'was about my feelings towards people dear to me; about my relationships with them; my perpetual pity for them and my own inadequacy – my feeling of duty left unfulfilled.'[56] For Tarkovsky art served partly to heal the scars left by obligations left undischarged – by the sense of having failed, or betrayed, the hopes and expectations of those dearest to us. These are the psychic forces that compel Wordsworth. The impact of 'Point Rash-Judgement' derives partly from the fact that the encounter at its heart leads to a sudden, and rather horrible, insight the poet could have done without. The rash judgement is more than a momentary failing, just as Perceval's failure to ask the right question at the right time is more than an oversight. It is

---

[54] *The Complete Romances of Chrétien de Troyes*, trans. David Staines (Bloomington: Indiana University Press, 1993), pp. 396–7. I find no evidence that Wordsworth ever read Chrétien, though he read Malory prior to composition of 'Point Rash-Judgement'; see *WR* ii 140.

[55] Ibid. 384.

[56] Andrey Tarkovsky, *Sculpting in Time: Reflections on the Cinema* trans. Kitty Hunter-Blair (London: Bodley Head, 1986), p. 134

evidence of another of those psychological features not under conscious control – the capacity to betray. Perceval's crimes can be traced to unacknowledged guilt at his mother's death; similar feelings haunt Wordsworth's poetry, most notably in the waiting for the horses episode. In that important respect 'Point Rash-Judgement' is a distinctively Wordsworthian treatment of an encounter that takes us back to a theme that he regarded as stemming from his creative sources. It does not intellectualize, preferring to focus emphatically on psychological truth.

> I will not say
> What thoughts immediately were ours, nor how
> The happy idleness of that sweet morn,
> With all its lovely images, was chang'd
> To serious musing and to self-reproach.
>
> (ll. 72–6)

Wordsworth's art lies in encapsulating the drama in a mere glance. In terms of narrative action almost nothing has happened; everything takes place within the mind. And he leaves the emotional work to the reader: 'I will not say / What thoughts immediately were ours.' He is eschewing the 'false secondary power' of the intellect, forcing us to locate the poem's meaning in an emotional reality that we must imagine. As the poem concludes, Wordsworth offers a few lines of commentary.

> Nor did we fail to see within ourselves
> What need there is to be reserv'd in speech,
> And temper all our thoughts with charity.
> – Therefore, unwilling to forget that day,
> My Friend, Myself, and She who then receiv'd
> The same admonishment, have called the place
> By a memorial name, uncouth indeed
> As e'er by Mariner was giv'n to Bay
> Or Foreland on a new-discover'd coast,
> And POINT RASH-JUDGMENT is the name it bears.
>
> (ll. 77–86)

The memorial name is loaded with emotion, enshrining the self-reproach of the moment. It is 'uncouth' in that it is hitherto unknown, strange; indeed the entire story, though set in his backyard, has taken us into another world, like the travel books Wordsworth and Coleridge devoured at this period. But the important thing is that its attachment to a feature in the landscape, 'A narrow girdle of rough stones and crags', turns the name into a permanent physical reminder of the emotional resonances arising from what happened, a reiteration of ideas that occur as early as 'The Vale of Esthwaite', where Wordsworth summed up the argument in a line borrowed from Shakespeare: '[From] every rock would hang a tale.'[57]

Indeed, this process transforms the locale into something unexpected. On one level the poem is decidedly concerned with physical space; in 1836 Wordsworth attached a note to line 5 saying that 'A new road has destroyed this retirement.'[58] And he repeated this when in 1843 he told Isabella Fenwick that 'The character of the eastern shore of Grasmere Lake is quite changed since these verses were written, by the public road being carried along its side.'[59] Though painful to him, that was in a sense irrelevant because the map plotted by the poem is impervious to change. No matter that the road's course is altered, nor that today we can only speculate as to the precise location of the point of 'jutting land' on which the angler stood – what counts is process. Absorbed into the imagination, the shores of Grasmere lake are forever established as one of those 'permanent and beautiful forms of nature' with which the poet's passions are incorporated.[60] Why should this move us? Because the space of art is the ideal one of fiction. In it, things never decay; one cannot walk into the world of a poem as one walks the shores of the real Grasmere lake. Poetry is incorruptible and in some sense innocent. Its component parts are the rudiments of Paradise, the building blocks of a system that has no relationship to our bodies except through the ocular perception of the printed word. They serve to trace an imaginary topography – not just in the poems on the naming of places, but in nearly all the poems of *Lyrical Ballads* volume two – that bears into times more disturbed and alienated than those known to the poet a crucial warning of what it is to lose sight, for a moment, of our shared humanity. And if we cannot resist the feeling that we are complicit with the poet and his companions at the moment of recognition – that, reliant on direct observation, he has given to the anxieties awakened by the encounter the density of objects – it must also be that this most morally undeceived of poems possesses all the depth and ambiguity of real life. It might almost be argued that 'Point Rash-Judgement' confronts us with a mystery to which there is no solution, refusing to gloss its author's serious musing and self-reproach, backing away from any comment on the act of recognition at its centre.

Understanding this, or something like it, Lady Beaumont told Coleridge 'that the night before last as she was reading your Poem on Cape RASH

---

57 'The Vale of Esthwaite' 353.
58 Cornell *Lyrical Ballads* 248.
59 Cornell *Lyrical Ballads* 399.
60 Wordsworth had only recently completed the Preface; *Prose Works* i 124.

JUDGEMENT, had you entered the room, she believes she should have fallen at your feet.'[61] Given the circumstances, it cannot have been easy for Coleridge to make this report to Wordsworth; and even for someone with Wordsworth's self-confidence, he might have reflected, at least for a moment, that the poem which had given so much pleasure to Lady Beaumont might at one stage have been written by Coleridge. Which leads me to suggest another context in which the poem might be understood. The only authorial comment on the central event occurs in lines 77–9:

> Nor did we fail to see within ourselves
> What need there is to be reserv'd in speech,
> And temper all our thoughts with charity.

When copied out by Dorothy in the second week of October 1800 these lines were *not* included as they had not then been composed. On 19 December 1800 Wordsworth wrote to the printer to insert them: 'These three lines are absolutely necessary to render the po[em] intelligible.'[62] Significantly, they were copied out by Coleridge. Were they also *composed* by him? James Butler and Karen Green believe so.[63] It would make sense; their urge to explain is Coleridgean. It reminds us that he is a partner in both conception and composition, as well as being a character within its drama.

His presence extends into the poem's mythic subtext. In Arthurian legend the Fisher King is in search of the regenerative principle; his lands are barren, and he is in continual pain from his wounds. Coleridge's situation was analogous. He was unable to write verse, and had been wounded by the cancellation of *Christabel*. Physically he was ailing; among other things, on 28 November Dorothy mentioned in her journal the 'Great Boils upon his neck'[64] that obliged him to take to bed at Dove Cottage rather than return to Keswick. These ailments stemmed partly from the depression into which the rejection of *Christabel* had plunged him. Coleridge and the Fisher King were both afflicted and in different ways condemned – and as Wordsworth composed the poem passed on to him by his friend's inertia, the 'idle man' at its centre might have seemed eerily familiar. That would have placed Wordsworth in the role of traitor, and turns the poem into an expression of subliminal guilt at Coleridge's plight.

---

[61] Griggs ii 957.
[62] *EY* 311.
[63] Cornell *Lyrical Ballads* 732.
[64] *Grasmere Journals* 33.

8

'I yearn towards some philosophic song'

Wednesday, Jan. 4th / in the highest & outermost of Grasmere Wordsworth read to me the second Part of his divine Self-biography – [1]

It was a risky thing for Wordsworth to be doing at the start of 1804. However divine the 'poem to Coleridge' it lacked the pressing importance of 'The Recluse' on which he had conspicuously done nothing since abandoning 'Home at Grasmere' nearly four years previously. If his 'Self-biography' was divine, how much more so, would the ailing Coleridge have argued, was the still unwritten philosophical poem? Wordsworth can only have responded with a pledge of his good intentions. It is likely that this recitation in the highest and outermost of Grasmere (somewhere in Easedale, perhaps?) initiated a further spate of exhortations to proceed with the great work for which Coleridge thought Wordsworth destined.

What had brought them to this point? As recently as October 1803 Coleridge had in no uncertain terms denounced *Lyrical Ballads* in an unbuttoned letter to Poole, by way of noting that Wordsworth has finally 'yielded to my urgent & repeated – almost unremitting – requests & remonstrances – & will go on with the Recluse exclusively'.[2] Coleridge probably had been 'unremitting' in his remonstrances, but Wordsworth was certainly *not* writing 'The Recluse' at that moment (though he may have agreed to do so in order to get some peace). If this is anything to go by, meetings must have been strained. Hardly surprising, then, that when in August 1803 Sir George Beaumont gave Wordsworth a smallholding in Applethwaite near Keswick so that he could be closer to Coleridge, he turned it down. As he explained to his brother Richard:

---

[1]   *Notebooks* i 1801.
[2]   Griggs ii 1013.

By the bye, I ought to have mentioned to you that Sir George Beaumont made
me a present last summer of a few old houses with two small fields attached to
them in the Vale of Keswick, value 100£, it was for me to patch up a house there
if I liked to be near Mr Coleridge. But this I decline, though he insists on my
keeping the land, so you see I am a freeholder of the County of Cumberland.
(*EY* 427)

Dove Cottage was already beginning to feel overcrowded. Besides William
and Dorothy it was now the home of Mary and baby Johnny (born 18 June
1803); Sara and Joanna Hutchinson were frequent guests. There was reason
to take Beaumont's offer seriously, as Wordsworth acknowledged in February
1804 when he said that he 'would be glad to get a ready built house *cheap*,
with a little Land'.[3] In that light the decision to decline Applethwaite was
pointed.

Nor was this the first time such a possibility had arisen. In the new year of
1801 William Calvert, recently retired from the militia, had been in the process of rebuilding his house at Windy Brow and invited the Wordsworths to
come and share it with him. The obvious incentive, besides the fact that William
and Dorothy got on with Calvert, was to be close to Coleridge, who lived half
a mile away. This plan excited Coleridge, who told Humphry Davy that
Wordsworth was 'strongly inclined to adopt the scheme'.[4] No doubt that was
what Wordsworth said to Coleridge, but it cannot have seemed entirely desir-
able because, after some dithering, the offer was turned down in late March
1801.[5] It is not clear what excuse was given to Coleridge, but it would certainly have taken some explaining. Two years later the refusal of another domi-
cile near Keswick must have reminded all concerned of what had happened in
1801.

On top of this, the Scottish tour of August 1803 had failed not because of
Coleridge's health (admittedly unstable) but because he had fallen out with
Wordsworth. As he reported to his wife, '[Wordsworth's] Hypochondriacal
Feelings keep him silent, & [self]-centered.'[6] To Poole he remarked: 'I went
into Scotland with Wordsworth & his Sister; but I soon found that I was a
burthen on them / & Wordsworth, himself a brooder over his painful hypochondriacal Sensations, was not my fittest companion.'[7] In his notebook he
recorded an observation that indicates something of the tensions between

[3] *EY* 439.
[4] Griggs ii 670.
[5] As a sort of thank-you present Wordsworth sent Calvert a copy of *Lyrical Ballads* (1800);
see *Supp.* 3–4.
[6] Griggs ii 978.
[7] Griggs ii 1010.

them: 'My words & actions imaged on his mind, distorted & snaky as the Boatman's Oar reflected in the Lake.'[8] As I have argued in the previous chapter, Wordsworth's pain in his side may have been a symptom of anxiety over 'The Recluse'. Coleridge's assurance to Poole in October that Wordsworth would be continuing with it suggests that he lobbied him before, during and after the Scottish tour. Wordsworth was probably angry about this, but as usual repressed his feelings for fear of what he would say if he opened his mouth. The same thing had happened in 1799 and 1800, and its recurrence would eventually destroy their friendship in 1810. Writing to Sir George in October, Wordsworth put a brave face on things and drily observed: 'Mr Coleridge, I understand, has written to you several times lately, so of course he will have told you when and why he left us. I am glad he did, as I am sure the solitary part of his tour did him much the most service.'[9] It was a tart comment on the failed expedition; there is no record of what Sir George made of it. To De Quincey Wordsworth remarked that their pleasure 'was not a little dashed by the necessity under which Mr Coleridge found himself of leaving us, at the end of something more than a fortnight, from ill health; and a dread of the rains'. A diplomatic comment this time, but Wordsworth undermines Coleridge's excuses by adding: 'The weather however on the whole was excellent, and we were amply repaid for our pains.'[10]

If there was ever a moment for Wordsworth to have gone his own way it was autumn 1803. As in 1799, strains had appeared in the relationship with Coleridge at the same time as he had begun to recognize afresh the inherent impossibility of getting on with 'The Recluse'. For his part Coleridge reflected in private on Wordsworth's selfishness, and on the sad fact that he himself 'had been long, long idle owing perhaps in part to his Idolatry' of Wordsworth.[11] But as in 1799, Coleridge could not let 'The Recluse' slip out of sight. He later claimed he had intended to visit Dove Cottage only for a day,[12] but that cannot be right. It was ostensibly a Christmas visit, as he set out from Keswick on 20 December 1803 with Derwent. Biographers note his presence at this time, but refrain from analysing his motives, of which there were at least three. It is clear from his notebooks[13] (though again biographers seem not to have noticed) that Sara Hutchinson also passed the festive season

8   *Notebooks* i 1473.
9   *EY* 409.
10   *EY* 453.
11   *Notebooks* i 1606.
12   See the letter to Beaumont of 30 January 1804, Griggs ii 1049.
13   See, for instance, *Notebooks* i 1793, 1815, and 1820: 'o dear Dorothy – & O dear Sara Hutchinson'.

at Dove Cottage. He had been besotted with her since 1799, and desperately wanted to see her again. Secondly, he needed money to travel to the Mediterranean for his health (at the moment he had in mind 'a year's residence in Madeira');[14] during his stay at Grasmere Wordsworth agreed to lend him £100 with interest of 5 per cent for ten months. The third and final reason was to exhort Wordsworth to write 'The Recluse'.

Did he really intend to visit only for a day? I doubt it. There was a convenience in the fact that illness detained him at Dove Cottage for longer than he expected, although as he afterwards told Poole he had been 'very, very ill – for days together so weak, as scarcely to be able to smile with tenderness & thanks on Mrs Wordsworth & Dorothy, who have nursed me with a Mother's Love'.[15]

Coleridge had cause to make himself agreeable to Wordsworth, and not just because he needed money. He could be very perceptive, particularly about Wordsworth, and probably sensed that as in October 1799, when he had decided to join Joseph Cottle on his first visit to the Lakes, this was a decisive moment in their relationship. He knew that his friend had to be won over and as before his charm worked its magic. Wordsworth took him on walks, and in this mood of renewed affection recited Part II of *The Prelude* to its dedicatee (no doubt at Coleridge's request). Coleridge's praise for the poem can only have led back to 'The Recluse'. Although it had caused tensions between them, it was flattering to Wordsworth to consider, as Coleridge insisted, that as the great philosophical poet of the age he was the only man qualified to write it. Wordsworth still felt the need to satisfy Coleridge, and at the same time confident only of his ability to continue *The Prelude*. We shall probably never know who proposed that *The Prelude* should become part of 'The Recluse'; it was an ingenious solution that would enable Wordsworth to extend the work he could write while apparently making progress on the one he couldn't. It was another agreement designed to re-institute the optimism they had shared at Alfoxden – and succeeded, at least for a time.

Coleridge suddenly recovered his health on 14 January and left Dove Cottage for Kendal, heading ultimately for London, where he would work with John Rickman on the census while preparing his Mediterranean tour. During his time in Grasmere he had managed to return Wordsworth's attentions to 'The Recluse', so that when writing to Richard Sharp the day after his departure he could affirm that Wordsworth

no more resembles Milton than Milton resembles Shakespere – no more resembles Shakespere than Shakespere resembles Milton – he is himself: and I dare

[14] Griggs ii 1035.
[15] Ibid.

affirm that he will hereafter be admitted as the first & greatest philosophical Poet – the only man who has effected a compleat and constant synthesis of Thought & Feeling and combined them with Poetic Forms . . .[16]

Coleridge ranked Wordsworth high in the literary pantheon partly because 'The Recluse' was felt to be imminent, as in December 1799. His time at Dove Cottage had not been wasted. He and Wordsworth once more had an understanding: 'The Recluse' was now redefined as 'a Faithful Transcript of his own most august & innocent Life, of his own habitual Feelings & Modes of seeing and hearing'.[17] This was new and reveals the nature of their agreement – that *The Prelude* would henceforth be part of 'The Recluse'.[18] It was the ideal way for Wordsworth to justify work on the 'poem to Coleridge'; by 13 February Dorothy was describing it as 'an appendix to the Recluse'.[19]

The idea of prefacing the great philosophical poem of the age with a self-portrait of its esteemed author seemed entirely tenable to Coleridge, and he continued to meditate on it after leaving Wordsworth. In the Mediterranean on 30 April he scribbled in his notebook: 'Mem. To write to the Recluse that he may insert something concerning *Ego* / its metaphysical Sublimity'.[20] The egotistical sublime to which Keats was later to take exception was calculated, and from this early point integral to the larger project on which Wordsworth was embarked.

This intensified the pressure to begin work, and as soon as Coleridge had gone Wordsworth applied himself. By that time he had reconceived *The Prelude* as a five-book work, which he described to John Thelwall in mid-January 1804 as 'a Poem of considerable labour'.[21] Within a day or so of Coleridge's departure he had mapped it out as follows.[22] (He would have known most about Books One and Two, because they were based closely on poetry already written.)

Book One would incorporate most of Part I of the 1799 *Prelude*. It could not begin with 'was it for this . . . ?' – hardly appropriate for a work beginning to merge in Wordsworth's mind with the high aspirations of 'The Recluse' –

[16] Griggs ii 1034.
[17] Ibid.
[18] It is surely no coincidence that at this moment Coleridge claimed to have finalized the plan for his own 'literary Life' (Griggs ii 1036).
[19] *EY* 440.
[20] *Notebooks* ii 2057.
[21] *EY* 432.
[22] It should be acknowledged that the plan that follows is conjectural, based on extant but imperfect manuscript evidence; scholars continue to debate the precise structure of the poem.

so he decided to preface it with a 54–line blank verse passage he had composed in December 1799. The so-called 'Glad Preamble' had been written
over four years before and was unpublished. He may have thought when it
was first written that he could use it in 'The Recluse' at some point; if so, he
now realized that this celebration of liberation 'from a house / Of bondage,
from yon city's walls set free'[23] was the ideal start to the expanded poem to
Coleridge. This would be followed by a lengthy discourse in which he specu-
lated on the appropriate subject for an epic poem before settling on 'some
philosophic song / Of truth that cherishes our daily life' (the post-Preamble).[24]

The Glad Preamble and post-Preamble would be followed by Part I of the
two-part poem, lightly revised, minus the three culminating spots of time (the
drowned man of Esthwaite, the lost child and the waiting for the horses).

Book Two would be Part II of the two-part poem, lightly revised.

Book Three would be a new piece of poetry recalling Wordsworth's undergraduate years, set in Cambridge and the Lake District.

Book Four would concern education and books, and though largely comprising new verse would incorporate three passages already in existence: 'There
was a boy', published in *Lyrical Ballads* (1800); 'The Discharged Soldier',
composed in January 1798 though not yet in print; and the drowned man of
Esthwaite. It is possible (though scholars debate the point) that it might have
contained the Arab dream, which eventually wound up in Book V of the
Thirteen-Book Prelude.[25]

Book Five was hazier in conception, and Wordsworth would have guessed
that it would be by far the most demanding. There was one reason for this: if
the poem to Coleridge was prefatory to 'The Recluse', Book Five would be
both transitional and introductory. It would provide readers with a stepping-
off point into the great philosophical poem that would follow and therefore

---

[23] *The Five-Book Prelude* i 6–7.

[24] Ibid., i 228–9. It is symptomatic that the phrase 'philosophic song' could apply as
much to 'The Recluse' as to *The Prelude* – and critics are divided as to its meaning; Robert
Woof reads it as *The Prelude* while Jonathan Wordsworth suggests 'The Recluse'. See Woof,
'Presentation of the Self in the Composition of *The Prelude*', in *Presenting Poetry: Composition, Publication, Reception*, ed. Howard Erskine-Hill and Richard A. McCabe (Cambridge:
Cambridge University Press, 1995), p. 148; Norton *Prelude* 40n7; and *Five-Book Prelude*
48n33. De Selincourt pointed out that the reference was probably to *The Prelude* on the
grounds of Coleridge's echo of these lines in 'To William Wordsworth' (OET *Prelude*
515).

[25] Jonathan Wordsworth maintains that the Arab dream had no part in the five-book
scheme, and I have followed him in my conjectural text. It has to be said, though, that the
matter is undecided.

contain material relating directly to 'The Recluse'. Given the imperfections of 'Home at Grasmere', the prospect of having to compose it would have given Wordsworth pause.

As a kind of insurance policy he provided himself with as many 'handholds' as he could. In reserve he still retained two spots of time from Part I of the two-part *Prelude* (the lost child and the waiting for the horses) and would use them as the climax to Book Five. For the opening of Book Five he would write a new piece of poetry describing a new spot of time: the climbing of Snowdon. This would have the virtue of being directly autobiographical, and was at the same time symbolic of the upward struggle of mankind described by the progressive philosophy of 'The Recluse'.

This redesigned *Prelude* would tell the story of its author's life up to 1791, though skipping everything between the summers of 1789 and 1791. The two-part version of 1799 had attempted to narrate the development of the mind in the face of grief at his parents' – principally his father's – deaths. The five-book version would extend its narrative so as to cover the remainder of Wordsworth's teenage years and early adulthood. It was the story of progression towards the flowering of genius. Though largely positive, it would present the temptations of Cambridge life as potentially damaging, and give prominence to his father's death by placing the waiting for the horses at its conclusion. He would have understood that it needed some counterweight for the sublime optimism that the poem to Coleridge, as preface to 'The Recluse', needed to espouse. The as yet unconceived thirteen-book poem would place further emphasis on threats to imaginative power – city life, the French Revolution, and the romantic entanglement implied by the Vaudracour and Julia episode, to name but a few. However, the poet's path in the five-book *Prelude* is comparatively uncluttered. As he began he must have believed that Cambridge, occupying all of Book Three, would be sufficient to represent the various struggles he had surmounted.

That resolved, Wordsworth set himself to compose the climbing of Snowdon as a matter of urgency. In view of the structural importance of Book Five as a whole he needed to write as much of it as he could before turning to Books Three and Four. The sophistication of the poetry from its earliest draft indicates that he had thought it out thoroughly before putting pen to paper. In a letter to an unknown correspondent in 1840 he recalled the occasion which inspired it as vividly as ever:

> More than 50 years have passed, since, in the course of a pedestrian tour with a lamented friend, a native of North Wales, I first had a sight of Bethgellert, and the beautiful country around, and in the neighbourhood of the Village. From an Inn, a humble one it was at that time, I set off from the Village about 10 oc at night for Snowden and reached its summit under the most favorable circumstances . . . (*LY* iv 110)

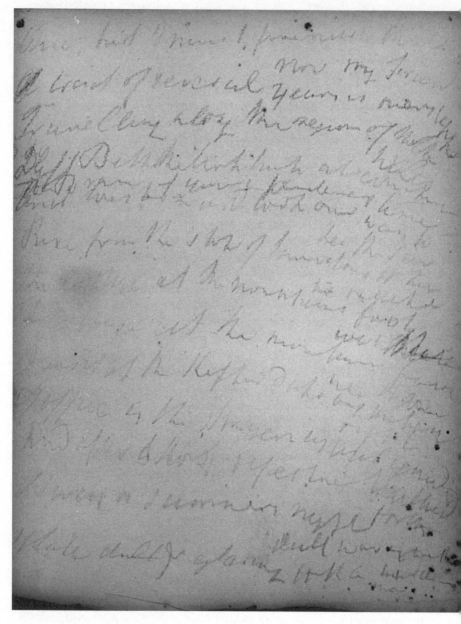

Figure 15. DC MS 43, 19v. *The Five-Book Prelude*: initial, rough draft in pencil of the climbing of Snowdon, *c.*February 1804.

With this experience etched deeply in his memory, enhanced by imagination, he sat down in February 1804 with a pencil and two leaves from a dismantled notebook used during the Scottish tour[26] and entered the first version of one of the most important pieces of poetry he would ever write.[27]

> Once, but I must premise that now my Friend
> A tract of several years is overstepped
> Travelling along the region of North Wales
> We left Bethkelerts huts at couching time
> [?Then] [?a pair of] young wanderers
> And westward took our way to see the sun
> Rise from the top of Snowdon. When we reachd
> The cottage at the mountains foot we there
> Rousd up the Shepherd who by antient right
> Of office is the strangers usual guide
> And after short refreshment sallied forth
> It was a summers night dull warm withal
> White dull & glaring with a dripping mist
> Low hung & dull that coverd all [?the] sky
> And threatened storm & rain. Yet on we went
> Uncheckd being gay & young & [having trust *del.*]
> In our tried pilot. Little could we see
> And after ordinary travellers [?talk][28]
> With the old shepherd silently we sank
> Each into commerce with his private thoughts
> Thus briskly did we mount & by myself
> With nothing either seen or heard the while
> That took me from my musing save that once
> The Shepherds cur did to his own great joy
> Unearth a Hedgehog
> Round which he made a barking turbulent
> This small adventure for even such it seemed
> In that wild place & in the dead of nigh[t]

---

[26]   Mark Reed judges that the notebook was dismantled prior to composition of the five-book poem; Cornell *13–Book Prelude* i 19.

[27]   My transcription of the draft draws on readings provided by Reed, Cornell *13–Book Prelude* ii 246–8. The draft is very difficult and for the convenience of the reader I have aimed to provide a clean reading text. Deletions are accepted when alternatives are entered; when they are not, I have retained the original reading, while indicating that the deletion has been made. Where alternative readings are entered but no deletion made, I have entered the alternative.

[28]   The original reading at this point is 'And after some [?brief] commonplace discourse'.

Being over & forgotten, on we went
In silence as before, with the face towards
The hill as if in opposition set
Against [an] enemy I panted up
With eager steps & no less eager thought[s]
When the ground on which [my] eyes were set
As if in spell did in a gentle sort
Appear to brighten so at least it seemed
In the half dream in which my thoughts were wrappd
Nor had I time to ask if it were so[29]

This is where the draft breaks off although Wordsworth probably continued on the next folio, which has not survived.[30]

It is the revised version of this passage, from the beginning of Book XIII of the *Thirteen-Book Prelude*, that attracts critical attention; to the best of my knowledge nothing has been said about this early draft. The variations are revealing. For one thing Coleridge, the 'Friend' of the opening line, is a strongly felt presence. Though eliminated from the equivalent lines in the *Thirteen-Book Prelude*, at this early moment Wordsworth is conscious of the need to placate Coleridge's demands for 'The Recluse'. That need is a driving force behind the passage and the poem as a whole, and would become increasingly compelling as Coleridge's health declined.

Wordsworth's admission that he has 'overstepped' several years to arrive at Snowdon, also eliminated from the Book XIII text, indicates unease about having skipped the years 1789–91. It would become so irksome that in March it compelled him to abandon the poem in favour of a plan for fourteen books (later altered to thirteen), with its account of the turbulent 1790s.

The overwhelming impression, though, is of fluency. Even in this initial sketch the manipulation of the verse is masterly, the work of someone confident in his powers with high hopes for the task ahead. He is thinking in terms of a five-Book structure long enough to require an extensive 250–line preamble about the most appropriate choice of subject for an epic (see *Five-Book Prelude* i 55–269). The climbing of Snowdon is in this sense more typical of the five-book *Prelude* than of any subsequent version; it is the expression of a writer recently embarked on a mission in which he believes. *The Prelude*, begun as a fugitive work, the articulation of possessions 'wholly, solely mine', had been converted into part of the grandiose scheme projected by Coleridge. This was convenient because it would help appease Coleridge's demands – but at a cost. The revisions required to convert the two-part poem into a

[29] MS WW, 19v–20v.
[30] See Reed's diagram of MS WW as it originally stood, Cornell *13–Book Prelude* i 20.

preface to 'The Recluse' were sweeping, and may be argued to have distorted it. Coleridge's 'Recluse'-centred view of Wordsworth had penetrated so deeply that if he was to expand *The Prelude* he could do so only by amalgamating the two. First and foremost, the climbing of Snowdon stands as a pledge of Wordsworth's commitment to this.

Within the context of the poetry of the Hawkshead and Cambridge years Snowdon returns obliquely to the leitmotif of the underworld journey. I argued in the first three chapters of this book that Wordsworth's classical models were tragic; Aeneas and Orpheus descend into the underworld so as to re-experience loss. The principal discovery of the Cambridge sonnets and *An Evening Walk* is that such patterns can be inverted so that they describe redemption; hence the visionary poet at the climax of *An Evening Walk* is symbolically reunited with the dead, witnessing 'Fair spirits'. As Wordsworth had written in a juvenile notebook, 'the dead friend is present in his shade.'

Those insights underpin the climbing of Snowdon. Instead of conducting us beneath the mountain he takes us up a mountain's summit. It was a device he and Coleridge had inherited from late eighteenth-century poets such as James Beattie[31] and William Crowe. Crowe's *Lewesdon Hill* (1788) had been set in the landscape around Racedown Lodge, and began with the lines:

> Up to thy summit, LEWESDON, to the brow
> Of yon proud rising, where the lonely thorn
> Bends from the rude South-east, with top cut sheer
> By his keen breath, along the narrow track
> By which the scanty-pastured sheep ascend
> Up to thy furze-clad summit, let me climb . . .
>
>   (ll. 1–6)[32]

Wordsworth had reworked the mountain ascent in *Descriptive Sketches* (published in 1793) and Coleridge returned to it in 'Reflections on Having Left a Place of Retirement' (composed in 1795).[33] By February 1804 Wordsworth would have felt the weight of a minor literary tradition bearing down on him. One way of offsetting that burden was to emphasize specific biographical detail, so he introduced Robert Jones as his companion; sets the scene firmly, and accurately, in north Wales (Beddgelert remains a favoured setting-out

---

[31] The precedent in Beattie's *The Minstrel* has been usefully discussed by Jonathan Wordsworth, *Borders of Vision*, chapter 10.

[32] Wordsworth read *Lewesdon Hill* in November or December 1795 at Racedown; see *WR* i 42.

[33] Coleridge appears to have met William Crowe at the Royal Institution on 28 March 1804 (Griggs ii 1106).

point for Snowdon today); is definite about the time of day (bed-time or 'couching time'); and heightens other aspects of local colour, notably the 'tried pilot' and his dog.

Remaining details are much as they appear in the Book XIII version. As in that text, the dog makes a 'barking turbulent' round the unfortunate hedge-hog in the midst of the ascent. Wordsworth's dog poetry is often comic.[34] 'The Dog' (written in 1786) had spun a Miltonic elegy about Ann Tyson's rough terrier of the hills, and when describing his walks with it in Book IV of the five-book poem Wordsworth would refer to 'a breath-like sound, / A respiration short and quick',[35] parodically invoking the correspondent breeze in Book I. Here too the dog is an opportunity for comedy. The Miltonic inversion of 'barking turbulent' is mock-heroic, like the inflated diction of 'tried pilot', and tells us about the psychology of the perceiving mind. Like his language, the poet's expectations are mistakenly puffed up, geared to the pos-sibility of extraordinary incident; they refer us back to the grander models in the rewritten Book One, where he mentions such possibilities for epic verse as Mithridates, Odin, Sertorius, Dominique de Gourges, Gustavus I and William Wallace.[36]

Wordsworth tells us that the sky 'threatened storm & rain', and as he climbs finds himself 'with the face towards / The hill as if in opposition set / Against [an] enemy'. He and Jones are 'Uncheckd being gay & young' a few lines earlier, much in the manner of two gallant knights. And like a contender in a heroic tale, he finds himself turning to face '[an] enemy'. That foe is the mountain, but it is also the challenge of composing 'The Recluse'. This makes sense if one bears in mind that at this moment much of the Five Books re-mains unwritten; he has started at the end. He is not aware that the poem will be restructured in Fourteen (and then Thirteen) Books within a few weeks, nor that the task he proposes is greater than he suspects. All the same, it is appropriate that the climbing of Snowdon, with its image of battle 'Against [an] enemy', describes the struggle towards creation of an epic masterwork. That theme is developed at greater length, and more explicitly, in the post-Preamble.[37]

A leaf is missing from the notebook at this point, containing approximately twenty lines. They would have comprised an early version of this passage, copied out by Mary Wordsworth shortly after being drafted.

---

[34] There are obvious exceptions, most notably 'Fidelity' and the 'famous Sheep-dog' in 'Home at Grasmere' MS B, 729.

[35] *Five-Book Prelude* iv 55–6.

[36] See *Five-Book Prelude* i 175–226.

[37] A. D. Nuttall comments helpfully on this in *Openings: Narrative Beginnings from the Epic to the Novel* (Oxford: Clarendon Press, 1992), chapter 4.

For instantly a light before my eyes
Fell like a flash. I looked about, and lo!
The moon stood naked in the heavens at height
Immense above my head, and on the shore
I found myself of a huge sea of mist,
That meek and silent rested at my feet.
A hundred hills their dusky backs upheaved
All over this still ocean; and beyond,
Far, far beyond, the vapours shot themselves
In headland, tongues, and promontory shapes,
Into the sea – the real sea, that seemed
To dwindle and give up its majesty,
Usurped upon as far as sight could reach.
Meanwhile, the moon looked down upon this show
In single glory, and we stood, the mist
Touching our very feet. And from the shore
At distance not the third part of a mile
Was a blue chasm, a fracture in the mist,
A deep and gloomy breathing-place through which
Mounted the roar of waters, torrents, streams
Inseparable, roaring with one voice.
The universal spectacle throughout
Was shaped for admiration and delight,
Grand in itself alone, but in that breach
Through which the homeless voice of waters rose,
That dark deep thoroughfare, had Nature lodged
The soul, the imagination of the whole.

(*The Five-Book Prelude* v 39–65)

The perceiving mind has transferred the 'majesty' of the real sea to the vapours that mimic its shapings, a haunting image that recalls 'Now ye meet in the cave', the Hawkshead poem discussed in chapter 2 in which a woman was buried by her husband and sons in 'the salt sea' (see pp. 37–9). That had attempted to deal with overwhelming grief, and it is not unreasonable to think that, while talking about the great ambition of 'The Recluse' through Snowdon, Wordsworth wanted to remain in touch with those feelings. Besides echoing the fountain of *Kubla Khan*, the incipient rush of which sounds 'As if this earth in fast thick pants were breathing', the image of the sea is a reminder of the intense, unresolved feeling at the heart of Wordsworth's poetry, explicitly referred to in the waiting for the horses episode at the end of Book Five. The chasm in the sea of mist thus gives access both to imaginative power and its origins in Wordsworth's past. It remains obscure and mysterious, alluding indirectly to the act of mourning.

That said, the overall impression given by this passage is one of confidence, even euphoria. It was true to the impulse of the moment in that it reflected his ease at knowing that the poem to Coleridge was no longer a free-standing piece of poetry composed out of sight of its dedicatee, but part of the millenarian epic he had been commissioned to write. The vision on the top of the mountain is rich in significance because of the authority it confers on him. It licenses Wordsworth as a mighty prophet, seer blest. It is his qualification for being able to tackle 'The Recluse', bringing its complex message to the rest of humanity. He had reason to be persuaded, for at this moment his poetic abilities were at their peak. The period during which he composed, and perhaps completed, the five-book *Prelude* was also that when he finished his 'Ode':

> We will grieve not, rather find
> Strength in what remains behind,
> In the primal sympathy
> Which having been must ever be,
> In the soothing thoughts that spring
> Out of human suffering,
> In the faith that looks through death,
> In years that bring the philosophic mind.

(ll. 182–9)

Until 1797 he had been the poet of human suffering, the poet for whom grief was the medium through which the world was perceived. Thanks to Coleridge's influence, and the sense that he was appointed as the true philosophical poet of the age, Wordsworth was now capable, in the 'Ode' and the extended versions of *The Prelude*, of verse in which 'human suffering' was seen as productive of 'soothing thoughts' rather than further distress; in which death was something to be 'looked through' as if it were a mere dream; in which grief could be transcended by 'the philosophic mind'. These sentiments would have been an affront to the Wordsworth of June 1797 and before, but in the context of spring 1804 they need no justification.

Such unshakeable certainty is a kind of madness and cannot be maintained for ever. Not long would pass before 'the faith that looks through death' would be found wanting. And although at the time he felt that the climbing of Snowdon was a success, there is cause for suspecting that it would give rise to misgivings. Before long the image of the mist and its chasm may have come to symbolize insubstantial, false hopes, so that by 1809–12, when he composed Book II of *The Excursion*, a similar vision is attributed to the Solitary by way of revealing how misguided he is. In his case the city that materializes out of the clouds is literally a castle in the air, its brilliant, 'molten' colours 'Con-

---

[38]   *The Excursion* ii 890.

fused, commingled, mutually inflamed'[38] in a manner that says much about his state of mind. Describing the byzantine complexity of his New Jerusalem, the Solitary comments:

> Fantastic pomp of structure without name,
> In fleecy folds voluminous, enwrapp'd.

(ii 894–5)

The fantastic, pompous vision is a symptom of his own sickness, and the enwrapping of the fleecy clouds describes blindness. Although we must be careful not to muddle the two passages, it is hard not to read the Solitary's New Jerusalem as a comment on Snowdon, especially in view of the verbal echo of the *Prelude* passage, where Wordsworth writes that the mountainside as it lightened became 'More bright in that half dream which *wrapp'd* me up' (my italics). The echo suggests that the Wordsworth of 1809–12 felt some unease about the *Prelude* episode. It may have been something he sensed as early as 1805, when he dropped the line about being wrapped in dreams from the thirteen-book *Prelude*.

For the moment, however, in February 1804, Wordsworth was content with this pledge of his commitment to 'The Recluse'. He proceeded to Books Three and Four before returning to Book Five early in March after Mary had copied the Snowdon passage into MS W. He knew how Book Five would end, and had known for two or three weeks how it began; now he had to work out what would go in the middle. It was a problem. Indeed, since composing the climbing of Snowdon the Five-Book structure as a whole had become problematic. Book Three did not completely work as an account of struggle, while Book Four (dependent as it was on a number of discrete passages already in existence) was lacking in coherence and stability – did it, or didn't it, include the Arab Quixote? The uncertainty of scholars over this question probably reflects the fact that Wordsworth himself was undecided. His one consolation was that he would have felt confident about the quality of Books One and Two. A great deal depended, therefore, on Book Five.

Mary had copied the early drafts of the climbing of Snowdon from the first notebook into another used mainly for Book Four. He reread and revised it, sharpened his quill, and continued it at the top of a new page.[39] For a self-reflexive poet like him it was natural to comment on his uncertainties, and that was what he proceeded to do. The 140–odd lines (now known as the analogy passage) which he then wrote consisted of a series of miniature spots of time meant to affirm his imaginative vision; but that strategy was implicitly

---

[39]   MS W, 37v; for facsimile see Cornell *13–Book Prelude* ii 396.

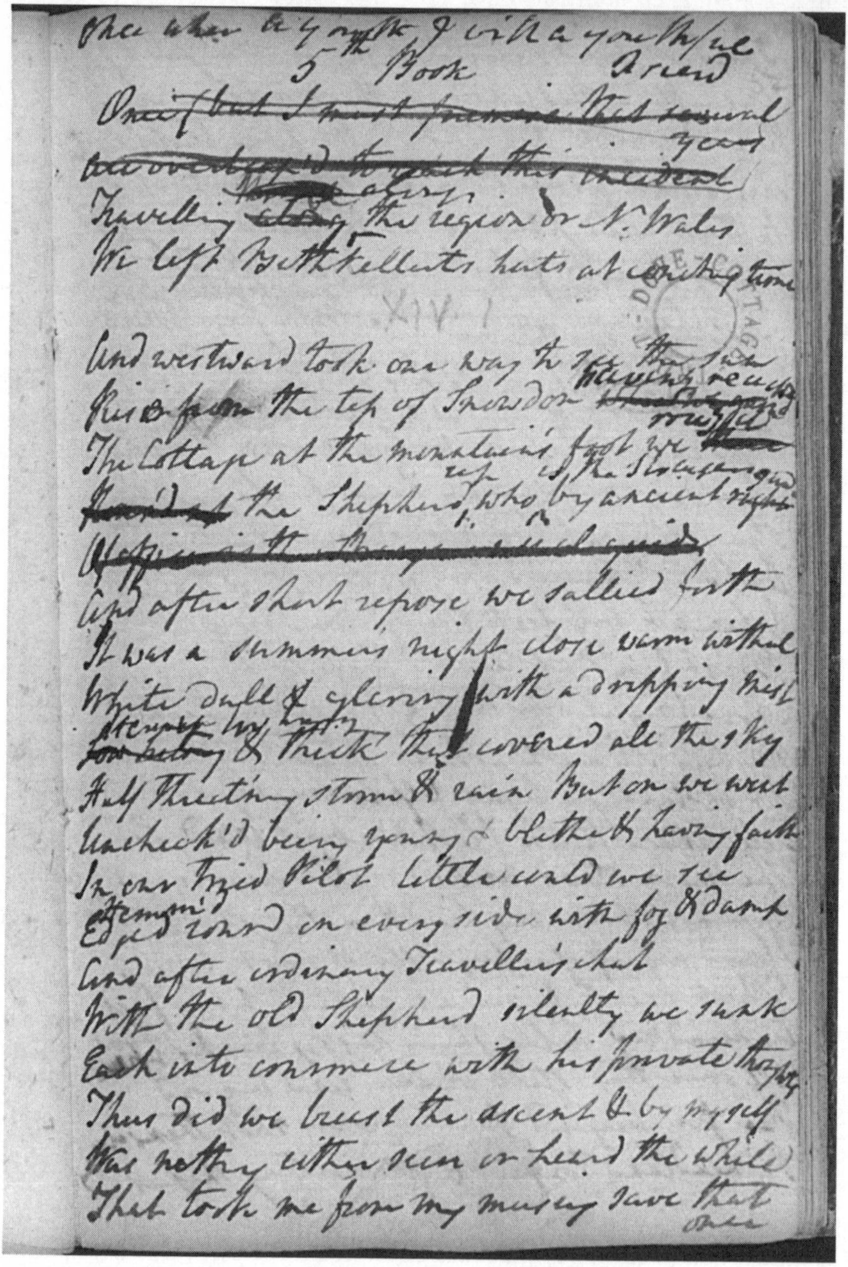

Once when in youth I with a youthful friend
5th Book
~~Once (but I must premise that several years~~
~~Are overleap'd to reach this incident)~~
Travelling along the region of N. Wales
We left Bethkelleths huts at couching time

And westward took our way to see the sun
Rise from the top of Snowdon. Having reach'd
The Cottage at the mountain's foot we rous'd
the Shepherd, who by ancient right
~~Of office is the Stranger's usual guide~~
And after short repose we sallied forth
It was a summer's night close warm withal
White dull & glaring with a dripping mist
Low hung & thick that covered all the sky
Half threat'ning storm & rain But on we went
Uncheck'd being young & blithe & having faith
In our tried Pilot little could we see
Hemm'd round on every side with fog & damp
And after ordinary Traveller's chat
With the old Shepherd silently we sunk
Each into commerce with his private thoughts
Thus did we breast the ascent & by myself
Was nothing either seen or heard the while
That took me from my musings save that once

Figure 16. DC MS 38, 36r. *The Five-Book Prelude*: revised fair copy of the Snowdon episode, late February or early March 1804. Note the deleted opening lines: 'Once (but I must premise that several years / Are overleap'd to reach this incident'.

an admission of doubt. Only someone wondering whether they were up to the task would have done it. As if registering its author's discomfiture the draft became increasingly hesitant, not unlike the catalogue of countryfolk in the middle of 'Home at Grasmere'. It caused such trouble that he stopped and redrafted it, and was eventually forced to discard it. But it is of interest for various reasons, and has been discussed by numerous critics;[40] for my purposes it is interesting primarily for the way in which it begins:[41]

> Even yet wilt thou vouchsafe an ear, oh friend,
> And something too of a submissive mind,
> As in thy mildness thou I know hast done,
> While with a winding but no devious song
> Through [   ] processes I make my way
> By links of tender thought.

(ll. 1–6)

By contrast with Snowdon these lines suffer from a stilted, tentative quality related to the difficulties I have just mentioned. It begins with another reference to Coleridge, often a symptom of authorial anxiety in *The Prelude*. His function in 'The Recluse' was hardly uncontroversial. The characterization of him as 'submissive' and 'mild', while no doubt referring accurately to his appreciation of Part II the previous month, is probably true more to Wordsworth's wishes than to life. There had, after all, been friction between them in the recent past.

This unevenness insinuates itself into Wordsworth's assessment of the five-book poem which, we are assured, is winding but not devious. Why should it be thought devious? Because Wordsworth knew his praise of Coleridge to be less than straightforward? Or was it that the climbing of Snowdon, which on a figurative level symbolized the aspirations of 'The Recluse', could not be followed up with philosophical verse that would satisfy Coleridge's high expectations? 'Home at Grasmere', which he probably had not shown to Coleridge, had stalled for precisely that reason.

Coleridge's presence is intriguing because it is really a form of absence. In the Glad Preamble of Book One Wordsworth had suggested that although his guide might be no more than 'a wandering cloud, / I cannot miss my way';[42] no such certainty is to be found here. Coleridge, who had conceived the philosophical scheme on which 'The Recluse' was based, his health now

---

[40]   Commentary by Kenneth Johnston, Mary Jacobus, and Joseph Kishel is reproduced in the Blackwell *Five-Book Prelude*.
[41]   My text is that given in Appendix I of the Blackwell *Five-Book Prelude*.
[42]   *The Five-Book Prelude* i 18.

so bad he was thought to be dying, was several hundred miles away in London and planned to distance himself further. He was the natural 'guide' for this poem, but his advice was not to be had. In the letter to Coleridge which announced his imminent intention to return to Book Five Wordsworth added

> I am very anxious to have your notes for the Recluse. I cannot say how much importance I attach to this, if it should please God that I survive you, I should reproach myself for ever in writing the work if I had neglected to procure this help.[43]

This dates from 6 March within four or five days of which the five-book poem had been abandoned. It had become clear to Wordsworth (and is implicit in the analogy passage) that if Book Five was to live up to his standards and provide a convincing introduction to 'The Recluse', he needed Coleridge's help. This was all the more pressing, given that *The Prelude* and 'The Recluse' had now become companion works – a point made implicitly in an alternative reading to line 3 of the analogy passage, 'As to this *prelude* thou I know hast done' (my italics). This explicit reference to the reading of the two-part *Prelude* Part II in the highest and outermost of Grasmere in January provides final confirmation, were any needed, that Wordsworth thought of the poem to Coleridge as prefatory to 'The Recluse'. No longer was it (as in 1799) written in defiance of Coleridge's wishes. It was legitimized by its relation to 'The Recluse', but with that shift in function came the worrying burden that the larger work couldn't be written without his friend's advice. In his absence Wordsworth is dependent on 'links of tender thought' rather than on the analysis contained in Coleridge's 'notes'. Coleridge later claimed to have given them to a friend, Major Ralph Adye (b. 1764), to convey to Wordsworth. Unfortunately Adye died of plague *en route* to England on 22 October 1804 and his possessions dealt with accordingly; as Coleridge reported, 'My Ideas respecting your Recluse were burnt as a Plague-garment.'[44]

Vexed as these lines are, the analogy passage continues unexpectedly with some of the most memorable lines about nature that Wordsworth would ever write.

> My present aim
> Is to contemplate for a needful while
> (Passage which will conduct in season due
> Back to the tale which we have left behind)

---

[43] *EY* 452.
[44] Griggs ii 1169.

> The diverse manner in which Nature works
> Ofttimes upon the outward face of things;
> I mean so moulds, exalts, endues, combines,
> Impregnates, separates, adds, takes away,
> And makes one object sway another so,
> By unhabitual influence or abrupt,
> That even the grossest minds must see and hear
> And cannot choose but feel. The power which these
> Are touched by, being so moved, which Nature thus
> Puts forth upon the senses (not to speak
> Of finer operations), is in kind
> A brother of the very faculty
> Which higher minds bear with them as their own.
> These from their native selves can deal about
> Like transformation, to one life impart
> The functions of another – interchange,
> Trafficking with immeasurable thoughts.
>
> (ll. 6–26)

Though apparently concerned with nature, Wordsworth is really describing the imagination. Nature possesses the ability to generate new imaginative realities, abstracting qualities from one object and transferring them to others – an 'interchange'. It is representative of an ability possessed by everyone, and is divine ('Impregnates' alludes to Milton's holy ghost which, brooding over chaos, 'mad'st it pregnant').[45] Given its date of composition – on or shortly after 6 March 1804 – this is a remarkably sophisticated piece of writing with a fairly intricate argument. It represents an advance on the disquisitions on imagination in the Preface to *Lyrical Ballads* and the infant babe passage, and establishes the basis on which Wordsworth will discuss imagination in his 1815 Preface. He must have known that it worked, and when he discarded the analogy passage retained these lines as part of the commentary on Snowdon (see *Five-Book Prelude* v 66–85). It would survive, lightly revised, into the *Thirteen-Book Prelude*.[46]

Had the analogy passage continued at this pitch Wordsworth might have concluded Book Five with a feeling of deserved satisfaction and attempted to perfect Books Three and Four; fortunately it failed, and by the time he rejected it was close to ceasing work on the poem altogether. On his return to Book Five he had at first revised the opening lines of the Snowdon episode to

---

[45] *Paradise Lost* i 22.
[46] See *The Thirteen-Book Prelude* xiii 77–84. It survives only in partial form in the 1818–20 C-Stage text (see Cornell *13–Book Prelude* ii 223–4) and is drastically revised in the *Fourteen-Book Prelude* (see Cornell *14–Book Prelude* 259).

read, 'Once (but I must premise that several years / Are overleap'd to reach this incident) . . .', before eliminating the parenthesis altogether (see figure 16, p. 204 above). What he could not eliminate was the knowledge that the years omitted from his narrative were essential to it, or that those which followed were equally full of formative experience (his residence in France, the Revolution, attachment to Godwinism, first meeting with Coleridge, and so forth). In this light the decision to scrap the five-book poem in favour of a much larger scheme in fourteen (and later thirteen) books seems less surprising. The manuscripts indicate that Books Four and Five caused him trouble, and may have been in a continuing state of flux. The five-book plan was flawed; he needed a larger canvas on which to work. The poem was reconceived between 6 and 12 March.

It was a way of raising the stakes. He would either make this poem succeed on an even larger scale or abandon 'The Recluse' for good and return to the small poems, the 'Lanes & allies' about which Coleridge had been so scathing several months before.[47] The challenge galvanized him, and in an incredible burst of energy Wordsworth cannibalized the drafts prepared for the five-book *Pre-lude*, converting them into an early but recognisable version of *Thirteen-Book Prelude* Books I–V.

A new fourteen-book scheme made more sense, and would release a new reserve of energy. He redesigned the poem very quickly. Books I–III would remain much the same as in the five-Book poem. The drafts he had prepared for Books Four and Five were now dismembered, rearranged, and new materials composed. The new Book IV concentrated more rigorously on the first long vacation from Cambridge of 1788, retaining 'The Discharged Soldier' as one of its episodes. The new Book V concerned reading, and incorporated the Arab dream. The old Book Five was discarded, with the aim of deploying the spots of time and climbing of Snowdon at the climax of the thirteen-book poem. This was done with remarkable alacrity; within less than a week of abandoning the five-book plan, *Thirteen-Book Prelude* I–V was on 18 March dispatched to Coleridge in more or less its ultimate form.[48] Just over a week later Coleridge was able to lend Books I and II to Lady Beaumont.[49] Fair-copy materials relating to the five-book *Prelude* (if they existed) were destroyed, leaving only the two notebooks used for drafting (MSS WW and W). At the same time a copy of the new Books I–V was prepared for Wordsworth's

---

[47] Griggs ii 1013.
[48] Coleridge issued detailed instructions for the sending of fair copies in letters of 8 and 15 February (Griggs ii 1060, 1065).
[49] Griggs ii 1104.

own use from which he produced a number of corrections sent to Coleridge on 29 March, by which time he was drafting *Thirteen-Book Prelude* Book VI – about the European walking tour of 1790.[50]

The five-book *Prelude* remains neglected partly because scholars continue to debate its contents, something the publication of a conjectural text in 1997 did nothing to resolve. It is widely agreed that Wordsworth was working to a five-book plan from February to early March 1804, and that the texts discussed in these pages were composed for it during that phase of composition. We disregard them at our peril. This was the moment at which the poem to Coleridge effectively became part of 'The Recluse', and when the tension between the Coleridgean notion of Wordsworth as the author of the great millenarian poem of the age, and Wordsworth's understanding of himself as the poet of grief, guilt and betrayal, was resolved – at least for the moment. What he may not have wanted to admit was that a longer *Prelude* would increase pressure to get on with 'The Recluse', to which, until now, he had been a fair-weather friend. Bits had been written at Alfoxden, and a serious but unsuccessful effort made to start it in 1800. There had been nothing since. Expansion and consolidation of *The Prelude* would commit him once and for all to 'The Recluse', interdependent as the two works had become. It is tempting to think of it as a trap sprung by Coleridge; if so, this was the moment when it firmly caught Wordsworth within its teeth, not to release him for another thirty years.

[50]   *EY* 463–5.

9

'That vast Abiding-place'

If we suppose for a moment that Coleridge was not read Part II of *The Prelude* in January 1804, that he visited the Wordsworths on 20 December 1803 and left the next day, as he claimed to have intended, and that *The Prelude* was never shackled, as henceforth it would be, to 'The Recluse' – is there any reason to think, had it been revised, that it would have been any different from the poem we have now?

The answer must be 'yes'. The five-book, thirteen-book and fourteen-book versions as written are conceived as adjuncts to 'The Recluse', and for that reason designed to expound ideas relating to it. The only version not so conceived was that of 1799, and it is consequently a very different work from the others – darker, more sombre, concerned more with psychological process than philosophical abstraction. Part I contains episodes intended to reconnect Wordsworth with his sources of power; those in Part II that describe the onset of his love for nature are brooding and subdued, as if its path were overshadowed by tragedy.

The confidence and optimism normally ascribed to *The Prelude* isn't characteristic of the two-part version, and in later ones derives from its association with 'The Recluse'. 'The Recluse' was supposed to preach a gospel of salvation. It was necessary for the poem that would introduce to absorb the darker passages of the 1799 poetry into a brighter work culminating in an epiphanic vision on the top of a mountain that confirmed Wordsworth's sense of election. Coleridge had convinced him that he was the only true philosophical poet of the age, a flattering thought that legitimized *The Prelude* and thereby produced some great poetry, including the most accomplished Wordsworth ever wrote. But this exalted manner was achieved only through Coleridge's influence. Left to his own devices, Wordsworth would have developed differently. This is not to downgrade *The Prelude* – it is ratified and made potent by its association with 'The Recluse' – but it is to say that some of the qualities Coleridge brought to it have little to do with the trajectory Wordsworth had been following up to June 1797, or with the subject-matter he rediscovered while composing the 1799 version. At the same time, much of *The Prelude*, almost in spite of the larger design of 'The Recluse', refers back to the concerns of *The Borderers* and 'The Ruined Cottage' MS B. One example I have already given is the climbing of Snowdon, where the mist recalls the sea in 'Now ye meet in the cave', the Hawkshead poem about a dead mother and her surviving family.

Other passages expose Wordsworth's unease about 'The Recluse' and its ambitions. The portrayal of London would be a particular challenge. Cities were fundamental to the doctrines of 'The Recluse'. It was in industrial conurbations that its natural religion was most badly needed, and to that audience, more than to country folk, that the author of 'The Recluse' needed to present his millenarian gospel. When in May 1815 Coleridge wrote his reproachful letter reminding Wordsworth what 'The Recluse' was supposed to have concerned he was clear about this; foremost among its various themes he mentioned 'Fallen men contemplated in the different ages of the World, and in the different states – Savage – Barbarous – Civilised – the lonely Cot, or Borderer's Wigwam – the Village – the Manufacturing Town – Sea-port – City – Universities'.[1] Although he didn't go into detail, Coleridge was clear that 'The Recluse' was to examine fallenness within the context of city life, partly as a means of prophesying redemption for its inhabitants. For that to happen *The Prelude* needed to bear out Wordsworth's claims to be fully part of the world, aware of the potential for good and evil. It would be a balancing act. City life was on the one hand a dehumanizing, corrupting thing of which the poet had to claim experience while at the same time remaining untainted, capable of rousing its denizens to transcendence. He would need to argue that the city was as appropriate a setting for elevated thoughts as the mountains of Cumbria.

The extent of this challenge is underlined by the fact that prior to 1804 Wordsworth's portrayal of cities had been far from complimentary.[2] When he composed the Glad Preamble in late 1799 they were the site of detention and, by implication, spiritual emptiness; addressing the correspondent breeze he had written:

> O welcome Messenger! O welcome Friend!
> A Captive greets thee, coming from a house
> Of bondage, from yon City's walls set free,
> A prison where he hath been long immured.
>
> (*The Thirteen-Book Prelude* i 5–8)

---

[1] Griggs iv 575.
[2] See, among others, Lucy Newlyn, '"In City Pent": Echo and Allusion in Wordsworth, Coleridge, and Lamb, 1797–1801', *RES* 32 (1981) 408–28.

Scholars have long debated the identity of this city, candidates ranging from London to Goslar. But Wordsworth is less literal-minded than his editors, and in truth the city of late 1799 is part of a self-constructed myth of imprisonment and liberation. The allusion to Moses – 'Remember this day in which ye came out from Egypt, out of the house of bondage'[3] – hints at its archetypal status. That bleak view of cities is corroborated by the 'lonely rooms' of 'Tintern Abbey' and the depiction of London in *Frost at Midnight* – where Coleridge is a prisoner, 'pent 'mid cloisters dim'.[4] Between 1798 and 1800 Wordsworth and Coleridge cast the city, especially London, as a spiritual hell.[5] Setting about an extended *Prelude* in 1804, Wordsworth would have understood that this judgement needed to be qualified and, if possible, revised.

Book VII of the thirteen-book poem, entitled 'Residence in London', describes a city whose qualities are ambiguous at best. Its portrayal of Bartholomew Fair is a work of poetic genius in which its hectic charm gives way to a harsh judgement: 'what a hell / For eyes and ears!', 'O blank confusion'.[6] Nor is there consolation in the figure of the London beggar whose written label describing his life stood as 'a type, / Or emblem, of the utmost that we know, / Both of ourselves and of the universe'.[7] Book VII stands as a testimony to how alienating and reductive Wordsworth found the city. It didn't help the cause of 'The Recluse', and on rereading it he would have known that he had to return to the subject in Book VIII, the significance of which he underscored by subtitling it 'Retrospect. Love of Nature leading to love of Mankind'. In that book the task of dignifying London begins with an apostrophe: 'Preceptress stern, that didst instruct me then . . .' As a means of arguing that the city was a spiritual teacher, he recalled his first sight of her when he was an undergraduate:

> On the Roof
> Of an itinerant Vehicle I sate,
> With vulgar men about me, vulgar forms
> Of houses, pavement, streets, of men and things,
> Mean shapes on every side . . .
>
> (viii 693–7)

3　Exodus 13:3.
4　*Frost at Midnight* 52.
5　Coleridge's former acolyte Charles Lloyd by contrast found London 'pleasant' in his 'London', published in *Blank Verse by Charles Lamb and Charles Lloyd* (1798). See in this regard Lucy Newlyn, 'Lamb, Lloyd, London: A Perspective on Book Seven of *The Prelude*', *CLB* NS 74 (January 1991) 33–52.
6　*The Thirteen-Book Prelude* vii 559–60, 696.
7　*The Thirteen-Book Prelude* vii 618–20.

The poetry is emphatic. In line 695, 'vulgar', twice repeated by Wordsworth, takes the stress; in fact, the line breaks in half with that repetition: 'With vulgar men about me, / Vulgar forms'. The other important word is 'men', repeated in lines 695–6; this is particularly significant, as it is one half of the formulation, 'Love of Nature leading to love of Man'. Humanity is at this moment equated with meanness, vulgarity, an unspecified but generally acknowledged common-place quality (although it did not then have the pejorative meaning it does now). Almost immediately, however, Wordsworth steps back:

> but at the time
> When to myself it fairly might be said,
> The very moment that I seem'd to know,
> The threshold now is overpass'd — Great God!
> That aught external to the living mind
> Should have such mighty sway! yet so it was . . .
>
> (ll. 697–702)

One of Wordsworth's virtues is the way in which his blank verse appears to mimic the rhythms and quirks of the spoken word. This is one such moment. He is describing something sublime and ineffable, but it steals upon him una-wares, and that sense of being overwhelmed, overtaken by something other, with a determining will greater than one's own, is perfectly evoked. That per-ceiving self, which has just noted the lowliness and vulgarity of the rural sub-urbs seen from the rooftop of the Cambridge to London stagecoach, is allowed a complacent enough observation; 'The threshold', that of the city, 'is overpass'd', when the cosy, self-fulfilling assumptions behind its impatient wish to sweep by are blown apart. That breakdown is matched by syntactic disruption at line 700:

> Great God!
> That aught external to the living mind
> Should have such mighty sway! yet so it was . . .

Not only does the poet's failure to complete his sentence mimic the impact of the inner experience, it makes the unfolding drama compelling by its refusal to answer, only to ask, questions of the reader. What external power has over-turned the lazy judgements passed in the first half of the sentence? But there is another surprise — the poetry has modulated from the banal to the sub-lime. It is the characteristic Wordsworthian shift, from a bough of wilding, a bottle of elder sticks, a peasant girl in a field — to what lies beyond. From the roof of the London stage we are given a fine view, but all the devices by which it was framed have been removed at a stroke, and we find the lie of the land to be utterly different from what we thought.

A weight of Ages did at once descend
Upon my heart, no thought embodied, no
Distinct remembrances; but weight and power,
Power, growing with the weight . . .

(ll. 703–6)

From the 'houses, pavement, streets', vulgar as they are, our gaze, and that of the poet, has been redirected to the inward landscape of the mind. Its susceptibility is not, on this occasion, to a precise image or recollection; instead, again by virtue of repetition, Wordsworth credits 'weight' – the 'weight of Ages' – and 'power'. It will not be reduced to an easy paraphrase; Wordsworth's terminology is at once too vague and monumental to allow it. What we can say is that the power and the weight are nothing to do with physics: this is the language of the spirit. Its imprecision, its denial of our readerly quest for clarity and resolution, is what pulls the poet up short:

alas! I feel
That I am trifling: 'twas a moment's pause,
All that took place within me came and went
As in a moment, and I only now
Remember that it was a thing divine.

(ll. 706–10)

The verse imitates the tentative, faltering steps taken by the mind; the calculated irregularity in his use of run-on line; the conspiratorial, but only half-acknowledged, address to the reader; and, to begin with, the confession of failure: 'alas! I feel / That I am trifling.' He is doing nothing of the sort: the verse is masterly in its manipulation of tone. The phrasing is imprecise: the experience remains 'a thing divine' – as resistant to definition as before. His one concession to narrative logic is to vouchsafe the knowledge that the 'thing divine' occupied no more than a 'moment'; and yet that snippet of hard fact serves only to compound our difficulties. The 'weight of Ages', so biblical, so elemental in its associations, has taken a moment to register. In fact, a series of paradoxes – 'That aught external to the living mind / Should have such mighty sway!', 'A weight of Ages', ''twas a moment's pause' – have been assembled so as to intrigue, while giving away the minimum of information. The genius of the verse resides in its understatement, its determination not to betray the essence of the thing. Understatement brings us closer to the unexpectedness of the first encounter, as well as to the poet in his own displaced fictional present, making a new discovery about the past as he relives it: 'I only now / Remember that it was a thing divine' (ll. 709–10). If the poem is to work London has to assume something of that divinity.

With that we are brought to a crisis. Wordsworth has already despaired of his ability to describe what happened, and yet the diction, evocative but vague, leaves him no choice but to conduct us over the threshold.

> As when a traveller hath from open day
> With torches pass'd into some Vault of Earth,
> The Grotto of Antiparos, or the Den
> Of Yordas among Craven's mountain tracts . . .
>
> (ll. 711–14)

The extended simile is literally, and figuratively, preoccupied with enlightenment and the problem of seeing – appropriately, since the passage is about Wordsworth's difficulty in comprehending the inner grandeur of London. In order to account for it he must take us somewhere more exotic. There's nothing accidental about the choice of location; the traveller becomes a wanderer through time and space as he echoes the Wordsworth who in May 1800 visited the cave of Yordas in Yorkshire with his brother John. Although that first-hand experience is uppermost, there are a number of literary sources in the background, notably such travel books as Gilpin's *Observations on the Highlands of Scotland* (1789) and Housman's *Descriptive Tour* (1802).[8] It is not known how he knew about the Grotto of Antiparos,[9] but that exotic name is evocative of the world of myth. The anonymous traveller who steps into it is at once the reader; the figure of the poet; the protagonist of one of the many travel books Wordsworth had read – Christopher Columbus, Sir Humphrey Gilbert or Mungo Park;[10] – and a legendary character such as Ulysses.

[8] See Nicola Trott and Duncan Wu, 'Three Sources for Wordsworth's *Prelude* Cave', *N&Q* 38 (1991) 298–9. In addition to those sources, Wordsworth would have known of the description of Yordas in West's *Guide to the Lakes* (3rd edn, London, 1784), pp. 244–6, which provides a digest of literary caves, from Ovid to Addison to Milton.
[9] On this point I am grateful to Jane Renfrew, who informs me that the Cave of Antiparos was the scene for the celebration of midnight Mass in the middle of the night, Christmas Day 1673, by the Marquis de Nointel, and that a Latin inscription on the base of a sort of pyramid used as an altar records the event. The Marquis de Nointel was the French Ambassador to the Porte. He was also an archaeologist who travelled widely and enriched the French museums with his collections. He spent three days over Christmas 1673 in the Cave, accompanied by 500 persons. The cave was illuminated by a hundred large torches of yellow wax and 400 lamps burning night and day, and trumpets sounded to announce the Mass to the world. Fortunately there was a spring of fresh water in the cave. The whole event is described in Joseph Pitton de Tournefort, *Relation d'un voyage au Levant* (2 vols, Paris, 1717) translated by John Ozell in 1718. It is possible that, as John Spedding suggests to me, Wordsworth read Tournefort's volume in France.
[10] All mentioned in the analogy passage of the five-book *Prelude*; see *Five-Book Prelude* 201–3.

> He looks and sees the Cavern spread and grow,
> Widening itself on all sides, sees, or thinks
> He sees, erelong the roof above his head,
> Which instantly unsettles and recedes . . .
>
> (ll. 715–18)

As it emerges from darkness the cavern seems to grow in size, one illusion replaced by another as it ripples overhead. Its unsettling gives away the traveller's state of mind. In fact the perceived image is an index of mood, for Wordsworth's metaphor has, in some strange way, taken us inside his own brain. The traveller is no longer atop the roof of a coach, but within, looking up at that overhead almost as if in some surreal cartoon his eyes were gazing at the interior of his own skull. Our path is, once again, inward, an impression supported by the underworld vision that ensues:

> Substance and shadow, light and darkness, all
> Commingled, making up a Canopy
> Of Shapes and Forms, and Tendencies to Shape,
> That shift and vanish, change and interchange
> Like Spectres . . .
>
> (ll. 719–23)

The roof of the cavern is replaced for a moment by a canopy 'Of Shapes and Forms, and Tendencies to Shape', but is not to be trusted; they 'shift and vanish, change and interchange / Like Spectres'. It is the Orphean underworld in which what is passionately loved can evaporate from one's clutches at a whim; the universe in which rash judgements, trite reflections of morality, may be blown away at a second glance. It is the antithesis of that idealized Wordsworthian universe in which concrete objects, embodying our emotions, aspire to permanence. Here, despite the semblance of vitality, everything is deliquescent, tending to shapes 'That shift and vanish'.

> . . . ferment quiet, and sublime;
> Which, after a short space, works less and less
> Till every effort, every motion gone,
> The scene before him lies in perfect view,
> Exposed and lifeless as a written book.
>
> (ll. 723–7)

The printed volume was to Wordsworth the exhaustion of artistic vitality; he preferred, whenever possible, not to publish. Where it could not be avoided, he returned compulsively to emend the printed text in later editions as if its continuing susceptibility to revision guaranteed its vitality. That anxiety – the fear of creative death – underwrites the simile up to this point.

At the same time the poetry engages with another kind of death. The echo of Virgil, 'aut videt, aut videsse putat', at lines 716–17 – he 'sees, or thinks / He sees' – refers us to Aeneas' encounter with Dido's spectre in Hades.[11] That meeting precipitates guilt when Aeneas realizes he was to blame for her fate. The allusion to a work Wordsworth studied at Hawkshead is inextricably attached to the terrible event – his father's death – that took place while he was a schoolboy there. Aeneas' uncomfortable encounter cannot help but remind us of the grief arising from John Wordsworth Sr's demise in 1783. The rash judgement then had been Wordsworth's impatience as he waited for the horses to take him home for holidays. Here it is paralleled by the arrogant observations of the undergraduate as he gazes down from the roof of the Cambridge stage, seeing 'vulgar men about me, vulgar forms / Of houses, pavement, streets, of men and things, / Mean shapes on every side' (ll. 695–7). After a moment he is silenced by the 'weight of Ages' that descends upon him. That the shift in perspective is not purely aesthetic is confirmed by the cave simile, which alludes to a bleak hinterland of loss. In the midst of a book which was supposed to validate the city and its citizens as the subject of the philosophical optimism of 'The Recluse', Wordsworth has reverted to the subject of grief, and in so doing steers the poem away from the sublime optimism of the millennial work towards the wellsprings of his imaginative power.

It is hardly surprising that those 'shapes and forms' that 'change and interchange / Like spectres' should invoke Dido. Aeneas is permitted to meet her in Hades so as to explain what had happened by way of pleading forgiveness. Christopher Pitt's translation of the *Aeneid* had been known to Wordsworth at Hawkshead;[12] this is how he translates the relevant passage in Virgil, which describes events after Aeneas has spoken:

> Nought to these tender words the fair replies,
> But fixt on earth her unrelenting eyes,
> The chief still weeping: with a sullen mien,
> In stedfast silence, frown'd th' obdurate queen.
> Fixt as a rock amidst the roaring main,
> She hears him sigh, implore, and plead in vain.
> Then, where the woods their thickest shades display,
> From his detested sight she shoots away;
> There from her dear Sichaeus in the grove,
> Found all her cares repaid, and love return'd for love.

---

[11]   Wordsworth would also have known Milton's reworking of Virgil at *Paradise Lost* i 783–4.
[12]   Wordsworth's copy is now in the possession of Paul F. Betz. See *WR* i 140–1.

> Touch'd with her woes, the prince with streaming eyes
> And floods of tears, pursues her as she flies.
>
> (vi 649–60)[13]

Pitt plays up Aeneas' need to explain and Dido's dismissal of him. Indeed her sullenness, frowning and subdued hostility are largely his addition, and as a means of emphasizing the point he supplies an interpretive commentary: 'she scorns to hold conference with him, who, in her own opinion, had basely forsook her; and, by her silent retreat, shews her resentment, and reprimands Aeneas more than she could have done in a thousand words.'[14] Aeneas goes on his way unforgiven – without expiation or the succour of mutual recognition; Dido's separation is absolute, and the underworld journey is resolved only with his painful recognition of its finality. Aeneas is not only bereft, but abandoned to the throes of intense, passionate and unmitigated grief:

> Touch'd with her woes, the prince with streaming eyes
> And floods of tears, pursues her as she flies.

The 'streaming eyes' and 'floods of tears' do not appear in Virgil; they are Pitt's interpolation, designed to elucidate emotions merely implied by the Latin text.

Wordsworth's cave simile both alludes to Aeneas' encounter with Dido and runs parallel to it. Up to line 727 it too presents an underworld descent followed by an audience with the 'shapes' and 'forms' that 'change and interchange / Like Spectres'. In mythic terms they *are* spectres, but before the protagonist can reclaim those dearest to him, who are restored for just a moment,

> The scene before him lies in perfect view,
> Exposed and lifeless as a written book.
>
> (*The Thirteen-Book Prelude* viii 726–7)

Just as Dido fled from Aeneas, the dead are removed from reach, and Wordsworth is left gazing up at the arid, unyielding surface of the rocky cavern. The fineness of the verse resides partly in its understatement of the emotional subtext, which is nonetheless implicit in the disappointment expressed in line 727: 'Exposed and lifeless as a written book'.

The cave simile as it appears in Book VIII is work of autumn 1804.

---

[13] *The Works of Virgil*, trans. Christopher Pitt and Joseph Warton (4 vols, London, 1763).
[14] Ibid., iii. 164.

However, an early version of it was drafted in early April 1804 for Book VI. Between 6 and 12 March Wordsworth had abandoned the five-book *Prelude*, partly because he was unhappy about the fact that it skipped the years 1789–90, to say nothing of the years 1790–1804. His first task was to rewrite what he had already written to form the thirteen-book *Prelude* Books I–V. Then in late March he began work on Book VI, which would concern the 1790 walking tour of the continent with Robert Jones, his undergraduate friend. A week or so into composition, he drafted the cave simile. That early version survives in MS WW, the dismembered rough notebook used for Books Four and Five of the five-book *Prelude*. In this context the cave simile is very different, although the draft is very close to the later version in Book VIII. The early version is an attempt by Wordsworth to describe the disappointment he and Jones felt when they were informed by a Swiss peasant that they had unwittingly crossed the Alps. For the purposes of my transcription I have aimed to present the draft as it stood on completion, but due to the chaotic nature of the entry it has sometimes been necessary to retain deleted words or letters (these are clearly marked), or to insert words or letters omitted in the heat of the moment (enclosed within square brackets). Omissions (usually of rough scrawls and early drafts) are indicated by ellipses. The passage begins with Wordsworth and Jones sheltering in a 'rude outhouse' from a shower high in the mountains; for the reader's convenience I have marked in square brackets, on the right hand of the page, the equivalent lines in the final text of the thirteen-book *Prelude*:[15]

	[25v]	a Peasant chanced to pass	[VI, 513]
		From who we learnd that we had missed our [?road]	
		Which lay within the river's bed [?]	
		For a few steps & then along [?its] course	
5		In short that all [the road *del.*] before us [?hence]	
		Was downward, or to give [in] brief	
	[26r]	The substance of this was the Alps were crossd	[VI, 524]
		As when a Traveller from the light of day	[VIII, 711]
		Hath pass[ed] in to som[e] high & gloomy cave	
10		The Grottoe of Antiparos or the den	
		Of Yordas among Craven's mountain tracts	
		He looks up & sees the cavern slowly spread	
		Widening itself in darkness sees or thinks	[VIII, 716]
		He sees ...	
15	[27r]	at length the roof	

[15] Facsimiles and transcriptions of the notebook pages from which this transcription has been made can be found in Cornell *13–Book Prelude* i 356–61, ii 254–8 and figure 17, p. 221.

```
              A mass of solid stone yet all alive
              With [?restless] fermentation
              The effort & the quality of smoke
              Substance & shadow light & darkness all
20            Commingling making up a canopy                    [VIII, 720]
              Of Shapes & forms that [?change & interchange]
     [27v]    Like spectres, ferment quiet & sublime
              That work [less] & less . . .
              Till every effort every motion gone               [VIII, 725]
25            The vault before him lies in perfect view
              He reads distinctly as a written book . . .       [VIII, 727]
              And grieves at the remembrance of his loss . . .
     [28r]    Imagination! rising up at once                    [VI, 525]
              Like an unfatherd vapour here
30            I paused was lost awhile as in
              A cloud . . .                                      [VI, 529]
     [28v]    Have found [my] strength & I have broken through
              The darkness that was [?upon] me
              And populous images before me stand               [VII, 350]
```

As he drafted these lines, Wordsworth understood the connection between the thwarting of imaginative expectation (in August 1790), profound feelings of grief stemming from his parents' deaths, and the sudden surge of inspiration in the present (early April 1804). The emotional burden of the Virgilian echo at lines 13–14 (present from the first and throughout consecutive redraftings on the dismembered leaves) is reinforced by the comparison of the shapes with spectres (ll. 21–2), which survived into Book VIII, and a line which didn't survive the revision: 'And grieves at the remembrance of his loss' (l. 27). That line appears in two drafts of the passage at MS WW, 27v,[16] and indicates that Wordsworth understood visionary power to be connected to bereavement. The opposition he poses is that between the material world and the imagined, the invisible, the intuited. What is seen plainly can no longer be susceptible to imaginative power, which derives authority from our emotions; indeed, the function of the draft is to assert the primacy of the imagination. That is why a living thought is preferable to 'a written book'. Wordsworth's implication is that through intensity of vision we may reclaim the dead – a thought consistent with the Hawkshead and Cambridge poetry (see chapters 1 to 3 above).

If this is indeed to be suggested, Wordsworth needs a more optimistic re-solution to the passage, so he apostrophizes the imagination, claiming to have

---

[16]   See Cornell *13–Book Prelude* i 360, ii 257.

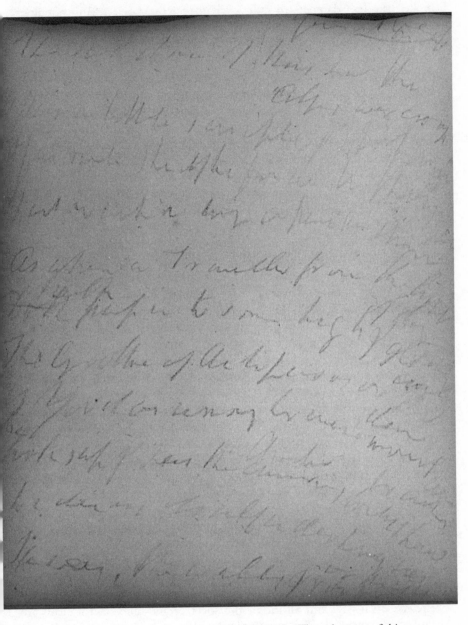

Figure 17. DC MS 43, 26r. *The Thirteen-Book Prelude*: 'The substance of this was the Alps were crossed . . .' Very rough draft in pencil of the Cave of Yordas passage, composed as part of the crossing of the Alps in Book VI.

broken through darkness to rediscover imaginative power, 'And populous images before me stand' (l. 34). By this means the image of past loss is turned into one of present gain, and the dead are symbolically restored.

As so often with early *Prelude* materials, the poetry can be fully understood only within the context of its composition. Wordsworth is writing in early April 1804, on the crest of a wave of inspiration that had commenced with Coleridge's departure for London on 14 January. Coleridge's departure for the Mediterranean on 6 April had turned the expansion and completion of *The Prelude* into a sacred trust. He who had conceived 'The Recluse' was thought to be dying, and in his last letter before departure, written on 29 March but not sent until 3 April, Wordsworth had promised to get on with *The Prelude* (now considered part of 'The Recluse'): 'I am now after a halt of near three weeks started again; and I hope to go forward rapidly. Adieu again and again – and again. . . . We entreat you to write for ever and ever, and at all opportunities. But this request must be unnecessary. We shall be so distressingly anxious.'[17] Whatever else might be said, this anxiety could be channelled into creativity, and it may have helped that Coleridge was no longer in a position to harass him about 'The Recluse'. The other revelation of Wordsworth's letter is that in the days prior to 29 March he had resumed composition after a break of nearly three weeks; Mark L. Reed estimates that composition had therefore ceased around 12 March.[18] In that case the cave simile can be read (and is read as such by Wordsworth himself) as describing the creative exhaustion that began at that time; the claim at its conclusion to having 'found [my] strength & . . . broken through' refers specifically to his resumption of work at the end of the month. It is a thanksgiving for renewed power as he embarks on the thirteen-book *Prelude* – a much greater challenge than the five-book version which did not succeed. Like all poets he is uncomfortably conscious of the precariousness of inspiration, and is wondering whether he can continue the spate of writing that has brought him three-quarters of the way through MS WW, with just over five books of the thirteen-book poem in draft. He thinks also of imaginative potency – not something he could depend on – and on a psychic level feels an obligation to the dead (and perhaps the soon-to-be-dead) to complete 'The Recluse'.

When in the autumn he moved the cave simile to Book VIII Wordsworth realized that the change of context meant that the poetry had to be, to some extent, depersonalised. The simile is no longer part of a thanksgiving for renewed creativity, and although the spectres and allusion to Virgil are allowed to remain, the line mentioning grief 'at remembrance of his loss' is

---

[17]   *EY* 465.
[18]   Reed ii 255.

eliminated, so reducing the extent to which it invokes Wordsworth's past. He otherwise follows the earlier draft closely, describing the gradually subsiding movement of shapes and shadows until they lie 'Exposed and lifeless as a written book'. He must have known, when he decided to move it to Book VIII, that he would have to extend it. It could not conclude with an image of death, not just because that would be untrue to its original context, but because it needed to say something positive about the city. 'The Recluse' had entered the city's walls, and once there would need to see it and its inhabitants as susceptible of redemption. The classical model had to be reversed, preferring retrieval to loss, plenitude to dearth.

> But let him pause a while, and look again
> And a new quickening shall succeed, at first
> Beginning timidly, then creeping fast
> Through all which he beholds: the senseless mass
> In its projections, wrinkles, cavities,
> Through all its surface, with all colours streaming,
> Like a magician's airy pageant, parts,
> Unites, embodying every where some pressure
> Or image, recognis'd or new, some type
> Or picture of the world; forests and lakes,
> Ships, rivers, towers, the Warrior clad in Mail,
> The prancing Steed, the Pilgrim with his Staff,
> The mitred Bishop and the thronèd King,
> A Spectacle to which there is no end.
>
> (*The Thirteen-Book Prelude* viii 728–41)

The new lines serve further to detach the simile from its personal context, and take it deeper into the realm of archetype. The figures that emerge from the wrinkles and cavities of the 'senseless' rock provide a tableau of London society in medieval times not unlike Blake's famous image of Chaucer's Canterbury pilgrims – a human embodiment of the 'weight of Ages' that descends on the young poet at line 703. This at least is the reading demanded if the simile is to explicate, as it ought, Wordsworth's experience as he gazed at the 'vulgar forms' of suburban London. But its significance extends beyond the rhetorical, as it resonates with images and characters encountered elsewhere:

> . . . forests and lakes,
> Ships, rivers, towers, the Warrior clad in Mail,
> The prancing Steed, the Pilgrim with his Staff,
> The mitred Bishop and the thronèd King,
> A Spectacle to which there is no end.

If the 'forests and lakes' refer us back to Cumbria, the 'Ships, rivers, towers' echo London as it appeared in 'Composed Upon Westminster Bridge': 'Ships, towers, domes, theatres, and temples lie / Open unto the fields, and to the sky' (ll. 6–7). That panorama had been both static and imaginatively heightened, more sublime than Eden at its creation: 'Never did sun more beautifully steep / In his first splendour valley, rock, or hill' (ll. 9–10). So it is that the revived vision in the cave aspires to a similarly ideal status. 'The mitred Bishop and the thrònèd King' have an iconic quality that recalls the 'cross-legged Knight / And the stone Abbot' at Furness Abbey.[19] They are figures from distant history, the dead symbolically resurrected, like Dunmail and his sons in the vision of the Battle of Dunmail Raise in 'The Vale of Esthwaite'. The 'Pilgrim with his Staff' is perhaps the most redolent, invoking Bunyan's hero, but is also a version of the leech-gatherer, Matthew with his bough of wilding, and the starving angler in 'Point Rash-Judgement'. The prancing steed is straight out of Ariosto, Tasso or Spenser, emblematic of a tradition as much as of a particular work.

All these figures remain indistinct, generic, as if they were the raw material of imaginative thought, plucked from the world of myth in which patterns of loss and retrieval were originally forged. What in Virgil was the site of grief and self-excoriation has been recast as that of imaginative potency or creative process. It is an implicit rebuke to the undergraduate who had judged harshly of the place in which he found himself, and a warning that it is as magical and enchanted as any of those in which he had been raised. In adapting Virgilian myth Wordsworth has re-inscribed his own.

The transplanted simile works because it derived power from the intense emotions that inspired it when it was first composed in April – the awareness of Coleridge's delicate state of health, the feeling of obligation towards the dead, and the intense desire to begin work on 'The Recluse'. The passage added in the autumn fused those concerns with others that revealed London to be a crucible of historical, political and spiritual forces that still held sway. In so doing it sought to give London the importance it needed within the grandiose scheme of 'The Recluse', for it was in the metropolis, in the midst of vice, that Wordsworth would locate the first glimmerings of an all-embracing, redemptive love. He comments repeatedly on the degradation of city life because it was vital to 'The Recluse' that its prescription for millennial harmony be rooted in reality.

---

[19]   *The Two-Part Prelude* ii 120–1.

                              Neither guilt nor vice,
        Debasement of the body, or the mind,
        Nor all the misery forced upon my sight
        Which was not lightly pass'd, but often scann'd
        Most feelingly, could overthrow my trust
        In what we may become, induce belief
        That I was ignorant, had been falsely taught,
        A Solitary, who with vain conceits
        Had been inspired, and walk'd about in dreams.

                                              (ll. 802–10)

London remains a stern preceptress to the last; misery, vice, debasement and, intriguingly, guilt, are 'forced' upon him as part of his tempering as poet of 'The Recluse'. They almost guarantee his sense of mission, his 'trust / In what we may become'. And yet it is impossible to ignore the note of self-doubt, the fear that he might be a madman who 'walk'd about in dreams'. Such admissions are essential to the nature of the poem: *The Prelude* is a sustained act of self-examination in which Wordsworth both questions and establishes his right to compose 'The Recluse'. The irony is that though *The Prelude* is in those terms a success, highlighting Wordsworth's strengths as the poet of the vague, the indistinctly seen, and the half-intimated, it reveals why 'The Recluse' was beyond him. That work would have no room for equivocation; it was to be a synthesis of poetry and philosophy that aspired, with biblical confidence, to the status of revelation. It is not that Wordsworth was incapable of perceiving inner truths, but that the creation of 'The Recluse' would be willed, systematic and analytical. When admonishing Wordsworth for the failure of *The Excursion* in 1815 Coleridge told him that as far as he was concerned 'The Recluse' was supposed to be 'the *first* and *only* true Phil. Poem in existence':

> Of course, I expected the Colors, Music, imaginative Life, and Passion of *Poetry*; but the matter and arrangement of *Philosophy* – not doubting from the advantages of the Subject that the Totality of a System was not only capable of being harmonized with, but even calculated to aid, the unity (Beginning, Middle, and End) of a *Poem*. Thus, whatever the Length of the Work might be, still it was a *determinate* Length: of the subjects announced each would have it's own appointed place, and excluding repetitions each would relieve & rise in interest above the other – . (Griggs iv 574)

Coming over a decade after Wordsworth had asked Coleridge for his notes to 'The Recluse'[20] this was exceptionally unhelpful. The unkind references to a

---

[20] In his letter of early March 1804; see *EY* 452.

'*determinate* length' align Coleridge with Jeffrey who, in his devastating review of November 1814, had made heavy weather of the fact that *The Excursion* 'fairly fills four hundred and twenty good quarto pages'.[21] It also reveals that the poem Coleridge had devised was impossible for Wordsworth to have written. None of his poems were composed to a prearranged menu. It was not how he worked or thought because his gift was to intuit rather than intellectualize. He was consequently not well read in the realms of philosophy. There is no clear evidence of his ever having read Locke, Hartley or Berkeley (though from his use of their ideas it seems entirely possible that he did), let alone the Germans. There is no cause to question his insistence that he had 'never read a word of German metaphysics, thank Heaven!'[22] – a statement corroborated by other uncomplimentary remarks, not least that recorded by Caroline Fox: 'Kant, Schelling, Fichte; Fichte, Schelling, Kant: all this is dreary work and does not denote progress.'[23] *The Thirteen-Book Prelude* is designed to bear out the view that, despite everything, Wordsworth is the author of 'The Recluse', but all the features that enable such passages as the cave simile to work their magic confirm that he was no philosopher, and had little inclination for systematic or analytic thought.

There was in Wordsworth, as in Shelley, a deeply messianic streak. Whatever his qualifications he wanted to think that he was the only person capable of writing 'The Recluse', and that determination echoes throughout *The Prelude* like the beat of a drum. You can hear it in the stentorian tones occasionally adopted by the verse, and it is the rationale by which he constructs the bogus history that takes us from Cumbria to Cambridge, then to France, the Alps and, finally, Snowdon – an uphill journey towards a sense of divine appointment. It is a trajectory (more fiction than fact) by which 'The Recluse' becomes the logical culmination of his creative life. And it is the combination of realist and Messiah that explains why, when Wordsworth discusses love of nature leading to love of man in Book VIII, the verse oscillates between censoriousness and piety, between the world as it is and as it might be.

So it is that the London of the cave simile is imaginatively transformed, free of the low-life characters glimpsed in Book VII. And for that reason it fails to argue that the 'degeneracy and vice' of city life could give way to 'a redemptive process in operation', as Coleridge put it.[24] You could argue that the transformation of London within the poet's imagination is a form of redemption, but 'The Recluse' was supposed to have established its authority within

---

[21]   *Edinburgh Review* 24 (November 1814) 1–30, p. 1.
[22]   *LY* iv 49.
[23]   Quoted in Peacock 76.
[24]   See CC *Table Talk* i 308.

the real world. As he worked towards the conclusion of Book VIII Wordsworth seems to have been aware that the problem remained unresolved and in a final effort to address it attempted to argue that even among the alienating crowds in London he had seen things that confirmed 'the unity of man, / One spirit over ignorance and vice / Predominant'.[25]

> In the tender scenes
> Chiefly was my delight; and one of these
> Never will be forgotten. 'Twas a Man
> Whom I saw sitting in an open Square
> Close to the iron paling that fenced in
> The spacious Grass-plot: on the corner-stone
> Of the low wall in which the pales were fix'd
> Sate this one Man, and with a sickly Babe
> Upon his knee, whom he had thither brought
> For sunshine, and to breathe the fresher air.
> Of those who pass'd, and me who look'd at him,
> He took no note; but in his brawny Arms
> (The Artificer was to the elbow bare
> And from his work this moment had been stolen)
> He held the Child, and, bending over it,
> As if he were afraid both of the sun
> And of the air which he had come to seek,
> He eyed it with unutterable love.
>
>   (ll. 842–59)

On arrival in London Wordsworth had dismissed the people around him as 'vulgar'. This passage extends the revision to which that rash judgement has already been subject – again through the filter of the imagination. Preserved forever in a spot of time, the artificer and his child become representative figures, symbolic of the ennobling effect of parental love. They provide Wordsworth with hope that despite their outward vulgarity the populace may be persuaded of the philosophy of 'The Recluse'. The artificer and his child are natural counterparts of the infant babe and his mother, and inevitably recall Wordsworth's parents. As artificer the father echoes the iconic figure of Christ the carpenter – perhaps the Unitarian Christ whose humanity makes him as susceptible and fallible as anyone else. But that association remains undeveloped. What is important is that it is on the mean streets of London that Wordsworth finds the emblem of his own destiny as well as a sign of promise for those he is to address. For the other artificer of *The Prelude* is Wordsworth himself. In that persona he simultaneously confirms his sense of

---

[25]   *The Thirteen-Book Prelude* viii 827–9.

election and his place in London life. The artificer is, finally, evidence that Wordsworth's hopes for universal betterment are not misplaced.

The passage recalls one of Wordsworth's models for 'The Recluse'. In 1815 Coleridge would invoke *De rerum natura* as its model by way of pointing out Lucretius' inadequacies: 'Whatever in Lucretius is Poetry is not philosophical, whatever is philosophical is not Poetry: and in the very Pride of confident Hope I looked forward to the Recluse, as the *first* and *only* true Phil. Poem in existence.'[26] Lucretius was an evangelist for a particular brand of Epicureanism, and his poem was designed to convert; similarly, 'The Recluse' would aim to change how people perceived themselves and their relation to the world. But Wordsworth and Coleridge would have found Lucretius' ideas anathema.[27] Lucretius regarded nature as dead and the universe as matter in motion. As a means of arguing against a designing principle in the world he asked a series of questions that would have caught Wordsworth's attention (I quote from the translation of Lucy Hutchinson, the seventeenth-century writer whose *Memoirs* of her husband were so admired by Wordsworth and Coleridge,[28] and to whom Wordsworth's wife Mary was related):

> Why are such generall contagions bred
> When seasons of the yeare intemperate be?
> Why rageth such unripe mortallitie?
> Besides, when nature doth with paynefull throes
> A wretched infant first to light expose,
> He, like a ship-wrackt saylor cast on shore
> By raging billows, naked, helplesse, poore,
> With cries, which well his future woes become,
> Lies on the earth, cast from his mothers womb.
>
> (v 237–45)

Lucretius' case is that the innate hostility of the natural world to humanity disproves the existence of a nurturing divinity. Wordsworth takes the same image – that of the infant child – and uses it twice in Book VIII to argue the opposite. The second time it is used is in the passage describing the artificer. The first time is in its opening lines, which describe the Grasmere summer fair, a passage probably composed early September 1804.[29]

---

[26]   Griggs iv 574.

[27]   Paul Kelley has usefully discussed Lucretius' influence on Wordsworth's early poetry in 'Wordsworth and Lucretius' *De Rerum Natura*', *N&Q* 30 (1983) 219–22. Among other things, as he points out, Lucretius provides the epigraph for *Descriptive Sketches*.

[28]   *WR* ii 115.

[29]   Cornell *13–Book Prelude* i 55.

What sounds are those, Helvellyn, which are heard
Up to thy summit? Through the depth of air
Ascending, as if distance had the power
To make the sounds more audible: what Crowd
Is yon, assembled in the gay green Field?
Crowd seems it, solitary Hill! to thee,
Though but a little Family of Men,
Twice twenty, with their Children and their Wives
And here and there a Stranger interspersed.

(ll. 1–9)

It was as optimists for human nature that Wordsworth and Coleridge formulated the ideas behind 'The Recluse'; they believed that humanity was engaged in continual progress up the ascent of being. How appropriate, then, that *Prelude* Book VIII, devoted to an elucidation of its central principle, should begin with an image of elevation. As the noise of the crowd rises into the heavens, it becomes more rather than less audible, seeming to acquire power in some sense analogous to the spiritual aspirations that provide Wordsworth with his ideal. The 'little Family of Men . . . with their Children and their Wives' is more than a random collection of people; the village, close enough to comprise a single family, is an image of the millenarian community Wordsworth and Coleridge wanted to create.[30] As he supplies detail, the image of a close-knit group bound by ties of mutual dependence becomes clearer: the aged hawker is a regular visitor to the fair, the fruit-seller is a local girl, the old man becomes generous, and children rich. It is a glimpse of society devoid of illness, poverty and deprivation – a rural paradise regained.

Immense
Is the Recess, the circumambient World
Magnificent, by which they are embraced.
They move about upon the soft green field:
How little They, they and their doings seem,
Their herds and flocks about them, they themselves
And all which they can further or obstruct!
Through utter weakness pitiably dear,
As tender Infants are: and yet how great!

(ll. 46–54)

In 'Home at Grasmere' MS B Wordsworth had expressed the wish that 'here / Should be my home, this Valley be my World' (ll. 42–3); likewise, in *Prel-*

---

[30] In this light Reed is surely correct to suggest that it is a 'countervision' to Bartholomew Fair in Book VII; see Cornell *13–Book Prelude* i 55.

ude Book VIII, Grasmere is a microcosm of the millennial ideal, presided over by a benevolent landscape that literally embraces its inhabitants, 'Through utter weakness pitiably dear, / As tender Infants are'. That nurturing relationship between the circumambient world and the villagers prefigures the artisan and his baby at the end of Book VIII, and echoes the image first used by Lucretius. It provides a living illustration of Wordsworth's theme: how the closeness of man and nature enables people to live in Edenic peace and child-like innocence. There is a pagan element too, reminiscent of the pantheism of the 1798 poetry:

> For all things serve them; them the Morning-light
> Loves as it glistens on the silent rocks,
> And them the silent Rocks which now from high
> Look down upon them; the reposing Clouds,
> The lurking Brooks from their invisible haunts,
> And Old Helvellyn, conscious of the stir,
> And the blue Sky that roofs their calm abode.

(ll. 55–61)

Everything is instinct with life – the light, rocks, clouds, brooks – bristling with affection for humanity. It is not unlike Ben Jonson's paradisal vision in 'To Penshurst', in which the partridge is so attuned to the needs of humanity that it 'is willing to be killed'.[31] Natural things are humanized by Wordsworth's language: sunlight 'loves', clouds repose, brooks lurk. Old Helvellyn, an ancient force risen out of the earth (which Wordsworth had encountered directly in 'The Vale of Esthwaite'), tacitly approves of the hubbub, while the blue sky provides the villagers with a 'roof'. That paradox, by which the sky relinquishes its power to threaten and becomes a shelter, recalls the cave in which Wordsworth saw 'A spectacle to which there is no end'. For now, the vale of Grasmere and its bustling citizens are unified in a harmony that foreshadows the 'future glory and restoration' to be predicted by 'The Recluse'.

Villages were one thing; cities were another. Although the city could be argued to be a sublime 'Preceptress' (with the help of the cave simile, transferred from its original context), Wordsworth could not comprehend city-dwellers in the same paradisal context as the Grasmerians. This tender portrait of village life was to be the closest Wordsworth would get to conceiving the paradisal brotherhood predicated by 'The Recluse'. The artisan and his child are evidence that the sustaining love of a parent was possible in the city, but they are a far cry from the 'little Family of Men' in the Vale of Grasmere.

---

[31] 'To Penshurst' 30. Wordsworth certainly knew Jonson's poem by February 1802; see *WR* ii 121.

10

'*I only look'd for pain and grief*'

As he set out from Portsmouth as Captain of the *Earl of Abergavenny* in late January 1805 John Wordsworth told his brother William that 'I shall make a very good voyage of it if not a *very great* one – at least this is the general opinion.'[1] He meant that he expected it to be profitable; the ship's cargo was valued at £200,000, and besides 200 crew members the ship was carrying nearly another 200 people as passengers. If all went well the voyage would bring him close to his dream of retiring to the Lake District with William and Dorothy.

The ship set sail from Portsmouth on 5 February 1805 but while off Portland Bill, barely an hour into its journey, it ran into a severe westerly gale. A pilot was taken on board to guide her into the safety of Portland Roads, the natural harbour between Weymouth and the Isle of Portland. There seems to have been a delay in obtaining the pilot and by the time he was on board they had lost the benefit of a flood tide. The difficult challenge facing him was to clear the Shambles, but he underestimated the clearance required by a fully-laden ship. John Wordsworth did not trust pilots, having previously mentioned to William that 'it is a joyful time for us when we get rid of them.'[2] This one miscalculated[3] and as the ship rounded the eastern end of the Shambles into Portland Roads her way was unexpectedly becalmed. At about 5 p.m. the wind dropped and she was swept onto the rocks. A terrifying evening followed as the ship was successively swept on and off the reef. Finally at around 7.30 p.m. she beat her way clear of the Shambles and despite being

---

[1] Ketcham 155.
[2] *EY* 563–4.
[3] This at least was Wordsworth's view, as reported by Southey to John Rickman on 1 May 1805: 'there was no misconduct whatever, except in the pilot for running her aground' (Warter i 321). In one of the various pamphlets concerning the wreck, John Wordsworth was reported to have cried, when the ship struck the rock, 'Oh pilot! pilot! you have ruined me' (*EY* 564n1).

waterlogged steered towards Weymouth sands. She was too flooded to remain afloat and, shortly after 11, two miles offshore, sank in 66 feet of water. Other ships were nearby, but it was too dangerous for them to approach. John had by this time ascended to the 'hen-coop', the highest part of the ship, where he was heard to utter his last words, 'Let her go! God's will be done.' Shortly after he was washed overboard and for five minutes struggled desperately for his life in a cold and violent sea.[4] Of the 387 people aboard 155 survived. John's body was recovered on 20 March and buried the following day in Wyke-Regis.

Unaware of what had happened three days after the wreck, Wordsworth was busily making progress with the thirteen-book *Prelude* – though at this stage he was still working to a plan of fourteen books, Book X at that time comprising two books. By the end of 1804 the entire work was mapped out and mostly written. There were some gaps between Book X, line 567, and the end of Book XIII, but much of this Wordsworth knew would comprise a redevelopment of materials already composed.[5] It is not known what he was working on when he wrote confidently to Richard Sharp on 8 February, three days after his brother's death, but it is likely to have been some of the earlier drafts in MS Z towards Book X or Book XI.[6]

> My Poem advances quick or slow as the fit comes; but I wish sadly to have it finished in order that after a reasonable respite I may fall to my principal work. . . . By the Bye I ought not to forget that we had a Letter from my Brother The Captain a few days ago from Portsmouth, speaking very favourably of his hopes and in good spirits.[7]

John's 'Letter' had been sent on 24 January. It praised 'Tintern Abbey', 'Michael' and the poems on the naming of places, while taking exception to 'a harshness'[8] in some of Wordsworth's as yet unpublished poems. Critics have argued over what this 'harshness' might be; I suspect John had in mind the sublime confidence of some of the *Prelude* poetry as it is clear that he preferred the compassionate manner of 'The Mad Mother' and 'Complaint of a Forsaken Indian Woman'. By his 'principal work' Wordsworth meant 'The Recluse', which he was expecting shortly to begin, the conclusion of the fourteen (soon to become thirteen) book *Prelude* being within sight.

---

[4] Wordsworth discussed the length of time for which John struggled in a letter to Richard Wordsworth, *EY* 583.
[5] I follow Mark L. Reed; see Cornell *13–Book Prelude* i 56.
[6] See Cornell *13–Book Prelude* ii 435ff.
[7] *EY* 534–5.
[8] Ketcham 156.

A few days later, on Monday 11 February, he and Mary went out for a walk. They returned to Dove Cottage at around 2 p.m. to find that Sara Hutchinson had arrived with news of John's death, plunging Dorothy into a state of terrible distress. His absence had meant that, as Wordsworth told his brother Richard later that day, 'I had no power of breaking the force of the shock to Dorothy or to Mary. They are both very ill.'[9]

This was no exaggeration. On 4 March Wordsworth told Richard that 'I cannot say that the burthen of our affliction in this house is yet much lighter; to time we must look for ease.'[10] Three days later he told Walter Scott that 'we have neither strength nor spirits for any thing.'[11] On 26 March, shortly after hearing of the recovery of John's body, Sara Hutchinson told her friend Mrs Cookson that 'we cannot stir from the house without meeting a thousand fresh remembrances of our loss.'[12] She referred to the fact that John had planted many of the trees and shrubs in the garden at Dove Cottage – a point reiterated by Mary in a letter of 7 March.[13]

The tragedy took a heavy toll on Dorothy in particular; she was described as looking unwell for weeks afterwards and found consolation by meditating on John's last words, as she reported to Christopher: 'a thousand times have I repeated to myself his last words "The will of God be done," and be it so.'[14] In her letter of mid-March to Jane Marshall she repeated those words with the comment: 'I have no doubt when he felt that it was out of his power to save his life, he was as calm as before if some thought of what we should endure did not awaken a pang.'[15] She was a focus of some anxiety made all the worse by the presence of two infant children, John and Dora, who would have witnessed her distress, and whom it was her task to look after. As late as mid-March she reported her inability to cope with John's boisterousness.[16] William and Mary's support was necessary to keep her on an even keel. As she told Richard on 27 February, 'William and Mary have done all that could be done to comfort me, and I have done my best for them.'[17] Later that day she wrote to Christopher, saying 'let us who are left cling closer to each other.'[18]

[9] *EY* 540.
[10] *EY* 552.
[11] *EY* 553.
[12] *The Letters of Sara Hutchinson*, ed. Kathleen Coburn (London: Routledge and Kegan Paul, 1954), p. 7.
[13] *EY* 569n1; see also Dorothy's letter to Jane Marshall, 15 and 17 March 1805, *EY* 560.
[14] *EY* 550.
[15] *EY* 559.
[16] *EY* 567, 570.
[17] *EY* 549.
[18] *EY* 550.

But who was comforting Wordsworth, and what was he suffering? I have suggested in earlier chapters that he had a natural tendency to suppress intense emotion. This is a not uncommon way for Englishmen to behave today; it was more widespread then. I have also suggested that his father's death may have generated feelings of anger.[19] Wordsworth confessed to being 'of a stiff, moody, and violent temper' as a boy,[20] and that passionate nature followed him into adulthood. John's death brought that intensity to the fore. It seems likely that, given Dorothy's state, he was compelled to sacrifice his own comfort from the outset. The day the news came through he reported to Beaumont that they were all 'in miserable affliction, which I do all in my power to alleviate; but heaven knows I want consolation myself.'[21] His tone was almost fearful when he added: 'I shall do all in my power to sustain my Sister under her sorrow, which is and long will be bitter and poignant.'[22] Mary hints at the strain on him in her letter to Catherine Clarkson of 7 March:

> Our beloved William! My dear friend you would love him more than ever, could you but know how he has exerted himself to comfort us and, after all, as he tells us, his, is the greatest loss . . . (Burton 2)

Nearly a month into their grief it is clear that Wordsworth felt in need of comfort and may not have received it. As the letter to Beaumont indicates, one of his main outlets was correspondence, and it is here that one finds most evidence of how he managed his feelings.

The day after writing to Beaumont he responded to a letter of condolence from Southey by saying that 'grief will, as you say, and must, have its course.'[23] There is a certain reluctance, if not resentment, in Wordsworth's reiteration of Southey's platitudinous observation; it was as though he felt his head bowed to a yoke. In a letter to Thomas Clarkson on 16 February he again commented: 'We shall endeavour to be resigned: this is all I can say; but grief will have its course.'[24] The same day he told his brother Christopher that 'We have done all that could be done to console each other by weeping together.

---

[19] See chapter 6 above, p. 132.

[20] *Prose Works* iii 372.

[21] *EY* 541. Wordsworth once told Thomas Moore that, 'such was his horror of having his letters *preserved*, that in order to guard against it, he always took pains to make them as bad and dull as possible' (*Memoirs, Journal, and Correspondence of Thomas Moore* ed. Rt. Hon. Lord John Russell, MP (8 vols, London, 1853–6) vii 198). The exceptions to this were the letters he wrote to Beaumont, as those quoted in this chapter demonstrate.

[22] *EY* 542.

[23] *EY* 543.

[24] *EY* 544.

I trust we shall with the blessing of God grow calmer every day.'[25] Again, there is a certain hollowness in that expression of trust, and it would prove futile, at least at first. His letter to Southey was answered by a visit to Dove Cottage when their grief was at its height, 13–15 February, which 'comforted us much', as Wordsworth told Thomas Clarkson.[26] The benefit of Southey's presence was that it relieved pressure on Wordsworth and provided another party to whom he could articulate his feelings. As rivals for Coleridge's affections they hadn't been close before this, but Southey's kindness marked the beginning of a deep and genuine friendship that lasted until his death. It certainly altered Dorothy's opinion. Before this, she told Lady Beaumont, Southey had seemed to possess 'nothing of the dignity or enthusiasm of the Poet's Character', but while at Dove Cottage 'he wept with us in our sorrow, and for that cause I think I must always love him.'[27] Southey later recorded that he had been 'dreadfully shocked' by John's death.[28] His visit lasted only a few days, and the deep reservoir of grief that had built up within Wordsworth had still to find release after his departure.[29]

The Wordsworths had learnt to share their grief in 1787, when delayed mourning for their parents had overcome John, Christopher, Dorothy and William thanks to the delay in sending horses to carry the brothers to Penrith. In 1805 their pain was worse for the fact that it was the loss of one of their number that had revived the process. The mourning of 1805 was different in other ways from that of 1787. In 1805 Dorothy's reliance on him made it harder for Wordsworth to express his feelings, and he channelled them instead into metaphysical questions. This began with the letter to Beaumont of 11 February in which he exclaimed 'Alas! what is human life!'[30] The next day to Southey he exclaimed, 'human life! after all, what is it!'[31] In both cases this was half-exclamation, half-question. Irritated by misleading reports in the newspapers in which John's conduct had been maligned, he was inspired in a letter to Beaumont of 12 March to amplify this:

[25] *EY* 543.
[26] *EY* 544.
[27] *EY* 577.
[28] Warter i 318.
[29] Southey made a second visit to Dove Cottage *c*.20 February, which he reported to William Taylor on 9 March: 'Poor Wordsworth is almost heart-broken by the loss of his brother in the Abergavenny, – his best and favourite brother. I have been twice over with him, and never witnessed such affliction as his and his sister's' (*A Memoir of the Life and Writings of the Late William Taylor of Norwich*, ed. J. W. Robberds (2 vols, London, 1843), ii 77).
[30] *EY* 541.
[31] *EY* 543.

Why have we sympathies that make the best of us so afraid of inflicting pain and sorrow, which yet we see dealt about so lavishly by the supreme governor? Why should our notions of right towards each other, and to all sentient beings within our influence differ so widely from what appears to be his notion and rule, if every thing were to end here? Would it be blasphemy to say that upon the supposition of the thinking principle being destroyed by death, however inferior we may be to the great Cause and ruler of things, we have *more of love* in our Nature than he has? The thought is monstrous; and yet how to get rid of it except upon the supposition of *another* and a *better world* I do not see. (*EY* 556)

The obvious answer to the last of these questions is 'yes'. So often thought of as the most pious and god-fearing of the Romantic poets, Wordsworth was fully capable of blasphemous thoughts. Grief compelled him to face up to his deepest feelings in response to the question, 'what is life?', posed in earlier letters. This comment to Beaumont shows that in framing it Wordsworth wanted to know what kind of justice underlay a divinely ordered system in which, as he had written in 'Ruined Cottage' MS B, 'the good die first, / And they whose hearts are dry as summer dust / Burn to the socket.'[32] In 1797 no answer had been given, and Margaret's tragedy was understood to be a fact of life. In the letter to Beaumont Wordsworth goes further, implying that human beings are mere playthings of whatever 'governor' ruled the planet.

This important letter goes on to extol John's many virtues before adding, 'and we see what has been his end!'[33] Wordsworth suggests that there is little point in being virtuous if the reward is an early death; again, he implicitly points an accusing finger at God. He turns immediately to a proxy, Edward Young, and copies out a passage from *Night Thoughts*. The appeal of this particular poem is clear. Young had written, 'Our Birth is nothing but our Death begun.'[34] In that belief he had set out to compose a poem of consolation, designed to show how the orthodox Christian might live a virtuous life in the hope of eternal reward. When he read Young shortly before writing to Beaumont, Wordsworth must have been seeking reassurance. He probably began reading *Night the Seventh*, 'The Infidel Reclaim'd', from the start, and then thought it worth copying out the following passage:

> When to the grave we follow the renown'd
> For valour, virtue, science, all we love,
> And all we praise; for worth, whose noon-tide beam,
> Enabling us to think in higher style,

[32] Ll. 150–2.
[33] *EY* 556.
[34] *Night Thoughts* v 719.

Mends our ideas of ethireal powers;
Dream we, *that* lustre of the moral world
Goes out in stench, and rottenness the close?
Why was he wise to know, and warm to praise,
And strenuous to transcribe in human life
The mind almighty? Could it be that fate
Just when the lineaments began to shine
And dawn the Deity, should snatch the draught,
With night eternal blot it out?

(EY 556, from Night Thoughts vii 205–17)

For Young these questions were rhetorical. The implication for him and his readers was that we are all divine and each contain some spark of immortality; stench and rottenness were not 'the close'. In the context of Wordsworth's letter, however, the tone is less persuasive. No doubt he would like to believe, with Young, that God had a divine purpose and that it was beneficial to John, but coming immediately after the suggestion that 'we have *more of love* in our Nature than he [i.e. God] has,' *Night Thoughts* reads more like a statement of doubt than of belief.

It is interesting that Wordsworth concludes his copy at line 217, because Young's sentence continues for another line or so:

. . . With Night eternal blot it out, and give
The Skies Alarm, lest Angels too might die?

(Night Thoughts vii 217–18)

Wordsworth may have chosen to omit this because it articulated his own fear too closely. Young is after all postulating something that must have seemed heretical. With John's death an angel *had* been condemned to death – something as inexplicable as Fate's snuffing out of the shining 'Lineaments' of the virtuous. Paradoxically Young, who had sought to promote Christian belief, had helped Wordsworth open up an avenue of doubt and scepticism.

In 1796 Coleridge told Thelwall that Wordsworth was 'at least a *Semi-atheist*',[35] which may have been another of way of saying that he had no need of a redeemer, as Wordsworth later claimed.[36] It is worth bearing in mind that when described as a semi-atheist Wordsworth had only recently renounced his adherence to the philosophy of Godwin, who was described by Coleridge as 'the very High priest of Atheism'.[37] According to the thirteen-book

---

[35] Griggs i 216.
[36] Morley i 158.
[37] Griggs i 215.

Prelude it was not atheism that led to that renunciation but the interminable interrogation of the mind.[38] In the wake of the Terror, there is good reason to think that, besides reacting against Godwin, Wordsworth also rejected outright atheism. At Racedown he read Louvet's *Narrative*, which warned against 'atheism reduced to principle'.[39] And during his residence in London he was a regular visitor to Joseph Fawcett's sermons at the dissenters' meeting-house at Old Jewry in the city. He later remembered that Fawcett's 'Xtianity was probably never very deeply rooted, &, like many others in those times of like shewy talents, he had not strength of character to withstand the effects of the French revolution & of the wild & lax opinions which had done so much towards producing it & far more in carrying it forward in its extremes.'[40] These are the judgements of Wordsworth in his seventies, so it is not surprising that they are implicitly critical of Fawcett. In the 1790s, however, there is reason to think that as a semi-atheist Wordsworth was intrigued by Fawcett's religious views, which were influenced by Plato. In a sermon on omnipresence Fawcett described God as

> the living soul that inhabits, and animates every living thing; that propels every drop through every vein; that produces every pulsation of every artery, every motion of every limb, every action of every organ, throughout the whole animal kingdom. . . . He is the life of the world: at once the maker, the inspector, and the mover of all things.[41]

Platonic notions of God occur throughout Wordsworth's poetry, and he was well-acquainted with them; at some point prior to 1810 he took possession of Coleridge's copy of Thomas Taylor's translation of *Cratylus, Phaedo, Parmenides, and Timaeus*.[42] They provided a useful way of conceiving of the unifying cosmic force that would bring about the millenarian enlightenment envisaged in such 1798 'Recluse' fragments as 'There is an active principle'. Indeed, there is good evidence for believing that Wordsworth's religious notions were in some ways Platonic. When dismissing German metaphysicians to Caroline Fox in 1844 he pulled back slightly from his criticisms: 'However, they have much of Plato in them, and for this I respect them: the English,

---

[38] *The Thirteen-Book Prelude* x 888–904.
[39] Jean Baptiste Louvet de Couvray, *Narrative of the Dangers to which I have been exposed* (London, 1795), p. 70. For details of Wordsworth's reading see *WR* i 89.
[40] *FN* 80.
[41] As quoted in Leslie Chard, *Dissenting Republican* (The Hague: Mouton, 1972), p. 151.
[42] See *WR* ii 167–8.

with their devotion to Aristotle, have but half the truth; a sound Philosophy must contain both Plato and Aristotle.'[43]

All the same, these ideas remain general, and Wordsworth tended to refrain from saying anything more specific. One of the most perceptive comments on his religious views dates from 1815, when Henry Crabb Robinson said that Wordsworth's religion was 'like [that] of the German metaphysicians, a sentimental and metaphysical mysticism in which the language of Christianity is used, which is a sort of analogy to this poetic and philosophical religion'.[44] That may be about as close as anyone ever got to pinning him down on matters which were probably, as in many people at the time, constantly under review and subject to revision.

What evidence there is suggests that in 1805 Wordsworth's creed was by no means conventional, and that he was capable of the questioning to which John's death appears to have given rise. Belief where it occurred in Wordsworth's early work had been located principally in the hope that the dead might be reclaimed through intense communion with natural things. Although there is abundant evidence of a belief in that kind of imaginative vision, there is none in an intervening deity. So it is that human tragedy takes its inevitable course in 'The Ruined Cottage' MS B and *The Borderers*, the beneficent God of Coleridge's verse being absent. 'The Recluse' was to preach the virtues of a divine agency and in refashioning himself as its author Wordsworth had found it necessary to postulate something like the Coleridgean creator – hence the recurrence of 'God' in poetry of 1798 onwards. All the same, I suspect that Robinson was correct in suggesting that for Wordsworth God was a means of referring to an innate, metaphysical divinity that resided within the mind.

John's death stripped away any ability to pretend, and made it impossible for Wordsworth to fudge questions of fundamental conviction. One aspect of this was to address the question of his own culpability. 'Poor blind Creatures that we are!' he told Richard Sharp, 'how he hoped and struggled and we hoped and struggled to procure him this voyage.'[45] Like the guilt he had felt in 1787, the sense that he had somehow been complicit in the events that destroyed his brother may have been related to the anger of the moment which, though frequently suppressed, is almost invariably present in his written statements. This quickly mellowed into acceptance. As Wordsworth told one of the survivors of the wreck: 'It was God's Will that he should not return to us and we must reconcile ourselves to our loss and make it of use to us to

---

[43]   Peacock 76.
[44]   Morley i 158.
[45]   *EY* 572.

prepare us for similar separations.'[46] John's last words, which Dorothy had repeated thousands of times since their first utterance, had become embedded in Wordsworth's tormented emotions.

His poetic vocation was intricately entwined with his feelings for John. On the day the news came through he described John as 'meek, affectionate, silently enthusiastic, loving all quiet things, and a Poet in every thing but words'.[47] That was fundamental to his response to the death, and would be repeated. It was no flight of fancy. In succeeding weeks he commented that 'I never wrote a line without a thought of its giving him pleasure, my writings printed and manuscript were his delight and one of the chief solaces of his long voyages.'[48] This is borne out by John's extant letters, and by Wordsworth's comment to Mary and Dorothy that the 'loss of John is deeply connected with his *business*'.[49] As late as 1812 he told Lord Lonsdale that 'My Brother had entirely sympathised with my literary pursuits, and encouraged me to give myself entirely to that way of Life, with assurance that [if] I stood in need of assistance, and he proved fortunate, it should ever be ready for me.'[50] At the very least Wordsworth regarded his brother as a partner and a patron. It would not be fanciful to suggest that he felt he owed John his vocation and what success he had enjoyed: 'he encouraged me to persist, and to keep my eye steady on its object.'[51] It was natural that he should commemorate him in verse. In mid- to late April, having written no poetry since 11 March, he

> had a strong impulse to write a poem that should record my Brother's virtues and be worthy of his memory. I began to give vent to my feelings, with this view, but I was overpowered by my subject and could not proceed: I composed much, but it is all lost except for a few lines, as it came from me in such a torrent that I was unable to remember it; I could not hold the pen myself, and the subject was such, that I could not employ Mrs Wordsworth or my Sister as my amanuenses. (*EY* 586)

Wordsworth's grief, which had produced anger, now became the source of inspiration, as in 1787 when 'The Vale of Esthwaite' had radically altered course subsequent to the delayed mourning for his father. When he returned to *The Prelude* in late April 1805 he was similarly changed. The poem to Coleridge was largely complete, but important passages had yet to be com-

---

[46] *EY* 579.
[47] *EY* 541.
[48] *EY* 565.
[49] Burton 2.
[50] *Supp.* 104.
[51] *EY* 547.

posed. He told Beaumont that he had two books to write, probably referring
to Books XII and XIII.[52] As he drafted the first of these in MS Z, he found an
opportunity to pay his first tribute in verse to his brother with a passage which
envisages his ideal audience – those who 'read the invisible soul':

> . . . men for contemplation fram'd,
> Shy, and unpractis'd in the strife of phrase,
> Meek men, whose very souls perhaps would sink
> Beneath them, summon'd to such intercourse:
> Theirs is the language of the heavens, the power,
> The thought, the image, and the silent joy;
> Words are but under-agents in their souls;
> When they are grasping with their greatest strength
> They do not breathe among them: this I speak
> In gratitude to God, who feeds our hearts
> For his own service, knoweth, loveth us
> When we are unregarded by the world.
>
> (*Thirteen-Book Prelude* xii 266–77)

This purports to describe an entire class of men but is a portrait of John. It
was he who, as Wordsworth told Beaumont, was 'modest; and gentle: and
shy, even to disease'.[53] To such people words are 'strife', a conflict from which
they retreat. Instead, as honorary poets, they speak the higher language of the
inspired when their souls are at their zenith. Only in the light of John's demise does the concluding statement make sense. Wordsworth's claims are
made 'In gratitude to God', who nourishes our spirits for his 'own service'.
That service and its larger purpose remains beyond our comprehension. But
as he wrote Wordsworth consciously attempted to build within himself a trust
in providence. That meant compelling himself to pay homage to a higher will
and accept that John's death must have had its logic.

Confronted once again with *The Prelude*, he found himself increasingly out
of sympathy with the self that had written it. Much had been composed in a
mood of proud hope, spurred on by the irrevocable knowledge that he was
the poet-prophet of 'The Recluse'. In the wake of John's death that hope
seemed empty, and on concluding *The Prelude* about 20 May he told Beaumont
that it 'seemed to have a dead weight about it, the reality so far short of the
expectation'.[54] That disappointment left its mark on the manuscript. Above
the title-page of Book XI in MS Z he commented: 'This whole book wants

---

[52] I follow Reed; see Cornell *13–Book Prelude* i 58.
[53] *EY* 548.
[54] *EY* 594.

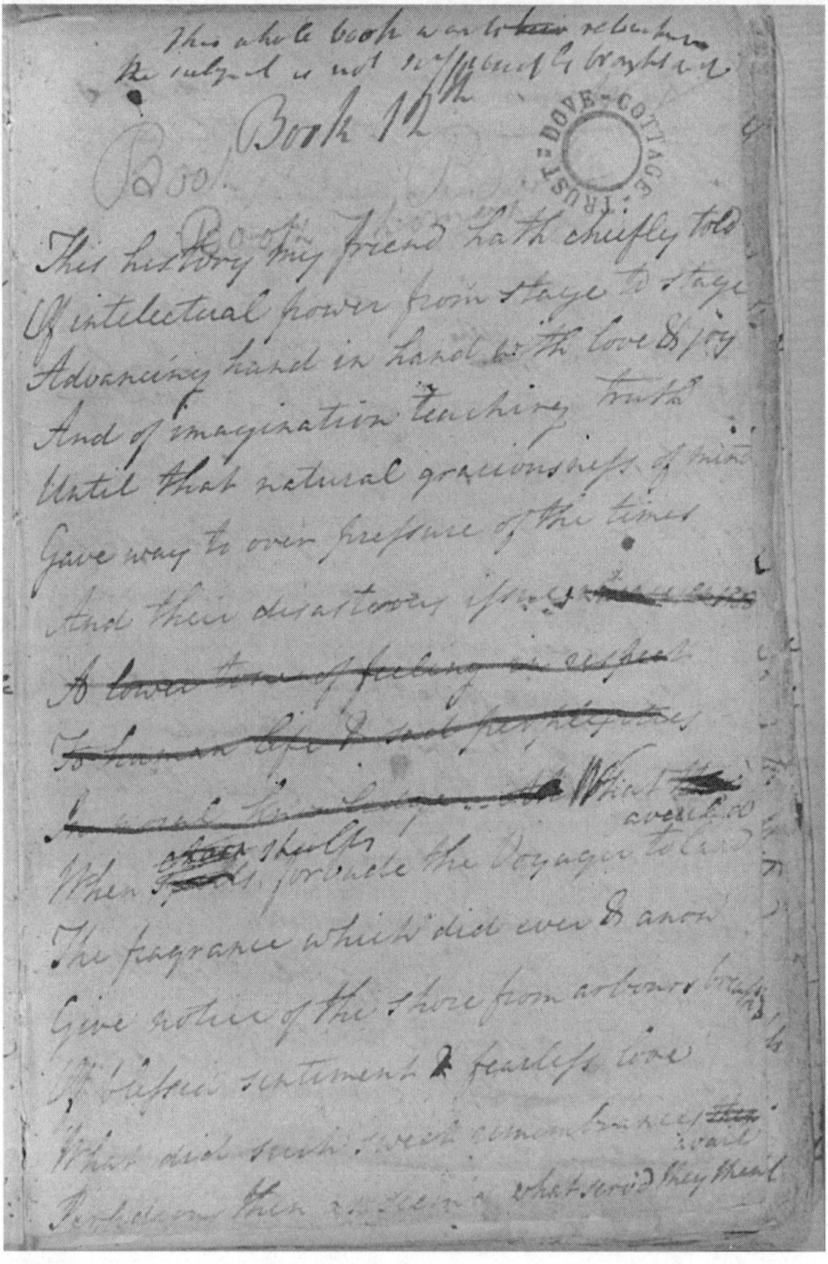
Book 12th
This history my friend hath chiefly told
Of intellectual power from stage to stage
Advancing hand in hand with love & joy
And of imagination teaching truth
Until that natural graciousness of mind
Gave way to over pressure of the times
And their disastrous issues
The fragrance which did ever & anon
Give notice of the shore

Figure 18. DC MS 49, 5r. *The Thirteen-Book Prelude*: 'Book 12th'; note the deleted lines in which Wordsworth criticizes his Godwinian self harshly in the wake of John's death.

retouching the subject is not sufficiently brought out.'[55] Further indications of how grief had altered him appear further down on the same page where five lines are deleted from the text, in which he criticized himself for his attachment to Godwinism,

> whence ensu'd
> A lower tone of feeling in respect
> To human life & sad perplexities
> In moral knowledge[56]

In the light of John's death Godwinism must have seemed more spurious than ever, for grief and suffering were devalued by it. That these harsh judgements were affected by thoughts of John is corroborated by the lines that follow:

> What avail'd,
> When Spells forbade the Voyager to land,
> The fragrance which did ever and anon
> Give notice of the Shore, from arbours breathed
> Of blessed sentiment and fearless love?
> What did such sweet remembrances avail,
> Perfidious then, as seem'd, what serv'd they then?
> My business was upon the barren seas,
> My errand was to sail to other coasts . . .
> (*The Thirteen-Book Prelude* xi 48–56)

In May 1805 Wordsworth could hardly have described himself as a mariner 'upon the barren seas' without thinking of John. Once again the idea of his being in John's situation is turned against himself. He becomes a stranger to 'blessed sentiment and fearless love', where John had been no such thing. Wordsworth is recalling Satan inhaling 'odorous sweets' as he approaches Eden,[57] but even Satan had been commendably attracted to their source. As he looks back, Wordsworth sees himself as having been alienated from the 'sweet remembrances' of family and friends, seduced by sterile systems of thought.

The new perspective forced upon him had distanced him further than ever from the optimism of the 1790s, leading him to regard that younger self less sympathetically than he would otherwise have done. John's death reminded

---

55 See figure 18 opposite.
56 Ibid.
57 *Paradise Lost* iv 156–66.

him of why he became a poet and of the forces that once inspired him – grief, guilt and betrayal. By comparison with that the redemptive plan of 'The Recluse' must have seemed meretricious and etiolated. Completion of *The Prelude* gave him scant pleasure because it wasn't something he wished any longer to have written. What was more, he told Beaumont,

> the doubt whether I should ever live to write the Recluse and the sense which I had of this Poem being so far below what I seem'd capable of executing, depressed me much: above all, many heavy thoughts of my poor departed Brother hung upon me; the joy which I should have had in shewing him the Manuscript and a thousand other vain fancies and dreams. (*EY* 594)

Alongside the sense in which John was a partner in the process of composition went the feeling that the preface to 'The Recluse' was a disappointment, 'far below' what he felt he could do. Its advocacy of the faith that looks through death, and the transcendental impulses that accompanied it, must have seemed like a betrayal of his brother's memory.

On 8 June Wordsworth went fishing with a neighbour at Grisedale Tarn where he had last parted from John. Overcome by emotion, he left his friend and 'in floods of tears'[58] composed the first of three elegies, which were written at around the same time: 'I only look'd for pain and grief', 'To the Daisy' ('Sweet Flower! belike one day to have') and 'Distressful gift! this Book receives'. 'For much it gives my soul relief / To pay the mighty debt of Grief,' he had written in 1787.[59] It proved so again, the debt now as then being both the composition of poetry and the shedding of tears:

> . . . And undisturb'd I now may pay
> My debt to what I fear'd.
> Sad register! but this is sure:
> Peace built on suffering will endure.
> ('I only look'd for pain and grief' 13–16)

These words are uttered in humility, and throughout the poems occasioned by the tragedy a similar tone recurs. He had learnt, directly from John, that God's will would be done. His anger had subsided and given way to pained submission. He had to learn to see it as a blessing; God had laid upon his brother 'A consecrating hand'.[60]

In the third of these confessional poems, and the least well-known, he turned

58   *EY* 599.
59   'The Vale of Esthwaite' 286–7.
60   'I only look'd for pain and grief' 60.

to a commonplace book left at Dove Cottage by John on his last departure
and mused on its contents. It concluded:

> But now – upon the written leaf
> I look indeed with pain and grief,
> I do, but gracious God,
> Oh grant that I may never find
> Worse matter or a heavier mind,
> For those which yet remain behind
> Grant this, and let me be resign'd
> Beneath thy chast'ning rod.
>
> (ll. 36–43)

It is a chilling sentiment, made all the more so by the original reading of the
second line: 'With heart oppressed by pain and grief'. The experiences of the
months since 11 February had oppressed Wordsworth, making him feel subject to the chastening hand of a stern master. Tragedy had brought his beliefs
into question. What did his brother's abrupt and tragic end say about the
nature of the universe? Was it harmonious with the idea of the 'redemptive
process in operation'[61] that 'The Recluse' was to illustrate? Could it be reconciled with the concept of a merciful God? Shortly before the elegies were
written Mary had copied a lightly revised version of the waiting for the horses
episode into Book XI of the thirteen-book *Prelude* where his father's death

> With all the sorrow which it brought appear'd
> A chastisement; and when I call'd to mind
> That day so lately pass'd, when from the crag
> I look'd in such anxiety of hope
> With trite reflections of morality,
> Yet in the deepest passion, I bow'd low
> To God, who thus corrected my desires . . .
>
> (xi 369–75)

Wordsworth read these lines before writing the elegies to John, and it is likely
that they helped him comprehend his loss as the exercise of divine power. But
where in *The Prelude* the perspective is partly that of a boy whose imagination
has generated unreal connections between disparate events, the elegies for
John establish the chastening rod of the Almighty as a reality, brought to bear
on a sensibility that had forgotten the value of humility. There was no irony in
this, as there arguably had been in the *Prelude* spot of time, where the 'trite

---

[61] CC *Table Talk* ii 177.

reflections' were responsible for the vengeance of a tyrannical God; in the elegies Wordsworth is attempting to express genuine meekness towards a divine power whose acts he cannot understand. How shallow the sublime aspirations of the Snowdon passage must have seemed to a poet whose most personal and heartfelt utterance of the moment was in the name of resignation 'Beneath thy chast'ning rod'.

We do not know exactly when Wordsworth first saw Beaumont's painting, *A Storm: Peele Castle*, but it must have been at least a year after John's death. Beaumont's original pen-and-wash study had been engraved by Thomas Hearne in 1783, and by 1806 had given rise to two oil paintings of the scene. Wordsworth visited London in spring 1806, arriving on 4 April. During his stay he was based in Grosvenor Square, close to Beaumont, at whose house he may have seen one of the oils before it was hung in the Royal Academy. Wordsworth saw it again at the Academy on 2 May.[62] He also saw the pen-and-wash study, and told Beaumont that it was the better of the two.[63] 'The picture was to me a very moving one,' he told him, 'it exists in my mind at this moment as if it were before my eyes.'[64] It would have brought back to him the days he spent at Rampside in 1794, close to Piel Castle, its wrecked ship recalling John's fate. Scholars scrupulously date Wordsworth's 'Elegiac Stanzas, Suggested by a Picture of Peele Castle, in a Storm' to 'between *c.*20 May and 27 June 1806',[65] to indicate that it was composed shortly after Wordsworth's departure from London. Beaumont read it by the end of June, and confessed himself 'not a little elated' by it.[66]

> I was thy Neighbour once, thou rugged Pile!
> Four summer weeks I dwelt in sight of thee:
> I saw thee every day; and all the while
> Thy Form was sleeping on a glassy sea.
>
> So pure the sky, so quiet was the air!
> So like, so very like, was day to day!
> Whene'er I look'd, thy Image still was there;
> It trembled, but it never pass'd away.

---

[62] His ticket was supplied by Joseph Farington; see Farington vii 2742.
[63] See Reed ii 321–2.
[64] *MY* i 63.
[65] Reed ii 43.
[66] Quoted in Felicity Owen and David Blayney Brown, *Collector of Genius: A Life of Sir George Beaumont* (New Haven and London: Yale University Press, 1988), p. 123.

How perfect was the calm! it seem'd no sleep;
No mood, which season takes away, or brings:
I could have fancied that the mighty Deep
Was even the gentlest of all gentle Things.

Ah! THEN, if mine had been the Painter's hand,
To express what then I saw; and add the gleam,
The light that never was, on sea or land,
The consecration, and the Poet's dream;

I would have planted thee, thou hoary Pile!
Amid a world how different from this!
Beside a sea that could not cease to smile;
On tranquil land, beneath a sky of bliss:

Thou shouldst have seem'd a treasure-house, a mine
Of peaceful years; a chronicle of heaven: –
Of all the sunbeams that did ever shine
The very sweetest had to thee been given.

A Picture had it been of lasting ease,
Elysian quiet, without toil or strife;
No motion but the moving tide, a breeze,
Or merely silent Nature's breathing life.

Such, in the fond delusion of my heart,
Such Picture would I at that time have made:
And seen the soul of truth in every part;
A faith, a trust, that could not be betray'd.

So once it would have been, – 'tis so no more;
I have submitted to a new controul:
A power is gone, which nothing can restore;
A deep distress hath humaniz'd my Soul.

Not for a moment could I now behold
A smiling sea and be what I have been:
The feeling of my loss will ne'er be old;
This, which I know, I speak with mind serene.

Then, Beaumont, Friend! who would have been the Friend,
If he had lived, of Him whom I deplore,
This Work of thine I blame not, but commend;
This sea in anger, and that dismal shore.

Oh, 'tis a passionate Work! – yet wise and well;
Well chosen is the spirit that is here;
That Hulk which labours in the deadly swell,
This rueful sky, this pageantry of fear!

And this huge Castle, standing here sublime,
I love to see the look with which it braves,
Cased in the unfeeling armour of old time,
The light'ning, the fierce wind, and trampling waves.

Farewell, farewell the Heart that lives alone,
Hous'd in a dream, at distance from the Kind!
Such happiness, wherever it be known,
Is to be pitied; for 'tis surely blind.

But welcome fortitude, and patient chear,
And frequent sights of what is to be borne!
Such sights, or worse, as are before me here. –
Not without hope we suffer and we mourn.

The most successful of the elegies to John, 'Elegiac Stanzas' speaks of the change wrought on Wordsworth by his brother's death. It is in the first place a personal testimony to his grief, but is also about the morality of aesthetics.

Wordsworth looks back on an earlier self whose confidence and mood were such that had he been a painter he would have depicted the Castle as a sublime eminence in the midst of Elysian quiet. He is really talking about a way of seeing the world – a vision that favours the transcendent, the sublime, the imaginatively enhanced. He readily acknowledges the seductiveness of that vision, his diction ('tranquil', 'dream', 'sunbeams') admitting the idealizing faculty of the imagination, something that remained with him from Hawkshead days until the near completion of the thirteen-book *Prelude* in early 1805. What else had the climbing of Snowdon been about, or the cave simile, or indeed the spots of time? That had seemed at the time a trust that could not be betrayed; now it was exposed as a 'fond delusion of my heart' that left him 'in a dream'. It was he who, implicitly, had been betrayed, led away from the truth. He looks back affectionately at his old self and sublime tendencies, but distress has been the occasion for renunciation. Attractive they may have been, but those impulses were false. Grief has humanized him, stripped him of the ruthless and not entirely human urge to aestheticize. A year after his loss, the pain is as keen as ever, and unchanging. It has permeated his understanding, returning him to solid earth.

The tempestuous weather and stricken vessel of Beaumont's painting is an index of this undeluded perspective. As he gazed upon it Wordsworth comprehended the Castle (which he once imagined in a sun-drenched spot of time) as symbolic of fortitude in the face of sorrow – 'The light'ning, the fierce wind, and trampling waves'. It is a new understanding that makes him feel sorry for anyone blind enough to continue pursuing childish dreams.

Wordsworth had been resident at Rampside in his mid-twenties, but this poem really looks back on an aesthetic predisposition he had possessed until John died – the power that had enabled him to compose *The Prelude*. It had been betrayed by events and, by implication, revealed him to have been a teller of falsehoods – a traitor, in other words, to the truths he had understood in 1787. Recognizing that, the poem embraces a more grounded knowledge of the place of suffering in human life. 'Elegiac Stanzas' is about the abdication of a certain kind of imaginative vision – 'A power is gone, which nothing can restore' – and is as much an elegy for that as for his brother. As in the elegies composed the previous year, he strives to inculcate a proper humility towards a divine order he cannot understand, but which has demonstrated the centrality of pain in human life. It has become a sacred obligation to John that he submit to this 'new controul'. Wordsworth had never been far from the memory of grief as it had struck him in 1787, but over the years it had become a submerged force in his work. It would be hidden no longer. From now on, it was a principal determinant in his aesthetic. The acceptance of fortitude and patience is a way of signalling that the psychological background to his work, while important, is to be valued for itself, not as part of a transaction whereby engagement with nature led automatically to some sort of superficial reward.

In this light the hope in the last line seems attenuated until one recalls the Collect for the Order for the Burial of the Dead in the *Book of Common Prayer*, where we are instructed 'not to be sorry, as men without hope, for them that sleep in him'.[67] That counsel bears comparison with the Pedlar's command to be 'wise and chearful', when the poet is stricken with grief at Margaret's fate at the conclusion of 'The Ruined Cottage' MS D. The difference is that by 1805 Wordsworth's hope occurs within the context of a declaration that he continues to suffer and to mourn. Grief will not be assuaged by assurances that the dead are at peace; on the contrary, it accepts bereavement as permanent and enduring, and refuses to expiate it with transcendent experience. This insight could have come only with age, and was one of the few blessings (if that is the correct term) for the tragedy of John's death.

The anger that had erupted in semi-blasphemous declarations to Beaumont in summer 1805 (a year before) had been reconfigured as trust in the wisdom

---

[67] For further discussion of this allusion see Edward Wilson, 'An Echo of St Paul and Words of Consolation in Wordsworth's "Elegiac Stanzas"', *RES* 43 (1992) 75–80.

of a higher order – although Wordsworth does not invoke God by name. However, its promise of eternal life commended Christianity as a means of consolation, and as time passed he would become increasingly reliant on it, and more explicit in reference to it, on those grounds.

Before hearing of John's death Wordsworth had declared that when *The Prelude* was complete 'I may fall to my principal work.'[68] That may have been a realistic hope on 7 February 1805, but by 3 June he was doubting whether 'I should ever live to write the Recluse'.[69] Such doubt was a warning. Aware of it or not, his altered way of thinking and feeling was inimical to the composition of his 'principal work'. Its mission had been to describe 'the necessity for and proof of the whole state of man and society being subject to and illustrative of a redemptive process in operation – showing how this Idea reconciled all the anomalies, and how it promised future glory and restoration'.[70] For someone who had bidden farewell to the idealizing faculty so as to bow his head to 'frequent sights of what is to be borne' this would be an uphill struggle. It had been difficult enough to conclude *The Prelude*, which had been no more than a preface to 'The Recluse', unburdened as it was by the weight of philosophical exegesis required to make sense of Coleridge's redemptive philosophy. What's more, most of *The Prelude* had been written before John's death. It could not have been written now, leaving 'The Recluse' further from reach than ever.

As Stephen Gill suggests, 'The Recluse', impossible though it was, 'became a trust, made sacred by his brother's death'.[71] John had believed in Wordsworth's greatness, perhaps more than Coleridge, and Wordsworth felt duty-bound to demonstrate that such faith had not been misplaced. Incidentally, he was at this point no less persuaded of radical principles than in earlier times; the journalist John Taylor, having met Wordsworth in May 1806, found him 'strongly disposed towards Republicanism':

> His notions are that it is the duty of every Administration to do as much as possible to give consideration to the people at large, and to have *equality* always in view; which though not perfectly attainable, yet much has been gained towards it and more may be.[72]

This summary of Wordsworth's political notions, though seldom cited, is an important one. By comparison with the views even of the enlightened Whigs

[68] *EY* 534.
[69] *EY* 594.
[70] CC *Table Talk* i 308.
[71] Gill 241.
[72] Farington vii 2785.

among whom he circulated, Wordsworth was understood to be radical. The term underlined here, 'equality', was still associated with the French Revolution, which by 1806 was seen to have led lamentably to the rise of Napoleon, crowned Emperor two years previously. Although Wordsworth did not support Napoleon, he remained attached to the ideals for which the Revolution had been fought. This went hand in hand with a distrust of those in power; according to Dorothy in March 1806, he believed that 'there is no true honour or ability amongst them.'[73] His prevailing determination to go forward with 'The Recluse' arose as much out of those convictions as out of intense feelings over his brother's death.

In the absence of Coleridge's notes, now said to have been destroyed, Wordsworth in December 1805 set himself to read 'for the nourishment of his mind, preparatory to beginning' work. However, Dorothy observed, in her letter to Lady Beaumont, 'I do not think he will be able to do much more till we have heard of Coleridge.'[74] Coleridge was still felt to possess the key to 'The Recluse' and its theories. Though expected to return to England upon hearing of John's death, he dallied in the Mediterranean, much to Wordsworth's distress. 'We have lately had much anxiety about Coleridge,' he told Beaumont, 'What can have become of him?'[75] By July 1806 Coleridge's continuing silence was, Wordsworth told Walter Scott, 'very vexatious and distressing'.[76] The standard edition of Coleridge's letters contains nothing whatever between 21 August 1805 and 17 June 1806 – an astonishing hiatus for such an inveterate letter-writer. No one but Coleridge seemed to understand the reason for the delay or refusal to communicate; Mary Lamb composed a poem about it, 'Why is he wandering o'er the sea? / Coleridge should now with Wordsworth be.'[77] All the same, his absence conveniently provided an excuse for not writing 'The Recluse', leaving Wordsworth free to 'meditate'. As Dorothy reported in January 1806, 'his thoughts are employed upon the Recluse.'[78] In all likelihood he was reviewing the manuscripts of 'Home at Grasmere' which had broken down in 1800. By 23 July he had begun to reorganize them and by early September had a more or less finished copy.[79] How much was written during those months? Scholars continue to deliberate, but it seems likely that despite telling Beaumont that he had written 'nearly

73 *MY* i 11.
74 *EY* 664.
75 *MY* i 8.
76 *MY* i 52.
77 Marrs ii 166.
78 *MY* i 2.
79 The datings derive from letters; *MY* i 58, 79. Scholars continue to dispute precise details of composition; see Cornell *Home at Grasmere* 16–22.

1000 lines', most were actually composed in 1800, work during summer 1806 consisting largely of reorganization and some revision.[80] There was cause to be generous to himself in progress reports to his patron, who set as much store by 'The Recluse' as Coleridge.

Wordsworth nurtured the expectation that Coleridge would shortly return and approve of his labours, bless them, and furnish him, at least verbally, with instructions and advice as to how to continue. On 1 August he promised Beaumont: 'Should Coleridge return so that I might have some conversation with him upon the subject, I should go on swimmingly.'[81] There is a tactical advantage in his insistence that continuation of 'The Recluse' depend on Coleridge's safe return and co-operation – something far from guaranteed. (Incidentally, these facts support the hypothesis that Coleridge had not been told about or shown 'Home at Grasmere' in 1800 or since; otherwise Wordsworth would not have told a mutual friend, Beaumont, that it had been largely written in 1806 – something Coleridge would have been able to contradict had he seen it before.)

By early August Coleridge was not far distant. His ship was in quarantine off Plymouth on 11 August and landed in Kent on the 17th. Even then he delayed getting in touch. The Wordsworths fondly invented reasons why; Dorothy told Catherine Clarkson: 'No doubt C. has not written himself because he is afraid to enquire after us,' alluding to their grief over John.[82] Coleridge resided in London, writing spasmodically (and unrevealingly) to the Wordsworths without committing himself to a meeting. The situation was similar to that in 1799, when on return from Germany he abstained from travelling north until a chance meeting with Cottle.

By 1806 it is likely that Coleridge preferred London life to the less comfortable existence in the Lake District, and if the truth be known felt no desire to see the Wordsworths. He couldn't say that and instead excused himself in a manner that roused almost as much contempt as if he had. Wordsworth wrote to Beaumont from Grasmere on 8 September:

> he dare not go home, he recoils so much from the thought of domesticating with Mrs. Coleridge, with whom, though on many accounts he much respects her, he is so miserable that he dare not encounter it. What a deplorable thing! I

---

[80]   James A. Butler concurs. He observes that *Home at Grasmere* was worked on in 1806, with transitions added and parts stitched together. But the bulk of it draws on material composed in 1800. In particular, MS R of the poem is likely to date from 1800, and a certain amount of poetry composed for 'Michael' in 1800 may have been considered by Wordsworth as part of *Home at Grasmere*.

[81]   *MY* i 64.

[82]   *MY* i 71.

have written to him to say that if he does not come down immediately I must insist upon seeing him somewhere. If he appoints London, I shall go.[83] (*MY* i 78–9)

But Wordsworth had a while yet to wait. No doubt Coleridge was quite sincere in not wanting to cohabit with his wife, but his lack of enthusiasm at the prospect of seeing Wordsworth was underlined by a continuing reluctance to agree a time and place either in London or elsewhere. One possible explanation, Molly Lefebure proposes, is that morphine addiction had now reduced him to a state of organic psychosis: 'His body's chemistry was radically altered by his drug, completely orientated to morphine and thus totally disorientated to all else.'[84]

No fortuitous encounter with Cottle would impel Coleridge northwards. What caused him to jump on the Carlisle stage was sex. His Mediterranean tour and its various distractions, which had included a flirtation with the opera singer Cecilia Bertozzoli, had given rise to a string of sexual fantasies which added fuel to his hopeless passion for Sara Hutchinson,[85] whom he was convinced was in love with him. In a notebook entry on 10 April 1805 he had written of how in sleep images were 'forced into the mind by the feelings that arise out of the position & state of the Body and its different members', adding that so far 'Sleep has never yet desecrated the images, or supposed Presences, of those whom I love and revere.'[86] In another notebook entry, beneath Sara's name, he wrote a phrase from a play he had recently read: 'This *dwelling* Kiss'.[87]

He began the journey north with the intention of tracking her down. Disembarking at Penrith, he found out that she was with the Wordsworth ménage, at that moment at Kendal *en route* to Coleorton where they were to spend the winter at the Beaumonts' country seat. I suspect that Molly Lefebure surmises accurately that Coleridge had little genuine interest in seeing the Wordsworths at that moment – quite the opposite in fact, if as seems likely his objective was Sara Hutchinson.[88] Having ascertained her whereabouts he dashed to Kendal and, instead of taking a room in their hotel, booked into another nearby. From there he sent for Wordsworth, with whom he wished to discuss his decision to separate from his wife. It was 26 October 1806, more than two months after his return to England. Something of his feeling for Sara at this time may be gathered from a notebook entry written a month later:

---

83 This letter survives; *MY* i 80.
84 *Bondage of Opium* 447.
85 Discussed by Lefebure, ibid., pp. 428–9; *Darker Reflections* 35–7, 41, 43.
86 *Notebooks* ii 2543.
87 *Notebooks* ii 2961.
88 *Bondage of Opium* 448.

I know, you love me! – My reason knows it, my heart feels it / yet still let your
eyes, your hands tell me / still say, o often & often say, My beloved! I love you
/ indeed I love you / for why should not my ears, and all my outward Being
share in the Joy – the fuller my inner Being is of the sense, the more my outward
organs yearn & crave for it / O bring my whole nature into balance and harmony. (*Notebooks* ii 2938)

This was pure fantasy. Sara could not stand to be close to him, and on seeing
him again in Kendal she, like William and Dorothy, was horrified by what had
become of him. Molly Lefebure says that morphine led Coleridge to declaim
'in his puppet's voice'.[89] If so, the performance would have been disturbing.
As Dorothy told Catherine Clarkson,

> We all went thither to him and never never did I feel such a shock as at first sight
> of him. We all felt exactly in the same way – as if he were different from what we
> have expected to see; almost as much as a person of whom we have thought
> much, and of whom we had formed an image in our own minds, without having
> any personal knowledge of him. . . . He is utterly changed; and yet sometimes,
> when he was animated in conversation concerning things removed from him, I
> saw something of his former self. But never when we were alone with him. (*MY*
> i 86)

Dorothy was acutely aware that they were in the company of a sick man: 'that
he is ill I am well assured. . . . His fatness has quite changed him – it is more
like the flesh of a person in a dropsy than one in health; his eyes are lost in it.[90]
   They remained with him from Sunday evening till Tuesday morning, when
Dorothy, Mary and the children departed for Coleorton. Sara and Wordsworth
remained with Coleridge one more night. It was an unconventional and
potentially scandalous thing for Sara to have done,[91] and there must have
been good reason for it. We do not know what they discussed, but it must
have had something to do with Coleridge's feelings for her. It had been decided that he would move in with the Wordsworths when they moved house,
and perhaps he and Sara needed to work out some *modus vivendi* before that
took place. Whatever they discussed, Coleridge believed after that meeting
that Sara loved him as much as he loved her.
   It is doubtful as to whether Coleridge was able to discuss artistic matters
with Wordsworth. This was not the man who in early 1804 had inspired the

[89] *Bondage of Opium* 449.
[90] *MY* i 87.
[91] Richard Holmes suggests that Wordsworth acted as go-between for Coleridge and
Sara; see *Darker Reflections* 76–7.

five-book, and then the thirteen-book *Prelude* by proposing its new function as preface to 'The Recluse'. Nor was he the man whose notes – verbal or written – would describe its philosophical content. It is not surprising that Wordsworth chose not to show him 'Home at Grasmere' either now or later. The reason cannot have been disappointment with the poem as he had expressed satisfaction with it in letters to Beaumont a month before; it was disappointment with Coleridge. He could not see how he would be able to judge the poem, let alone suggest how to develop it. As his illusions evaporated, Wordsworth must have begun to doubt the quality of what he had done and question the entire project. Before long 'Home at Grasmere' was no more than a quarry from which he would mine parts of *The Excursion*. Anxiety about 'The Recluse' had effectively been displaced by anxiety about Coleridge. Two weeks later Wordsworth wrote to him from Coleorton saying that he was 'most anxious to hear of you', adding of the Beaumonts that 'their love of you is very great and they are most anxious to hear from you.'[92]

Having announced their separation to his wife, Coleridge joined the Wordsworths at Coleorton where, on a series of evenings concluding 7 January 1807, William read all thirteen Books of *The Prelude* to Coleridge as the conclusion to the task first envisaged in early 1804. Years later Coleridge remembered that 'thro'' the whole of that Poem "με Αΰρα τις εἰσέπνουσε μυστικωτάτη"' – 'a certain most mystical breeze blew into me.'[93] In response he wrote his last great poem, 'To William Wordsworth', which in 1815 Wordsworth asked him not to publish as its 'commendation would be injurious to us both'.[94] It was a revealing request (which, incidentally, Coleridge would disregard, including the poem in *Sibylline Leaves* (1817)). The suppression of both *The Prelude* and the adulatory poem it inspired was necessary by 1815, given the perceived failure of *The Excursion* and the increasingly provisional nature of 'The Recluse'.

Even at Kendal in late October 1806, Wordsworth must have felt, all the more acutely for its proximity to John's death, the impact of loss. He had been looking earnestly forward to reunion with Coleridge, and the chaotic meeting in Kendal did not meet his expectations. That Coleridge was so strangely altered would have intensified the feeling that their relationship was no longer mutually inspiring. Soon after the encounter he composed a lament for the confidence they had once shared.

---

[92]   *MY* i 90–1.
[93]   Griggs iv 574. The quotation is from Aristophanes, *The Frogs* 313–14.
[94]   *MY* ii 238.

A COMPLAINT.

There is a change – and I am poor;
Your Love hath been, nor long ago,
A Fountain at my fond Heart's door,
Whose only business was to flow;
And flow it did; not taking heed
Of its own bounty, or my need.

What happy moments did I count!
Bless'd was I then all bliss above!
Now, for this consecrated Fount
Of murmuring, sparkling, living love,
What have I? shall I dare to tell?
A comfortless, and hidden WELL.

A Well of love – it may be deep –
I trust it is, and never dry;
What matter? if the Waters sleep
In silence and obscurity.
– Such change, and at the very door
Of my fond Heart, hath left me poor.

11

'*Forbearance & self-sacrifice*'

While preparing to travel down to London in February 1808 Wordsworth wrote to Charles Lamb from Grasmere. On the 26th Lamb relayed the contents of Wordsworth's letter to Thomas Manning in typically jocular fashion: 'Wordsworth the great poet is coming to town. . . . He says he does not see much difficulty in writing like Shakespeare, if he had a mind to try it. It is clear then nothing is wanting but the mind. Even Coleridge a little checked at this hardihood of assertion.'[1]

Critics usually cite this famous quotation to Wordsworth's detriment, but if understood as part of the unfolding struggle to get down to 'The Recluse' it reveals something quite different. There is a weight of evidence to indicate that Coleridge was partly responsible for Wordsworth's repeated claims to greatness. As early as July 1797 he hailed him as 'a very great man – the only man, to whom *at all times* & in *all modes of excellence* I feel myself inferior'.[2] In 1799 he reproached Poole for warning him against 'prostration' before Wordsworth, and in early 1804 told Richard Sharp that Wordsworth 'no more resembles Milton than Milton resembles Shakespere – no more resembles Shakespere than Shakespere resembles Milton'.[3] He doesn't say that Wordsworth is better than either Shakespeare or Milton, but the implication is clear: his genius is of the same ilk. In the earliest version of 'To William Wordsworth' Coleridge had hailed the thirteen-book *Prelude* as

> An Orphic tale indeed,
> A tale divine of high and passionate thoughts
> To their own music chaunted!
>
> (ll. 38–40)[4]

---

1   Marrs ii 274–5.
2   Griggs i 334.
3   Griggs ii 1034.
4   From the text published in my *Romanticism: An Anthology* (1998), p. 515. These lines were quoted by Coleridge as part of a description of *The Prelude* in *The Friend* (CC *Friend* i 368).

That testimonial dates from January 1807, just over a year before Lamb's disparaging report of Wordsworth's high opinion of himself.

From the moment he first came to know Wordsworth, the promotion of his talents to the level of those of Milton and Shakespeare had been essential to Coleridge's campaign to persuade him to assume the mantle of epic poet. Not that Wordsworth was incapable of taking a favourable view of his own talents without his help, but it is to say that Coleridge's energetic endorsements had been decisive in compelling him to focus the next thirty years of his life on 'The Recluse'. In order to make the high ambitions of that work a reality it was necessary for Wordsworth to accept the comparisons with Milton and Shakespeare and remake himself in that image. As I have argued, this was a departure from the areas of concern cultivated prior to 1797. The female vagrant of 'Salisbury Plain', the sailor of 'Adventures on Salisbury Plain', Mortimer in *The Borderers* and Margaret in 'The Ruined Cottage' are proof of a consistent preoccupation with political oppression, injustice, and the suffering produced by it.

The effort of refashioning himself as the philosophical poet of the age inevitably meant measuring up against eminent forebears and thinking more about the Coleridgean theme of transcendence. *The Prelude* in all its forms is no less emotionally 'true' than the poems Wordsworth wrote in the mid-1790s, but the five-book and thirteen-book versions are principally concerned with the poet's upward journey towards spiritual enlightenment, as symbolized by the Snowdon ascent. And because *The Prelude* (as part of 'The Recluse') had an optimistic burden to carry it needed to place social and political injustice within the larger context of 'a redemptive process in operation'.[5] Wordsworth needed to convince himself, and everyone else, that this perspective, which did not come naturally to him, was his own; claims to supersede Milton were part of this. And yet from the outset Coleridge understood that although Wordsworth was capable of philosophizing, there were respects in which he was ill-suited to the task – hence his observation to Hazlitt in 1798 that at Alfoxden Wordsworth

was not prone enough to belief in the traditional superstitions of the place, and that there was something corporeal, a *matter-of-fact-ness*, a clinging to the palpable, or often to the petty, in his poetry, in consequence. His genius was not a spirit that descended to him through the air; it sprung out of the ground like a flower, or unfolded itself from a green spray, on which the gold-finch sang. He said, however . . . that his philosophic poetry had a grand and comprehensive spirit in it, so that his soul seemed to inhabit the universe like a palace, and to discover truth by intuition, rather than by deduction. (Wu ix 104–5)

[5] CC *Table Talk* i 308.

A tendency to cling to the palpable meant that he was hardly the ideal candidate for 'The Recluse', but Coleridge reckoned that his ability to intuit philosophical truths would see him through. How frank was he with Wordsworth about this? It is difficult to be sure, but Coleridge had a knack of saying one thing to someone's face and something quite different behind their back. This is probably what happened at Alfoxden. He seems to have praised Wordsworth more or less unremittingly so as to persuade him to take on 'The Recluse', while providing more balanced assessments elsewhere.

It was equally disingenuous to confess himself taken aback by Wordsworth's 'hardihood of assertion'. He knew he was partly responsible for having created the self-image Wordsworth was projecting and that it was a natural by-product of the determination to write 'The Recluse'. Lamb's waggish remarks to Manning are thus less revealing of Wordsworth than they are of Wordsworth's strained relations with Coleridge. A decade before, Coleridge had sung paeans to 'The Giant Wordsworth – God love him!';[6] now his feelings were so warped that he was happy to surrender to ridicule the talent he had once adored.

Morphine addiction was partly to blame, as was Coleridge's hopeless love for Sara Hutchinson, with whom he imagined Wordsworth to be intimately involved.[7] When Wordsworth wrote to Coleridge in May or June 1808 to reprove him for 'giving by voice and pen to your most lawless thoughts, and to your wildest fancies, an external existence',[8] it was in response to an accusation of that kind. It was at this moment that Coleridge composed 'Ad Vilmum Axiologum', which rebuked Wordsworth for forcing him to 'submit to the sight of Asra's estranged eyes'.[9] This unsatisfied longing can only have been aggravated by his flirtation with Charlotte Brent in February 1808, which having gone a little too far for decency culminated in a grovelling apology when he was compelled to excuse himself on account of 'the mere *light-headedness* of a diseased Body, and a heart sore-stricken'.[10] On a professional level too, he was demoralized. His lectures on the principles of poetry for the Royal Institution had faltered after the delayed second lecture on 5 February, when, crippled with bowel trouble (probably brought on by temporary withdrawal from opium), he retired to his bed for almost two months, not to deliver the third lecture until 30 March.[11] The Wordsworths had never been

---

6   Griggs i 391.
7   See *Notebooks* ii 2001.
8   *MY* i 240.
9   *Notebooks* ii 3231 and n. Coburn dates it 1807–10, though 1808 seems likely.
10   Griggs iii 73. For more information on this curious episode see *Notebooks* iii 3235, 3236 and 3237.
11   Full details provided by R. A. Foakes in his excellent introduction to the lectures, CC *Literature* i 11–21.

encouraging about Coleridge's lecturing projects on the grounds of his frag-
ile health; when he mooted a series on the fine arts in 1806 Wordsworth
warned him 'not on any account [to] entangle yourself with any engagement
to give Lectures in London',[12] and following his collapse after the second of
the 1808 lectures Dorothy reported with some relief that 'he has been obliged
to give up the attempt.'[13] It cannot have made Coleridge feel any better about
himself that Wordsworth then set out to 'prevail upon him to return with him
to this Country'.[14] Ignominious retreat to the household where he was tormented by glimpses of his beloved cannot have been what Coleridge felt would
do him most good (Sara Hutchinson decided to move permanently to Grasmere in April). On every level, therefore, there was cause for him to feel em-
bittered, and to direct some of that hard feeling at Wordsworth. Lamb's letter
merely echoes that resentment.

Wordsworth was also under pressure. He had completed the thirteen-book
Prelude in early 1806, after which it had been his avowed intention to return
to 'The Recluse'. Instead he had tinkered with 'Home at Grasmere' but, still
not satisfied, had kept it from Coleridge. *Benjamin the Waggoner*, complete
by 29 March 1806, did not relate to 'The Recluse'; it was by Wordsworth's
own account 'purely fanciful',[15] and it is no discredit to the poem to describe
it as a very engaging *jeu d'esprit*. Henry Crabb Robinson compared it with
'Tam O'Shanter',[16] and that is the obvious precedent, both poems seeking to
cultivate a similar sense of earnest playfulness.

The publication of *Poems in Two Volumes* in April 1807 may have partly
salved any feeling that he was doing nothing; as he told Walter Scott, 'I had a
thoroughly idle summer; and part of the Autumn was idle.'[17] But the need to
renew his labours was pressing, and out of an excursion to Yorkshire in July
came the idea for a poem. *The White Doe of Rylstone* could hardly be regarded
as part of 'The Recluse', but it might serve the interests of that work in a way
which *Benjamin the Waggoner* and *Poems in Two Volumes* could not. In later
years he placed considerable importance on it; he told Justice Coleridge that
it was, 'in conception, the highest work he had ever produced'.[18]

The first version was composed between late October 1807 and 16 January
1808 in six parts comprising over 1,700 lines. Financial need made Dorothy
keen to see it published at the earliest opportunity, and when Wordsworth

12 *MY* i 90.
13 Ibid. 198.
14 Ibid.
15 Henry Crabb Robinson, as quoted by Paul Betz, Cornell *Benjamin* 22.
16 Ibid.
17 *MY* i 191.
18 *PW* iii 548.

visited London in late February 1808, having written to Lamb of his intention to outdo Shakespeare, he intended to get the poem into print. Longman got so far as to offer Wordsworth 100 guineas per thousand copies of the work sold. But it was not to be. A series of circumstances, including an unsympathetic reception from Lamb and Coleridge, led him first to revise it during April and May 1808, then to withdraw it completely.[19] It was subjected to considerable revision over the next seven years before publication in 1815.

This reveals a great deal about the evolution of Wordsworth's talent and his work on 'The Recluse'. The manuscript of the 1808 *White Doe* exists today only in fragmentary form. From what survives we may deduce that it was an intriguingly distinct work from that eventually published; a text of the 1808 version may be found in the appendix to this volume. Its narrative may be reconstructed as follows:

Part One is set in the present day (1808) at the ruins of Bolton Priory, the physical remains of the Norton family's Catholic faith, where all that remains is the tower and small chapel. It is the sabbath, and the congregation have arrived for a service, in the middle of which the white doe wanders into the graveyard and settles down beside one of the grave-mounds. When the congregation emerges they stare at her in amazement, 'Gazing, doubting, questioning'.[20]

Part Two looks back to the Catholic rebellion of 1569 when the inwardly-resistant Emily Norton obeys the wishes of her father by designing the banner that would reignite the cause at key moments and later betray her brother Francis. Prior to their departure from the family seat, Rylstone Hall, Francis attempts in vain to dissuade his father and brothers from joining the wars. After they have left he is inspired by the spirit of prophecy and predicts to Emily the destruction of the family and the laying waste of their fortunes. Pointing to the white doe in the grounds of their estate, he predicts that it will 'to her peaceful woods / Return',[21] reverting to the life she led before being domesticated. With that he exhorts her to 'Be strong, be worthy of the grace / Of God,'[22] and leaves to pursue their father.

Part Three describes the approach of the Norton family to the rebel stronghold at Brancepeth Castle, where Norton senior proclaims that 'For the Old and holy Church we mourn, / And must in joy to her return.'[23] He holds up

---

[19]   As these events have been analysed by the Cornell editor at some length I make no effort to enlarge on her findings here; see Cornell *White Doe*, Introduction.

[20]   1808 text, Fragment 1, 285.

[21]   1808 text, Fragment 2, 25–6.

[22]   1808 text, Fragment 2, 49–50.

[23]   1808 text, Fragment 2, 126–7.

the standard embroidered by Emily, which depicts the wounds of the cruci-
fied Christ, as a symbol of their struggle – 'by this we live or die.'[24] It inspires
all those who see it to cry out with 'A voice of uttermost joy'.[25] Unfortunately
the royal army has mustered a much larger force of 30,000 from York alone,
and when they first encounter each other, the rebel leaders retreat, leaving
Norton and his sons alone in the field. At this point they are joined by Francis,
who attempts for a second time to persuade his father to withdraw from battle
and return home. Norton senior rejects him as a coward.

At this point the 1808 text diverges markedly from that published in 1815.
In 1815 Canto Four starts here; in 1808 Part Three continues, describing
how the rebel cause failed, partly because the crown had so promptly suppressed it. The insurgents scatter, some (including the Nortons) hoping to
regroup on the Scottish border, pursued by Francis. The 1808 manuscript
breaks off here,[26] and it is possible only to guess what followed. Surviving
drafts indicate that Francis made a third attempt to persuade his father to give
up the rebellion, as fruitlessly as before. Coleridge provides a hint of what
came next: 'The whole of the Rout and the delivering up of the Family by
Francis I never ceased to find not only *comparatively* very heavy, but to me
quite obscure, as to Francis's motives.'[27] On this basis it is safe to conjecture
that Parts Three and Four described how Francis gave up his family to their
enemies. The likely rationale is that he was deceived into thinking that such
drastic measures would at least save their lives even if it could not detain them
from prison. Francis's Protestant sympathies lend some support to this
(Coleridge describes him as a 'Protestant Malcontent',[28] presumably because
of Francis's observation that he and Emily 'have breathed the breath / Together, of a purer faith'[29] than their father).

My guess is that Part Three described Francis's rationale for this action, and
the successful capture and imprisonment of the Nortons was described in Part
Four, of which only the last eighteen lines survive.[30] In them, an old friend of
Norton senior tells Emily of the family's fate, and the final execution of her
father and brothers. He adds that Francis is still living and will return.

No trace of Part Five is to be found among Wordsworth's manuscripts. The
equivalent lines in 1815 describe Francis's journey home with the standard,
his apprehension by government troops and summary execution near Bolton

[24]   1808 text, Fragment 2, 144.
[25]   1808 text, Fragment 2, 157.
[26]   Cornell *White Doe* 330–1.
[27]   Griggs iii 108.
[28]   Ibid.
[29]   1808 text, Fragment 2, 34–5.
[30]   Cornell *White Doe* 334–5.

Abbey. When the villagers carry his corpse to the priory for burial Emily realizes what has happened and is consumed with grief. The Cornell editor surmises that this was little revised in 1815.[31]

What survives of Part Six suggests that it followed the same course as Canto VII in 1815, describing Emily's grief, the solace derived from her close relationship with the white doe, and her death. It returned, finally, to the present day, and the numinous form of the doe beside Emily's grave.

So far as we can tell, the most important difference between the early and published texts is Francis. Where in 1815 he is a wholly sympathetic character, becoming in effect a martyr to pacifism, his counterpart in 1808 is the more ambiguous figure of the traitor. This is significant because it helps explain why in 1808 Wordsworth had been drawn to the story.[32]

In large part the tale of the *White Doe* appealed to Wordsworth because of all that had happened since his brother's death, one of the consequences of which was a complete reassessment of his aesthetic practices. In the 'Elegiac Stanzas' of 1806 he had bidden farewell to 'the Heart that lives alone, / Hous'd in a dream, at distance from the Kind!', preferring 'fortitude, and patient chear'.[33] The solitary heart at distance from humanity had created a poetry of aspiration in *The Prelude*; if fortitude and patient cheer were now to govern his poetry that would have consequences. It is best understood as an inevitable stage in the maturing of his poetic genius. John's death taught him that his poetry had lost sight of the emotions to which it gave rise. One of his first poems after the tragedy concluded with the pious prayer to be 'resign'd / Beneath [God's] chast'ning rod'.[34] Such self-abasement was diametrically opposed to the optimism of earlier years by which the individual had the power to change the world through an act of will. Henceforth he would comprehend tragedy as an inevitability to be borne with dignity. The *White Doe* was a manifesto for this view and after completing the poem he drafted a short 'Advertizement' to be prefaced to the published text, in which he hoped 'that what I write will live & continue to purify the affections & to strengthen the Imaginations of my fellow beings'.[35] What he meant was that the poem would teach the reader how suffering may be embraced, that it may enrich the imagination. It would expound this philosophy by illustration.

---

[31] Ibid. 36.

[32] It was precisely this aspect that Coleridge disliked, for religious reasons. In his letter to Wordsworth he said that 'it seemed to require something in order to place the two Protestant Malcontents of the Family in a light, that made them *beautiful*, as well as virtuous' (Griggs iii 108).

[33] 'Elegiac Stanzas' 53–4, 57.

[34] 'I only look'd for pain and grief' 42–3.

[35] Cornell *White Doe* 196–9.

In setting out on this project he placed three figures at the thematic heart of the poem: Francis, Emily and the doe.

Francis's situation reworks that of Mortimer in *The Borderers*. Like Mortimer, he is a tragic figure in that fate leaves him with no choice but to act as he does, even if it makes him morally culpable. Wordsworth goes to great lengths to demonstrate that Francis did everything he could to avoid surrendering his family to the crown. In what survives of the 1808 text he twice pleads with his father to give up the fight, and as the manuscript breaks off is about to plead a third time:

> 'Tis Francis! – much he longs to entreat
> (For he hath cause of dread this night)
> That they would urge their weary feet
> To yet a further, further flight . . .
>
> (1808 text, Fragment 3, 86–9)

When this failed Francis seems to have realized that the only way of saving his father and brothers was to bargain with the government, agreeing to their surrender in return for clemency. That they were hiding in the border country only strengthens parallels with Wordsworth's play.[36] Only in retrospect is Mortimer's abandonment of Herbert proved to have been an error; likewise, Francis would have recognized his blunder only after it had been committed. At the time, Mortimer and Francis take what they believe to be the one course open to them. Wordsworth recognized the comparisons from the outset, and when in 1832 he revised the *White Doe* he used some lines from the play as its epigraph:

> Action is transitory – a step, a blow,
> The motion of a muscle – this way or that –
> Tis' done; & in the after-vacancy
> We wonder at ourselves like men betrayed:
> Suffering is permanent obscure & dark,
> And has the nature of infinity.
>
> (Cornell *White Doe* 77)[37]

---

[36]   In lines with no equivalent in the 1815 text, we are told that 'hope doth yet with some remain / The Scottish Border thus to gain' (1808 text, Fragment 3, 68–9).

[37]   In the 1836–7 edition Wordsworth commented on these lines: 'This and the five lines that follow were either read or recited by me, more than thirty years since, to the late Mr Hazlitt, who quoted some expressions in them (imperfectly remembered) in a work of his published several years ago' (Cornell *White Doe* 158). Hazlitt quoted phrases from these lines on numerous occasions: for instance, in *Characters of Shakespear's Plays* (1817); *Lectures on the English Poets* (1818); *Lectures on the English Comic Writers* (1819) and *Table Talk* (1821–2) (Wu i 320; ii 370; v 407; vi 302–3).

This quotation speaks of moral blindness: only in the 'after-vacancy', when it is too late, does the tragic hero understand his mistake. The same motif occurs in Shakespeare. As he smothers the wife who loves him, Othello asserts his righteousness: 'O balmy breath, that dost almost persuade / Justice to break her sword'.[38] Lear sees no alternative but to disown Cordelia, and spends the rest of the play paying the price; further in the past, it was as the victim of a similar misapprehension that Oedipus killed Laius and married Jocasta.

Wordsworth always thought of the *White Doe* as related to something that had recurred in his poetry since Hawkshead days – the sense that the destruction of our loved ones is something for which we are responsible, irrespective of the facts. It had inspired the earliest version of the waiting for the horses in 'The Vale of Esthwaite' when he lamented the failure to grieve sufficiently for his parents at the time of their decease: 'I mourn because I mourn'd no more.' Delayed mourning had left him feeling complicit in their deaths – a sense that blossomed, in the two-part *Prelude*, into the belief that their demise was wrought by a God angered by his trite reflections inspired by the horses' failure to fetch him from school. Death brought in its wake a sense of betrayal for those who survived. That knowledge was reawakened by John's death in 1805, and so not surprisingly, the *White Doe* of 1808 (though not 1815) sought a way of expressing it through the depiction of Francis's treachery towards his father and brothers.

In the fragmentary 1808 text there are several clues to the fact that Francis will unwittingly cause his family's downfall, notably in Wordsworth's use of dramatic irony. After his father and brothers have left Rylstone Hall for the wars, Francis is described alone 'in the vacant Hall' as he feels his first intimation of the disaster to come – the strange sensation that the hall is 'A phantasm . . . like a dream of night'.[39] When that has passed he walks into the grounds of the hall and hears 'A sound of military chear, / Faint':

> There stood he leaning on a lance
> Which he had grasp'd unknowingly,
> Had blindly grasp'd in that strong trance,
> That dimness of heart-agony . . .
> (1808 text, Fragment 1, 396, 398–401)

Despite the attempt to deter the Nortons from battle, he has seized a weapon without being aware of what he was doing: he will be just as culpable as the others, if not more so. There is a hint, in the use of that word 'unknowingly', of the inadvertent part he is to play in the ruin he envisions.

---

[38] *Othello* V i 16–17.
[39] 1808 text, Fragment 1, 384, 386–7.

His farewell speech to Emily survives only in part in the manuscript, leaving us with no choice but to supplement our readings with passages from the 1815 text. He begins by saying that the Nortons are 'misled', and that 'our tears to-day may fall / As at an innocent funeral.'[40] This is richly ironic; the Norton brothers are indeed to die as innocents, thanks to Francis. It is a tragedy in which he will be instrumental. A moment later he tells Emily that

> With their's my efforts cannot blend,
> I cannot for such cause contend;
> Their aims I utterly forswear;
> But I in body will be there.
>
> (1815 text, 511–14)

In the light of subsequent events this is overweening. Forsworn he may be, but that fact will lead to the Nortons' execution at their enemies' hands, and his own botched flight and execution. The essence of his situation is that, despite clear-sightedness when acknowledging the futility of the rebellion, Francis fails to anticipate the extent of his own involvement in its failure. 'On kind occasions I may wait,' he tells Emily, 'See, hear, obstruct, or mitigate.'[41] This is his most ironic utterance of all. His conduct towards his family will be anything but kind and his duties, though intended to mitigate, will in fact condemn. He is, in fact, to betray his kind.

His tone changes when he throws down the weapon seized during his trance – another symbolic touch – and tells of the ruin to come. There is no irony here. Among other things, he tells Emily that 'we / Are doomed to perish utterly':[42]

> Espouse thy doom at once, and cleave
> To fortitude without reprieve.
>
> (1808 text, Fragment 2, 9–10)

Francis is closest to Wordsworth as he speaks these words. The poet who in the depths of grief had in 1806 bowed to the chastening rod of God's ordinance has fully integrated 'fortitude without reprieve' into the moral framework of his verse. It is all the more sincere for the fact that Emily's espousal to 'doom' is the only marriage she can have. It will not be given to her to 'cleave' to a living husband; she will die maiden, destiny her only spouse. None of the Nortons will be granted the reprieve they might have sought, all of them

---

[40] 1815 text, 466, 472–3.
[41] 1815 text, 517–18.
[42] 1815 text, 536–7.

wedded to their fate. This was not something Wordsworth might have wished to write about in 1804, though now felt to be central. Francis explains:

> If on one thought our minds have fed,
> And we have in one meaning read –
> If, when at home our private weal
> Hath suffered from the shock of zeal,
> Together we have learn'd to prize
> Forbearance, and self-sacrifice –
> If we like combatants have fared,
> And for this issue been prepared –
> If thou art beautiful, and youth
> And thought endue thee with all truth
> Be strong, be worthy of the grace
> Of God and fill thy destined place
> A soul by force of sorrows high
> Uplifted to the purest sky
> Of undisturb'd humanity.
>
> (1808 text, Fragment 2, 41–53)

Like William and Dorothy in the midst of grief, Francis and Emily are united by a belief-system that holds 'Forbearance, and self-sacrifice' to be exemplary, and like the Wordsworths they would learn that their grief was an 'issue' for which their shared education had prepared them. For Emily this is a blessing: as Francis leaves her 'He kiss'd the consecrated Maid.'[43] Her consecration – a religious rite, first and foremost – consists as much of her acceptance of his advice as it does of his kiss.

In opposition to the 'zeal' of their father and brothers, Francis's philosophy is to bow to God's will however harsh and unforgiving; Emily's significance is that she illustrates it. This is borne out by her conduct after being cast out of her family home:

> Upon a primrose bank, her throne
> Of quietness, She sits alone . . .
> Behold her like a Virgin Queen
> Neglecting in imperial state
> These outward images of fate,
> And carrying inward a serene
> And perfect sway, through many a thought
> Of chance and change that hath been brought

---

[43] 1808 text, Fragment 2, 57.

To the subjection of a holy
Though stern and rigorous melancholy!
(1808 text, Fragment 5, 14–15, 22–9)

Though stripped of everything, she remains queenly, the spiritual counterpart of Elizabeth I. She has become mistress of her grief, capable of subjecting fate and worldly change to the rule of 'stern and rigorous melancholy'. Those contending terms 'inward' and 'outward' are fundamental, and recall 1 John 2:17: 'And the world passeth away, and the lust thereof: but he that doeth the will of God abideth for ever.' Though not a queen in a material sense, Emily's inner world is abundantly rich. Her serenity is proof that self-rule has exalted her beyond the reach of the outside world; it bestows on her the authority ('perfect sway') of a monarch:

Her soul doth in itself stand fast
Sustained by memory of the past
And strength of Reason; held above
The infirmities of mortal love,
Undaunted lofty, calm, and stable,
And awfully impenetrable.
(1808 text, Fragment 5, 55–60)

What has happened thus far is important only in having led to this. Francis's betrayal of his father and brothers, their execution, and his own death, has bereaved Emily of her worldly identity, compelling her fully to realize her inner self. The testing of her soul has exalted her far beyond mere mortals.

It was audacious of Wordsworth to devote so much of the poem – three-quarters of the 1808 text – to events prior to this, something that provided Coleridge with the most undermining of his criticisms:

In my re-perusals of the Poem it seemed always to strike on my feeling as well as judgement, that if there were any serious defect, it consisted in a disproportion of the Accidents to the spiritual Incidents, and closely connected with this, if it be not indeed the same, – that Emily is indeed talked of, and once appears; but neither speaks nor acts in all the first 3 fourths of the Poem . . . . In short, to express it *far* more strongly than I *mean* or *think* in order, in the present anguish of my spirits, to be able to express it [at] all, that ¾ths of the Work is every thing rather *than* Emily; *then*, the last almost a separate (& doubtless most exquisite Poem) wholly *of* Emily. (Griggs iii 107–8)

He was right, in that Part Six of the 1808 text (Canto VII in 1815) is the poem's *raison d'être*. The lengthy preamble, as Coleridge observes, threatened to unbalance the poem. The criticism is serious because it was an attack on the poem's design. What was Wordsworth up to?

'The moving accident is not my trade,' Wordsworth had written in early 1800,[44] and in the *White Doe* it is of little significance compared with the life of the spirit. That is why he dismissed comparisons with Scott: 'Sir Walter pursued the customary & very natural course of conducting an action, presenting various turns of fortune, to some outstanding point on which the mind might rest as a termination or catastrophe.'[45] Wordsworth's language is plainly condemnatory: 'action', 'turns of fortune', 'catastrophe' – all are to do with manipulation of narrative, and reduce Scott's skill to that of a storyteller. To Scott's face, Wordsworth could be equally brutal. In August 1808, after deciding not to publish the *White Doe*, he wrote a cantankerous letter to him about *Marmion*,[46] recently published, in which he commented: 'I think your end has been attained; that it is not in every respect the end which I should wish you to propose to yourself, you will be well aware from what you know of my notions of composition, both as to matter and manner.'[47] Again, the cause of his disfavour is Scott's propensity for concentrating on 'moving accident' at the expense of all else. Wordsworth's criticism was consistent with the views expressed in the Preface to *Lyrical Ballads*, but his disapprobation must have been fuelled by having just withdrawn what he felt to be a great poem from the press while *Marmion* sold in huge quantities. It can be no accident that, while visiting London in 1808 to publish the *White Doe*, Wordsworth was contemplating work on an essay entitled 'Why bad poetry pleases',[48] a subject on which Coleridge was also meditating (a notebook entry praises 'a small and thinking Minority, the Recluses of the World', and criticizes the 'false reputation' of the rest).[49] Wordsworth repeated his criticism of Scott's exclusive preoccupation with 'moving accident' many times in subsequent years, remarking in 1844 that he 'has never in verse written anything addressed to the immortal part of man'.[50]

While he was writing the 1808 text of the *White Doe* Scott supplied 'interesting particulars' about the Nortons that conflicted with Wordsworth's chief source – 'The Rising in the North', a ballad in Percy's *Reliques*.[51] Wordsworth

[44]   'Hart-Leap Well' 97.
[45]   *FN* 32–3.
[46]   For Wordsworth's reading of it see *WR* ii 185–6.
[47]   *MY* i 264.
[48]   Morley i 10.
[49]   *Notebooks* iii 3282.
[50]   Peacock 340. Wordsworth could be ruder still; in 1815 he told Farington that Scott's poetry was 'like a machine made to amuse children which turns round seeming to unravel something but to which there is no end' (Peacock 339).
[51]   *MY* i 237.

rejected them, saying that 'so far from being serviceable to my Poem they would stand in the way of it.' Had Scott been as touchy as his correspondent he may have felt the implied snub: Wordsworth was interested less in fact than in spiritual truth, which spoke to 'the immortal part of man'. The *White Doe* took a heroic subject *à la* Scott but dealt with it in a Wordsworthian manner – that is to say, it took historical events and from them extrapolated an alternative, spiritual narrative. Emily's beatification in Part Six is the culmination of everything that has gone before it – the magical appearance of the doe in Part One, Francis's prophecy in Part Two, the zealotry of the Nortons (to which it is contrasted) and Francis's struggle to return the banner to Bolton Abbey. Each ingredient contributes to her apotheosis. Wordsworth would have argued that the reason why Part Six doesn't unbalance the poem is because it retrospectively transforms what precedes it: far from being the climax of a historical narrative of the kind retailed by Scott, it turns the entire poem into a spiritual odyssey. This renders Coleridge's argument redundant. There can be no disproportion between the outward history and inward journey because the two are complementary, the latter lending the former a significance it would otherwise lack.

This is a daring idea partly because it is only in retrospect, after the entire work is digested, that we understand that Emily has throughout been the chief protagonist even when absent from the drama. It placed the burden of interpretation squarely on the shoulders of the sympathetic, meditative reader – not one that either Coleridge or Lamb wished to bear. And if they could not be depended on, there was little chance that a public whose taste for narrative poetry had been conditioned by Scott would be. As Wordsworth remarked to Dorothy, 'I am so thoroughly disgusted with the wretched and stupid Public, that though my wish to *write* for the sake of the People is not abated yet the loathing at the thought of publication is almost insupportable.'[52] And sure enough, when published in 1815 the poem was greeted with expressions of incomprehension and ridicule.[53] Jeffrey began his review with a famous opening sentence: 'This, we think, has the merit of being the very worst poem we ever saw imprinted in a quarto volume.'[54]

When he defended the poem to Coleridge, Wordsworth pointed out that

> all the action proceeding from the will of the chief agents, was fine-spun and inobtrusive, consonant in this to the principle from which it flowed, and in harmony with the shadowy influence of the Doe, by whom the poem is introduced, and in whom it ends. It suffices that everything tends to account for the

---

[52]   *Supp.* 11.
[53]   A summary of the critical response is given by Dugas, Cornell *White Doe* 60–1.
[54]   *Edinburgh Review* 25 (October 1815) 355–63, p. 355.

weekly pilgrimage of the Doe, which is made interesting by its connection with a human being, a Woman, who is intended to be honoured and loved for what she *endures*, and the manner in which she endures it; accomplishing a conquest over her own sorrows (which is the true subject of the Poem) by means, partly, of the native strength of her character, and partly by the persons and things with whom and which she is connected; and finally, after having exhibited the 'fortitude of patience and heroic martyrdom', ascending to pure etherial spirituality, and forwarded in that ascent of love by communion with a creature not of her own species, but spotless, beautiful, innocent and loving, in that temper of earthly love to which alone she can conform, without violation to the majesty of her losses, or degradation from those heights of heavenly serenity to which she has been raised. (*MY* i 222)

The doe embodies all the virtues displayed by Emily in grief – fortitude, patience, endurance, strength of character. As distinct from the passing shows of being elsewhere in the poem, those qualities are permanent. So it is that the doe never deserts her, separating itself from the herd as it rushes by to look on her with 'pure benignity'.[55] So it is that the doe that appears in the present (1808) is apparently the same as that known to Emily in the sixteenth century, at least 250 years before. It doesn't matter whether they are the same – only a pedant like Scott would have worried over that – the point is that it symbolizes the immortality to which Emily aspires when her soul 'Rose to the God from whom it came!'[56]

Wordsworth's hurt at the scorn poured on the *White Doe* by Coleridge and Lamb is understandable. Of all his circle, they might have been expected to read it sympathetically. Wordsworth was scathing about their failure to do so. 'Let Lamb learn to be ashamed of himself in not taking some pleasure in the contemplation of this picture,' he told Coleridge.[57] Why had he expected so much of Lamb? Partly because Charles and Mary had been so compassionate towards the Wordsworths at the time of John's death. Lamb went so far as to gather statements from John's shipmates and send them to Dove Cottage.[58] It was not unreasonable in that light for Wordsworth to hope that Lamb would see what the doe signified:

> White she is as lilly of June
> And beauteous as the silver moon
> When out of sight the clouds are driv'n
> And she is left alone in heaven

---

[55] 1815 text, 1676.
[56] 1815 text, 1887.
[57] *MY* i 222.
[58] He sent three within the space of a month; see Marrs ii 157–65.

> Or like a Ship, some gentle day
> In sunshine sailing far away
> A glittering Ship that hath the plain
> Of Ocean for her own domain
>   (1808 text, Fragment 1, 60–7)

This simile, which survives in the 1815 text, reveals that the doe has a personal resonance as the medium between Wordsworth and his dead brother. By gathering eyewitness accounts of John's last moments Lamb had performed a similar function, bringing Dorothy and William closer to him in their distress. The deeply-felt need to retrieve him, though revealed symbolically, explains why they both repeated the mantra of his last words – 'His will be done.' The doe performs the same function for Emily; still grieving for Francis, she sees it emerge from the woods, 'A single One in mid career'.[59] An echo recalls her dead brother who has just been referred to as 'the solitary One'.[60] Through communion with it she ascends, as Wordsworth puts it, 'to pure etherial spirituality'. Its mediating presence is the means of her beatification and implied reunion with her brother.

Wordsworth would have hoped that Lamb would have noticed the nautical imagery by which the numinous creature is twice associated with John Wordsworth:

> In quietness she lays her down
> Gently as a weary wave
> Sinks when the summer breeze hath died
> Against an anchor'd Vessel's side
> Even so without distress doth she
> Lie down in peace and lovingly.
>   (1808 text, Fragment 1, 144–9)

Through the image of the doe settling among the dead, the poet momentarily revives that of his brother's ship, at rest in a summer sea, beyond the reach of heartache and 'distress'. It is the means by which he may aspire towards the peace vouchsafed to Emily, and the rarefied spirituality that is his ultimate consolation.

Wordsworth's dismay at Coleridge and Lamb's fault-finding was deeply felt, and the consequences were lasting. He eventually forgave Lamb, who was partly following Coleridge's lead. But it was Coleridge's reaction that troubled him most, and which in the end led to the decision not to publish, at

---

[59]   1815 text, 1662.
[60]   1815 text, 1556.

least for the present. Why did Coleridge take against it? Besides the personal difficulties between them, he had cause to regard the *White Doe* as a distraction from 'The Recluse'. He did not say as much, preferring to express anxiety that the poem would prove less popular with the public than *Peter Bell*, 'The Ruined Cottage', or 'Salisbury Plain'.[61] All the same, he must have felt that it was trivial compared with the great task ahead;[62] if so, he failed to see that the *White Doe* was a declaration of intent. Wordsworth could not have written it before 1805, and probably would not have wanted to. Like virtually everything else he wrote, it is overshadowed by *The Prelude*, which in its five- and thirteen-book manifestations is a young man's poem, full of the confidence and optimism with which Coleridge had charged him in early 1804. The *White Doe* is the work of an older and wiser poet who has bowed his head in humility while remaining hopeful of God's grace. If less appealing than *The Prelude* to those who live in a faithless world, it was important to Wordsworth for its inauguration of a new aesthetic developed out of the renewed experience of grief. For that reason it returned him to subjects rooted in the childhood traumas that had inspired so much of his pre-Alfoxden verse. This reorientation can only have been a boon to 'The Recluse', the contents of which had never been entirely clear to him. John's death and its impact on his poetry had opened a vein of thought that had been there all along, which would feed naturally into the millenarian project formulated a decade before. That's partly why he set such store by the *White Doe*, as an entry in Benjamin Robert Haydon's diary confirms:

> One day Wordsworth in a large Party, at a moment of silence, leaned forward & said, '*Davy*, do you know the reason I published *my* White Doe in *Quarto*?' 'No,' said Davy, rather blushing. 'To express my own opinion of it,' he replied.[63]

This is the same kind of story with which this chapter began; it doesn't on the face of it reflect very well on Wordsworth. But if one reads the *White Doe* as a harbinger of his future work on 'The Recluse', Wordsworth's comment may be understood less as self-flattery than as a pledge of conviction in the task ahead. Accordingly, Coleridge's criticisms were discouraging for the way in which they effectively refuted Wordsworth's evolving ideas for 'The Recluse'.

---

[61]   Griggs iii 112.
[62]   He entered a note for 'A fine subject to be introduced in William's great poem' in his notebooks in summer 1809 (*Notebooks* iii 3538).
[63]   *The Diary of Benjamin Robert Haydon*, ed. Willard Bissell Pope (5 vols , Cambridge, Mass., 1960–3), ii 470. The most likely date for this episode is June 1820 (see also Reed ii 602n23).

Besides Dorothy, the only people to appreciate the poem were Lady Beaumont and her sister, Frances Fermor.[64] But Wordsworth would not allow the cold water poured on his work by Coleridge and Lamb to detain him. He was still revising the manuscript of the *White Doe* when in early April 1808 he turned to another notebook and wrote three new poems for 'The Recluse'.

[64]   *Supp.* 13.

12

'O teach me calm submission to thy will'

~~To my God~~ *To my Friends.*
Conscious, I am dying, I feel unutterable consolation from the sense of the intensity and the [*words obliterated*] distinctness of

(*Notebooks* iii 3273)

When Coleridge made this entry in his notebook in early February 1808 illness had just brought his lectures on the principles of poetry to a halt.[1] Concern for his health was Wordsworth's 'sole errand' in London,[2] although it was probably at Dorothy's insistence that he took with him the manuscript of the recently completed *White Doe* for publication. Coleridge appears not to have been mortally ill as feared; what Wordsworth could not have guessed was how diseased his imagination had become, thanks to his addiction. While preparing for the lectures he had written a notebook entry about how Wordsworth had 'wantonly stripped me of all my comfort and all my hopes'.[3] This stemmed from his frustrated affection for Sara Hutchinson. On 27 December 1806 he thought he saw Wordsworth in bed with her. The image, which he later admitted to have been fantasy, brought with it the suspicion that Wordsworth was detaining him from Sara so as to keep her for himself. It corrupted further contact between them and recurs throughout Coleridge's notebooks. At 2.30 on the morning of 13 September 1807 Coleridge awakened in the midst of an opium-induced slumber in tears, and wrote a long, tortured essay on his doomed love for Sara in which he lamented that she had come to 'learn from <u>W</u> – to pity & withdraw herself from my affections. Whither? – O agony! O the vision of that Saturday Morning – of the Bed / –

---

[1] Molly Lefebure surmises that the illness was brought on by sudden withdrawal from opium prior to the lectures; *Bondage of Opium* 456.
[2] *MY* i 213.
[3] *Notebooks* iii 3232.

O cruel!'[4] Where his feelings for Sara were concerned, Coleridge believed that Wordsworth came between them on the grounds of his innate superiority: 'W. is greater, better, manlier, more dear, by nature, to Woman, than I – I – miserable I!'[5] Six months later these rancid, self-pitying emotions had fermented further, remaining as potent as ever. The withdrawal of the *White Doe* from the press in May was a particularly anxious time. The peremptory manner in which Wordsworth did it – neglecting to explain matters to Coleridge, who was preparing to correct proofs[6] – seems to have revived the unpleasant image of Sara and Wordsworth in bed, as Coleridge confided to his notebook:

> O that miserable Saturday morning! The thundercloud had long been gathering, and I had been now gazing, and now averting my eyes, from it, with anxious fears, I scarcely dared be conscious ~~of~~. But *then* was the first Thunder-Peal!
> But a minute and a half with ME – and all that time evidently *restless & going* – An hour and more with [Wordsworth] *in bed* – O agony!'[7]

Two pages are torn from the notebook at this point, probably containing further rantings. These poisoned sentiments lay behind the vituperative letter he sent to Wordsworth on 12 May, accusing him of 'High Self-opinion pampered in a hot bed of moral & intellectual Sympathy' and unwarranted 'indignation' at criticism of his poems (specifically the *White Doe*). The notebook entry which outlines the contents of this letter (not extant) also reveals the true cause of Coleridge's ire: 'I did not mention the affair of [*word obliterated*], because that is too sore a point.'[8] The word struck from the sentence is probably 'Asra', and the 'affair' is probably Wordsworth's supposed relations with her, as biographers have suggested.[9]

Wordsworth had more important matters at hand. While in London he met for the first time Henry Crabb Robinson, who reported that 'My Esteem for W's *mind* his philosophic & poetic view of things is confirmed and strengthened.'[10] It would be wrong to place too much emphasis on this, but the mention of 'his philosophic & poetic view of things' supports the idea that 'The Recluse' was not far from either his mind or conversation. As I have argued in previous chapters, renewed grief at John's death, and Coleridge's increasing estrangement, left him with no option but to find a new way of

---

4   *Notebooks* ii 3148 f45v.
5   Ibid., f46.
6   Griggs iii 114.
7   *Notebooks* iii 3328.
8   Ibid., 3304.
9   *Bondage of Opium* 458; *Darker Reflections* 139.
10 *Robinson Correspondence* i 52.

thinking about 'The Recluse'. He had bidden farewell to the proud confidence of *The Prelude* and sought instead a philosophy of forbearance and a trust in God. With the *White Doe* he had made that breakthrough, and in its concluding lines written of how on visiting Bolton Abbey he was inspired by intimations of the millenarian brotherhood which 'The Recluse' would help bring about:

> When, left in solitude, erewhile
> We stood before this ruined Pile,
> And, quitting unsubstantial dreams,
> Sang in this Presence kindred themes;
> Distress and desolation spread
> Through human hearts, and pleasure dead, –
> Dead – but to live again on Earth,
> A second and yet nobler birth . . .
>
> (1815 text, 1857–64)[11]

Rejecting the 'unsubstantial dreams' of his earlier verse, Wordsworth's attentions are seized by the connection between 'Distress and desolation' and 'A second and yet nobler birth', which he glosses as 'The re-ascent in sanctity!'[12] The *White Doe* of 1808 was a vehicle by which Wordsworth could hail the spiritualizing effects of suffering – effects he believed to be inextricably part of the general progress of the human species which 'The Recluse' was to promote. This was why he hoped for a sympathetic reading from Coleridge, and was probably something he wanted to discuss with him.

Fluctuating relations with Coleridge affected the fortunes of 'The Recluse' as always. The poem had been firmly in Wordsworth's sights since early 1804, when Coleridge had left for London and the Mediterranean for health reasons, and its completion then had been a trust made sacred by his proximity to death. With the passage of time the obligation had intensified; 'The Recluse' was now a sacred tribute to be paid to John's memory, and Wordsworth almost certainly raised it with Coleridge. This is supported by the fact that Coleridge mentions it in a notebook entry dating from March, during Wordsworth's visit.[13] Strained relations must have made 'The Recluse' all the more pressing; it had been formulated by them both, and completion may have seemed to Wordsworth to be a way of retrieving the intimacy they shared a decade before.

---

[11]   These lines were revised for the published text of 1815, but it is reasonable to suppose that they reworked sentiments present in 1808; see Cornell *White Doe* 366–9.
[12]   1815 text, 1866.
[13]   *Notebooks* iii 3238.

When he left Coleridge's London lodgings on the evening of 3 April, he was in a 'very thoughtful and melancholy state of mind'.[14] Heading east, up the Strand into Fleet Street and past St Dunstan in the West, he glanced up to see St Paul's Cathedral at the top of Ludgate Hill, 'solemnised by a thin veil of falling snow'.[15] His worries made him peculiarly sensitive to its imaginative potential, and he could not forget it. A few days later, on return to Grasmere, he described it in a letter to Beaumont:

> I cannot say how much I was affected at this unthought-of sight, in such a place and what a blessing I felt there is in habits of exalted Imagination. My sorrow was controlled, and my uneasiness of mind not quieted and relieved altogether, seemed at once to receive the gift of an anchor of security.(*MY* i 209)

Although he was still embroiled in negotiations over publication of the *White Doe*, this epiphanic moment marked the beginning of serious work on 'The Recluse'. In odd moments he was working on revisions for the *White Doe* under Coleridge's direction, but as he thought about the image he realized that it was the basis of a new poem. Shortly after arrival in Grasmere, where paper was in short supply, he grasped the nearest notebook to hand – the first manuscript of *Peter Bell* – and entered the draft.

> Press'd by conflicting thoughts of love and fear
> I parted from thee, Friend! and took my way
> Through the great City, walking with an eye
> Downcast, ear sleeping, and feet masterless,
> That were sufficient guide unto themselves
> And step by step went pensively. Now mark,
> Not how my trouble was entirely hush'd
> That might not be, but how [b]y sudden gift
> Gift of Imagination's holy power!
> My Soul in her uneasiness received
> An anchor of security. – It chanc'd
> That, while I thus was pacing, I rais'd up
> My heavy eyes, and instantly beheld
> Saw at a glance in that familiar place
> A visionary scene: a length of Street
> Laid open in its morning quietness
> Deep, hollow, unobstructed, vacant, smooth
> And white with Winter's purest white, as fresh
> And fair and spotless as he ever sheds

[14] *MY* i 209.
[15] Ibid.

On field or mountain. – Moving form was none
Save here & there a dusky Passenger
Slow, shadowy, soundless, dusky: and beyond
And high above this winding leng[t]h of street
This noiseless and unpeopled avenue
Pure, silent, solemn, beautiful, was seen
The Huge Majestic Temple of St Paul
In awful sequestration, through a veil
Through its own sacred veil of falling snow.[16]

'St Paul's' reworks ideas from earlier poems: the 'instant' vision recalls the 'instantaneous light' that falls upon the 'musing [man]' in 'A Night-Piece'.[17] The pensiveness that precedes the vision is familiar from 'Resolution and Independence', where the poet is stricken by 'fears, and fancies' – again related to Coleridge.[18] Its overall design and diction recalls another London poem, 'Composed upon Westminster Bridge', where the city in early morning also 'lie[s] / Open'.[19] Other details reveal how peculiar 'St Paul's' was to this moment in his career.

For one thing, distress and anxiety is more potent than ever; from the outset Wordsworth is 'Press'd by conflicting thoughts', and in the first rough draft '*Oppressd* with heavy thoughts of Love and fear' (my italics).[20] Those ominous tones return again and again. The parting in line 2 is implicitly worrying; is it a final parting of the ways, as feared when Coleridge went south in early 1804? The 'Downcast' eye, unhearing ear, and 'masterless' feet reveal how distracted he was as he made his way from the Strand into Fleet Street. As with his earliest verse, he is interested in the history or science of feelings – psychology, in other words. He is careful to say that what happened to him did not entirely calm him,

but how [b]y sudden gift
Gift of Imagination's holy power!
My Soul in her uneasiness received
An anchor of security.

[16] This is a transcription of the earliest complete draft of the poem in DC MS 18. Alternative readings are not included. A facsimile of the relevant page in the MS can be found in Cornell *Tuft* 102–3.
[17] 'A Night-Piece' 7.
[18] 'Resolution and Independence' 27.
[19] 'Composed upon Westminster Bridge' 6–7.
[20] Cornell *Tuft* 104–5.

Did this precede his letter to Beaumont, where he remarked: 'My sorrow was controlled, and my uneasiness of mind not quieted and relieved altogether, seemed at once to receive the gift of an anchor of security'? My guess is that it did – that he knew what had been said in the poem and was able to paraphrase it in prose. Either way, the letter and the poem are close in time, perhaps written within hours of each other, *c*.8 April 1808. The nautical imagery is familiar from the poem which was partly the cause of Wordsworth's anxiety – the *White Doe*, where the doe sinking onto the grass at the Priory is likened to a wave 'Against an anchor'd Vessel's side'.[21] Of course the anchor is a traditional symbol, but it had a personal resonance given John's profession of sea-captain. It was now part of a new philosophy for 'The Recluse'; as in the *White Doe*, where Emily's grief is transformed to 'a serene / And perfect sway',[22] the visionary of 'St Paul's' encounters a sight in the natural world that, imaginatively transformed, helps him manage an emotion that threatens to overwhelm him. This was no part of Wordsworth's thinking before John's demise but had become integrated into the millenarian philosophy that, in the absence of Coleridge's putative notes, he had been forced to formulate for himself.

It is a vision of perfection, 'white with Winter's purest white, as fresh / And fair and spotless as he ever sheds / On field or mountain'. Imaginative engagement with the world has become a purgative experience; Emily too had gone from 'fair to fairer; day by day / A more divine and loftier way!'[23] Her beatification was proof of the ability of the imagination to cleanse the spirit through its handling of grief. Sequestered, set apart from the rest of the city – and indeed the world – the cathedral has been transformed likewise, and in the process gives security to the perceiving mind of the poet. An act of imaginative perception has also been one of worship. Nearly two months later Wordsworth told Francis Wrangham that

> piety and religion will be best understood by him who takes the most comprehensive view of the human mind, and that for the most part, they will strengthen with the general strength of the mind; and . . . this is best promoted by a due mixture of direct and indirect nourishment and discipline. (*MT* i 249)

For Wordsworth psychology was the key to the soul. If you understood the workings of the mind, you could understand the spirit. What is so interesting about this is the emphasis it places on strength derived from 'nourishment and discipline'. St Paul's is precisely an image of that quality – of what remains when the grieving is over.

---

[21]   1808 text, Fragment 1, 147; Cornell *White Doe* 246–7.
[22]   1808 text, Fragment 5, 25–6.
[23]   1815 text, 1867–8.

In 'St Paul's' Wordsworth chose to sing the praises of a cathedral. To the best of my knowledge this is the first such building he celebrated in this way. Like Furness Abbey in *The Prelude*, it is not there because of its ecclesiastical significance, but because it speaks of the sacred in nature. It is for that reason abstracted in 'awful sequestration' like a natural object, 'field or mountain'.

When he completed the draft he felt a glimmer of his former confidence. He was writing semi-autobiographical blank verse. With *The Prelude* out of the way, that could mean only one thing: he was working on 'The Recluse'. That elusive work felt once more within reach, and he turned to another page in the manuscript to compose an address to the clouds reprising some of the central ideas behind the 'correspondent breeze' and 'The Eolian Harp'; it culminated with a description of the sun shining on the clouds, 'A Vision of beatitude and light'.[24] Its invocation of Emily's apotheosis at the end of the *White Doe* implies a hope that her experience can be symbolized by the movements of the elements and made more widely available. Turning to yet another page, Wordsworth composed a further poem about a tuft of primroses, which turned out to be the longest.

The *White Doe* had been abandoned when, probably in June or July, he opened a fresh manuscript and entered fair copies of all three. The Cornell editor presents them as 'St Paul's', 'To the Clouds' and 'The Tuft of Primroses', but, as he observes, their close association reflects 'Wordsworth's intention to make them parts of a single, larger, design: his "long Poem," *The Recluse*'.[25] With this in mind, it was typical of Wordsworth to have begun with the vision of St Paul's, for that would have made a good climax for an extended poetic work (in much the same way he had begun work on the extended *Prelude* of 1804 with the Snowdon passage). 'To the Clouds', an invocation to the elements, would make a good opening; and 'The Tuft of Primroses' would have been a substantial part of what came in between. Altogether they amount to nearly 700 lines, and if he had found a way of welding them into a whole might have formed an acceptable second book of 'The Recluse'. In the event he abandoned 'The Tuft of Primroses' before it was complete, to pillage it in 1809–10 for parts of *The Excursion*, and of the three would publish only 'To the Clouds' during his lifetime, in substantially revised form (in 1842).[26] He never published 'St Paul's', which made its first appearance in print, with 'The Tuft of Primroses', in de Selincourt's Clarendon edition of the works, 1940–9.

Wordsworth's first rough draft towards 'The Tuft of Primroses' begins:

[24]   1808 text, 88.
[25]   Cornell *Tuft* 7.
[26]   Parallel texts of both versions are supplied in the Cornell edition.

> Fair tuft of Flower[s] most beautiful & bright
> Art living to be welcome[d] once again . . .
> The breath of Spring shall touch in vain this barren rock . . .
>
> (Cornell *Tuft* 138–9)

It begins hopefully, with the flowers' ability to regenerate. In the background there is a literary tradition that exploits the same motif – Vaughan and Herbert spring to mind[27] – but Wordsworth's context is distinct. At the time this rough draft was entered (probably in April 1808) the revised *White Doe* was still in play, and he is mindful of the prospect of 'A second and yet nobler birth' which springs from the thought of 'Distress and desolation spread / Through human hearts, and pleasure dead'.[28] As in that work, he seeks emblems of rebirth.

Wordsworth then turned to the next blank page he could find and continued:

> O pity if the gladsome Spring had breath[ed]
> Upon the bosom of this barren rock
> And found thee not but thou ar[t] here, reviv[e]d
> And beautiful as ever like a Queen
> Smiling on thy imperishable throne
>
> (Cornell *Tuft* 132–3)

These lines rework one of the most powerful images in the 1808 *White Doe*, where after the deaths of her father and brothers Emily is described

> Upon a primrose bank, her throne
> Of quietness . . .
> Behold her like a Virgin Queen . . .
>
> (Fragment 6, 14–15, 22)

She has merged with the primroses to become a symbol of permanence and 'imperishability', in serene command of the emotions that threatened to destroy her. Images and ideas from the *White Doe* were feeding directly into this new poem. It was not about the paradisal existence enjoyed by William and Dorothy in 'Home at Grasmere'; it was not a hymn of thanks for the poet's lot; nor was it 'the *first* and *only* true Phil. Poem in existence', as Coleridge had planned. John's death had been an admonition which had begun to shape

---

[27]   I doubt whether they influenced him in this case; he had read Herbert but not Vaughan (see *WR* ii 107–8, 263–4).
[28]   1815 text, 1864, 1861–2.

his thought. Emily's primrose bank provided a throne, an image of her power over grief; it tells us that the grace of the natural world helps her subject what she has experienced to the influence of 'stern and rigorous melancholy'.[29] When Wordsworth compares the primrose to a queen on its throne he does so with her in mind, for this is a poem about loss, and how to cultivate the self-rule of which Emily had been mistress; in effect, it is a commentary on the *White Doe*.

Wordsworth then discusses a series of deaths or near-deaths. First there is Sara Hutchinson who, suffering serious illness, feared to go on her favourite walks (ll. 36–47); then the 'lofty band of Firs'[30] in Bainriggs, and the sycamore and ash trees chopped down in 1807 (ll. 77–135); and then the Sympson family, who lived in a farmhouse near Dunmail Raise, all five of whom had died within the space of two years (ll. 135–234). He had begun with an image of regeneration, but his theme turns out to be loss. The tension is indicative of a confusion that will continue to disrupt the poem and finally bring it to an end. He is on safe ground when discussing Sara Hutchinson whose life was thought to be in danger but who had recovered, and the trees which, though a grievous loss, are not human. Difficulties arise when he gets onto the Sympsons.

The Revd Joseph Sympson, vicar of Wythburn, and his family lived at High Broadraine, a farmhouse on the Keswick road. They had been close friends of the Wordsworths and make frequent appearances in letters and journals; Sympson had been Johnny Wordsworth's godfather by proxy. He had died on 27 June 1807, while the Wordsworths were returning to Grasmere from Coleorton. The news was a shock, bringing back the trauma of John's drowning, and may have prompted the Wordsworths to go on their holiday to Yorkshire (and Bolton Abbey) in early July. In a letter to Catherine Clarkson of 19 July Dorothy laments the changes they had found in Grasmere, which her brother was describing in his poem:

> On our arrival here our spirits sank and our first walk in the evening was very melancholy. Many persons are dead, old Mr. Sympson, his son the parson, young George Dawson, the finest young Man in the vale, Jenny Hodgson our washerwoman, old Jenny Dockray and a little girl Dorothy's age who never got the better of the hooping-cough which she had when we went away. All the trees in Bainriggs are cut down, and even worse, the giant sycamore near the parsonage house, and all the finest firtrees that overtopped the steeple tower. (*MY* i 158–9)

---

29   1808 text, Fragment 5, 29.
30   L.79.

Their time in Leicestershire had refreshed them but they had come home to the renewed understanding that death and destruction were all-conquering. It made the task of envisaging the millenarian paradise of 'The Recluse' all the more difficult. But Wordsworth had begun 'The Tuft of Primroses' in defiant mood, and with some confidence, thanks to the relative success of 'St Paul's' and 'To the Clouds'. In spite of his grief at the fate of those around them, he had to deal with the thorny issue of death, and the Sympson family provided the occasion.

In Emily's case grief had been ameliorated by its subjection to fortitude – but she had been a fictional character. Wordsworth was now attempting to apply similar ideas to real people, and he discovered an unresolved tension between grief in the raw and the need to theorize about it. The first hint of this appears when he attempts to discuss Sympson. He has mentioned how, during his services, 'the Voice / Of the glad bells, and all the murmuring streams / United their soft chorus with the song':[31]

> Methinks that Emma hears the murmuring song
> And the pure Ether of her Maiden soul
> Is overcast, and thy maternal eyes
> Mary, are wet, but not with tears of grief[32]
> 'Twas but a little patience & his term
> Of solitude was spent . . .
>
> (Cornell *Tuft* 218–19)

The reference to Dorothy's 'Maiden soul' momentarily recalls Emily. But understatement pulls the poetry back from the emotion Sympson's passing had inspired: her soul is merely 'overcast', and Mary's tears are *not* those of grief. Why? Because grief is a threat. He is trying to discuss its aftermath and the process of forbearance that continues for the rest of one's life. Mary and Dorothy are to be honoured not for the intensity of their pain but for their endurance.[33] Wordsworth found this a plausible argument in Emily's circumstances which were imaginatively conceived; it was harder to realize when brought within range of real life.

This becomes clearer as he discusses Sympson's death. There is some awkwardness in the idea that his 'term / Of solitude was spent', as if relief from

---

[31] 'The Tuft of Primroses' 123–5.
[32] In the manuscript these four lines are set apart from the rest of the text by a line drawn round them. Its purpose was to move them from page 37r in the notebook to the bottom of page 35r, where Wordsworth earlier refers to the 'murmuring streams'. The Cornell editor apparently overlooks this (Cornell *Tuft* 210–11 and 218–19).
[33] *MY* i 222.

solitude by death were a blessing. Some twenty lines later his sufferings 'Fell with the body into gentle sleep / In one blest moment'.[34] These euphemisms endanger a proper appreciation of the emotions inspired by Sympson's demise. Wordsworth has set himself a difficult test; he needs to signal the strategy of forbearance while remaining faithful to the tragedy, and as a result the poetry oscillates between understatement and expressions of deep feeling. He recovers his poise at the conclusion of this section of the poem with a description of the 'Bower' planted by Sympson's daughter:

> I grieve to see that Jasmine on the ground
> Stretching its desolate length, mourn that these works
> Of love and diligence and innocent care
> Are sullied and disgrac'd; or that a gulf
> Hath swallowed them which renders nothing back;
> That they, so quickly, in a cave are hidden
> Which cannot be unlock'd; upon their bloom
> That a perpetual winter should have fallen.

(ll. 227–34)

Anyone sensitive to the echo of Milton's account of Eve's garden, where 'Iris all hues, roses, and jessamine / Reared high their flourished heads between, and wrought / Mosaic,'[35] will be conscious of the significance of the fallen jasmine in the Sympsons' garden: its fate is a correlative for that of the hands that tended it. Nor can there be much doubt of the precise subtext of this passage: the main verbs, 'mourn' and grieve', underline the fact that its focus is the impact of bereavement. This could not be further removed from 'The Ruined Cottage' MS D, where in another wild garden death had been an 'idle dream that could not live / Where meditation was'.[36] That conviction took its force from the Coleridgean ethos on which 'The Recluse' was based. It is an index of Wordsworth's maturity a decade later that death is not so easily dismissed, but he has nothing to offer in exchange for the optimistic philosophy that is now found wanting.

Where does that leave the millenarian project? Wordsworth's remaining weapon is his virtuosity as a poet; so it is that the primrose tuft is made to represent immortality – it sits on an 'imperishable throne . . . In splendour unimpaired'. Not surprisingly, therefore, in the base text of the manuscript draft, he modulates immediately from one of his most evocative descriptions of death to one of eternal life:

---

[34] Ll. 194–5.
[35] *Paradise Lost* iv 698–700.
[36] 'The Ruined Cottage' MS D, 523–4.

> . . . upon their bloom
> That a perpetual winter should have fallen,
> Fallen, while my little Primrose of the rock
> Remains, in sacred beauty, without taint
> Of injury or decay, is born again
> To reap one other pleasure, to proclaim
> Her charter in the blaze of noon . . .
>
> (Cornell *Tuft* 230–1)

This is necessary to validate the optimistic view by which 'The Recluse' was meant to be informed; accordingly Wordsworth's diction – 'born again', 'reap' – recalls scriptural prophecies of resurrection. But what distinguishes this poetry from that of 1798 is the same thing that distinguishes 'St Paul's' from 'A Night-Piece'. In 1808 Wordsworth is a step closer to orthodox Christian notions than he had been a decade before. As originally formulated, there had been nothing orthodox about 'The Recluse'. In one of the 'Pedlar' drafts he had proposed the existence of a cosmic spirit that 'circulates, the soul of all the worlds';[37] our ability to perceive it had underwritten a faith in man's redemptive power. By 1808 he is thinking differently; the primrose is protected by his belief in conventional notions of rebirth and eternal life.

On rereading these lines Wordsworth realized that they needed toning down; in the final draft the sentence ends after he has lamented that the Sympsons have fallen into a 'perpetual winter', and continues:

> Meanwhile the little Primrose of the rock
> Remains, in sacred beauty, without taint
> Of injury or decay, lives to proclaim
> Her charter in the blaze of noon . . .
>
> (ll. 235–8)

Divided from the Sympsons by a full stop, and no longer claimed to be 'reaping pleasure' or 'born again', this is less obviously an attempt to negotiate between the irrevocability of death and the optimism of 'The Recluse'. For the moment, the tension is suppressed. It is just one more symptom of Wordsworth's uncertainty. A few lines later he implicitly admits that the primrose is vulnerable and under threat, acknowledging that the voice of the mountain streams around him speaks 'In vain – the deafness of the world is here',

---

[37] 'There is an active principle' 11.

and the best
And Dearest resting places of the heart
Vanish beneath an unrelenting doom.

(ll. 275–9)

This is a major concession to the modern vision of the world as matter in motion in which nature is constantly susceptible to exploitation. In the Preface to *Lyrical Ballads* Wordsworth had referred to the 'beautiful and permanent forms of nature';[38] there is no such confidence here. It is symptomatic of his ebbing faith in those youthful tenets that 'The Tuft of Primroses' either questions or denies them.

Aware that the poem was under stress, he realized he had to redefine his aims. In an effort to pin down the kind of idealism he was prepared to espouse he turned to Cave's *Apostolici* and the story of St Basil, the founder of eastern monasticism, who as a young man fled Athens to live in a mountainous retreat similar to Grasmere. The great influences on Basil were his sister Macrina and his friend Gregory Nazianzen; as the Cornell editor explains, Wordsworth was attracted to the story by its parallels with his association with Dorothy and Coleridge.[39] Wordsworth begins by stating Basil's reasons for going into retreat:

What but this,
The universal instinct of repose,
The longing for confirm'd tranquillity,
Inward and outward, humble and sublime,
The life where hope and memory are as one,
Earth quiet and unchanged, the human soul
Consistent in self rule, and heaven revealed
To meditation in that quietness.

(ll. 301–8)

Who could argue with this? And that, perhaps, is the problem. Its ambitions are much diminished from what they had been in 1798, when the universalizing impulse of 'The Recluse' had seemed so credible. Then, among the 'Pedlar' drafts, he had written of a necessitarian philosophy by which a 'chain of good / Shall link us to our kind'.[40] 'Self rule', 'meditation' and 'tranquillity' are all fine things, but there is no suggestion of how, or whether, they will enable us to search for 'kindred love / In fellow-natures'.[41] That has diminished to 'self

---

[38] *Prose Works* i 124.
[39] Cornell *Tuft* 20–5.
[40] 'Not useless do I Deem' 40–1.
[41] Ibid. 10–11.

rule', a less consequential affair. Wordsworth's vision has been constricted. On an intellectual level it is to be hoped that the monastery will show the world how to live, but that function is an etiolated one undermined by a description of the many monasteries which have fallen into ruin or been destroyed.

If Wordsworth's account of Basil's monasticism has any weight, it is in its personal significance. The relationship between Basil and Gregory enables him to attempt to heal the hurt feelings between him and Coleridge. The first draft of the passage where Basil invites Gregory to join him is clearer about this than later ones:

> Come Nazianzen to these fortunate Isles
> This blest Arcadia to these purer fields
> Than those which Pagan superstition feigned
> For mansions of the happy dead – O come
> ~~I feel that wanting Thee I am alone~~
> To this enduring Paradise these walks
> Of contemplation piety &
>
> (Cornell *Tuft* 268–9)

'I feel that wanting Thee I am alone': Wordsworth could not allow this to stand because it so nakedly exposed the impulses behind the verse. Relations with Coleridge had become strained; that anxiety had led directly to the spot of time in Fleet Street and inspired this phase of 'Recluse' composition. By comparison with the Alfoxden year, Wordsworth indeed felt 'alone' and in need of his old friend. That was why he had gone down to London in the first place – to invite him back to the Lakes. In the purer realm of the imagination their relationship could be made whole, as they are reunited in a paradise that surpasses that 'which Pagan superstition feigned / For mansions of the happy dead'.

This is an overstatement based on Wordsworth's affection for Coleridge, and in alluding directly to the 'happy dead' recalls the retrieving impulse that runs through much of his poetry from 'The Vale of Esthwaite' onwards. As he proceeds to envisage Basil's mountain retreat it becomes increasingly idealized. 'The River swarms with fish' runs another line in the base text soon deleted, and a few lines later in the same draft 'the fruits that hang / In the primaeval woods'[42] provide the monastery with food. Wordsworth's model is Jonson's 'To Penshurst' where fish run into nets, eels 'leap on land, / Before the fisher, or into his hand', and 'orchard fruit . . . Hang on thy

---

[42] Cornell *Tuft* 272–3.

walls, that every child may reach'.[43] In the midst of this Wordsworth places Gregory:

> So shall thy frame be strong thy spirits light
> Thy own endeavour fill thy temperate board
> And thou be thankful.
>
> (Cornell *Tuft* 274–5)

These tender lines express the loving kindness he felt for his old friend, whose spirits seemed always heavy, and whose health had long been a cause for worry. They were quickly deleted, for the same reason as before – that they too obviously revealed the personal concerns that informed this ideal resort. Grasmere could never have lived up to such hopes. As he revised these lines he eliminated the comparison with Elysium.[44] In doing so he sought to ground the poetry in reality, abdicating wish-fulfilment where it conflicted with truth. Anything else would have been a betrayal. As with the admission that some of his most beloved spots 'Vanish beneath an unrelenting doom', the early manuscript draft now embarks on a description of the desecration of monasteries all over Europe, 'they that heard the voice / Of Rhone or Loire, of British Thames or Tweed'.[45] The earliest coherent rough draft of this passage runs as follows:

> Gone are they, levelld with ground, or left
> To encounter friendlessly the beating storm
> And perish under heaven of human care
> As ordaind, as an ever ready prey
> For hungry time to feed upon . . .
>
> (Cornell *Tuft* 306–7)

Wordsworth deleted these lines almost as soon as they were written because they contradict the claims made earlier. The notion that the monastery is 'an ever ready prey' to time rescinds the notion of its being 'quiet and unchanged', a symbol of permanence. Instead it has become the victim of transience and decay. In the first of the quoted lines, Wordsworth supplies 'dust' as an alternative for 'ground', with its echo of 'dust to dust, ashes to ashes', from the Order for the Burial of the Dead. The word 'perish' is potent too; unlike the primrose on its 'imperishable' throne, the monasteries, founded on the dreams of men, are doomed to fall, especially when entrusted to 'human care / As ordaind' – presumably an ironic reference to Henry VIII.

For all their apparent contradictions Wordsworth's thoughts are moving

---

[43] Jonson, 'To Penshurst' 31–44. For Wordsworth's reading of Jonson see *WR* ii 121–2.
[44] See 'The Tuft of Primroses' 358–64.
[45] Cornell *Tuft* 306–7.

consistently in one direction, accommodating themselves to scepticism. Basil's hopes though marvellous in theory were disproved by experience; while recognizing the attractions of wish-fulfilment, Wordsworth knew it to be a mirage. A powerful urge still made him want to speak on behalf of the dream and champion St Basil's ideals. But it was impossible. Grief had marked him too deeply. In the last coherent passage prepared for 'The Tuft of Primroses' before it came to a standstill he returned to memories of the Grande Chartreuse which he had visited in 1790, and written about in *Descriptive Sketches* and the thirteen-book *Prelude*. As in *Descriptive Sketches*, he describes the 'flash of arms . . . and yon military glare'[46] of the revolutionary soldiers who desecrated the monastery – and whom, incidentally, he had not seen.[47] The personified form of Nature then speaks in the building's defence:

> O leave in quiet this embodied dream,
> This substance by which mortal men have clothed,
> Humanly cloth'd the ghostliness of things,
> In silence visible and perpetual calm.
> Let this one Temple last – be this one spot
> Of earth devoted to Eternity.

> (ll. 538–43)

Wordsworth knows that Nature's pleas are to be ignored, the Chartreuse sacked and its inhabitants tortured and killed. By the time he has reached this point, hope is futile. Nature continues:

> let it be redeemed
> With all its blameless priesthood – for the sake
> Of Heaven-descended truth; and humbler claim
> Of these majestic floods, my noblest boast;
> These shining cliffs, pure as their home, the sky;
> These forests unapproachable by death,
> That shall endure as long as Man endures
> To think, to hope, to worship, and to feel;
> To struggle, – to be lost within himself
> In trepidation, – from the dim abyss
> To look with bodily eyes, and be consoled.

> (ll. 557–67)

Wordsworth assembles the virtues mentioned earlier (and in the *White Doe*) – purity, sublimity, meditation – and places them in the mouth of an ab-

---

46 'The Tuft of Primroses' 517–18.
47 See pp. 69–75.

straction with no authority. As Nature pleads for the redemption of the priesthood and the eternal life of the 'embodied dream', her words count for nothing. This ironic utterance is about the betrayal and destruction of an ideal. The
'Sister Streams of Life and Death' whisper to the narrator, as in *Descriptive
Sketches*,[48] but in vain: they are messengers of transience and loss. The tension
between Wordsworth's desire to believe in the ideals expounded by Nature and
his increasing inability to do so has become his subject. And, as Stephen Gill has
argued, it may be read as a repudiation of the revolutionary hopes of the 1790s,
or even as a confession of revolutionary guilt – the sense that his early political
affiliations made him complicit in the destruction of the Chartreuse, and perhaps other violent action.[49] He no doubt had such feelings; they would have
been fuelled by emotional traumas about which he had written in the 1799
Prelude and 'The Vale of Esthwaite' – the failure adequately to mourn his father
at the time of his death, and the obscure anxiety that he was in some way implicated in it. The Chartreuse is where the streams of Life and Death meet, and
where, symbolically, he might be expected to reconnect with those he has lost;
its impending destruction represents a denial of that hope. Such treachery is a
blow against the imagination. As a result the abyss in the last of the quoted lines
remains 'dim', and does not yield a redemptive vision; it allows the individual
only to be 'lost within himself / In trepidation'. Wordsworth had been far less
pessimistic in *Prelude* Book VI, where loss had been followed by affirmation:

> Imagination! lifting up itself
> Before the eye and progress of my Song
> Like an unfather'd vapour; here that Power,
> In all the might of its endowments, came
> Athwart me; I was lost as in a cloud,
> Halted without a struggle to break through,
> And now recovering to my Soul I say
> I recognize thy glory . . .
>
>   (*The Thirteen-Book Prelude* vi 525–32)

The soul's 'glory' in March 1804 had been the ability to 'break through' the
darkness of creative exhaustion, the feeling of being 'lost as in a cloud', so as
to reclaim imaginative power 'In all the might of its endowments'. Four years
later he yearns for such inspiration, but finds himself on the brink of an abyss
gazing into a darkness that will not give way. Gone is the certainty of the

---

[48]   See p. 76.
[49]   See Stephen Gill, '"Affinities Preserved": Poetic Self-Reference in Wordsworth', *SIR*
24 (1986) 531–49, p. 537. As regards revolutionary guilt, Nicholas Roe speculates that
Wordsworth may have been involved in the Bourdon affair, described in Johnston 371–2.

Prelude episode, where imagination descends on him like the holy ghost so as to confirm his sense of election as the poet of 'The Recluse'; instead the author of 'The Tuft of Primroses' is bereft and confused. The aspiration to preserve the 'embodied dream' represented by the monastery is irresistible, but he has chosen a historical episode the outcome of which is predetermined. The 'blameless priesthood' are not to be redeemed from their fate; 'Heaven-descended truth' will be denied and consolation no longer granted to those who go there. With those successive renunciations will go the confirmation Wordsworth seeks that he can go on with 'The Recluse'. That too will be denied and the poem would break down.

The poetry of earlier years had been that of belief: this is the voice of doubt. Loss, grief and the falling away of precious friendships had left him no longer capable of believing that love of nature would lead to love of mankind. He must have known, by the time he reached this point in the draft, that he could not continue. 'The Recluse' had not been designed as a poem of consolation, but by 1808 that is all he has to offer. He had abandoned it by 29 September, when he referred to it glumly as 'about 500 lines of my long Poem, which is all I have done'.[50]

'St Paul's' had been a success because it reworked earlier concepts unrelated to 'The Recluse'. It placed Wordsworth at the centre of things, as he had been when writing *The Prelude*, under no obligation to expound a philosophy. 'To the Clouds' had been a flight of fancy – an accomplished one no doubt, but hardly primary 'Recluse' material. When he began writing 'The Tuft of Primroses' he would have been aware of the challenge. The problem was that when he looked around he saw only death and decay where he sought sanctuary. Even the primroses are doomed to go the same way as the flowers once tended by Sympson: 'all are ravaged.'[51] Tragedy had shaped his view of the world, and he could not spread falsehoods in his poetry, however attractive they appeared.

Coleridge's letter to Daniel Stuart of June 1809, in which he describes Wordsworth's *The Convention of Cintra* as 'almost a self-robbery from some great philosophical poem, of which it would form an appropriate part, & be fitl[ier] attuned to the high dogmatic Eloquence, the oracular [tone] of impassioned Blank Verse',[52] appears at first to allude to 'The Tuft of Primroses', or at least to imply that he knew of its existence. There was ample opportunity for him to have seen it. From September 1808 he was a regular visitor, and later a resident, with the Wordsworths, who had by then moved to Allan Bank, remaining until May 1810. But he nowhere refers either to 'Home at Grasmere'

---

[50]   *MY* i 269.
[51]   Ibid. 217.
[52]   Griggs iii 214.

or 'The Tuft of Primroses'. In fact, the reference in the letter to Stuart describes a poem Wordsworth had not, and would not, compose. The 'high dogmatic Eloquence' typical of the 1798 poetry is absent from that of 1808, and there is nothing oracular about 'The Tuft of Primroses'. Coleridge may have got wind of the fact that Wordsworth had been working on 'The Recluse', but seems not to have seen it, now or later. Wordsworth almost certainly withheld the post-1800 'Recluse' poems from him because they fell short of expectation, preferring to quarry them for sections of *The Excursion* and *The Prelude*.[53]

This was not the end of 'The Recluse'. Serious work on *The Excursion* began in late 1809, and that, as Wordsworth ill-advisedly told his readers (and as his critics did not hesitate to remind theirs) was 'the second part of a long and laborious Work, which is to consist of three parts'.[54] It was in the Preface that Wordsworth likened the relationship of the still-unpublished *Prelude* and 'The Recluse' to that of an 'ante-chapel . . . to the body of a gothic church', adding that his shorter works, so long a bone of contention between him and Coleridge, may 'be likened to the little cells, oratories, and sepulchral recesses, ordinarily included in those edifices'.[55] Owen and Smyser, usually diplomatic in their views, describe this as a 'generally pompous document',[56] and there must have been occasions when Wordsworth regretted having published it, given the derision it provoked. More importantly, it misrepresented the evolution of his work, making it appear as if he had styled himself as the author of a great philosophical poem from the outset. Nor, for all its virtues, did the poem do him any favours, combining some of his finest writing with new composition of variable quality. The hostile reception was a further blow to his ambitions and left him reluctant to continue.[57] In 1822 he told Walter Savage Landor that

> *The Recluse* has had a long sleep, save in my thoughts; my MSS. are so ill-penned and blurred that they are useless to all but myself; and at present I cannot face

---

[53] The tragedy of the Sympsons (ll. 135–99) and part of St Basil's address to Gregory (ll. 365–70) became part of *Excursion* Book VII; part of the explanation of St Basil's calling (ll. 280–308) was absorbed first into Book V and then Book III. A version of lines 549–51, about the Chartreuse, was used in the 'Essay, Supplementary to the Preface' (1815), and the entire Chartreuse episode incorporated into the C-stage *Prelude* of 1818 (see Cornell *13-Book Prelude* ii 104–5, 995–7). In these works, Kishel argues, Wordsworth's ' "despondency" could be more effectively "corrected"' (Cornell *Tuft* 27). Similarly, parts of 'Home at Grasmere' were recycled for *The Excursion*: Book IV, 332–72 and Book VI, 1079–1191 derive from it. It also provided copy for the *Guide to the Lakes*, see Cornell *Home at Grasmere* 24.

[54] *Prose Works* iii 5.

[55] Ibid. 5–6.

[56] Ibid. 3.

[57] Prior to publication he expected the critics to 'vent their malice', but it would have been a blow all the same (*Supp.* 145).

them. But if my stomach can be preserved in tolerable order, I hope that you will hear of me again in the character chosen for the title of that Poem. (*LY* i 126)

It was a forlorn utterance made on the basis of declining confidence in his abilities. Against the odds he summoned the conviction in summer 1826 for another poem towards 'The Recluse' – 'Composed when a probability existed of our being obliged to quit Rydal Mount as a Residence', known also as 'Verses on Nab Well'. It was intended, he told Henry Crabb Robinson shortly after its completion, as 'an introduction to a portion of his great poem – containing a poetical view of water as an *element* in the composition of our globe'.[58]

This brief work of 101 lines (in its earliest form) reprised the conversation poem to remarkable effect. It may fall short of the great work of the late 1790s but is distinguished by its careful observation of the Rydal Mount environs. At its centre Wordsworth presents the image of a fern at the spring's edge, reflected in the water:

> Words should say,
> Could they but paint the wonders of thy cell,
> How often I have mark'd a plumy fern,
> Bending an apex towards its paler self,
> Reflected all in perfect lineaments,
> Shadow and substance kissing, point to point.
> A subtler operation may withdraw
> From sight the solid floor that limited
> The nice communion, but that barrier gone,
> Nought checks nor intercepts the downward shew
> Created for the moment: flowrets, plants,
> And the whole body of grey wall they deck,
> Reflected, but not there diminutive,
> There of etherial texture, and, thro' scale
> Of vision less and less distinct, descending
> To gloom impenetrable. So, in moods
> Of thought pervaded by supernal grace,
> Is the firm base of ordinary sense
> Supplanted, and the residues of flesh
> Are linked with spirit; shallow life is lost
> In being; to the idealizing soul,
> Time wears the colors of Eternity,
> And Nature deepens into Nature's God. –

(ll. 48–70)

---

[58] Morley i 339. Kishel notes that Wordsworth may be recalling the kind of grand epic scheme Coleridge had formulated by 1796 as a series of 'Hymns to the Sun, the Moon, and the Elements' (*Notebooks* i 174).

Wordsworth's vision of the imagination as it perceives and half-creates recalls the underworld journeys of earlier years. At Hawkshead and Cambridge he had reworked that myth in an attempt to find a new way of talking about 'the idealizing soul' and the emotional need that underpinned it. The Narcissus-like image of the fern as it kisses its reflection recalls Wordsworth's encounter with his *alter ego*, the spectre-guide in 'The Vale of Esthwaite' – a vision supplanting the reign of 'ordinary sense' consistent with the urge to lose consciousness 'In being'. 'Verses on Nab Well' restates emotions and desires that have always inspired him by focusing minutely on what is before his eyes – the 'perfect lineaments' of the plant, the 'downward shew' of its reflection and its 'scale / Of vision less and less distinct'. Such close attention to material reality leads to its deliquescence in 'etherial texture'. It is the perfect metaphor for the supplanting of 'ordinary sense' by 'spirit', made all the more effective by its unboastful manner, up to the final claim that 'Nature deepens into Nature's God.'

Wishing to make the most of what must have seemed like his last chance to compose 'The Recluse', Wordsworth put 'Verses on Nab Well' through no less than seven fair copies, expanding it from 101 lines to 182, and finally to 202 – including, among other things, a digression on Joan of Arc.[59] The revisions of the so-called 'Late Version' (given in the Cornell edition) are reductive, elucidating elements which in the earlier text are better for having been merely implied; for instance, the description of the fern and its reflection culminates in the final text with a gratuitous six–line disquisition on Narcissus. By the time he had watered down the quiet intensity of the early version, Wordsworth was as far as ever from completing his great work. 'Verses on Nab Well' had been in its earliest form a good poem, but did no more than present variations on the theme of loss. Like 'The Tuft of Primroses' it is valedictory, occasioned by the 'sad news'[60] that the Wordsworths were expected to vacate Rydal Mount by its owner, Lady Le Fleming. The attempt to assert a metaphysical connection with the landscape is inspired by threatened eviction rather than the desire to precipitate universal redemption of mankind; such ambitions are no longer part of his thinking. 'The Recluse' had become inextricably related to loss, death, transience.

'Verses on Nab Well' is not well-known, and was written at a period when, according to some, Wordsworth's was a 'desiccated' talent,[61] but it proves

---

[59] Late version, ll. 163–89. According to the Cornell editor, the episode is an attempt 'to rewrite a portion of his own life, thinly veiled in historical or mythic detail' (Cornell *Tuft* 29).
[60] *LY* i 416.
[61] Thomas McFarland condemns the poem as 'a banal effort' and writes of 'the desiccated 1820s'; *William Wordsworth: Intensity and Achievement* (Oxford: Clarendon Press, 1992), pp. 41–2.

that during his fifties he was capable of good poetry. It may be less flamboyant than earlier work, but is all the more impressive on that account. If only he had relinquished the high-flown aspirations of 1798 he might have accepted that there was a great poem to be written about subjects that mattered to him, but by comparison with 'The Recluse' they seemed inferior. As a result it seemed necessary to dress them up in the conflicting ideas that in the absence of Coleridge's notes had sprung up around the great philosophical poem of the age. The result was that his natural artistic development was distorted by frustration and a growing sense of failure intensified by the contempt of critics and parodists.[62] He never accepted that it was natural that age should distance him from the enthusiasm that had inspired him to write of the time when

> All things shall speak of man, and we shall read
> Our duties in all forms; and general laws
> And local accidents shall tend alike
> To quicken and to rouze, and give the will
> And power which by a [   ] chain of good
> Shall link us to our kind. No naked hearts,
> No naked minds, shall then be left to mourn
> The burthen of existence.
>
> ('Not Useless do I Deem' 36–43)

That was the 'high dogmatic Eloquence' Coleridge had praised, and led him to describe Wordsworth as a 'Giant'.[63] It envisages the end of the fallen world and the beginning of an era in which humanity will be infinitely receptive of the cosmic forces within the natural world, which will 'link us to our kind'. It is not just what Wordsworth is saying, but the sublime certainty with which it is said, that is so impressive. Within days, on 6 March 1798, he proudly informed James Webbe Tobin that

> I have written 1300 lines of a poem in which I contrive to convey most of the knowledge of which I am possessed. My object is to give pictures of Nature, Man, and Society. Indeed I know not any thing which will not come within the scope of my plan . . . . the work of composition is carved out for me, for at least a year and a half to come.[64]

---

[62] Parodists were drawn to Wordsworth's poetry like flies to honey. Before *Lyrical Ballads* had been formally published, in 1798, Thomas Beddoes was writing imitation Wordsworthiana; see my *'Lyrical Ballads* (1798): The Beddoes Copy', *The Library*, ser. 6, 15 (December 1993) 332–5.

[63] Griggs i 391.

[64] *EY* 212.

For the moment, Wordsworth knew precisely what 'The Recluse' would say, and how long it would take to write – eighteen months – that is, until the end of 1799. Perhaps it might have been written then, or at least largely completed. But *Lyrical Ballads* intervened and a lengthy train of obstacles followed. Whatever else could be said, it was not to be written over the next four decades, but that didn't stop those around him from hoping. It couldn't have helped that publication of *The Excursion* in 1814 revealed a marked disinclination among readers to hail the larger work of which it claimed to be part. Byron's reaction was typical; shortly after its publication he told Thomas Moore that Wordsworth 'has just spawned a quarto of metaphysical blank verse, which is nevertheless only part of a poem'.[65] Worse was to come. Wordsworth appears not to have read Byron's dedication to *Don Juan* Cantos I and II:

> And Wordsworth, in a rather long 'Excursion',
>   (I think the quarto holds five hundred pages)
> Has given a sample from the vasty version
>   Of his new system to perplex the sages:
> 'Tis poetry – at least by his assertion,
>   And may appear so when the dogstar rages;
> And he who understands it would be able
>   To add a story to the Tower of Babel.

(ll. 25–32)

If he had seen this in 1819 when it was written he would probably have been incensed, but by 1832, when it was published, Byron was long dead and Wordsworth had written him off as 'reprehensible, perverted, and vicious'.[66] In any case, by then he had all but given up hope of writing 'The Recluse'. In November 1829 Dorothy said that it was 'plain that his mind is set upon doing its best at the great Work',[67] but the following January she told Mary Lamb that 'he shrinks from his great work.'[68] In 1831 he was promising to return to 'The Recluse' during the winter, and was subsequently said to 'forget his meals and even his politics' while working on it. He was merely revising *The Prelude* and 'Home at Grasmere'.[69] In earlier years Coleridge's lobbying succeeded in making him anxious; that of his family proved no more constructive. By the mid-1830s even they were beginning to despair. On 17 May

---

[65]   Marchand iv 157.
[66]   Peacock 202. The remark dates from 1814.
[67]   *LY* ii 169.
[68]   Ibid. 191.
[69]   For details see the introduction to Cornell *14–Book Prelude* and Cornell *Home at Grasmere* 28–30.

1833 Dora told Edward Quillinan, '*I* don't believe the "Recluse" will ever be finished.'[70]

While touring Italy in 1837 with Henry Crabb Robinson he made one final attempt in the form of a blank verse description of St Francis. But it was brief and led to nothing more.[71] By the following year he had begun to accept that the task was beyond him. 'Why?' his American publisher, George Ticknor, asked in May 1838, to which Wordsworth answered:

> Why did not Gray finish the long poem he began on a similar subject? Because he found he had undertaken something beyond his powers to accomplish. And that is my case.[72]

'The Recluse' had never really been Wordsworth's poem, except perhaps in early 1798, when he wrote hundreds of lines towards it. It was Coleridge's, along with a host of other still-born notions which appear in list after list in the pages of his notebooks. Coleridge was good at foisting these ideas onto others. In 1796 he persuaded Joseph Cottle to write an epic poem called *Alfred*. It was published in 1799 to almost universal contempt, even from Coleridge; by his own account, Cottle 'suffered deeply from the very mean opinion, which I had frankly expressed to him of his Epic Poem'.[73]

On another occasion in 1800 Coleridge suggested to Humphry Davy that he and Thomas Beddoes write 'a compact compressed History of the Human Mind for the last Century – considered simply as to the acquisition of Ideas or new arrangement of them'.[74] Davy's plan to write an epic poem about Moses, concerned with 'man, nature and society', was probably also Coleridge's suggestion.[75] Unlike Cottle and Wordsworth, he wisely refrained from styling himself accordingly, and left the ideas in his notebooks, now at the Royal Institution. On yet another occasion in December 1799, Coleridge hatched an ambitious plan for Southey, instructing him to

> Bring together on your table or skim over successively – Brucker, Lardner's History of Heretics, Russel's Modern Europe, and Andrews' History of England – & write a History of Levellers and the Levelling Principle under some

---

[70] Cornell *Home at Grasmere* 30.
[71] The passage has not been published. The manuscript is in the possession of Paul F. Betz, to whom I am indebted for this information.
[72] Cornell *Home at Grasmere* 31. Gray's 'long poem' was the unfinished 'The Alliance of Education and Government', begun by August 1748 and abandoned by March 1749.
[73] Griggs i 586. Further discussion of Cottle's magnum opus may be found in my 'Cottle's *Alfred*: Another Coleridge-Inspired Epic', *CLB* NS 73 (January 1991) 19–22.
[74] Griggs i 557.
[75] I am grateful to Molly Lefebure for this information.

goodly Title, neither praising nor abusing them. Lacedaemon, Crete, and the attempts at agrarian Laws in Rome – all these you have by heart. (Griggs i 554)

Given the circumstances, Southey was remarkably indulgent to his old friend, saying in response: 'A History of the Levelling Principles – or Jacobinism – if it be a prettier title – I am able and willing to undertake – if a publisher chuses to engage me.'[76] Fortunately no one did, and that was that. A few months later Coleridge was chivvying Daniel Stuart to commission newspaper articles from Charles Lamb: 'if you want matter, Lamb has got plenty of "My Great Aunt's Manuscript".'[77] But within weeks Coleridge had returned to the Lakes, leaving Lamb to observe: 'With him have flown all my splendid prospects of Engagement with the Morning Post, all my visionary guineas.'[78]

Commissioning others to carry out his ideas was a compulsion, perhaps as compensation for an inability to realize them himself. In getting caught up with 'The Recluse' Wordsworth was walking a well-trodden path, though not one that would yield the recognition he desired. The peculiar psychological complex in which he had become enmeshed is revealed by the fate of the other work which Coleridge persuaded him to write: the Preface to *Lyrical Ballads*. Wordsworth later recalled that it was

> written at the request of Mr Coleridge out of sheer good nature. I recollect the very spot, a deserted Quarry in the Vale of Grasmere where he pressed the thing upon me, & but for that it would never have been thought of. (Little 62)

For his part, Coleridge claimed that the Preface '[arose from] the heads of our mutual Conversations &c – & the f[irst pass]ages were indeed partly taken from notes of mine / for it was at first intended, that the Preface should be written by me'.[79] In these respects, it is exactly comparable with 'The Recluse' with the exception that it was written shortly after it was suggested. In that sense it was also a success, but it wasn't seen in that light by Coleridge, who attacked it publicly, in impressively pompous terms, in *Biographia Literaria* (ostensibly a defence of Wordsworth):

> With many parts of this preface in the sense attributed to them and which the words undoubtedly seem to authorise, I never concurred; but on the contrary objected to them as erroneous in principle, and as contradictory (in appearance

---

[76]   Curry i 212.
[77]   Griggs i 581.
[78]   Marrs i 191. Stuart did publish Lamb in the *Morning Post* in 1802, shortly before he relinquished the proprietorship.
[79]   Griggs ii 811.

at least) both to other parts of the same preface, and to the author's own practice in the greater number of the poems themselves. (CC *Biographia* ii 9–10)

Critics are ill-advised to take this at face value. Coleridge had been implicated
in the Preface to the extent of allowing Wordsworth to work from his notes.
His lengthy repudiation of it – particularly its claim to employ what Coleridge
inaccurately describes as 'the language of *real* life'[80] – is disingenuous. On a
visit to London in December 1817, Wordsworth told Henry Crabb Robinson
that

> Coleridge's book has given him no pleasure, and he finds just fault with Coleridge
> for professing to write about himself and writing merely about Southey and
> Wordsworth. With the criticism on the poetry he is not satisfied. The praise is
> extravagant and the censure inconsiderate. (Morley i 213)

Coleridge was never satisfied with the job anyone made of projects he proposed because the finished object could not compare with his idealized notions. This had been obscured in the case of *Alfred* by the fact that it was a
genuinely bad poem. What Coleridge did with the Preface – in a public fo-
rum, no less – was probably what he would have done with 'The Recluse' had
it ever been composed; it was certainly what he did with *The Excursion*, as
Wordsworth discovered in a rather unpleasant way. On 3 April 1815 Coleridge
wrote to Lady Beaumont to tell her that *The Excursion* was not 'equal' to *The
Prelude*. Why? Because it articulated 'Truths, which the generality of persons
have either taken for granted from their Infancy, or at least adopted in early
life'.[81] Wordsworth visited London in May to supervise publication of *Poems*
(1815) and the *White Doe*, and was shown Coleridge's letter by Lady
Beaumont. Feeling 'perplexed [rather] than enlightened by your *comparative*
censure',[82] he wrote to Coleridge requesting an explanation. In his response
of 30 May Coleridge delivered some of the most damaging criticism
Wordsworth was ever to receive. He said that he was disappointed by *The
Excursion* because it did not conform to 'the Plan, I had supposed that you
were engaged on'.[83] This 'Plan' for 'The Recluse', rehearsed in painful and
meticulous detail, may have been true in spirit to what had been agreed in

---

[80]   Ibid. 8.
[81]   Griggs iv 564.
[82]   *MT* ii 238. In *MT* this important letter is reprinted from an earlier printed text rather
than the original. In November 1999 the manuscript surfaced and was sold at Bloomsbury
Book Auctions in London to 'an anonymous buyer' (*The Westmorland Gazette*, 26 November 1999).
[83]   Griggs iv 575.

spring 1798, but was also a highly developed amplification of it, rococo in its sophistication. Wordsworth had no way of knowing that this was what he had been expected to produce, for without Coleridge's notes there had been no way of divining it. In truth, no one but Coleridge could have known every detail in the 'Plan' for 'The Recluse' before it was spelt out in May 1815 (and perhaps not even he had). It was a ghost, a chimera, an opium-dream as intricate and involved as Piranesi's *Carceri d'Invenzione*,[84] the much-needed 'notes' for which were burnt as a plague-garment in a far-away place, long ago, if indeed they had ever existed. By harnessing his career to Coleridge's ideal, locked as it was in a constant state of evolution in a distant and impenetrable recess of his brain, Wordsworth lumbered himself with an impossible task there was no prospect of completing.

In the late 1820s Wordsworth told Henry Nelson Coleridge why he was unable to write 'The Recluse' by way of expressing regret that 'he had ever attempted such a subject':

> So long as he was called upon to operate with the imagination on the visible world, and to evoke the spirit that seems to lie hidden in its varied forms in sympathy with man, he felt he was able to do it; but to deal with [the world *del. to*] nature as it really in a religious view is, was what he could not manage. He thought himself entitled to avail himself as a verseman of many notions wch he was not prepared to defend literally as a proseman, and he complained of the way in wch he had been made answerable for mere plays of the Imagination.[85]

'If we abandon the old mythical conception of Gods and Nymphs &c. what can we substitute?' he had asked. Such pagan notions had no scientific credibility but they allowed discussion of nature's inner life – which was important to him. The problem, as Wordsworth saw it, was that 'it was impossible to reconcile the exact truth with poetry.' Where the imagination was involved, a kind of fiction was generated, which drew on such mythic concepts as the underworld journey and the Oedipus figure. They embodied a poetic truth, but not necessarily a factual one. Wordsworth was not a scientist, and the 'matter and arrangement of *Philosophy*' was too much to demand of him.[86] The 'mere plays of the Imagination' were vastly preferable, even if they led back to neo-classical ways of thought. It was another way of saying that 'The Recluse', with its burden of philosophical exegesis, did not play to his strengths.

---

[84]   The seventeen plates issued in 1745 that had seduced Beckford and De Quincey; see Robert Woof, *Thomas De Quincey 1785–1859* (Grasmere: The Wordsworth Trust, 1985), pp. 21–4.
[85]   CC *Table Talk* i 550.
[86]   Griggs iv 574.

This was nothing new; it was something he had known for years. In 1799, at a time when he had been moving away from 'The Recluse', he described intellect as 'the very littleness of life',

> that false secondary power by which
> In weakness we create distinctions, then
> Believe that all our puny boundaries are things
> Which we perceive and not which we have made

As he composed those lines, ostensibly for the two-part *Prelude*, Wordsworth knew that 'The Recluse' was not for him. It would be concerned with synthesized constructs unrelated to the divine spirit in nature, 'the one interior life / That lives in all things',

> In which all beings live with god themselves
> Are god existing in one mighty whole
> As undistinguishable as the cloudless east
> At noon is from the cloudless west when all
> The hemisphere is one cerulean blue
>
> (Cornell *1799 Prelude* 164–5)

Epilogue

Catherine Wordsworth died at 5.15 on the morning of 4 June 1812. She was not yet 4. Her parents were away from home, and by the time they returned to Grasmere her corpse was buried. Thomas Wordsworth, her brother, died on 1 December at the age of 6½. As Stephen Gill observes, these events had an impact on the Wordsworth household that lasted for the remainder of the poet's life.[1] Dorothy wrote on 31 December 1812, 'there is no comfort but in the firm belief that what God wills is best for all of us – though we are too blind to see in what way it is best.'[2] She was once again echoing John's last words, 'God's will be done,' reiterating the trust in providence that had developed out of it. For his part, Wordsworth struggled to maintain equilibrium, as he told Southey:

> I dare not say in what state of mind I am; I loved the Boy with the utmost love of which my soul is capable, and he is taken from me – yet in the agony of my spirit in surrendering such a treasure I feel a thousand times richer than if I had never possessed it. . . . O Southey feel for me! (*MY* ii 51)

When John died in 1805 there had been a period when taking care of those around him had led Wordsworth to feel that his own needs were being neglected. Once again, the pressure on him was intense, particularly in view of Mary's grief, which led her to lose weight and become depressed. The delayed mourning of 1787 had been a 'mighty debt'[3] paid to his father, though in arrears; the death of John wrought a further 'debt to what I fear'd'.[4] When Wordsworth thinks of Thomas as a 'treasure' to be surrendered to God, he is doing what literature and experience has taught him – enclosing painful feel-

---

[1] Gill 294–5.
[2] *MY* ii 59.
[3] 'The Vale of Esthwaite' 287.
[4] 'I only look'd for pain and grief' 14.

ings in concepts that prevent it from destroying him. It is consistent with the stoicism of Ben Jonson in 'On My First Son', where the boy's life has been 'lent to me, and I thee pay, / Exacted by thy fate, on the just day'.[5] Trapped beneath those tough monosyllables – 'pay', 'fate', 'just' – emotion is contained.

The art of such poetry is that it wears an expression of impassivity, as Yeats noticed in his 'General Introduction to my Work', where he says that tragic figures

> must be cold; no actress has ever sobbed when she played Cleopatra, even the shallow brain of a producer has never thought of such a thing. The supernatural is present, cold winds blow across our hands, upon our faces, the thermometer falls, and because of that cold we are hated by journalists and groundlings. There may be in this or that detail painful tragedy, but in the whole work none. I have heard Lady Gregory say, rejecting some play in the modern manner sent to the Abbey Theatre, 'Tragedy must be a joy to the man who dies.' Nor is it any different with lyrics, songs, narrative poems; neither scholars nor the populace have sung or read anything generation after generation because of its pain.[6]

Much of Wordsworth's poetry is tragic in the sense that it aspires to that condition where the emotional temperature, though high, barely registers. This was a lesson he seems to have understood from the outset, when in 'The Vale of Esthwaite' he wrapped grief at his father's death in wordplay: 'I mourn because I mourn'd no more.'[7] From that point onwards it became increasingly submerged beneath the surface of his verse, alluded to through symbolic re-enactments of the underworld journey, or by integrating representations of the dead into his vision of the natural world. The aim was simultaneously to contain and to articulate intense feeling.

The post-Preamble composed for Book I of *The Prelude* made heavy weather of chewing over what might be the most appropriate subject for his work; when *The Excursion* was close to completion, grief reclaimed him once again, and was revealed as his natural theme.

> Surprized by joy – impatient as the Wind
> I wished to share the transport – Oh! with whom
> But thee, long buried in the silent Tomb,
> That spot which no vicissitude can find?
> Love, faithful love recalled thee to my mind –

---

[5] Ll. 3–4.
[6] W. B. Yeats, *Selected Criticism and Prose*, ed. A Norman Jeffares (London: Pan Books, 1980), pp. 266–7.
[7] 'The Vale of Esthwaite' 289.

But how could I forget thee? – Through what power,
Even for the least division of an hour,
Have I been so beguiled as to be blind
To my most grievous loss? – That thought's return
Was the worst pang that sorrow ever bore,
Save one, one only, when I stood forlorn,
Knowing my heart's best treasure was no more;
That neither present time, nor years unborn
Could to my sight that heavenly face restore.

This inspired outpouring was addressed to Catherine at a moment when Wordsworth felt 'beguiled' by momentary joy into losing sight of 'my most grievous loss'. It works by reiterating, no less than four times, the fact of her death, as if it were something he had failed properly to comprehend. The first time is at line 4, where she is taken to a 'spot which no vicissitude can find'; then at line 9, where she is 'my most grievous loss'; a third time in line 10, where the thought's return becomes 'the worst pang that sorrow ever bore'; and finally the recollection of the moment when he knew she was dead and would never see her again (ll. 13–14). The convulsive action of grief is repeated as the mind struggles both to accept and resist the fact of loss.

It is a form of tautology, a technique pioneered by Wordsworth years before he first met Coleridge, in his translations from Virgil, where Orpheus had lamented Eurydice.[8] He had worked variations on it in the *Lyrical Ballads* of 1798 and the 1799 *Prelude* (see chapters 5 and 6), and here it is again, used as before in 'an attempt . . . to communicate impassioned feelings' while betraying 'the inadequateness of our own powers, or the deficiencies of language'.[9] Those deficiencies are elemental to the business of disclosing to the reader the intensity of emotion behind the utterance while keeping the outward temperature low.

We do not know exactly when 'Surprized by joy' was composed, though it was first published in Wordsworth's collected *Poems* of 1815. Line 3 prompts scholars to suggest that it was written 'a considerable time'[10] after Catherine's death and before late October 1814 (when the 1815 edition was ready for the printer). It probably postdates Wordsworth's other important response to Catherine's death. On 5 January 1813 Dorothy proudly told Catherine Clarkson that 'William has begun to look into his poem the Recluse within the last two days and I hope he will be the better for it.'[11] The link between

---

[8] See p. 26.
[9] Cornell *Lyrical Ballads* 351.
[10] Cornell *Poems 1807–20* 112.
[11] *MY* ii 64.

'The Recluse' and Wordsworth's experience of grief had been reinforced by
John's death, and it is significant that part of his response to the demise of his
children was to turn to the manuscripts of the largely complete *Excursion* and
compose a blank verse passage in which the Solitary describes the loss of his
daughter:

> Our blooming Girl
> Caught in the gripe of Dark with such brief time
> To struggle in as scarcely would allow
> Her cheek to change its colour was conveyed
> From us to regions inaccessible
> Where height or depth admits not the approach
> Of living man though longing to pursue.
>   ('Have you espied upon the dewy lawn', 21–7)

The living man who longs to pursue the dead is familiar from Wordsworth's
classical education at Hawkshead, an echo of Aeneas and Orpheus. But in
middle age the poet has relinquished hope of re-enacting their pursuit in his
verse. Where in 'The Vale of Esthwaite' he descended unhesitatingly into
Helvellyn's inmost womb and in *Prelude* Book VIII conducted us to the cave
of Yordas, the Elysian fields of *The Excursion* remain beyond reach, no more
than a 'longing' – the attraction of which is underlined by the tautology of the
last three quoted lines, which remark upon the inaccessibility of the dead and
then gloss it. As in 'Surprized by joy', powerful emotion is barely restrained
by language.

So redolent is it of Wordsworth's recent experience that it is easy to forget
that for the purposes of *The Excursion* he is writing 'in character', providing
the Solitary with a personal history. But as it proceeds, we are brought uncannily close to its author, especially when the Solitary breaks into an impassioned apostrophe to his dead daughter:

> – Departed Child! I could forget thee once
> Though at thy bosom nurs'd – this woeful gain
> Thy dissolution brings that in my soul
> Perpetually a Shadow doth abide
> That never never more shall be displaced
> By the returning Substance, seen or touchd,
> Seen by mine eyes or clasped in my embrace. –
> Absence and death how differ they! and how
> Shall I admit that nothing can restore
> What one short sigh so easily removed?
> Death, life, and sleep, reality and thought,
> Instruct me, God, their boundaries to know

And make my new condition fairly mine
– O teach me calm submission to thy will.

(ll. 38–51)

The most memorable lines of 'The Tuft of Primroses' are those which attempted to describe the state of non-being into which the Sympson family had fallen;[12] likewise, these are the highlight of the Solitary's recollection, flowing directly from the wellspring of Wordsworth's emotional reserves. Like 'Surprized by joy', they are concerned with the problem of apprehending death and its strange paradox for the survivor – the natural psychological reflex of thinking the departed to be present (the 'beguiling' in the sonnet), followed by the renewed awareness of nonexistence. Wordsworth's use of the opposition between shadow and substance, while traditional, is perfectly apposite –

> Perpetually a Shadow doth abide
> That never never more shall be displaced
> By the returning Substance, seen or touchd,
> Seen by mine eyes or clasped in my embrace. –

In the space of very few lines Wordsworth manages to hint at an entire philosophy of death and life. The 'Shadow', which recalls the 'shades' of the juvenile poetry, is a ghost – a very real one, at least for the survivor. It is the ghost we all possess, perceptible to those who know us during our lifetime, independently of our physical selves; while we are alive it may be retained by our loved ones, to be 'displaced' when we are present in body. The Solitary's daughter has left that ghost in her father's heart – but her returning substance, her physical self, will never again displace it, be 'seen or touchd'. The last line and a half,

> . . . seen or touchd,
> Seen by mine eyes or clasped in my embrace,

is another tautology, unnecessary in logical terms, but calculated to express the reluctance of the mind to accept the irrevocability of death – and perform the same function as Orpheus' repeated lament for Eurydice.[13] In glossing the most profoundly felt desires of the bereft father, that last line – 'Seen by mine eyes or clasped in my embrace' – is poignant because it offers, for a moment, the possibility of reclaiming the dead. It can be no accident that clasping in his

---

12 See pp. 283–6.
13 See p. 26.

arms is precisely what Orpheus had wanted to do with Eurydice, a desire painfully faithful to bereavement as it oscillates between incredulity at loss and the vain hope that the dead are not gone forever. No wonder the Solitary is so reluctant to concede death's finality:

> Shall I admit that nothing can restore
> What one short sigh so easily removed?

Placed at the end of the line, 'restore' takes an emphasis (as in the last line of 'Surprized by joy'), turning the question into a genuine enquiry. But it is rhetorical: the answer to the Solitary's question can only be 'no'. Grief may fill him with the hope of seeing her again, but the question has been posed to expose its futility. Restoration is impossible – nor, in the midst of this, are we offered the consolation of an afterlife. All we have is the finality of death, and the irrepressible reflex to deny it.

In some respects the most astonishing element is the Solitary's prayer:

> Death, life, and sleep, reality and thought,
> Instruct me, God, their boundaries to know
> And make my new condition fairly mine
> – O teach me calm submission to thy will.

The central argument of the post-1798 poetry was that the living might cross the boundaries of life and death in order to retrieve some higher wisdom agreeable to the optimistic notions of 'The Recluse'. In that belief the 'Ode' had espoused the Platonic belief in pre-existence – 'Our birth is but a sleep and a forgetting' – and found strength in

> the soothing thoughts that spring
> Out of human suffering,
> In the faith that looks through death,
> In years that bring the philosophic mind.

> (ll. 186–9)

Attractive though such notions might have been, they are superficial com-pared with the more realistic, and quite un-visionary, ideas in this draft for *The Excursion*. Not only is the Solitary not interested in looking through death, but any such idea is displaced by a desire to 'know' – that is, to acknowledge and respect – those boundaries. There is no thought of transgressing them; Wordsworth understands their absolute nature and bows down to them: 'O teach me calm submission to thy will.' Who is speaking – the Solitary or the poet? In all likelihood, both; the Solitary is articulating the philosophy be-queathed by John – God's will be done.

Modern critics see Wordsworth either as a believer in radical causes or as a dried-up Tory. But the force that exerted most influence on his poetic life was grief, and for much of his adulthood he was the victim of successive bereavements that left him with little to believe in but the need to bow his head to the ordinance of God, however severe. It was a terrible challenge to have set because it left him vulnerable to doubt. At the back of his mind there lurked the question articulated in the letter written to Beaumont after John's death: 'Would it be blasphemy to say that upon the supposition of the thinking principle being destroyed by death, however inferior we may be to the great Cause and ruler of things, we have *more of love* in our Nature than he has?'[14] In 1805 it had seemed likely, and although his subsequent work attempted to retreat from the notion, there is a perceptible tendency in his poetry towards scepticism. 'The Tuft of Primroses' had attempted to affirm the idea of a millenarian brotherhood by discussing monastic seclusion, but had undermined that with memories of the Grande Chartreuse and its desecration by the revolutionary guard. *The Excursion* of all poems was expected to reaffirm the aspirations of 'The Recluse', but this passage with its account of death and bereavement was unlikely to deliver the Coleridgean message of universal redemption. Instead Wordsworth offers a prayer to 'teach me calm submission to thy will' – a force which remains beyond human comprehension. No wonder he decided to omit it from the poem.

The draft continues with recollections of the dead child and a detailed account of the grief of the Solitary's wife, based heavily on that of Mary Wordsworth.[15] As it concludes, the Solitary describes her as she pays her daily obsequies at the graveside:

> the Mother did not miss
> Dear consolation, kneeling on the turf
> In prayers and blending with this solemn rite
> Of pious hope the vanities of grief.

(ll. 130–3)

Not bestowed by an external agent, consolation is derived exclusively from physical and spiritual submission to the Almighty, with which grief by comparison is vain and futile. Like the poet himself, the Solitary's wife can only submit to the will of a higher power whose ways are incomprehensible. It is an etiolated hope alongside that of 1798. Then, grief 'Appeared an idle dream

---

[14] *EY* 556.
[15] In the Fenwick Note to 'Maternal Grief' he noted, '*for private notice solely*', that the mother's behaviour was 'faithfully set forth from my Wife's feelings & habits after the loss of our two children within half a year of each other' (*FN* 67–8).

that could not live / Where meditation was'[16] because life and death were
perceived as part of a cosmic perspective whereby physical nonexistence was
part of a larger spiritual existence that was infinite. But by 1813–14 it could
not be so glibly written off. If indeed it was a real, tangible force with which
he had to grapple, and the boundaries of life and death were to be recognized
as immovable and remote, the godlike perspective of the 1798 poetry was
untenable. By 1813–14 he is compelled to assume a more humble posture,
honouring God's inscrutable will and signalling his resignation to it. He says
as much in Thomas Wordsworth's epitaph, composed at the same period:

> Six months to six years added, He remain'd
> Upon this sinful earth, by sin unstain'd.
> O blessed Lord, whose mercy then remov'd
> A Child whom every eye that look'd on lov'd,
> Support us, teach us calmly to resign
> What we possess'd and now is wholly thine.

This isn't really about Wordsworth's dead son, but about those left behind –
those who have not yet learnt to 'resign' their love. As with the Solitary, the
pain of the epitaph rests in its admission that the living do not wish to relinquish the dead. It is there in the claim that the child was loved by all who saw
him, in the reluctant tone of 'teach us calmly to resign', and the unwelcome
recognition that Thomas 'is wholly thine'. In that sense the last three lines are
tautological, as they reiterate the wish to retain the child while admitting that
he must be returned to God.

   Throughout these works God is venerated while at the same time resented.
The lesson that the Solitary had to 'resign / What we possess'd' is placed in
the future, and will be a hard one. Similarly, the image of his wife praying over
her child's grave as she weeps is starkly unconsoled, particularly in view of the
undesirable knowledge that her grief is vain. In strict Christian terms it was,
because of the afterlife, but the phrase 'vanities of grief' cannot help but seem
peremptory, especially as it concludes the draft; Wordsworth realized this when
in 1841–2[17] he worked the passage into an independent poem, 'Maternal
Grief', adding an explanation to cushion the blow:

> For such, by pitying Angels and by Spirits
> Transferred to regions upon which the clouds

---

[16] 'The Ruined Cottage' MS D, 523–4.
[17] The Cornell editor notes that Wordsworth may have been working on it from March
1841 onwards.

Of our weak nature rest not, must be deemed
Those willing tears, and unforbidden sighs,
And all those tokens of a cherished sorrow,
Which, soothed and sweetened by the grace of Heaven
As now it is, seems to her own fond heart,
Immortal as the love that gave it being.

('Maternal Grief' 74–81)

The 'pitying Angels' that endorse this judgement are probably the weakest feature of the verse, no more persuasive than the girl's spirit which has apparently been 'transferred' elsewhere. If anything the mother's tears and sighs are less credible for being willed and unforbidden, and her sorrow no more acceptable by being cherished. These epithets serve to heighten her self-indulgence, especially when she promotes her sorrow to the level of immortality. As in the case of *King Lear*, her fondness is a form of foolishness.[18] The attempt to soften the toughness of the 1813–14 text succeeds in belittling the mother's feelings, while the machinery introduced to assist the poet – the angels, clouds and 'grace of Heaven' – confer on it an insalubrious sentimentality absent from the earlier version.

The weakness of the revisions stems from the ambiguity surrounding 'the vanities of grief'. When in 1813–14 he composed the draft, besides indicating that the mother's feelings take no account of conventional Christian teaching, it could have been taken to imply that the belief in an afterlife was itself an illusion, and that grief is vanity because as it is ineffectual. This would not be an unreasonable interpretation. After all, 'Have you espied upon the dewy lawn' conspicuously does not conclude with an allusion to God or eternal life, which had been part of the *White Doe* and the 'Elegiac Stanzas'. The final image of the mother praying and weeping over her daughter's grave in her search for 'Dear consolation' is all we are offered. It is unmediated. There is no indication of whether her 'solemn rite / Of pious hope' was valuable for any other reason than the comfort it gave her – but the implication could be that it was as vain as her grief. So potent is that word 'vanities' that it threatens to undermine all else in those concluding lines. 'Vanity of vanities, saith the preacher, vanity of vanities; all is vanity.'[19] It wouldn't be too far-fetched to suggest that the verbal ambiguity is evidence of emotional equivocation in Wordsworth: he acknowledges the necessity to bow down before God's will but at the same time resents its implementation, and what he sees as the wanton deaths of the pure-hearted and innocent. In that light it is not possible for

[18] 'I am a very foolish fond old man'; *King Lear* IV vii 59.
[19] Ecclesiastes 1:2.

him to go further than the troublesome phrase, 'vanities of grief' – and although the passage is entered in the *Excursion* manuscripts, no more than seven lines from it were to find their way into the published poem.[20] The rest too nakedly exposed the morbid behaviour of Mary Wordsworth and his anger at the force that had decreed Catherine's death; it was obviously unpublishable.

Even so, *The Excursion* lacked the proud hope of the pre-1805 poetry. It was, as Gill has observed, 'an uncertain and troubled work, for what Wordsworth offered – and continued to offer – was not a *confessio fidei* but an exploration of faith'.[21] That exploratory tone is more pronounced in the 1813–14 passage than elsewhere. Who could blame Wordsworth for being moved to doubt or anger at the deaths of his young children, as he tried and failed to understand by what logic they had forfeited their lives? 'Surprized by Joy' works because it backs away from those feelings, focusing narrowly on the incredulity of the bereaved mind. In its final line it seems unpersuaded by the traditional Christian promise; Wordsworth stands forlorn, knowing

> That neither present time, nor years unborn
> Could to my sight that heavenly face restore.

He is granted no more solace than the Solitary's wife – bereft, aggrieved, compelled to recognize the unforgiving force of death and the enduring nature of loss. True to the mood of the moment, there is nothing about an afterlife or universal redemption – nothing of the philosophical resolution that 'The Recluse' would have provided, for it no longer seemed true or authoritative.

The pain of Catherine and Thomas' deaths never faded. Nearly forty years later Aubrey de Vere said that Wordsworth described the 'details of their illnesses with an exactness and impetuosity of troubled excitement, such as might have been expected if the bereavement had taken place but a few weeks before'.[22] The pain was revived with the death of his daughter Dora in July 1847. When Henry Crabb Robinson came for his Christmas visit Wordsworth was helpless with grief; after being coaxed out on walks he would 'retire to his room sit alone & cry incessantly':

> I witnessed several such bursts of grief occasioned by the merest accidents, such as my proposing to call with him on Mrs Arnold – He was unable to take leave of me for sobbing when I came away – During my three weeks stay, it was very

---

[20]   *The Excursion* (1814) iii 646–52.
[21]   Gill 295.
[22]   Quoted Gill 294.

seldom that I could engage him in any conversation. (*Robinson Correspondence* ii 657–8)

By February 1848 he was no better. Mary told Isabella Fenwick that

he is bowed to the dust – and our dear comers and goers seem rather to have increased, than dissipated his dejection. His mind and spirits . . . [are] in the lowest state of *humiliation* and deep sorrow. But I doubt not you will agree with me in the hope that this must work for good and that time will bring comfort – May the Almighty in his mercy see fit to send support ere long. (Burton 293)

Wordsworth was reacting in the same way as before, submitting to the higher will that had ordained Dora's death, in a spirit of '*humiliation* and deep sorrow'. That submissive posture was his only means of coming to terms with the deaths of those closest to him. At the same time there is the unavoidable sense that Dora's death had revived unresolved feelings of loss and abandonment first generated by his parents' deaths in the 1780s. That would help explain why, when Mary was able to depend on her faith for support, she recognized that her husband was unable to recover from the blow; as she told Kate Southey, his 'spirits are so overwhelmed that I can fix upon nothing.'[23] The situation was so desperate that when offered consolation by his gardener James, Wordsworth was unable to accept it, as James reported to Robinson:

'Ah! Sir And so I took the liberty of saying to Master – He merely said – "Oh she was such a bright creature – And then I said *"But Sir don't you think she is brighter now than she ever was*, And then Master burst into a flood of tears.(*Robinson Correspondence* ii 661)

Thirty years earlier the knowledge that he could still pour his energies into 'The Recluse' had provided consolation; with John's death it had become a sacred trust, and when Catherine and Thomas died he had turned to *The Excursion*. By 1847 'The Recluse' was a lost cause, leaving nothing into which his grief for Dora could be displaced. Nor, in her state of health, was Dorothy able to comfort him. There was only a vacuum where once the great philosophical poem of the age had been; no wonder he told Isabella Fenwick that he read his poetry 'less than any other – and often think that my life has been in a great measure wasted.'[24] He seems to have written nothing after Dora's death, except the 'Installation Ode', at the behest of Prince Albert, who had

23 *LY* iv 865.
24 *LY* iv 776.

been appointed Chancellor of Cambridge University (though even that was ghosted by Wordsworth's son-in-law, Edward Quillinan).

It would be easy to think of grief as a disabling force in Wordsworth's life but that is not the argument of this book. 'Poetry is passion: it is the history or science of feelings,' he once wrote.[25] Cushioned from the full impact of his father's death by the kindness of his landlady Ann Tyson and her husband, Wordsworth did not fully understand its implications until he left the comparative shelter of Hawkshead and the school he loved so much. He had intense feelings before that, but seems not to have understood their place in his creative life. The unexpected catharsis of summer 1787, shared with his sister and brothers, brought home the centrality of emotion to his work, particularly the feelings connected to his parents' decease. Those feelings never left him; in fact, they intensified until they seemed to define him. Though on a conscious level he subscribed to the tenets of Christian theism, the poet in old age knew only that those who meant most to him – his parents, John, Catherine, Thomas and Dora – had been taken in their prime, and nothing could console him for that loss. Loss forced him into devotion to a God whose ways he did not understand. In that situation there was no way he could have written as His spokesman.

It is tempting to think of 'The Recluse' as one of the big red herrings of the Romantic period, a ruin, or an epic that never was. But that is not my argument either. It was, correctly speaking, two things: an idea in Coleridge's mind (not a word of which was ever written); and an organizing principle (which was at times inspirational) in Wordsworth's. Both are instrumental to a full understanding of Wordsworth's life and work. As such they were productive of some of his greatest poetry – 'The Ruined Cottage', 'The Pedlar', 'Not Useless do I Deem', 'There is an active principle', the various *Preludes*, 'Home at Grasmere', 'The Tuft of Primroses', 'To the Clouds', *The Excursion* and 'Verses on Nab Well'. And when Wordsworth claimed that his shorter poems bore the same relation to 'The Recluse' as the 'little cells, oratories, and sepulchral recesses'[26] to a Gothic church, he was not far from the truth. The *White Doe* and the *Lyrical Ballads* were consistent with his ambitions for 'The Recluse' at the time they were composed, and could not have been produced without knowledge of the larger project.

Wordsworth's last known poem, besides the 'Installation Ode', was a prayer, 'On the Banks of a Rocky Stream', composed before Dora's death, in late 1846. It is a worthy final utterance for a poet whose mind aspired to repose.

---

[25] Note to 'The Thorn', Cornell *Lyrical Ballads* 351.
[26] *Prose Works* iii 6.

In these lines the urge to write arises not from contentment but from turbulence both in the past and present. For Wordsworth it was focused by grief and given impetus by the ambition to write a poem that would change the world for the better.

> Grant me, o blessed Lord a mind
> In which my thoughts may have a quiet home
> Thoughts which now fret like balls of foam
> That in a whirlpool each the other chase
> Around and around and neither find
> An outlet nor a resting place. —[27]

---

[27] This poem was published in revised form in 1847.

Appendix
The White Doe of
Rylstone *(1808 Text) and*
its 'Advertizement'

The White Doe of Rylstone of 1808 ranks as one of the great lost works of
Wordsworth's career – lost because it was dismembered and revised shortly
after its completion to form a new text that was never published and may
never have been completed. Today it survives only in fragments in two manuscripts at the Wordsworth Library in Grasmere, MSS 61 and 62. MS 61 is a
home-made notebook used for drafting between 2 December 1807 and 3
January 1808; MS 62 contains printer's copy completed by 16 January, towards a text of about 1700 lines.

A further manuscript copy of the poem (no longer extant) was given to
Southey, who liked it;[1] Coleridge and Lamb, however, were highly critical of
it, and their remarks led to revision during summer 1808 for a printed edition
(which at one stage was to include 'Benjamin the Waggoner' and *Peter Bell*)
which failed to materialize.[2] The poem was published in a further revised form
in 1815 by Longman.[3]

The manuscripts contain several layers of composition of which three are
discernible. The earliest dates from the first phase of work (late October 1807
to 16 January 1808); the second was entered in the wake of Coleridge and
Lamb's criticisms of the poem (between mid-April and 12 May 1808); the
third is subsequent to that, preparatory to the 1815 published text.

---

[1] Southey was apparently the first to see it, probably when he visited Dove Cottage in
early February; unlike Coleridge and Lamb he thought it 'incomparably fine' (Reed ii 372n4).
[2] The revisions of summer 1808 are discussed in helpful detail, Cornell *White Doe* 48–50.
[3] For a detailed account of the poem's composition see Reed ii 700–2 and Cornell *White
Doe*, Introduction.

In this appendix I have attempted to retrieve the text of the poem when first completed, *c.* 16 January 1808; revisions postdating that moment are not incorporated. Copy text is MS 62, except where MS 61 is the only witness. When in doubt my policy has been conservative, in the sense that I favour earlier readings except where the revision or deletion was executed during the phase of composition that concluded in January 1808. Emendations are accepted only where they are clearly corrections. Minor errors of the pen are silently corrected, but archaic spellings allowed to stand. Punctuation is authorial, though it has on occasion been necessary to supply closing quotation marks and essential pointing, such as full stops, when they are omitted by Wordsworth or his copyist. Ampersands are expanded to 'and'. I have footnoted original or deleted readings where they are of critical interest, along with occasional points of information. For ease of reference each fragment is numbered, and line numbers provided within them. Equivalent line numbers in the 1815 text are given in square brackets on a separate indent.

The reader can trace my footsteps by reference to facsimiles of the relevant manuscripts in Cornell *White Doe* 226–341. MS 61 also contains the earliest known draft of 'The Force of Prayer', which was probably composed in September 1807 and therefore antedates the 1808 *White Doe*; it has been transcribed by the Cornell editor and is there presented as a parallel text with the draft contained in a letter of 18 October 1807 from Dorothy Wordsworth to Jane Marshall; see Cornell *White Doe* 383–9.

Fragment 1

Part 1st

From Bolton's old monastic Tower
The Bells ring loud with gladsome power[1]
The sun is bright the fields are gay
With people in their best array
Of stole and doublet, hood and scarf   5   [5]
Along the banks of the crystal Wharf
Through the vale retired and lowly
Trooping to that summons holy
And up among the moorlands see
What sprinklings of blithe company   10   [10]
Of Lasses and of Shepperd-grooms
That down the steep hills force their way

---

[1] The base text reads: 'The morning bells from Bolton tower / Are speaking with a voice of power' (1r); see figure 19 overleaf.

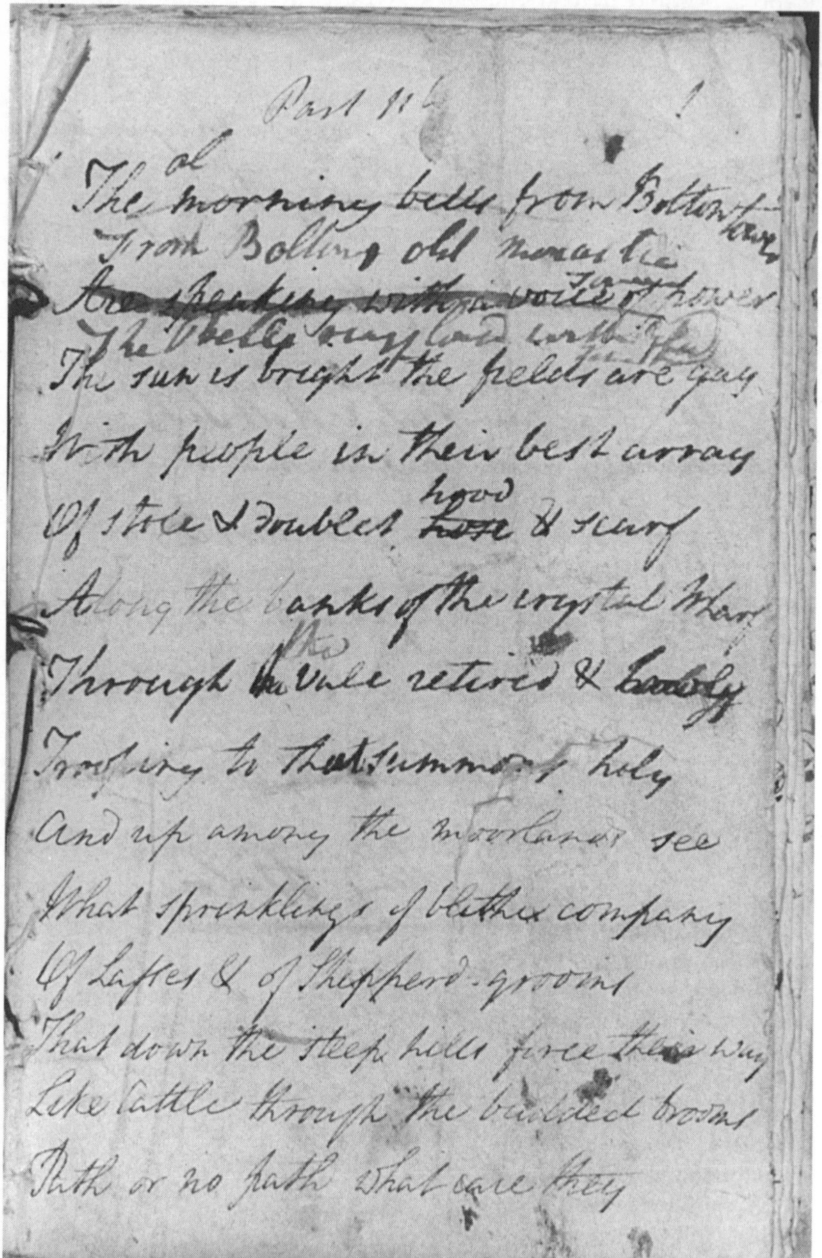

Figure 19. DC MS 61, 1r. *The White Doe of Rylstone*: early draft of the opening lines, composed December 1807–January 1808.

Like Cattle through the budded brooms
Path or no path what care they
And thus in joyous mood they hie   15   [15]
To Bolton's mould'ring Priory

What would they there? full fifty years
That Pile with all its stately Peers[2]
Too harshly hath been doom'd to taste
The bitterness of wrong and waste   20   [20]
Its courts are ravaged but the Tower
Is standing with a voice of power
That ancient voice which wont to call
To mass or some high festival
And in the shatter'd Fabric's heart[3]   25   [25]
Remaineth one protected part
A rural chapel neatly drest
In Covert like a little nest
And thither young and old repair –
This Sabbath-day for praise and prayer   30   [30]

Fast the Church-yard fills – anon
Look again and they all are gone
The cluster round the Porch and the folk
That sate in the shade of the Prior's Oak
But scarcely[4] have disappeared   35   [35]
Ere the prelusive hymn is heard
With one consent the People rejoice
Filling the Church with a lofty voice
They sing a service which they feel
For tis the sunrise now of Zeal   40   [40]
And faith and hope are [in] their prime
In great Eliza's golden time.

A moment end the fervent din
And all is hush'd without and within
For though the Priest with calmer glee   45   [45]
Begins the holy liturgy
You cannot hear his voice – 'tis drown'd
In the neighbouring Rivers sound
When, soft! the dusky trees between
And down the path through the open green   50   [50]

2   The MS contains an alternative reading: 'That sumptuous Pile with all its Peers'.
3   shatter'd Fabric's heart] The original reading is 'Ruin's mouldring heart'.
4   But scarcely] The original reading is 'All like Faries' – which does scan.

Where is no living thing to be seen
And through the gate which is the bound
Of the Church-yard's private ground
And right across the verdant sod   [55]
Towards the very house of God   55
Comes gliding in with lovely gleam
Comes gliding in serene and slow
Soft and silent as a dream
A solitary Doe.   [60]
White she is as lilly of June   60
And beauteous as the silver moon
When out of sight the clouds are driv'n
And she is left alone in heaven
Or like a Ship, some gentle day   [65]
In sunshine sailing far away   65
A glittering Ship that hath the plain
Of Ocean for her own domain.

Lie silent in your graves ye dead
Lie quiet in your Church-yard bed   [70]
Ye living tend your holy cares   70
Ye multitude pursue your prayers
And blame not me if my⁵ heart and sight
Are occupied with one delight
Tis a work for Sabbath hours   [75]
If I with this bright Creature go   75
Whether she be of forest bowers
Of the bowers of earth below
Or a Spirit for one day giv'n
A gift of grace from purest heaven.   [80]
What harmonious pensive changes   80
Wait upon her as she ranges
Round and through this Pile of state
Overthrown and desolate
Now a step or two her way   [85]
Is through space of open day   85
Where the enamoured sunny light
Brightens her that was so bright
Now doth a delicate shadow fall
Falls upon her like a breath.   [90]

From some lofty arch or wall   90
As she passes underneath

⁵ my] the copyist originally wrote 'your', which was quickly corrected to 'my'.

Now some gloomy nook partakes
Of the glory that she makes
High-ribb'd vault of stone, or cell   [95]
With perfect cunning fram'd as well   95
Of stone and Ivy and the spread
Of the elder's bushy head
Some jealous and forbidding cell
That doth the living stars repel   [100]
And where no flower hath leave to dwell.   100
The presence of this Milk-white Doe
Fills many a damp obscure recess
With radiance of a saintly shew
And reappearing, she no less   [105]
To the open day gives blessedness   105
But say amongst these holy places
Which thus assiduously she paces
Comes she with a Votary's task
Rite to perform or boon to ask   [110]
Fair Pilgrim! harbours she a sense   110
Of sorrow or of reverence
Can she be grieved for quire or shrine
Crush'd as if by wrath divine?
For what survives of house where God   [115]
Was worshipp'd or where Man abode   115
Old magnificence undone
Or for the gentler work begun
By nature softening and concealing
And busy with a hand of healing   [120]
The altar whence the cross was rent   120
Now rich with mossy ornament
The dormitory's length laid bare
Where the wild-rose blossoms fair
And sapling ash whose place of birth   [125]
Is that lordly chamber hearth   125
There low now he lurketh but proud will he be
When the North wind shall rock him a far-spreading tree
She sees a Warrior carv'd in stone
Among the thick weeds stretch'd alone
A warrior with his shield of pride   130
Cleaving humbly to his side   [130]
And hands in resignation press'd
Palm to palm on his tranquil breast[6]

---

[6]   The stone warrior, which is Wordsworth's invention, echoes the 'cross-legged knight' in
Two-Part Prelude ii 120.

Methinks she passeth by the sight
As a common Creature might   135
If she be doom'd to inward care   [135]
Or service it must lie elsewhere
But hers are eyes serenely bright
And on she moves with pace how light
Nor spares to stoop her head and taste   140
The dewy turf with flowers bestrown   [140]
And in this way she fares, till at last
Beside the ridge of a grassy grave
In quietness she lays her down
Gently as a weary wave   145
Sinks when the summer breeze hath died   [145]
Against an anchor'd Vessel's side
Even so without distress doth she
Lie down in peace and lovingly.

The day is placid in its going   150
To its tranquil measures bound   [150]
As the River in its flowing,
Can there be a softer sound?
So the balmy minutes pass
While this radiant Creature lies   155
Couched upon the sacred grass   [155]
Pensively with downcast eyes
When now again the people rear
A voice of praise with awful Chear
It is the last the parting song   160
And from the Temple forth they throng   [160]
And quickly spread themselves abroad
While each pursues his several road
But some a variegated band
Of middle-aged and old and young   165
And little children by the hand   [165]
Upon their leading Mothers[7] hung
Turn with obeisance gladly paid
Towards the spot where full in view
The lovely[8] Doe of whitest hue   170
Her Sabbath couch hath made.   [170]

[7] Mothers] the original reading, which was deleted to 'Grandsires', which was deleted in turn.
[8] lovely] originally 'famous', which was deleted to 'Peerless'.

It was a solitary mound
Which two spears length of level ground
Did from all other graves divide
As if in some respect of pride   175
Or sorrow that retains her mood,
Still shy of human brotherhood
Or guilt that humbly would express
A penitential loneliness.

'Look there she is, my Child, draw near,   180
She fears not, wherefore should we fear?   [180]
She means no harm', but still the Boy
To whom the words were softly said
Hung back, and smiled, and blush'd with joy
A shame-fac'd blush of glowing red.   185
Again the Mother whisper'd low,   [185]
'Now you have seen the famous Doe
From Rillestone⁹ she hath found her way
Over the hills this sabbath day
Her work, whate'er it be, is done   190
And she will depart when we are gone   [190]
Thus doth she keep from year to year
Her sabbath morning, foul or fair.'

This knows the blissful Boy full well
This knows the Country far and near   195
But, Matron! there is more to tell
For, certes, if I rightly trace
The characters of every face
A thousand earnest thoughts are here
An ample creed of love and fear   200
Repose of heart, and truth that sees
A world of fond remembrances
That do the gentle Creature wrong.

That bearded staff-supported Sire   [220]
Who in his youth hath often fed   205
Full chearily on Convent bread
And heard old tales by the kitchen fire
That Old Man's mind, I guess, hath turn'd
To days far off, hath mounted high

⁹ Rillestone] Wordsworth's spelling, corrected by his copyists; it was apparently the spelling he found in his sources.

To Albemarle and Romilly   210
When Lady Aaliza mourn'd
Her Son, and felt in her despair   [230]
The pang of unavailing prayer,
Her Son in Wharf's abysses drown'd,
The noble Boy of Egremound.[10]   215
From which affliction when God's grace
At length had in her heart found place   [235
]A pious Structure fair to see
Rose up, this stately Priory,
The Lady's work, but now laid low   220
To the grief of her soul that doth come and go
In the beautiful Form of this milk-white Doe.   [240]

Pass, he who will, the Chauntry door   [245]
And thro' the chink in the fractured floor
Look down, and see a grisly sight,   225
A Vault where the Bodies are buried upright
There face by face, and hand by hand
The Claphams and Mauleverers stand,   [250]
And in his place among Son and Sire
Is John de Clapham, that fierce Esquire,   230
A valiant Man, and a name of dread
In the ruthless Wars of the White and Red,
Who dragg'd Earl Pembroke from Banbury Church   [255]
And smote off his head on the stones of the Porch.
Look down and thro' the pavement see   235
A glimpse of this dismal Family
Look down among them if you dare
The white Doe oft is peeping there
And for no good – A Dame of blood
Thinks thus, that Dame with the haughty air   240
Who hath a Page her book to hold
And wears a Frontlet edged with gold
A [   ] by birth and she
Loves not the [Hall] of Bethmesley
That slender Youth a Scholar pale   245
From Oxford come to his native Va[le]
He also hath his own conceit
It is, thinks he, the gracious Fairy   [270]
Who loved the Shepherd Lord to meet

[10] Wordsworth found this story in Whitaker's *History of Craven* and used it as the inspiration for 'The Force of Prayer', composed prior to the *White Doe*.

In his wanderings solitary   250
And taught him signs, and shew'd him sights
In Craven's Dens,[11] on Cumbria's Heights
When under cloud of fear he lay,
A Shepherd clad in homely grey,
Nor left him at his later day   255   [285]
And hence when he with spear and shield
Rode full of years to Flodden Field[12]
His eye could see the hidden springs
And how the current was to flow,
The fatal end of Scotland's King,[13]   260   [290]
And all that hopeless overthrow.
But not in wars did he delight
This Clifford wish'd for worthier might
Nor in broad pomp or courtly state
Him his own thoughts did elevate,   265   [295]
Most happy in his shy recess
In Barden's humble quietness.

And rich in studious friends was he
Who standing on the Old Church Tower   [300]
In many a calm propitious hour   270
Perused, with him the starry sky
Or in their cells with him did pry
For other lore their strong desire
Searching the earth with chemic[14] fire   [305]
But they and their good works are fled   275
And all is now disquieted,
And peace is none for living or dead.

[11] In Craven's Dens] In *Thirteen-Book Prelude* Book VIII Wordsworth had referred to 'the Den / Of Yordas among Craven's mountain tracts' (ll. 713–14) which he had visited in May 1800 with his brother John.
[12] Flodden Field] The subject of Scott's *Marmion*, published in 1808, but which Wordsworth did not read until after completing the *White Doe*; see *WR* ii 185. Scott lent Wordsworth an earlier poem about Flodden Field in September 1807; see *WR* ii 88–9.
[13] Scotland's King] James IV (1473–1513).
[14] chemic] The original reading is 'chemy'd', revised to 'chemyc'. I have adopted the orthography of the 1815 printed text. The phrase 'chemic fire' is an intriguing one which points to Wordsworth's awareness of the work of Humphry Davy, who was at this point lecturer and director of the laboratory of the Royal Institution, London. Davy was much on his mind at this moment as he had been ill and Coleridge had communicated details of his recovery to Wordsworth during composition of the *White Doe*; see *MY* i 182. Davy's first Bakerian lecture in 1806 was on 'some chemical agencies of electricity'.

Ah! pensive Scholar, think not so
But look again at the radiant Doe   [310]
What quiet watch she seems to keep   280
Alone beside that grassy heap.

Why mention other thoughts unmeet
For a vision that is so sweet
While stand the people in a ring,   [315]
Gazing, doubting, questioning,   285
Yea many overcome in spite
Of recollections clear and bright
Which yet do unto some impart
An undisturb'd repose of heart   [320]
And all the Assembly own a law   290
Of orderly respect and awe
To a superior Presence due.
But now they dwindle to a few
These also vanish one by one
And, last, the Doe herself is gone.   295

Harp sound the truth upon thy strings
For a Spirit with angel wings
Is near us, and a Spirit's hand;
A Voice is with thee, a command   [335]
To chaunt in strains of heavenly glory   300
A tale of tears, a mortal story.

[Part Two]¹⁵

The Harp in lowliness obey'd,
And first we sang of the greenwood shade
And a solitary Maid,   [340]
Beginning where the Song must end   305
With her and with her sylvan Friend,
The Friend who stood before her sight,
Her only unextinguish'd light,
Her last upholder, in a dearth   [345]
Of love upon a hopeless earth.   310

For she it was, this Maid who wrought
Meekly, with foreboding thought

¹⁵ Part Two] not in the MS.

In vermil Colours and in gold,
 An unbless'd work, which standing by,
 [350]Her Father did with joy behold,   315
Exulting in its imagery,
A Banner, one that did fulfil
Too perfectly his headstrong will
For on this Banner had her hand   [355]
Embroider'd (such was the command)   320
The sacred Cross, and figured there
The five dear wounds our Lord did bear
Full soon to be uplifted high,
And float in rueful company.   [360]

It was the time when England's Queen   325
Ten years had reign'd,[16] a Sovereign dread,
Nor yet the restless Crown had been
Disturb'd upon her virgin head
But now the inly-working North   [365]
Was ripe to send her thousands forth,   330
A potent Vassalage, to fight
In Percy's and in Neville's right,[17]
Two Earls fast leagued in discontent –
Who gave their wishes open vent,   [370]
And boldly urged a general plea   335
The rites of ancient piety,
To be by force of arms renewed,
Glad prospect for the multitude
And that same Banner on whose breast   [375]
The blameless Lady had express'd   340
Memorials chosen to give life
And sunshine to a dangerous strife,
This Banner, waiting for the Call
Stood quietly in Rillestone Hall.   [380]

It came, and Francis Norton said   345
'O Father! rise not in this fray
The hairs are white upon your head
Dear Father hear me when I say
It is for you too late a day   [385]
Bethink you of your own good name!   350

16   The year was, therefore, 1569.
17   Thomas Percy (1528–72), seventh Earl of Northumberland; Charles Neville (1543–
1601), sixth Earl of Westmoreland – both notorious Catholic sympathizers.

A just and gracious Queen have we,
A pure religion, and the claim
Of peace on our humanity
'Tis meet that I endure your scorn   [390]
I am your Son your eldest born   355
But not for Lordship or for land
My Father do I clasp your knees
The banner touch not, stay your hand
This multitude of men disband   [395]
And live at home in blissful ease   360
For these my Brethren's sake for me
And most of all for Emily'.
Loud noise was in the crowded Hall
And scarcely could the Father hear   [400]
That name which had a dying fall,[18]   365
The name of his only Daughter dear
And on the Banner which stood near
He glanced a look of holy pride,
And his wet eyes were glorified.   [405]
Then seiz'd the Staff; and thus did say   370
'Thou, Richard, bear'st thy Father's name,
Keep thou this Ensign till the day
When I of thee require the same
Thy place be on my better hand   [410]
And seven[19] as true as Thou I see   375
Will cleave to this good cause and me',
He spake, and eight brave Sons straightway
All follow'd him, a gallant Band,
Forth, when Sire and Sons appear'd   [415]
A gratulating shout was rear'd   380
With din of arms and minstrelsy
From all his warlike tenantry
A shout to which the Hills replied.[20]   [420]

But Francis in the vacant Hall
Stood silent under dreary weight,   385
A phantasm in which roof and wall
Fell round him like a dream of night.   [425]
And dreaming, walking, desolate,
He found his way to a postern gate

---

[18]   a dying fall] an allusion to *Twelfth Night* I i 4.
[19]   seven] Wordsworth alludes to the Seven against Thebes, the seven Argive heroes who attempted to wrest Thebes from Eteocles in Aeschylus' play.
[20]   These two lines were heavily revised in summer 1808; see Cornell *White Doe* 278–9.

And when he waked, at length his eye   390
Was on the calm and silent sky
With air about him breathing sweet   [430]
And verdant grass beneath his feet
Nor did he fail ere long to hear
A sound of military chear,   395
Faint, but it reach'd that shelter'd spot,
He heard, and it disturb'd him not.   [435]

There stood he leaning on a lance
Which he had grasp'd unknowingly,
Had blindly grasp'd in that strong trance,   400
That dimness of heart-agony.
There stood he, cleansed from the despair   [440]
And sorrow of this fruitless prayer
The past he calmly hath review'd
But where will be the fortitude   405
Of this brave Man when he shall see
That Form beneath the spreading Tree   [445]
And know that it is Emily
Oh! hide them from each other, hide,
Kind Heaven! this Pair severely tried.   410

He saw the Maid where full in view
She sate beneath the spreading yew   [450]
And thitherward he turn'd straitway
And, greeting her, did firmly say
'Might ever Son command a Sire   415   [455]
The act were justified today
Gone are they – they have their desire
And I with thee one hour will stay,   [460]
To give thee comfort if I may'.

He paused her silence to partake   420
And long it was before he spake
Then all at once his thoughts turn'd round

[Five leaves are missing from the manuscript at this point (see Cornell *White Doe* 282–3). The draft in MS 61 recommences with the equivalent of line 556 in the 1815 published text. I begin, however, with lines equivalent to 1815, ll. 540–55, from in MS 62.]

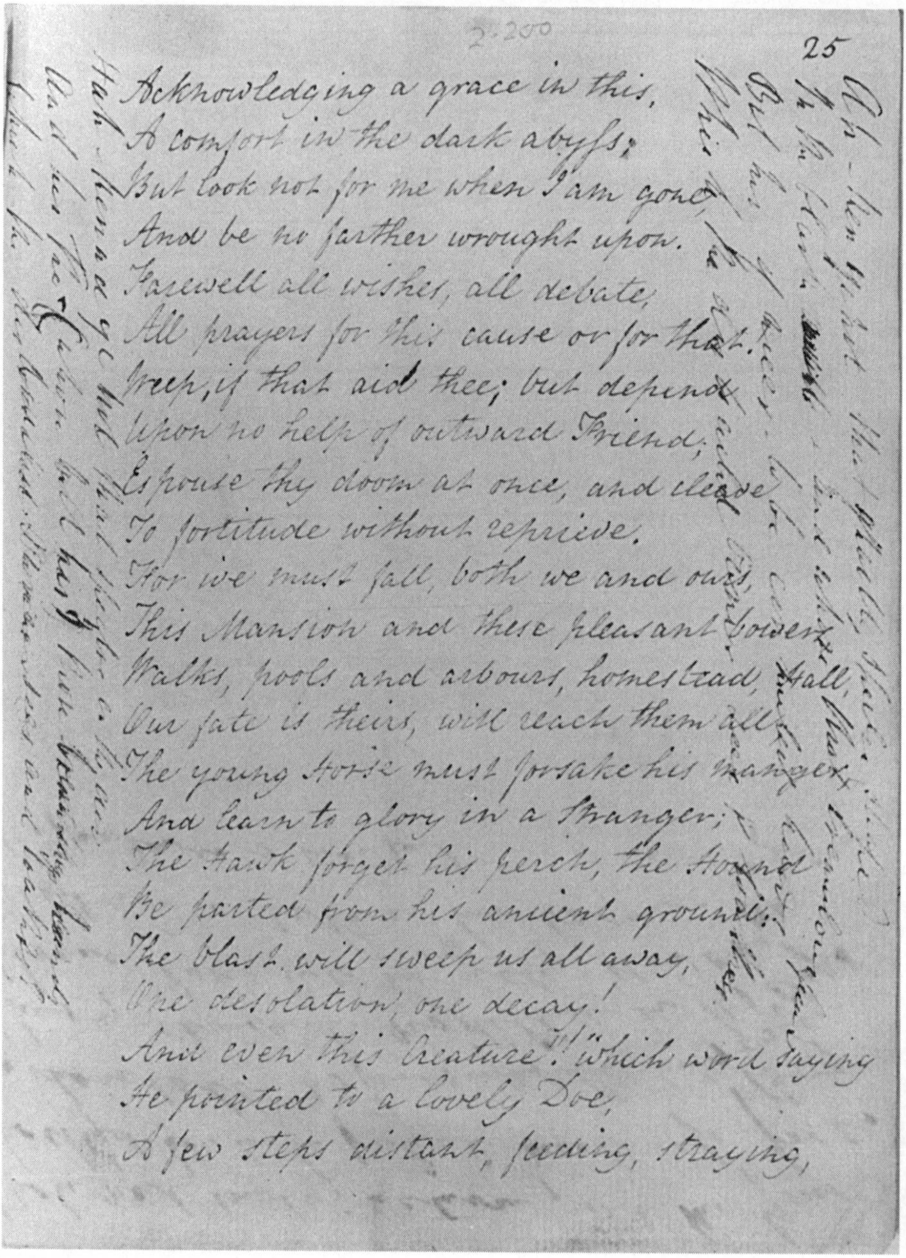

Acknowledging a grace in this,
A comfort in the dark abyss;
But look not for me when I am gone,
And be no farther wrought upon.
Farewell all wishes, all debate,
All prayers for this cause or for that!
Weep, if that aid thee; but depend
Upon no help of outward Friend;
Espouse thy doom at once, and cleave
To fortitude without reprieve,
For we must fall, both we and ours,
This Mansion and these pleasant Bowers
Walks, pools and arbours, homestead, Hall
Our fate is theirs, will reach them all;
The young Horse must forsake his manger
And learn to glory in a stranger;
The Hawk forget his perch, the Hound
Be parted from his ancient ground;
The blast will sweep us all away,
One desolation, one decay!
And even this Creature!" which word saying
He pointed to a lovely Doe,
A few steps distant, feeding, straying,

Figure 20. DC MS 62, 25r. *The White Doe of Rylstone*: fair copy dating from before 16 January 1808.

Fragment 2: from *Part Two*

... Acknowledging a grace in this,   [540]
A comfort in the dark abyss:
But look not for me when I am gone,
And be no farther wrought upon.
Farewell all wishes, all debate,   5
All prayers, for this cause or for that!   [545]
Weep, if that aid thee; but depend
Upon no help of outward Friend;
Espouse thy doom at once, and cleave
To fortitude without reprieve.   10
For we must fall, both we and ours,   [550]
This Mansion and these pleasant bowers,
Walks, pools and arbours, homestead, Hall,
Our fate is theirs, will reach them all;
The young Horse must forsake his manger,   15
And learn to glory in a Stranger;   [555]
The Hawk forget his perch,
the Hound Be parted from his ancient ground:
The blast will sweep us all away,
One desolation, one decay!   20
And even this Creature!' which word saying   [560]
He pointed to a lovely Doe,
A few steps distant, feeding, straying,
'Fair Creature, and more white than snow!
Even she will to her peaceful woods   25
Return, and to her murmuring floods   [565]
And be in heart and soul the same
She was before she hither came,
Ere she had learnt to love us all,
Herself beloved in Rylstone Hall.   30
– But thou, my Sister, doom'd to be   [570]
The last leaf which by Heaven's decree
Must hang upon a blasted tree,
If not in vain we breathed the breath
Together, of a purer faith –   35
If hand in hand we have been led   [575]
And thou (O happy thought this day!)
Not seldom foremost in the way
– If on one thought our minds have fed,
And we have in one meaning read –   40
If, when at home our private weal   [580]
Hath suffered from the shock of zeal,

Together we have learn'd to prize
Forbearance, and self-sacrifice
 – If we like combatants have fared,   45
And for this issue been prepared –   [585
]If thou art beautiful, and youth
And thought endue thee with all truth
Be strong, be worthy of the grace
Of God and fill thy destined place   50
A soul by force of sorrows high   [590]
Uplifted to the purest sky
Of undisturb'd humanity.
He ended, or She heard no more
He led her from the Eughtree shade   55
And at the mansion's silent door   [595]
He kiss'd the consecrated Maid
And down the valley he pursued
Alone the armed multitude.

Part Third

Now joy for you and sudden chear   60
Ye Watchmen upon Brancepeth Towers   [600]
Looking forth in doubt and fear,
Telling melancholy hours!
Proclaim it, let your Masters hear
That Norton with his band is near   65
Marching down the banks of Weir!
The stout earls heard and at once set free
From tremblings and perplexity,
They took their fate and hand and voice
With final pledge confirm'd the choice.   70

Said revered Norton to the pair
Gone forth to hail him on the plain,   [610]
'This meeting, noble Lords!
looks fair,I bring with me a goodly train;
Their hearts are with you: Hill and Dale   75
Have help'd us: Ure we crossed and Swale
And horse and harness followed – see   [615]
The best part of their Yeomanry!
Stand forth, my Sons! – these eight are mine,
Whom to this service I commend;   80
Which way soe'er our fate incline
These will be faithful to the end;   [620]

They are my all' – (voice failed him here),
'My all save one, a Daughter dear!
Whom I have left, the mildest birth   85
The meekest Child on this blessed earth.
I had – but these are by my side   [625]
These eight, and this is a day of pride;
The time is ripe – with festive din
Lo! how the People are flocking in,   90
Like hungry Fowl to the Feeder's hand
When snow lies heavy upon the land.'   [630]

He spake bare truth for far and near
From every side came noisy swarms
Of Peasants in their homely gear;   95
And, mix'd with these, to Brancepeth came
Grave Gentry of estate and name,   [635]
And Captains known for worth in arms,
And prayed the Earls in self-defence
To rise, and prove their innocence. –   100
'Rise, noble Earls, put forth your might
For holy Church, and the People's right!'   [640]
The Norton fixed, at this demand,
  His eye upon Northumberland,
And said, 'The minds of Men will own   105
No loyal rest while England's Crown
Remains without an Heir, the bait   [645]
Of strife, and factions desperate;
Who, paying deadly hate in kind,
Through all things else, in this can find   110
A mutual hope, a common mind,
And plot, and pant, to overwhelm   [650]
All ancient honour in the realm.
Brave Earls! to whose heroic veins
Our noblest blood is given in trust,   115
To you a suffering State complains,
And ye must raise her from the dust.   [655]
With wishes of still bolder scope
On you we look, with dearest hope,
Not only for redress of wrongs   120
In what to high or low belongs
Or to a Crown without an Heir
That hangs to drop we know not where
Even for our Altars, – for the prize
In Heaven, of life that never dies;   125
For the Old and holy Church we mourn,   [660]
And must in joy to her return.

Behold!' – and from his Son, whose stand
Was on his right: from that guardian hand
He took the Banner, and unfurled   130
The precious folds, – 'Behold', said he,   [665]
'The ransom of a sinful world,
Let this your preservation be,
The wounds of hands, and feet and side,
And the sacred Cross on which Jesus died!   135–
This bring I from an ancient hearth   [670
]These Records wrought in pledge of love
By hands of no ignoble birth,
A Maid o'er whom the blessed Dove
Vouchsafed in gentleness to brood   140
While she the holy work pursued.'   [675]
'Uplift the Standard!' was the cry
From all the Listeners that stood round,
'Plant it, – by this we live or die.'
The Norton ceas'd not for that sound,   145
But said, 'The prayer which ye have heard,   [680]
Much injured Earls! by these preferred
Is offered to the Saints,
the sigh Of tens of thousands, secretly.' –
'Uplift it!' cried once more the Band,   150
And then a thoughtful pause ensued.   [685]
'Uplift it!' said Northumberland –
Whereat, from all the multitude,
Who saw the Banner reared on high
In all its dread emblazonry,   155
With tumult and indignant rout   [690]
A voice of uttermost joy brake out:
The transport was rolled down the River of Were
And Durham, the time-honoured Durham! did hear,
The Towers of St Cuthbert[21] were stirred by the shout! 160

Now was the North in arms: they shine   [695]
In warlike trim from Tweed to Tyne
At Percy's voice: and Neville sees
His Followers gathering in from Tees,
From Were, and all the little Rills   165
Concealed among the forked Hills. –
Seven hundred Knights, Retainers all   [700]

[21]   The Towers of St Cuthbert] Durham Cathedral is dedicated to St Cuthbert, who is
buried there.

Of Neville, at their Master's call
Had sate together in Raby Hall![22]
Such strength that Earldom held of yore;   170
Nor wanted at this time rich Store   [705]
Of well appointed Chivalry. –
Not loth the sleepy Lance to wield,
And greet the old paternal Shield,
They heard the summons; – and, furthermore,   175
Came Foot and Horsemen of each degree,   [710]
Unbound by pledge of fealty;
Appeared, with free and open hate
Of novelties in Church and State;
Knight, Burgher, Yeoman, and Esquire;   180
And the Romish Priest, in Priest's attire.   [715]
And thus, in arms, a zealous Band
Proceeding under joint command,
To Durham first their course they bear;
And in St Cuthbert's ancient Seat185
Sung Mass, – and tore the Book of Prayer –   [720]
And trod the Bible beneath their feet.
Thence marching southward smooth and free,
They mustered their Host at Wetherby,
Full sixteen Thousand[23] fair to see;   190
The choicest Warriors of the North!   [725]
But none for undisputed worth
Like those eight Sons; who in a ring,
Each with a lance – erect and tall,
A falchion, and a buckler small,   195
Stood by their Sire on Clifford-moor,   [730]
In youthful beauty flourishing,
To guard the Standard which he bore,
With feet that firmly pressed the ground
They stood, and girt their Father round;   200
Such was his choice; no Steed will he   [735]
Henceforth bestride, – triumphantly
He stood upon the verdant sod,
Trusting himself to the earth, and God.
Rare sight to embolden and inspire!   205
Proud was the field of Sons and Sire; –   [740]
Of him the most; and, sooth to say,

[22] Raby Hall] large apartment above Raby Castle, held by the Neville family until 1570,
when it was seized by the Crown for Neville's part in the uprising.
[23] sixteen Thousand] thirteen thousand in MS 61.

No shape of man in all the array
So graced the sunshine of that day:
The monumental pomp of age   210
Was with this goodly Personage;   [745]
A Stature undepressed in size,
Unbent, which rather seemed to rise,
In open victory o'er the weight
Of seventy years, to higher height;   215
Magnific limbs of withered state, –   [750]
A face to fear and venerate, –
Eyes dark and strong, and on his head
Rich locks of silver hair, thick-spread,
Which a Brown Morion half-concealed,   220
Light as a Hunter's of the field;   [755]
And thus, with girdle round his waist,
Whereon the Banner-staff might rest:
At need, he stood, advancing high,
The glittering, floating Pageantry.   225

　　　　Who sees him? – many see, and One   [760]
With unparticipated gaze;
Who 'mong these Thousands Friend hath none,
And treads in solitary ways.
He, following wheresoe'er he might,   230
Hath watched the Banner from afar,   [765]
As Shepherds watch a lonely star,
Or Mariners the distant light
That guides them on a stormy night.
And now upon a chosen plot   235
Of rising ground, yon healthy spot!   [770]
He takes this day his far-off stand,
With breast unmailed, unweaponed hand.
– Bold is his aspect; but his eye
Is pregnant with anxiety,   240
While, like a Tutelary Power,   [775]
He stands there fixed, from hour to hour.
Yet sometimes, in more humble guise,
Stretched out upon the ground he lies,
As if it were his only task   245
Like Herdsman in the sun to bask,   [780]
Or by his Mantle's help to find
A shelter from the nipping wind;
And thus with short oblivion blest
His weary Spirits gather rest.   250
Again he lifts his eyes; and lo!   [785]

The pageant glancing to and fro;
And hope is wakened by the sight
That he thence may learn, ere fall of night,
Which way the tide is doomed to flow.   255

    To London were the Chieftains bent;   [790]
But what avails the bold intent?
A royal Army is gone forth
To quell the rising of the North;
They march with Dudley[27] at their head,   260
And, in ten day's space, will to York be led!   [795]
Can such a mighty host be raised
Thus suddenly and brought so near?
The Earls upon each other gazed;
And Neville was oppressed with fear;   265
For, though he bore a valiant Name,   [800]
His heart was of a timid frame;
And bold if both had been, yet they
Against so many might not stay.

    Word for retreat was giv'n – 'We yield'   270   [816]
Said Norton, 'then an unfought field;
Ev'n these poor eight of mine would stem'
(Half to himself and half to them
He spake) ' – would stem or quell a force
Ten times their number man and horse   275

[The 1808 text breaks off at this point in MS 61. The next fragment is drawn
from MS 62.]

Fragment 3: from *Part Three*

. . . She steeped, but not for Jesu's sake;
This Cross in tears: – by her, and One
Unworthier far, we are undone –
Her Brother was it who assailed   [885]
Her tender Spirit and prevailed.   5
While thus he brooded, music sweet
Was played to chear them in retreat;

[24] Ambrose Dudley, Earl of Warwick (1528–90), one of Elizabeth I's lieutenants appointed to suppress the uprising.

But Norton lingered in the rear: [895]
Thought followed thought – and, ere the last
Of that unhappy train was past,   10
Before him Francis did appear.

        'Now when 'tis not your aim to oppose',
Said he, 'in open field your Foes,   [900]
Now that from this decisive day
Your multitude must melt away,   15
An unarmed Man may come unblamed;
To ask a grace, that was not claimed
Long as your hopes were high; he now   [905]
May hither bring a fearless brow,
When his discountenance can do   20
No injury, may come to you.
Though in your cause no part I bear
Your indignation I can share;   [910]
Am grieved this backward march to see,
How careless and disorderly!   25
I scorn your Chieftains, Men who lead
And yet want courage at their need;
Then, look at them with open eyes!   [915]
Deserve they further sacrifice?
My Father! I would help to find   30
A place of shelter till the rage
Of cruel men do like the wind
Exhaust itself and sink to rest   [920]
Be Brother now to Brother joined!
Admit me in the equipage   35
Of your misfortunes, that at least,
Whatever fate remains behind,
I may bear witness in my breast   [925]
To your nobility of mind!'

        'Thou Enemy, my bane and blight!   40
Oh! bold to fight the Coward's fight
Against all good' – but why declare,
At length, the issue of this prayer?   [930]
Or how, from his depression raised
The Father on his Son had gazed;   45
Suffice it, that the Son gave way,
Nor strove that passion to allay;
Nor did he turn aside to prove   [935]
His Brothers' wisdom or their love;
But calmly from the spot withdrew,   50

The like endeavours to renew,
Should e'er a kindlier time ensue.[25]

Not otherwise than he had said,
As from the Royal power they fled
That followed close on their dismay,   55
Did this rash levy day by day
Dissolve; – while Neville's brow betrayed
A sadness visible to all;
For promise fails of Norfolk's aid,
Nor can Lord Dacre rise, the call   60
For him too suddenly was made.
Yet still in arms a few are left,
Though of their Chieftains now bereft;
And Norton to the last is true,
And, for the chearing of this few,   65
The Banner is by him displayed;
But what can save, who give them aid?
Though hope doth yet with some remain
The Scottish Border thus to gain.
And wandering in this wretched plight   70
Through wood, at fall of night,
In little knots, or Man by Man,
They seek for shelter where they can;
The Nortons who had chanced to espy
A Forest-lodge in a lonely glade,   75
Deserted now and half-decayed,
Turn to that shattered canopy
Their toil-worn steps, and together there
May sleep in covert from the air.

Yet One is left with unclosed eyes,   80
And, forced by anxious thought to rise,
Beside the door walks to and fro;
And yet Another, and the best,
Is near them in this time of rest,
A guard of whom they do not know,   85
'Tis Francis! – much he longs to entreat
(For he hath cause of dread this night)
That they would urge their weary feet
To yet a further, further flight,

---

[25] At this point the 1808 and 1815 texts diverge sharply. In 1815 Canto III ends here; 1808 continues with lines that have no equivalent elsewhere.

[The text in MS 62 breaks off here. We do not know how it continued but surviving drafts indicate that Francis made a third attempt to persuade his father to give up the rebellion, as fruitlessly as before. Parts Three and Four may then have gone on to describe Francis's yielding up of his brothers to the enemy (see pp. 264–6), and his own escape. Part Four concluded with the next fragment, from MS 62, which is almost the same as the equivalent lines in 1815.]

Fragment 4: from *Part Four*

These things, which thus had in the sight
And hearing past of him who stood
With Emily on the Watch Tower height,
In Rylstone's woeful neighbourhood,   [1365]
He told; and oftentimes with voice   5
Of power to encourage or rejoice;
For deepest sorrows that aspire
Go high, no transport ever higher.
'Yet, yet in this affliction', said   [1370]
The old Man to the silent Maid,   10
'Yet, Lady! heaven is good – the night
Shews yet a Star which is most bright,
Your Brother lives – he lives – is come
Perhaps already to his home;   [1375]
Then let us leave this dreary place.'   15
She yielded; and with gentle pace,
Though without one uplifted look,
To Rylstone Hall her way she took. –

[Part Four ended here, corresponding to the end of Canto V in the 1815 text. Nothing of 1808 Part Five is extant. The correspondent Canto VI in 1815 describes Francis' flight with the standard and his ignominious death at the hands of the soldiers near Bolton Abbey. The next fragment, from Part Six, is also from MS 62.]

Fragment 5: from *Part Six*

The walks and pools Neglect hath sown
With weeds, the bowers are overthrown,
Or have given way to slow mutation,   [1590]
While in their ancient habitation
The Norton name hath been unknown: 5

The lordly Mansion of its pride
Is stripped; the ravage hath spread wide
Through park and field, a perishing   [1595]
That mocks the gladness of the Spring!
And with this silent gloom agreeing   10
There is a joyless human Being,
Of aspect such as if the waste
Were under her dominion placed;   [1600]
Upon a primrose bank, her throne
Of quietness, She sits alone;   15
There seated may this Maid be seen,
Among the ruins of a wood,
Erewhile a Covert bright and green   [1605]
And where full many a brave tree stood,
That used to spread its boughs, and ring   20
With the sweet Birds' carrolling.
Behold her like a Virgin Queen
Neglecting in imperial state   [1610]
These outward images of fate,
And carrying inward a serene   25
And perfect sway, through many a thought
Of chance and change that hath been brought
To the subjection of a holy   [1615]
Though stern and rigorous melancholy!
The like authority, with grace   30
Of awfulness, is in her face,
There hath she fixed it; yet it seems
To o'ershadow by no native right   [1620]
That face, which cannot lose the gleams,
Lose utterly the tender gleams   35
Of gentleness and meek delight,
And loving kindness ever bright.
Such is her sovereign mien; – her dress,   [1625]
(A Vest, with woolen cincture tied,
A Hood of mountain wool undyed)   40
Is homely; fashioned to express
A wandering Pilgrim's humbleness.

    And she hath wandered, long and far,   [1630]
Beneath the light of sun and star,
Hath roamed in trouble and in grief,   45
Driven forward like a withered leaf;
Yea like a Ship, at random blown
To distant places and unknown.   [1635]
But now she dares to seek a Haven
Among her native wilds of Craven;   50

Hath seen again her Father's Roof,
And put her fortitude to proof;
The mighty sorrow hath been borne   [1640]
And she is thoroughly forlorn:
Her soul doth in itself stand fast   55
Sustained by memory of the past
And strength of Reason; held above
The infirmities of mortal love,   [1645]
Undaunted lofty, calm, and stable,
And awfully[26] impenetrable.[27]   60

        And so, beneath a mouldered Tree,
A self-surviving leafless Oak,
By unregarded age from stroke   [1650]
Of ravage saved, sate Emily.
There did she rest, with head reclined,   65
Herself most like a stately Flower,
(Such have I seen) whom chance of birth

[MS 62 breaks off at this point.]

The Prose 'Advertizement'

In addition to a working draft of the 1808 text, MS 61 contains fragments of
a prose 'Advertizement' entered during or immediately after composition of
the 1808 *White Doe*, which would have followed the poem had it been published at the time of its composition. Given the significance of what Wordsworth
says, which relates the poem back to *Lyrical Ballads*, and invokes some crucial
ideas associated with the Romantic imagination, it is remarkable that no effort
has previously been made to produce a reading text. To the best of my knowledge its only appearance in print is in the facsimiles and transcriptions of the
relevant manuscript pages at Cornell *White Doe* 185–203. A glance is sufficient to indicate one reason why academic editors have fought shy; it is fragmentary and chaotic, but not resistant to production of a clear reading text
(see figure 21 opposite).

---

[26] awfully] originally read 'wilfully'.
[27] In the Fenwick Note to this poem, Wordsworth remarked that Emily's triumph over
grief was gained 'not without aid from the communication with the inferior creature, which
often leads her thoughts to revolve upon the past with a tender and humanizing influence
that exalts rather than depresses her' (*FN* 33).

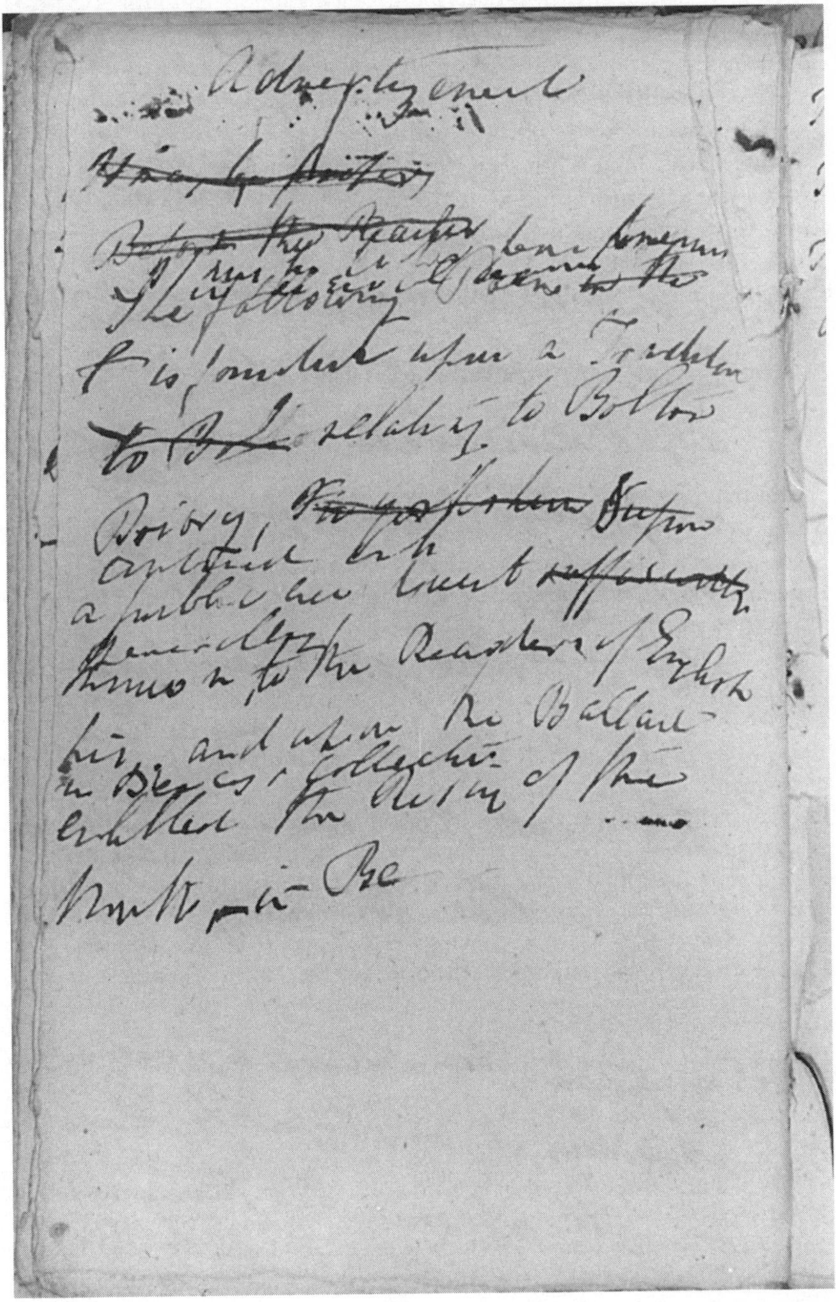

Figure 21. DC MS 61, 24v. *The White Doe of Rylstone*: rough draft of the 'Advertizement'.

My aim is to present the Advertizement as it might have appeared had Wordsworth used it as the basis for a final draft. As a rule I have respected deletions and accepted alternative readings when accompanied by cancellation marks. Interlined readings are accepted where accompanied by deletions or clear indication of their position within the text. On occasion, because of the nature of the draft, it has been necessary to retain deleted readings where Wordsworth has struck through particular words without providing replacements. All such readings are placed within square brackets. As above, authorial punctuation is retained, though on occasion it has been necessary to add essential pointing. Orthography is authorial, though ampersands are expanded to 'and'.

Fragment 1

Advertizement

The following Poem is founded upon a Tradition relating to Bolton Abbey, known to the Readers of English his[tories] and upon the Ballad in Percy's Collection entitled the Rising of the North.[1]
[Three or five stubs follow this page in the notebook.]

Fragment 2

I have thought it proper to annex the Ballad on which the for[e]going tale is partly founded, and with Dr Percy's prefatory account. I should reproach myself with ingratitude if I did not on the present occasion express my gratitude to Dr Percy for the pleasure which His *Reliques of Antient Poetry*[2] have given me, and for the instruction which I have derived from them: [3] [with this acknowledgment I shall at present rest contented and not give way [to][4] a strong inclination which I feel to give a history [of Poetry].[5] I am strongly tempted to add more but this is not the place.]

    Happening in the course of last summer to be on a visit to some Friends in

---

[1] This sentence seems to have provided the basis for another in the published text of 1815, which is the preface to a reprint of Percy's text; see Cornell *White Doe* 150–6.
[2] Wordsworth first read Percy at Hawkshead; see *WR* i 110. He did not acquire his own copy until 1798. He also comments on Percy in the Essay, Supplementary to the Preface, 1815 (*Prose Works* iii 75–7).
[3] Text from here to the end of the paragraph is deleted in the MS.
[4] to] 'by' in the MS, but emended for sense.
[5] Deleted in the MS.

Yorkshire I was by them conducted to Bolton Priory or Abbey as it is generally called; and from the impression of that day the foregoing owes its birth. The beautiful Ruin, the delicious Vale which it adorns, the River which flows by it, the chasm of the Strid and its accompanying history and tradition,[6] Barden Tower of Lord Clifford, the Shepherd whose History had interested me from my earliest childhood, upon all those objects I looked with that high delight which when it was afterwards recollected in tranquillity, I felt to be worthy of being recorded in Verse; [for the benefit of][7] my own affections; and of those who think and feel as I do. My own affections prompted me to this labour and I was confident that those who think and feel as I do would be grateful for the pleasure which I should impart to them, with new local beauties of landscape and local remembrances. I have mentioned a high moral purpose and with a high regard to this also I have the same confidence, as that I shall please those whose affections are pure and whose imagination is vigorous. Others I refer to the best models among the antient Greeks, to the Latin writers before the Augustan age, to Chaucer, Spenser, Shakespear and Milton, and lastly though of at least [as much][8] importance considered as a Composition to the Bible,[9] and when they have studied these
[This sentence is unfinished.]
Beyond this I have no wish except [. . .][10] an earnest that what I write will live and continue to purify the affections and to strengthen the Imaginations of my fellow beings.

Fragment 3

For though an anapestic verse of twelve syllables, with its four long and accompany[ing] eight short syllables does in fact take up more time to pronounce than a trochaeic Verse of seven, with its four, and accompanying three short syllables, nevertheless the rapidity or hurry given to the verse by the additional short syllables causes a delusion which however different as the Verses may be as to number of syllables reduces the two Verses as to the feeling of time within the same limits. As to the style after what has been said in the preface to the *Lyrical Ballads* I have nothing to add. The only Readers whom I wished to please are those whose affections are representative of the affections of human nature [clear healthy and independent].[11]

---

6 The chasm and its story provided the subject for Wordsworth's 'The Force of Prayer', published with the *White Doe* in 1815; see Cornell *White Doe* 147–9.
7 Deleted in the MS, but necessary for sense.
8 Not in the MS.
9 Bible] 'bibble' in the MS. Wordsworth praises tautology in the Bible in the Note to 'The Thorn' and in the 1815 Preface (Cornell *Lyrical Ballads* 351; *Prose Works* iii 34).
10 The draft is extremely confused at this point.
11 clear healthy and independent] deleted in the MS.

Fragment 4[12]

I cannot help availing myself of this opportunity of recommending to the notice
of all lovers of beautiful Scenery this truly enchanting spot and at the same time
must take the liberty of ex[h]orting improvers of grounds to study the example
which in the management of this place has been given by the Rev Mr Carr[13] who
has here wrought with an invisible hand of art, in the very spirit of nature. The
situation and neig[hbourhood] of Bolton Priory cannot be better described than
in the words of Dr W[hitaker] in his *His[tory] and Ant[iquities] of the De[a]nery
of Craven in the County of York* by far the best book of the kind I ever read.[14]

<hr />

[12]   At this point Wordsworth handed the pen to Mary Wordsworth and dictated the remainder of the Advertizement to her.
[13]   Wordsworth met the Revd William Carr again in London, in late March 1808, when he
told the poet that he was 'fatter than when he saw me at Bolton' (*Supp.* 12).
[14]   Wordsworth first saw the book in September 1807 at the earliest; see *WR* ii 239–40.

Bibliography

The bibliography lists works under the following headings:
1 Primary Texts: Coleridge, Southey and the Wordsworth Family
2 Primary Texts: Other Writers
3 Critical, Biographical and Bibliographical Sources

1   Primary Texts: Coleridge, Southey and the Wordsworth Family

Coleridge, Samuel Taylor. *The Collected Works of Samuel Taylor Coleridge*. General Editor: Kathleen Coburn. Bollingen Series 75. Princeton, NJ: Princeton University Press.
I *Lectures 1795 on Politics and Religion*, ed. Lewis Patton and Peter Mann. 1971.
II *The Watchman*, ed. Lewis Patton. 1970.
III *Essays on His Times*, ed. David V. Erdman. 3 vols. 1978.
IV *The Friend*, ed. Barbara Rooke. 2 vols. 1969.
V *Lectures 1808–1819 On Literature*, ed. R. A. Foakes. 2 vols. 1987.
VI *Lay Sermons*, ed R. J. White. 1972.
VII *Biographia Literaria*, ed. James Engell and W. Jackson Bate. 2 vols. 1983.
VIII *Lectures 1818–1819 On the History of Philosophy*, ed. J. R. de J. Jackson. 2 vols. 2000.
IX *Aids to Reflection*, ed. John Beer. 1993.
X *On the Constitution of the Church and State*, ed. John Colmer. 1976.
XI *Shorter Works and Fragments*, ed. H. J. Jackson and J. R. de J. Jackson. 2 vols. 1995.
XII *Marginalia*, ed. George Whalley and H. J. Jackson. 6 vols. 1980– .
XIII *Logic*. ed. J. R. de J. Jackson. 1981.
XIV. *Table Talk*, ed. Carl Woodring. 2 vols. 1990.
Fears in Solitude, France an Ode, and Frost at Midnight. London, 1798
The Letters of Samuel Taylor Coleridge, ed. E. L. Griggs. 6 vols. Oxford: Clarendon Press, 1956–71.
Coleridge's Miscellaneous Criticism, ed. Thomas Middleton Raysor. Cambridge, MA.: Harvard University Press, 1936.

The Notebooks of Samuel Taylor Coleridge, ed. Kathleen Coburn et al. Bollingen Series 50. 5 vols. New York: Pantheon Books, 1957–.

The Poetical Works of Samuel Taylor Coleridge, ed. E. H. Coleridge. 2 vols. Oxford: Clarendon Press, 1912.

Coleridge's Dejection, ed. Stephen Maxfield Parrish. Ithaca, NY: Cornell University Press, 1988.

Coleridge's Sonnets from Various Authors bound with Revd. W. L. Bowles' Sonnets, ed. Paul Zall. Glendale, CA: La Siesta Press, 1968.

Southey, Robert. *New Letters of Robert Southey 1792–1838*, ed. Kenneth Curry. 2 vols. New York and London: Columbia University Press, 1965.

The Life and Correspondence of the Late Robert Southey, ed. Revd Charles Cuthbert Southey. 6 vols. London: Longman, 1850.

The Letters of Robert Southey to John May, ed. Charles Ramos. Austin, TX: Jenkins, 1976.

Poems. Bristol: Joseph Cottle, 1797.

The Poetical Works of Robert Southey. Paris: A. & W. Galignani, 1829.

Selections from the Letters of Robert Southey, &c. &c. &c, ed. John Wood Warter. 4 vols. London: Longman, 1856.

Peter Mann. 'Two Unpublished Letters of Robert Southey'. *N&Q* NS 22 (1975) 397–9.

Wordsworth, William. *The Cornell Wordsworth*. General Editor: Stephen M. Parrish. Ithaca, NY: Cornell University Press.

Early Poems and Fragments, 1785–1797, ed. Carol Landon and Jared Curtis. 1997.

An Evening Walk, ed. James Averill. 1984.

Descriptive Sketches, ed. Eric Birdsall. 1984.

The Salisbury Plain Poems, ed. Stephen Gill. 1975.

The Borderers, ed. Robert Osborn. 1982.

The Ruined Cottage and The Pedlar, ed. James Butler. 1979.

Lyrical Ballads, and Other Poems, 1797–1800, ed. James Butler and Karen Green. 1992.

The Prelude, 1798–1799, ed. Stephen Parrish. 1979.

Peter Bell, ed. John Jordan. 1985.

Home at Grasmere, ed. Beth Darlington. 1977.

Poems in Two Volumes, and Other Poems, 1800–1807, ed. Jared Curtis. 1985.

The Thirteen-Book Prelude, ed. Mark L. Reed. 2 vols. 1991.

Benjamin the Waggoner, ed. Paul Betz. 1981.

The White Doe of Rylstone, ed. Kristine Dugas. 1988.

The Tuft of Primroses, with other late poems for The Recluse, ed. Joseph Kishel. 1986.

Shorter Poems, 1807–1820, ed. Carl H. Ketcham. 1989.

Translations of Chaucer and Virgil, ed. Bruce Graver. 1998.

Last Poems, 1821–1850, ed. Jared Curtis. 1999.

The Fourteen-Book Prelude, ed. W. J. B. Owen. 1985.

Butler, James A. 'Wordsworth, Cottle, and the *Lyrical Ballads*, Five Letters, 1797–1800'. *JEGP* 75 (1976) 139–53.

The Fenwick Notes of William Wordsworth, ed. Jared Curtis. London: Bristol Classical Press, 1993.

The Letters of William and Dorothy Wordsworth: The Early Years 1787–1805, ed. Ernest De Selincourt. rev. Chester L. Shaver. Oxford: Clarendon Press, 1967.

The Letters of William and Dorothy Wordsworth: The Middle Years 1806–1820, ed. Ernest De Selincourt; rev. Mary Moorman and Alan G. Hill. 2 vols. Oxford: Clarendon Press, 1969–70.

The Letters of William and Dorothy Wordsworth: The Later Years 1821–1853, ed. Ernest De Selincourt; rev. Alan G. Hill. 4 vols. Oxford: Clarendon Press, 1978–88.

The Letters of William and Dorothy Wordsworth: A Supplement of New Letters, ed. Alan G. Hill. Oxford: Clarendon Press, 1993.

The Love Letters of William and Mary Wordsworth, ed. Beth Darlington. Ithaca, NY: Cornell University Press, 1981.

Peacock, Markham L. *The Critical Opinions of William Wordsworth*. Baltimore, MD: Johns Hopkins University Press, 1950.

The Poetical Works of William Wordsworth, ed. Ernest De Selincourt and Helen Darbishire. 5 vols. Oxford: Clarendon Press, 1940–9.

The Prose Works of William Wordsworth, ed. Revd Alexander B. Grosart. 3 vols. London: Edward Moxon, Son, and Co., 1876.

The Prose Works of William Wordsworth, ed. W. J. B. Owen and Jane Worthington Smyser. 3 vols. Oxford: Clarendon Press, 1974.

The White Doe of Rylstone: A Critical Edition, ed. Alice Pattee Comparetti. Ithaca, NY: Cornell University Press, 1940.

William Wordsworth: The Five-Book Prelude, ed. Duncan Wu. Oxford: Blackwell, 1997.

William Wordsworth: The Prelude, or Growth of a Poet's Mind, ed. E. De Selincourt; rev. Helen Darbishire. 2nd edn. Oxford: Clarendon Press, 1959.

William Wordsworth: The PreludeThe 1805 Text, ed. Ernest De Selincourt, corrected by Stephen Gill. Oxford: Oxford University Press, 1970.

William Wordsworth: The Prelude 1799, 1805, 1850, ed. Jonathan Wordsworth, M. H. Abrams and Stephen Gill. New York, NY: W. W. Norton, 1979.

William Wordsworth: The Prelude The Four Texts (1798, 1799, 1805, 1850), ed. Jonathan Wordsworth. London: Penguin, 1995.

Wordsworth and Reed: The Poet's Correspondence with his American Editor: 1836–1850, ed. Leslie Nathan Broughton. Ithaca, NY: Cornell University Press, 1933.

Wordsworth: Poetical Works, ed. Thomas Hutchinson; rev. Ernest De Selincourt. Oxford: Oxford University Press, 1978.

Journals of Dorothy Wordsworth, ed. Ernest De Selincourt. 2 vols. London: Macmillan & Co. Ltd., 1941.

Dorothy Wordsworth: The Grasmere Journals, ed. Pamela Woof. Oxford: Clarendon Press, 1991.

Hutchinson, Sara. *The Letters of Sara Hutchinson*, ed. Kathleen Coburn. London: Routledge and Kegan Paul, 1954.

The Letters of John Wordsworth, ed. Carl H. Ketcham. Ithaca, NY: Cornell University Press, 1969.

The Letters of Mary Wordsworth 1800–1855, ed. Mary E. Burton. Oxford: Clarendon Press, 1958.

2   Primary Texts: Other Writers

Arnold, Matthew. *The Poems of Matthew Arnold*, ed. Kenneth Allott. London: Longman, 1965.

Beattie, James. *Dissertations Moral and Critical*. London, 1783.

—— 'An Extract from *Illustrations on Sublimity*, in the same Work'. *Annual Register* 26 (1783) ii 130–6.

—— *The Minstrel, in Two Books: with some other poems*. London, 1779.

—— *Original Poems and Translations*. London, 1760.

Beccaria Bonesara, Cesare. *An Essay on Crimes and Punishments*, trans. Anon. London, 1767.

Beckford, William. *Dreams, Waking Thoughts and Incidents*, ed. Robert Gemmett. Rutherford, NJ: Farleigh Dickinson University Press, 1971.

Blake, William. *The Complete Poetry and Prose of William Blake*, ed. David V. Erdman, commentary by Harold Bloom. Garden City, NY: Anchor Books, 1982.

Bowlby, John. *Attachment and Loss, Volume III: Loss, Sadness and Depression*. Harmondsworth: Penguin, 1981.

Bowles, William Lisle. *Fourteen Sonnets, Elegiac and Descriptive*. Bath, 1789.

—— *Sonnets Written Chiefly on Picturesque Spots During a Tour*. Bath, 1789.

Brydone, Patrick. *A Tour through Sicily and Malta in a Series of Letters to William Beckford, Esq. of Somerly in Suffolk*. 2 vols. Dublin, 1773.

Burke, Edmund. *A Philosophical Enquiry into the Origin of our Ideas of the Sublime and Beautiful*, ed. James T. Boulton. 2nd edn. Oxford: Basil Blackwell, 1987.

—— *A Letter from Mr Burke, to a Member of the National Assembly*. Paris and London, 1791.

Burns, Robert. *The Kilmarnock Poems*, ed. Donald A. Low. London: Dent, 1985.

Byron, George Gordon, Lord. *The Complete Poetical Works*, ed. Jerome J. McGann and Barry Weller. 7 vols. Oxford: Clarendon Press, 1980–93.

—— *Byron's Letters and Journals*, ed. Leslie A. Marchand. 13 vols. London: John Murray, 1973–94.

Collins, William. *Thomas Gray and William Collins: Poetical Works*, ed. Roger Lonsdale. Oxford: Oxford University Press, 1977.

—— *The Poems of Gray, Collins and Goldsmith*, ed. Roger Lonsdale. Longman Annotated English Poets Series. London: Longman, 1969.

—— *The Works of William Collins*, ed. Richard Wendorf and Charles Ryskamp. Oxford: Clarendon Press, 1979.

Constable, John. *John Constable's Correspondence*, ed. R. B. Beckett. 6 vols. Ipswich: Suffolk Records Society, 1961–8.

Cottle, Joseph. *Alfred*. London, 1800.

—— *Early Recollections, Chiefly Relating to the Late Samuel Taylor Coleridge, During his Long Residence in Bristol*. 2 vols. London, 1837.

—— *Reminiscences of Samuel Taylor Coleridge and Robert Southey*. London, 1847.

—— *Malvern Hills: A Poem*. London, 1798.

Cowper, William. *The Poems of William Cowper*, ed. John D. Baird and Charles Ryskamp. 3 vols. Oxford: Clarendon Press, 1980–95.

Crowe, William. *Lewesdon Hill.* Oxford, 1788.

Darwin, Erasmus. *Zöonomia.* 2 vols. London, 1794–6.

De Quincey, Thomas. *Collected Writings,* ed. David Masson. 14 vols. Edinburgh: A. & C. Black, 1889–90.

—— 'Lake Reminiscences, From 1807 to 1830. No. III. – William Wordsworth – Continued'. *Tait's Edinburgh Magazine* 6 (April 1839) 246–54.

Dryden, John. *Poems,* ed. James Kinsley. 4 vols. Oxford: Clarendon Press, 1958.

—— *Essays,* ed. W. P. Ker. 2 vols. Oxford: Clarendon Press, 1900.

Estlin, John Prior. *The Nature and the Causes of Atheism, Pointed out in a Discourse, Delivered at the Chapel in Lewin's-Mead, Bristol.* Bristol, 1797.

Farington, Joseph. *The Diary of Joseph Farington,* ed. Kenneth Garlick, Angus Macintyre and Kathryn Cave. 16 vols. New Haven: Yale University Press, 1979–84.

Farquhar, George, *The Beaux' Stratagem.* London, 1707.

Fawcett, Joseph. *The Art of War. A Poem.* London, 1795.

Field, Barron. *Barron Field's Memoirs of Wordsworth,* ed. Geoffrey Little. Sydney: Sydney University Press, 1975.

Freud, Sigmund. *The Standard Edition of the Complete Works of Sigmund Freud,* ed. James Strachey and Anna Freud. 24 vols. London: Hogarth Press and the Institute of Psycho-Analysis, 1953–74.

Gilpin, William. *Observations, Relative Chiefly to Picturesque Beauty, Made in the Year 1772, in Several Parts of England; Particularly the Mountains and Lakes of Cumberland and Westmoreland.* 2 vols. London, 1786.

—— *Observations, Relative Chiefly to Picturesque Beauty, Made in the Year 1776, on Several Parts of Great Britain; Particularly the High-Lands of Scotland.* 2 vols. London, 1789.

Godwin, William. *Caleb Williams,* ed. David McCracken. Oxford: Oxford University Press, 1982.

Gray, Thomas. *The Poems of Mr Gray,* ed. William Mason. 2 vols. York, 1775.

Haydon, Benjamin Robert. *The Diary of Benjamin Robert Haydon,* ed. Willard Bissell Pope. 5 vols. Cambridge, MA: Harvard University Press, 1960–3.

Hazlitt, William. *Selected Writings,* ed. Duncan Wu. 9 vols. London: Pickering and Chatto, 1998.

—— *Works,* ed. P. P. Howe. 21 vols. London: Dent, 1930–4.

Heaney, Seamus. *The Cure at Troy.* London: Faber and Faber, 1990.

Isola, Agostino. *Pieces Selected From the Italian Poets.* 2nd edn. Cambridge, 1784.

Jonson, Ben. *The Complete Poems,* ed. George Parfitt. Harmondsworth: Penguin, 1975.

Keats, John. *The Poems of John Keats,* ed. Jack Stillinger. Cambridge, MA: Harvard University Press, 1978.

Klein, Melanie. *The Selected Melanie Klein,* ed. Juliet Mitchell. Harmondsworth: Penguin, 1986.

Lamb, Charles. *The Letters of Charles and Mary Anne Lamb 1796–1817,* ed. Edwin W. Marrs, Jr. 3 vols. Ithaca, NY: Cornell University Press, 1975–8.

—— *The Letters of Charles and Mary Lamb 1796–1843,* ed. E. V. Lucas. London: Dent & Methuen, 1935.

Langhorne, John. *The Country Justice.* London, 1774–7.

—— *Owen of Carron.* London, 1778.

—— *Poetical Works*. 2 vols. London, 1766.

Lockhart, John Gibson. *Memoirs of the Life of Sir Walter Scott*. 2nd edn. Edinburgh, 1842.

Louvet de Couvray, Jean-Baptiste. *Narrative of the Dangers to Which I have been Exposed, since the 31st of May, 1793*, trans. Anon. London, 1795.

Lyttelton, George, Baron Lyttelton. *The Works of George Lord Lyttelton*. London, 1774.

Machiavelli, Niccolò. *Machiavel's Discourses upon the First Decade of T. Livius*, trans. Edward Dacres. 2nd edn. London, 1674.

Mackintosh, James. *Vindiciæ Gallicæ*. London, 1791.

Macpherson, James. *Fingal: An Ancient Epic Poem*. London, 1762.

—— *Temora: An Ancient Epic Poem*. London, 1763.

Marvell, Andrew. *The Poems and Letters of Andrew Marvell*, ed. H. M. Margoliouth, rev. Pierre Legouis with the collaboration of E. E. Duncan-Jones. 3rd edn. 2 vols. Oxford: Clarendon Press, 1971.

—— *The Works of Andrew Marvell, Esq*, ed. Thomas Cooke. 2 vols. London, 1772.

Milton, John. *The Poetical Works of John Milton*, ed. Helen Darbishire. 2 vols. Oxford: Clarendon Press, 1952–5.

—— *Paradise Lost. A Poem in Twelve Books*, ed. Thomas Newton. London, 1763.

—— *Paradise Lost and Complete Shorter Poems*, ed. Alastair Fowler and John Carey. 2 vols. 2nd edn. London: Longman, 1997–8.

Moore, Thomas. *Memoirs, Journal, and Correspondence of Thomas Moore*, ed. Rt. Hon. Lord John Russell, MP. 8 vols. London, 1853–6.

Ovid. *Ovid's Metamorphosis Englished*, trans. George Sandys. Oxford, 1632.

Percy, Thomas. *Reliques of Ancient English Poetry*. 3 vols. London, 1765.

Pope, Alexander. *The Twickenham Edition of the Works of Alexander Pope*. General editor John Butt. London: Methuen.

I *Pastoral Poetry and An Essay on Criticism*, ed. E. Audra and Aubrey Williams. 1961.
II *The Rape of the Lock*, ed. Geoffrey Tillotson. 3rd edn. 1962.
III i *An Essay on Man*, ed. Maynard Mack. 1950.
III ii *Epistles to Several Persons*, ed. F. W. Bateson. 2nd edn. 1961.
IV *Imitations of Horace*, ed. John Butt. 2nd edn. 1953.
VII–VIII *The Iliad*, ed. Maynard Mack. 1967.
IX–X *The Odyssey*, ed. Maynard Mack. 1967.

Racine, Jean. *Athaliah*, trans. William Duncombe. 2nd edn. London, 1726.

Robberds, J. W. (ed.) *A Memoir of the Life and Writings of the Late William Taylor of Norwich*. 2 vols. London, 1843.

Robinson, Henry Crabb. *Henry Crabb Robinson on Books and Their Writers*, ed. Edith J. Morley. 3 vols. London: Dent, 1938.

—— *Diary, Reminiscences, and Correspondence of Henry Crabb Robinson*, ed. Thomas Sadler. 3 vols. London, 1869.

—— *The Correspondence of Henry Crabb Robinson with the Wordsworth Circle (1808–1866)*, ed. Edith J. Morley. 2 vols. Oxford: Clarendon Press, 1927.

Schiller, Johann Christoph Friedrich von. *The Robbers*, trans. Alexander Fraser Tytler. London, 1792.

Shakespeare, William. *The Riverside Shakespeare*, ed. G. Blakemore Evans. Boston: Houghton Mifflin, 1974.

Shaw, Cuthbert. *Monody to the Memory of a Young Lady who Died in Child-bed.* London, 1768.

Shelley, Mary. *The Journals of Mary Shelley 1814–1844,* ed. Paula R. Feldman and Diana Scott-Kilvert. 2 vols. Oxford: Clarendon Press, 1987.

Smith, Charlotte. *Elegiac Sonnets.* 3rd edn. London, 1786.

Styron, William. *Darkness Visible: A Memoir of Madness.* London: Jonathan Cape, 1991.

Tarkovsky, Andrey. *Sculpting in Time: Reflections on the Cinema,* trans. Kitty Hunter-Blair. London: Bodley Head, 1986.

Tennyson, Alfred Lord. *The Poems of Tennyson,* ed. Christopher Ricks. London: Longmans, Green, 1969.

Troyes, Chrétien de. *The Complete Romances,* trans. David Staines. Bloomington: Indiana University Press, 1993.

Vaughan, Henry. *The Complete Poems,* ed. Alan Rudrum. Harmondsworth: Penguin, 1976.

Virgil. *Eclogues, Georgics, Aeneid, 1–6,* trans. H. Rushton Fairclough. Loeb Classical Library. 2nd edn. Cambridge, MA: Harvard University Press. 1986.

—— *Aeneid 7–12, The Minor Poems,* Trans. H. Rushton Fairclough. Loeb Classical Library. 2nd edn. Cambridge, MA: Harvard University Press. 1986.

—— *The Bucolicks of Virgil, with an English Translation and Notes,* trans. John Martyn. 2nd edn. London, 1749.

—— *The Georgicks of Virgil, with an English Translation and Notes,* trans. John Martyn. 3rd edn. London, 1750.

—— *Georgics Books I–IV,* ed. Richard F. Thomas. Cambridge Greek and Latin Classics. 2 vols. Cambridge: Cambridge University Press. 1988.

—— *The Works of Virgil. In English Verse. The Aeneid Translated By the Rev. Mr. Christopher Pitt, The Eclogues and Georgics, with Notes on the Whole, By the Rev. Mr Joseph Warton,* Trans. Joseph Warton. 4 vols. London, 1758.

Wilkinson, Joshua Lucock. *Political Facts, Collected in a Tour, in the Month of August, September, and October, 1793, Along the Frontiers of France; with Reflexions on the Same.* London, 1793.

—— *The Wanderer.* London, 1795.

—— trans. *State of France, in May, 1794, by Le Comte de Montgaillard.* London, 1794.

Williams, Helen Maria. *Poems.* 2 vols. London, 1786.

—— *Letters written in France in the summer of 1790.* London, 1790.

Yeats, William Butler. *Selected Criticism and Prose,* ed. A. Norman Jeffares. London: Pan Books, 1980.

Young, Edward. *Night Thoughts,* ed. Stephen Cornford. Cambridge: Cambridge University Press, 1989.

3 Critical, Biographical and Bibliographical Sources

Ashton, Rosemary. *The Life of Samuel Taylor Coleridge.* Oxford: Blackwell, 1996.

Averill, James H. *Wordsworth and the Poetry of Human Suffering.* Ithaca, NY: Cornell University Press, 1980.

Bartlett, Phyllis. 'A Critical and Textual Study of Wordsworth's An Evening Walk and Descriptive Sketches'. B.Litt. thesis, University of Oxford, 1928.

Bate, Jonathan. *Shakespeare and the English Romantic Imagination*. Oxford: Clarendon Press, 1986.

—— *Romantic Ecology*. London: Routledge, 1991.

Bateson, F. W. *Wordsworth: A Re-Interpretation*. London: Longman, 1954.

Bauschatz, Paul. 'Coleridge, Wordsworth, and Bowles'. *Style* 27 (Spring 1993) 17–40.

Beatty, Arthur. 'Joseph Fawcett: The Art of War'. *University of Wisconsin Studies in Language and Literature* 2 (1918) 224–69.

—— '"The Borderers" and "The Ancient Mariner"'. *TLS* (29 Feb. 1936) 184.

—— *William Wordsworth: His Doctrine and Art in Their Historical Relations*. Madison: University of Wisconsin, 1922.

Beer, John. 'William Ellery Channing Visits the Lake Poets'. *RES* 42 (1991) 211–26.

Betz, Paul Frederick. 'The Elegiac Mode in the Poetry of William Wordsworth: A Commentary on Selected Verse, 1786–1805, with a critical edition'. Ph.D. thesis, Cornell University, 1965.

Bewell, Alan. *Wordsworth and the Enlightenment: Nature, Man, and Society in the Experimental Poetry*. New Haven and London: Yale University Press, 1989.

Bicentenary Wordsworth Studies, ed. Jonathan Wordsworth. Ithaca, NY: Cornell University Press, 1970.

Boulger, James D. *The Calvinist Temper in English Poetry*. The Hague: Mouton, 1980.

Bromwich, David, *A Choice of Inheritance: Self and Community from Edmund Burke to Robert Frost*. Cambridge, MA: Harvard University Press, 1989.

—— *Disowned by Memory: Wordsworth's Poetry of the 1790s*. Chicago: University of Chicago Press, 1998.

—— 'Revolutionary Justice and Wordsworth's *Borderers*'. *Raritan* 13 (Winter 1994) 1–24.

Broughton, Leslie Nathan. *The Theocritean Element in the Works of William Wordsworth*. Halle: Max Niemeyer, 1920.

Butler, James A. 'Tourist or Native Son: Wordsworth's Homecomings of 1799–1800'. *Nineteenth-Century Literature* 51 (1996) 1–15.

Byatt, A. S. *Unruly Times: Wordsworth and Coleridge in their Time*. London: Hogarth Press, 1989.

Carlisle, Nicholas. *A Concise Description of the Endowed Grammar Schools in England and Wales*. 2 vols. London, 1818.

Carnall, Geoffrey. *Southey and His Age*. Oxford: Clarendon Press, 1960.

—— 'The Idiot Boy'. *N&Q* 201 (1956) 81–2.

Chandler, James. *Wordsworth's Second Nature: A Study of the Poetry and Politics*. Chicago: University of Chicago Press, 1984.

Chard, Leslie F., II. *Dissenting Republican: Wordsworth's Early Life and Thought in their Political Context*. The Hague: Mouton, 1972.

—— 'Joseph Johnson: Father of the Book Trade'. *BNYPL* 79 (1975–6) 51–82.

Christie, Ian R. *Stress and Stability in Late Eighteenth-Century Britain: Reflections on the British Avoidance of Revolution*. Oxford: Clarendon Press, 1984.

Clancey, Richard W. *Wordsworth's Classical Undersong: Education, Rhetoric, and Poetic Truth*. Basingstoke: Macmillan, 2000.

Clayden, P. W. *The Early Life of Samuel Rogers*. London, 1887.

Coe, Charles Norton. *Wordsworth and the Literature of Travel*. New Haven: Yale University Press, 1953.

Coleridge's Imagination, ed. Richard Gravil, Lucy Newlyn and Nicholas Roe. Cambridge: Cambridge University Press, 1985.

Cottle, Basil. 'The Life (1770–1853), Writings, and Literary Relationships of Joseph Cottle of Bristol'. Ph.D. thesis, University of Bristol, 1958.

Courtney, Winifred F. *Young Charles Lamb 1775–1802*. London: Macmillan, 1982.

Crum, M. C. 'The Life of Basil Montagu'. B.Litt. thesis, University of Oxford, 1950.

Curry, Kenneth. *The Contributions of Robert Southey to the Morning Post*. Alabama: University of Alabama Press, 1984.

Curtis, Jared. 'Wordsworth and Earlier English Poetry'. *Cornell Library Journal* 1 (1966) 28–39.

—— 'Wordsworth, Coleridge, and *Lines, left upon a Seat in a Yew-tree*'. *Bulletin of Research in the Humanities* 87 (1986–7) 482–8.

—— *Wordsworth's Experiments with Tradition: The Lyric Poems of 1802 with texts of the poems based on early manuscripts*. Ithaca, NY: Cornell University Press, 1971.

Davies, Hugh Sykes. *Wordsworth and the Worth of Words*. Cambridge: Cambridge University Press, 1986.

Duffy, Edward. *Rousseau in England*. London: University of California Press, 1979.

Erdman, David V. 'Coleridge, Wordsworth, and the Wedgwood Fund'. *BNYPL* 60 (1956) 425–43, 487–507.

—— *Commerce des Lumières: John Oswald and the British in Paris, 1790–1793*. Columbia: University of Missouri Press, 1986.

—— Immoral Acts of a Library Cormorant: the Extent of Coleridge's Contributions to the *Critical Review*'. *BNYPL* 63 (1959) 433–54, 515–30, 575–87.

Evans, Bergen, and Pinney, Hester. 'Racedown and the Wordsworths'. *RES* 8 (1932) 1–18.

Finch, John Alban. 'Wordsworth, Coleridge, and The Recluse, 1798–1814'. Ph.D. thesis, Cornell University, 1964.

Fink, Z. S. *The Early Wordsworthian Milieu*. Oxford: Clarendon Press, 1958.

—— 'Wordsworth and the English Republican Tradition'. *JEGP* 47 (1948) 107–26.

Foxon, D. F. 'The Printing of *Lyrical Ballads*, 1798'. *The Library*, ser. 5, 9 (1954) 221–41.

Frye, Northrop. *The Great Code: The Bible and Literature*. London: Routledge and Kegan Paul, 1982.

Fullmer, June Z. *Sir Humphry Davy's Published Works*. Cambridge, MA: Harvard University Press, 1969.

Gibson, Alexander Craig. *The Folk-Speech of Cumberland*. London and Carlisle, 1880.

Gilchrist, J., and Murray, W. J. *The Press in the French Revolution*. Melbourne and London: Cheshire and Ginn, 1971.

Gill, Stephen. *William Wordsworth: A Life*. Oxford: Clarendon Press, 1989.

—— *Wordsworth and the Victorians*. Oxford: Clarendon Press, 1998.

—— *Wordsworth: The Prelude*. Cambridge: Cambridge University Press, 1991.

—— '"Affinities Preserved": Poetic Self-Reference in Wordsworth'. *SIR* 24 (1986) 531–49.

—— 'Wordsworth's Poems: The Question of Text', *RES* 34 (1983) 172–89.

Gittings, Robert, and Manton, Jo. *Dorothy Wordsworth*. Oxford: Clarendon Press, 1985.

Gordon, Mary. *'Christopher North': A Memoir of John Wilson*. 2 vols. Edinburgh, 1862.

Graver, Bruce Edward. 'Wordsworth's Translations from Latin Poetry'. Ph.D. thesis, University of North Carolina, 1983.

——'Wordsworth and the Romantic art of Translation'. *WC* 17 (1986) 169–74.

Greaves, Margaret. *Regency Patron: Sir George Beaumont*. London: Methuen, 1966.

Hamilton, Paul. *Wordsworth*. Brighton: Harvester Press, 1986.

Hartman, Geoffrey H. *Wordsworth's Poetry 1787–1814*. New Haven: Yale University Press, 1964.

—— *The Unmediated Vision: An Interpretation of Wordsworth, Hopkins, Rilke, and Valéry*. New Haven: Yale University Press, 1954

—— *Beyond Formalism: Literary Essays 1958–1970*. New Haven: Yale University Press, 1970.

—— *The Unremarkable Wordsworth*. London: Methuen, 1987.

Hearn, Ronald B. *The Road to Rydal Mount: A Survey of William Wordsworth's Reading*. Salzburg: Universität Salzburg, 1973.

Holmes, Richard. *Coleridge: Early Visions*. London: Hodder and Stoughton, 1989.

—— *Coleridge: Darker Reflections*. London: HarperCollins, 1998.

Hunt, Bishop C., Jr. 'Wordsworth and Charlotte Smith'. *WC* 1 (1970) 85–103.

—— 'Wordsworth's Marginalia in Dove Cottage, to 1800: A Study of his Relationship to Charlotte Smith and Milton'. B.Litt. thesis, University of Oxford, 1965.

—— 'Wordsworth's Marginalia on *Paradise Lost*'. *BNYPL* 73 (1969) 167–83.

Jacobus, Mary. *Tradition and Experiment in Lyrical Ballads, 1798*. Oxford: Clarendon Press, 1976.

—— '"Tintern Abbey" and Topographical Prose'. *N&Q* NS 18 (1971) 366–9.

Jay, Eileen. *Wordsworth at Colthouse*. Kendal: Westmorland Gazette, 1981.

Jaye, Michael C., 'William Wordsworth's Alfoxden Notebook: 1798', in *The Evidence of the Imagination: Studies of Interactions between Life and Art in English Romantic Literature*, ed. Donald H. Reiman, Michael C. Jaye, and Betty T. Bennett, with the assistance of Doucet Devin Fischer and Ricki B. Herzfeld. New York: New York University Press, 1978, pp. 42–85.

Johnston, Kenneth R. 'Philanthropy or Treason? Wordsworth as "Active Partisan"'. *SIR* 25 (1986) 371–409.

—— *The Hidden Wordsworth: Poet, Lover, Rebel, Spy*. New York, NY: W. W. Norton, 1998.

—— 'The Politics of *Tintern Abbey*'. *WC* 14 (1983) 6–14.

—— *Wordsworth and The Recluse*. New Haven: Yale University Press, 1984.

Jones, Stanley. *Hazlitt: A Life*. Oxford: Oxford University Press, 1991.

Kelley, Paul. 'Charlotte Smith and *An Evening Walk*'. *N&Q* NS 29 (1982) 220.

—— 'Rousseau's *Discourse on the Origins of Inequality* and Wordsworth's *Salisbury Plain*'. *N&Q* NS 24 (1977) 323.

—— 'Wordsworth and Lucretius' *De Rerum Natura*'. *N&Q* NS 30 (1983) 219–22.

—— 'Wordsworth and Pope's *Epistle to Cobham*'. *N&Q* NS 28 (1981) 314–15.

Kennedy, Michael L. *The Jacobin Clubs in the French Revolution: The First Years*. Princeton, NJ: Princeton University Press, 1982.

—— *The Jacobin Clubs in the French Revolution: The Middle Years.* Princeton, NJ: Princeton University Press, 1988.

Kipling, Charlotte. 'A Note on Wordsworth's Mathematical Education'. *CLB* NS 59 (July 1987) 96–102.

Landon, Carol D. 'A Survey of an Early Manuscript of Wordsworth, Dove Cottage, MS 4, Dating from his School Days, and of Other Related Manuscripts, Together with an Edition of Selected Pieces'. Ph.D. thesis, University of London, 1962.

—— 'Some Sidelights on *The Prelude*'. in *Bicentenary Wordsworth Studies*, ed. Jonathan Wordsworth. Ithaca, NY: Cornell University Press, 1970, pp. 359–76.

—— 'Wordsworth, Coleridge, and the *Morning Post*: An Early Version of *The Seven Sisters*'. *RES* 11 (1960) 392–402.

—— 'Wordsworth's Racedown Period: Some Uncertainties Resolved'. *BNYPL* 68 (1964) 100–9.

Lawrence, Berta. *Coleridge and Wordsworth in Somerset.* Newton Abbot: David & Charles, 1970.

Lefebure, Molly. *Samuel Taylor Coleridge: A Bondage of Opium.* London: Gollancz, 1974.

—— *The Bondage of Love: A Life of Mrs Samuel Taylor Coleridge.* London: Gollancz, 1988.

Legouis, Emile. *The Early Life of William Wordsworth: 1770–1798*, Trans. J. W. Matthews. London: J. M. Dent, 1921.

Levinson, Marjorie. *Wordsworth's Great Period Poems.* Cambridge: Cambridge University Press, 1986.

Leyburn, Ellen D. 'Berkeleian Elements in Wordsworth's Thought'. *JEGP* 47 (1948) 14–28.

Lienemann, Kurt. *Die Belesenheit von William Wordsworth.* Berlin: Mayer & Müller, 1908.

Lindenberger, Herbert. *On Wordsworth's Prelude.* Princeton, NJ: Princeton University Press, 1963.

Lindop, Grevel. *A Literary Guide to the Lake District.* London: Chatto and Windus, 1993.

Locke, Don. *A Fantasy of Reason: The Life & Thought of William Godwin.* London: Routledge and Kegan Paul, 1980.

Lyon, Judson Stanley. *The Excursion: A Study.* New Haven: Yale University Press, 1950.

McElderry, B. R., Jr. 'Southey and Wordsworth's "The Idiot Boy"'. *N&Q* 200 (1955) 490–1.

McFarland, Thomas. *William Wordsworth: Intensity and Achievement.* Oxford: Clarendon Press, 1992.

MacGillivray, J. R. 'Wordsworth and J.-P. Brissot'. *TLS* (29 Jan. 1931) 79.

Maclean, C. M. 'Lewesdon Hill and Its Poet'. *Essays and Studies* 27 (1941) 30–40.

Martin, C. G. 'Coleridge and William Crowe's *Lewesdon Hill*'. *Modern Language Review* 62 (1967) 400–6.

Mayberry, Tom. *Coleridge and Wordsworth in the West Country.* Stroud: Alan Sutton, 1992.

Milton, the Metaphysicals, and Romanticism, ed. Lisa Low and Anthony John Harding.

Cambridge: Cambridge University Press, 1994.

Moorman, Mary. 'Ann Tyson's Ledger: An Eighteenth-Century Account Book'. *Transactions of the Cumberland and Westmorland Antiquarian and Archaeological Society* 50 (1950) 152–63.

—— *William Wordsworth: A Biography.* 2 vols. Oxford: Clarendon Press, 1957–67.

Newlyn, Lucy. *Coleridge, Wordsworth, and the Language of Allusion.* Oxford: Clarendon Press, 1986.

—— *Paradise Lost and the Romantic Reader.* Oxford: Clarendon Press, 1993.

—— *Reading, Writing, and Romanticism: The Anxiety of Reception.* Oxford: Clarendon Press, 2000.

—— 'Lamb, Lloyd, London: A Perspective on Book Seven of *The Prelude*'. *CLB* NS 74 (January 1991) 33–52.

—— '"In City Pent": Echo and Allusion in Wordsworth, Coleridge, and Lamb, 1797–1801'. *RES* 32 (1981) 408–28.

Nuttall, A. D. *A Common Sky: Philosophy and the Literary Imagination.* London: Chatto and Windus for Sussex University Press, 1974.

—— *Openings: Narrative Beginnings from the Epic to the Novel.* Oxford: Clarendon Press, 1992.

Owen, Felicity, and Brown, David Blayney. *Collector of Genius: A Life of Sir George Beaumont.* New Haven: Yale University Press for the Paul Mellon Centre for Studies in British Art, 1988.

Owen, W. J. B. 'Literary Echoes in *The Prelude*'. *WC* 3 (1972) 3–16.

—— 'Two Addenda'. *WC* 13 (1982) 98.

—— 'A Sense of the Infinite'. *WC* 21 (1990) 18–27.

—— 'Understanding *The Prelude*'. *WC* 22 (1991) 100–9.

—— *Wordsworth as Critic.* London: Oxford University Press, 1969.

—— *Wordsworth's Preface to Lyrical Ballads.* Copenhagen: Rosenkilde and Bagger, 1957.

Pares, Richard. *A West-India Fortune.* London: Longmans, Green, 1950.

Park, Roy, *Charles Lamb as Critic.* London: Routledge and Kegan Paul, 1980.

Parrish, Stephen. *The Art of the Lyrical Ballads.* Cambridge, MA: Harvard University Press, 1973.

—— 'The Whig Interpretation of Literature', *TEXT* 4 (1988) 343–50.

Pollin, Burton R. 'Permutations of Names in *The Borderers*, or Hints of Godwin, Charles Lloyd, and a Real Renegade'. *WC* 4 (1973) 31–5.

Potts, Abbie Findlay. *Wordsworth's Prelude: A Study of Its Literary Form.* Ithaca, NY: Cornell University Press, 1953.

Presenting Poetry: Composition, Publication, Reception, ed. Howard Erskine-Hill and Richard A. McCabe. Cambridge: Cambridge University Press, 1995.

Reed, Mark L. *Wordsworth: The Chronology of the Early Years: 1770–1799.* Cambridge, MA: Harvard University Press, 1967.

—— *Wordsworth: The Chronology of the Middle Years: 1800–1815.* Cambridge, MA: Harvard University Press, 1975.

—— 'Wordsworth on Wordsworth and Much Else: New Conversational Memoranda'. *Papers of the Bibliographical Society of America* 81 (1987) 451–8.

Roe, Nicholas. 'Citizen Wordsworth'. *WC* 14 (1983) 21–30.

—— *The Politics of Nature*. Macmillan Studies in Romanticism. London: Macmillan, 1992.

—— 'Radical George: Dyer in the 1790s'. *CLB* NS 49 (January 1985) 17–26.

—— *Wordsworth and Coleridge: The Radical Years*. Oxford: Clarendon Press, 1988.

—— 'Wordsworth's Account of Beaupuy's Death'. *N&Q* NS 32 (1985) 337.

—— '"Atmospheric Air Itself": Medical Science, Politics and Poetry in Thelwall, Coleridge and Wordsworth', in *1798: The Year of the Lyrical Ballads*, ed. Richard Cronin. Houndmills: Macmillan, 1998. pp. 185–202.

Sandford, Mrs Henry. *Thomas Poole and his Friends*. 2 vols. London, 1888.

Schneider, Ben Ross. *Wordsworth's Cambridge Education*. Cambridge: Cambridge University Press, 1957.

Shaver, Chester L. 'Wordsworth's Debt to Thomas Newton'. *MLN* 62 (1947) 344.

—— 'Wordsworth's Vaudracour and Wilkinson's Wanderer'. *RES* 12 (1961) 55–7.

Sheats, Paul D. *The Making of Wordsworth's Poetry, 1785–1798*. Cambridge, MA: Harvard University Press, 1973.

Simmons, Jack. *Southey*. London: Collins, 1945.

Smith, Christopher J. P. *A Quest for Home: Reading Robert Southey*. Liverpool: Liverpool University Press, 1997.

Stallknecht, Newton P. *Strange Seas of Thought: Studies in William Wordsworth's Philosophy of Man and Nature*. Bloomington: Indiana University Press, 1958.

Stein, Edwin. *Wordsworth's Art of Allusion*. University Park, PA: The Pennsylvania State University Press, 1988.

Stillinger, Jack. 'Textual Primitivism and the Editing of Wordsworth'. *Studies in Romanticism* 28 (1989) 3–28.

—— *Coleridge and Textual Instability* New York: Oxford University Press, 1994.

Stockwell, A. W. 'Wordsworth's Politics'. B.Litt. thesis, University of Oxford, 1950.

Storey, Mark. *Robert Southey: A Life*. Oxford: Clarendon Press, 1997.

Sultana, Donald. *Samuel Taylor Coleridge in Malta and Italy*. New York: Barnes and Noble, 1969.

Thomas, Gordon. '"Orphans Then": Death in the *Two-Part Prelude*'. *CLB* NS 96 (October 1996) 157–73.

Thomas, W. K., and Ober, Warren U.. *A Mind For Ever Voyaging: Wordsworth at Work Portraying Newton and Science*. Edmonton: The University of Alberta Press, 1989.

—— *Thomas Gray: Contemporary Essays*, ed. W. B. Hutchings and William Ruddick. Liverpool: Liverpool University Press, 1993.

Thompson, E. P. 'Disenchantment or Default? A Lay Sermon'. *Power and Consciousness*, ed. Conor Cruise O'Brien and William Dean Vanech. London: University of London Press, 1969. pp. 149–81.

—— 'Wordsworth's Crisis'. *London Review of Books* 10 (8 December 1988) 3–6.

Thompson, T. W. *Wordsworth's Hawkshead*, ed. Robert Woof. London: Oxford University Press, 1970.

Todd, F. M. *Politics and the Poet: A Study of Wordsworth*. London: Methuen, 1957.

Trott, Nicola, and Duncan Wu. 'Three Sources for Wordsworth's *Prelude* Cave'. *N&Q* NS 38 (1991) 298–9.

Tyson, Gerald P. *Joseph Johnson: A Liberal Publisher*. Iowa City: University of Iowa Press, 1979.

Bibliography

Watson, J. R. 'Lucy and the Earth-Mother'. *EIC* 27 (1977) 187–202.

West, Thomas. *A Guide to the Lakes, in Cumberland, Westmorland, and Lancashire.* 3rd edn. London, 1784.

Whalley, George. 'The Bristol Library Borrowings of Southey and Coleridge, 1793–8'. *The Library*, ser 5, 4 (1949) 114–32.

—— 'Coleridge Marginalia Lost'. *Book Collector* 17 (1968) 428–42.

Williams, John. *Wordsworth: Romantic Poetry and Revolution Politics.* Manchester: Manchester University Press, 1989.

Wilson, Douglas B. *The Romantic Dream: Wordsworth and the Poetics of the Unconscious.* Lincoln: University of Nebraska Press, 1993.

Woof, Robert Samuel. 'The Literary Relations of Wordsworth and Coleridge, 1795–1803: Five Studies'. Ph.D. thesis, University of Toronto, 1959.

—— 'Wordsworth's Poetry and Stuart's Newspapers: 1797–1803'. *Studies in Bibliography* 15 (1962) 149–89.

—— *Thomas De Quincey: An English Opium-Eater 1785–1859.* Grasmere: Trustees of Dove Cottage, 1985.

Wordsworth, Christopher, Jr. *Memoirs of William Wordsworth.* 2 vols. London, 1851.

Wordsworth, Jonathan. *The Music of Humanity.* New York: J. & J. Harper, 1969.

—— *William Wordsworth: The Borders of Vision* Oxford: Clarendon Press, 1982.

—— 'Wordsworthian comedy', in *English Comedy*, ed. Michael Cordner, Peter Holland and John Kerrigan. Cambridge: Cambridge University Press, 1994.

Worthington, Jane. *Wordsworth's Reading of Roman Prose.* Yale Studies in English 102. New Haven: Yale University Press, 1946.

Wu, Duncan. 'A Chronological Annotated Edition of Wordsworth's Poetry and Prose: 1785–1790'. D.Phil. thesis, University of Oxford, 1990.

—— *Wordsworth's Reading 1770–1799.* Cambridge: Cambridge University Press, 1993.

—— *Wordsworth's Reading 1800–1815* Cambridge: Cambridge University Press, 1995.

—— *Romanticism: An Anthology.* 2nd edn. Oxford: Blackwell, 1998.

—— 'Cottle's *Alfred*: Another Coleridge-Inspired Epic'. *CLB* NS 73 (January 1991) 19–21.

—— '*Lyrical Ballads* (1798): The Beddoes Copy'. *The Library*, ser. 6, 15 (1993) 332–5.

—— 'Three translations of Virgil read by Wordsworth in 1788'. *N&Q* NS 37 (1990) 407–9.

—— 'William Wordsworth and the Farish Brothers'. *Bodleian Library Record* 14 (1991) 99–101.

—— 'Wordsworth/Lamb/Elton: A New Literary Connection'. *CLB* NS 68 (Oct. 1989) 129–31.

—— 'Wordsworth's Copy of Smart's Horace'. *N&Q* NS 38 (1991) 303–5.

—— 'Wordsworth's *Orpheus and Eurydice*: The Unpublished Final Line'. *N&Q* NS 38 (1991) 301–2.

—— 'Wordsworth's Reading of Bowles'. *N&Q* NS 36 (1989) 166–7.

—— 'Wordsworth's Reading of Marvell'. *N&Q* NS 40 (1993) 41–2.

—— 'Wordsworth and *The Morning Chronicle*'. *N&Q* NS 40 (1993) 39–40.

Wylie, Ian. *Young Coleridge and the Philosophers of Nature.* Oxford: Clarendon Press, 1989.

Index

Within authors' entries the titles of poems and other works are listed in the order of the first main word, ignoring 'A', 'And' or 'The' at the start.

368 Index